'WHAT ELSE COULD

For my parents, Cathy and Joe

'WHAT ELSE COULD I DO?'

Single Mothers and Infanticide, Ireland 1900–1950

Clíona Rattigan

IRISH ACADEMIC PRESS
DUBLIN • PORTLAND, OR

First published in 2012 by Irish Academic Press

2 Brookside, Dundrum Road, Dublin 14, Ireland	920 NE 58th Avenue, Suite 300 Portland, Oregon, 97213-3786, USA

© Clíona Rattigan 2012

www.iap.ie

British Library Cataloguing in Publication Data
An entry can be found on request

ISBN 978 0 7165 3139 5 (cloth)
ISBN 978 0 7165 3140 1 (paper)

Library of Congress Cataloging-in-Publication Data
An entry can be found on request

Printed by Good News Digital Books, Ongar, Essex

Contents

List of Tables

List of Plates

6. The hollow where Rose E. said she buried her sister's infant daughter in October 1934. The baby's body was never located. Central Criminal Court, Co. Roscommon, 1935.

7. Trials Record Book entry for Mary Anne M. who was convicted of concealment of birth at the Central Criminal Court in July 1927. Trials Record Book, Central Criminal Court, Change of Venue Dublin June 1925 – December 1926.

8. Mary C. was convicted of concealment of birth at the Central Criminal Court in November 1943. Like many single women convicted of the same offence in post-independence Ireland, Mary C. agreed to serve her sentence in a convent rather than in prison. Central Criminal Court, City of Dublin, 1943.

9. Mary C. was convicted of soliciting in October 1940. Central Criminal Court, City of Dublin, 1943.

10. and 11. Wards in the South Dublin Union hospital where Mary C., who was recovering from a scabies infection, was employed as an inmate worker. Mary C. gave birth in the lavatory of Ward 23 in the Female Chronic Hospital in May 1943. Central Criminal Court, City of Dublin, 1943.

12. Marriage certificate documenting the marriage of nineteen-year-old Mary H. to the father of her infant, James M., a labourer nineteen years her senior in August 1931. Mary was convicted of concealment of birth but was released on condition that she marry James M. Central Criminal Court, Trials Record Book (Change of Venue cases) Nov 1927–June 1933.

13. Letter for Mary H.'s solicitor to the County Registrar in Dublin following her marriage to James M. Central Criminal Court, Trials Record Book (Change of Venue cases) Nov 1927 – June 1933.

14. Nora C. was convicted of manslaughter in July 1927. The entry in the Trials Record Book notes that she enter the High Park Convent in Dublin 'until the Superioress consents to her discharge'. Central Criminal Court, Trials Record Book, (Change of venue cases), June 1925– Dec 1926.

15. The entry in the Trials Record Book for Sarah M., convicted of manslaughter in December 1943, notes that she married the father of her deceased infant in January 1944. By marrying the father of her decesased infant Sarah M. avoided serving time in prison or in a religious institution. Central Criminal Court, State Book at Central Criminal Court 1941–45.

16. 23-year-old Mary B. gave birth in her bedroom in her mother's

home in May 1939. Mary's mother said she 'wanted the child removed' as soon as she learned that her unmarried daughter had given birth. Shortly after the baby was born the doctor who had attended to Mary made enquiries regarding the adoption of her infant and managed to find three addresses for her. However, by the time the doctor returned to the B. household Mary's infant had died. Mary claimed that her infant daughter died soon after she was born as the baby fell off the bed and hit her head against Mary's dressing table. She was found not guilty by direction at the Central Criminal Court, Dublin. Central Criminal Court, Co. Tipperary, 1939.

17. A market bag taken possession of by gardaí at the defendant's home and handed to the State Pathologist in a 1936 Co. Tipperary case. In this particular case the woman gave birth while cycling to a nearby town. She said that she put the infant's body in her market bag and later 'dumped it in a bucket' in the fowl house on the grounds of her aunt's home. Central Criminal Court, Co. Tipperary, 1937.

18. **Garda standing at the edge of the lake in Co. Cork where Eithna M. drowned her seven month-old son in September 1940.** In her statement the nineteen-year-old mother told gardaí that on 17 September 1940 she 'made up her mind to drown the child in G. lake as [she] [had] been annoyed from it since it was born'. Eithna M. spent the entire day at the edge of the lake after she had killed her son. According to Eithna's second cousin, with whom she and her baby lived, two days before the incident, when asked to attend to her baby, Eithna had remarked 'Am I going to be all my life watching the baby?' The young mother may well have been suffering from depression but, as there are no medical reports in her file, this is by no means certain. She may simply have resented the responsibility of motherhood and deliberately decided to take her son's life. Central Criminal Court, Co. Cork, 1941.

19. The lake in Co. Cork where Eithna M. drowned her infant son. Central Criminal Court, Co. Cork, 1941.

Acknowledgements

Many individuals and organisations have provided me with invaluable assistance and advice since this book began life as a PhD thesis a number of years ago. I am extremely grateful to them all, but there are a few who deserve special mention.

First of all, I would like to thank my PhD supervisor Professor David Dickson who provided a great deal of advice, support and encouragement. He was always interested in my work and gave generously of his time and expertise.

I have received encouragement and assistance from many people during my research on single mothers and infanticide. In particular, I would like to thank Professor Eunan O'Halpin, Dr Sandra McAvoy, Dr Leanne McCormick, Dr Karen Brennan, Dr Caitríona Clear, Dr Maryann Valiulis, Dr Deirdre McMahon and Professor Mary O'Dowd who generously shared references and advice.

I was fortunate to be able to exchange ideas with Professor Maria Luddy during my time as a Teaching Fellow at the University of Warwick. I am especially grateful to her for her encouragement and for her comments on the initial drafts of this book. My work benefited greatly from her invaluable insights.

I am grateful to the staff at all the libraries and archives that I have used, especially those at Trinity College, Dublin, the National Archives of Ireland and the Public Record Office of Northern Ireland. In particular, I wish to thank Gregory O'Connor at the National Archives of Ireland for his assistance and advice. I would also like to record my appreciation to the staff of the Public Record Office of Northern Ireland who assisted me in my successful application to the Northern Ireland Courts Service for permission to use the trial records currently closed to the public.

I wish also to thank the National Archives of Ireland for providing permission to publish the photographs used in this book. I wish especially to record my gratitude to the Irish Research Council for the Humanities and Social Sciences for providing funding for my PhD studies. My thanks are due especially to Lisa Hyde and the staff at Irish Academic Press who have been most patient and supportive throughout.

I would like especially to thank my parents Cathy and Joe Rattigan and my sister Aoife for their unflagging support, for their continuous encouragement, their generosity and their interest in my research. Their support has meant a great deal and I dedicate this book to them.

Thanks are also due to Dympna Kyne and Mick MacAree for their assistance and for always opening their home to me whenever I needed to return to Dublin. I would like to thank my fellow historians and good friends Mary Muldowney, Eve Morrison, Catriona Pennell, Jennifer Redmond and all my close friends who provided advice and encouragement throughout this project.

Finally, I would like to thank Nicolas. Not only did he provide constant encouragement but also helped in a practical way by introducing me to various Parisian libraries where I completed my writing. His steadfast commitment to his own studies has been a huge inspiration to me. Most of all, he made me laugh.

'The troublesome matter of unmarried mothers'[1]

Every year between 1900 and 1950 hundreds of single Irish women were faced with a huge predicament – unplanned pregnancy out of wedlock. Some women dealt with the dilemma by concealing the pregnancy, giving birth alone and committing infanticide shortly afterwards. Ena P., who was 20 years old, was arrested in the hotel where she was employed as a kitchen helper on Eden Quay in Dublin in March 1932. Ena's employer had noticed a bad smell coming from her room. On further investigation, the body of a newborn male was found on top of the wardrobe in Ena's room. The garda who arrested Ena stated that she appeared very frightened when apprehended. She told him that she was expecting to be arrested, and stated: 'I gave birth to a child. I killed it. What else could I do?' In her statement Ena said 'I could not help it' and again asked 'What could I do?'[2] Ena's passivity and sense of helplessness is quite striking. The judicial records of Irish infanticide trials suggest that, like Ena, many unmarried women, felt that they had no choice but to give birth in secret and to take the infant's life shortly after self-delivery. The options available to working-class women like Ena were certainly limited in Ireland between 1900 and 1950.

Most defendants felt unable to confide in anyone. They did their best to conceal signs of pregnancy from everyone they knew, perhaps even denying the pregnancy to themselves. They usually gave birth unattended. In the vast majority of cases, the illegitimate infants of unmarried women were killed within hours of being born. The infants of women who gave birth in a workhouse or county home were generally a week or two old before they were killed, as women were required to remain there for a short period of time after the birth.

Ena P. gave birth in her workplace, in the room she occupied in a hotel in central Dublin. She managed to deliver without arousing any suspicion; it was the odour from the infant's corpse that prompted her employer to investigate several days after the birth. Ena P. had been able to deliver indoors; not all single expectant women in the case files had been as fortunate. Others gave birth in even more strained circumstances, sometimes in unsanitary conditions outdoors. Only a very small proportion of defendants in the cases examined delivered in hospitals.

Bridget B., aged 25, had left her native place in Co. Galway some time before giving birth in a Co. Limerick field between Kilmallock and Bruff in June 1935. The expectant mother had been homeless towards the end of her pregnancy. Bridget seems to have slept out of doors in the days leading up to the birth of her infant son. She walked more than five miles following the onset of labour. After the birth she continued her journey to Limerick by foot and walked around the city for some time before taking shelter in a church. According to the doctor who examined her the day after she gave birth alone, Bridget appeared to have been very distressed at what had happened. Dr Molony was of the opinion that Bridget had 'suffered greatly both physically and mentally'. Gardaí managed to locate the field where Bridget had given birth. In his evidence, Sergeant Patrick McKenna explained that when he entered the field where Bridget had given birth alone and unassisted two days previously, he saw that the grass had been trampled upon. There was, he said, 'an impression made' on the ground 'as if some person had been lying there'.[3] On closer inspection, Sergeant McKenna found bloodstains on the grass. He also found a blood-stained lemon-coloured garment. It contained the afterbirth. Bridget was convicted at the Central Criminal Court of the manslaughter of her infant son. She was sentenced to three months' imprisonment but this was suspended on her agreeing to enter the Legion of Mary Hostel in Limerick and to spend three months there. The sentence was quite lenient when compared to other manslaughter cases in the same period; perhaps the circumstances in which Bridget had given birth affected the outcome.

What motivated unmarried women like Bridget B. to run away from home and to deliver out of doors in difficult circumstances? An editorial in the *Irish Independent* in February 1931 suggested that 'wicked mothers' murdered newborns in order 'to hide their shame or to save trouble'.[4] Shame, the stigma associated with single motherhood, poverty and the low value placed on children born out of wedlock were all important motivating factors. From the cases examined here, it is clear that many Irish people considered the murder of illegitimate children a lesser crime than the murder of children born within wedlock. In her study of infanticide in the 1920s, Ryan referred to the 'low value attached to illegitimate infant life'.[5] If unmarried motherhood was considered shameful and deviant at the time, it is perhaps only to be expected that people would not have held illegitimate children in high regard. At the trial of two Co. Roscommon sisters for the murder of the elder's infant daughter in 1935, Garda Joseph Christol testified that he overheard Rose remark to her sister that 'the child is better off dead anyway'.[6] Margaret F. did not seem to regret killing her infant. Her cousin Bridget described Margaret's detached attitude in her statements. Margaret had referred to her infant as a bastard shortly after the birth in June 1930 and expressed no remorse for her actions, as though a child born out of wedlock and associated with shame and dishonour did not deserve to live.[7] Motivating factors in infanticide cases involving single mothers will be explored throughout this study.

In 1900 the island of Ireland was an integral part of the United Kingdom and was governed as a single unit; by 1921 the country was partitioned. The Government of Ireland Act, 1920 provided for two Irish parliaments: one for the six north-eastern counties and another for the Twenty-Six Counties. While the north-eastern counties reluctantly accepted the agreement and the Six-County state of Northern Ireland was established, a Home Rule parliament in Dublin was not enough to satisfy the rest of the country and the War of Independence continued in the South until July 1921. In December 1921 the Twenty-Six County Irish Free State was established. The Twenty-Six County state was predominately Catholic. In 1922 92.6% of the newly independent state's population was Catholic. Protestants accounted for 7.4% of the population in the southern state in 1922, while in the six counties of Northern Ireland they accounted for about 66% of the population. Both Northern Ireland and the Irish Free State had strong religious identities.

The Catholic Church exerted a huge influence in Ireland throughout the period under review but particularly in the post-independence period when conservative social policies were introduced including bans on divorce and contraception along with a tightening of censorship. The Catholic Church's influence was felt in almost every sphere of Irish life, in education, health and politics as well as private matters of morality, and sexual morality in particular. Catholic religious orders ran hospitals, schools, orphanages, and other institutions. A new constitution which clearly reflected Catholic beliefs was introduced in 1937. Northern Protestantism was also morally conservative. Ferriter has noted that it was 'essentially similar to Southern Catholicism, without the obsession with birth control.'[8] Socially conservative legislation was also introduced in Northern Ireland; an Intoxicating Liquor Act, which restricted the sale of alcohol and banned the opening of public houses on Sundays, was introduced in 1923.

There was a high degree of poverty in Ireland during the period under review. Industrialisation in Ireland had been heavily concentrated in the north-east, while agriculture predominated in the south. Partition made clear the economic divide between Northern Ireland and the Twenty-Six County state which lagged significantly behind its northern neighbour and experienced high levels of emigration and unemployment. Following the Second World War the provisions of the Welfare State were extended to Northern Ireland and the gap widened between Northern Ireland and the Twenty-Six County state.

It is hardly surprising then that in a state with such a socially conservative outlook Irish women would find themselves defined as mothers and homemakers. Although the right to vote was extended to all women over the age of 21 in the Twenty-Six County state in 1922, reactionary legislation was passed in relation to women's employment and women's public role in the early years of the Irish Free State. As Cullen Owens has noted, 'early hopes that women would play a significant role in the new Ireland were soon quashed as a series of restrictive measures were introduced by government.'[9] During the period under review the hearth and home was regarded as the Irish woman's rightful sphere. As Valiulis has noted, 'Throughout the 1920s and 1930s, women were, in effect, barred from serving on juries, were forbidden to sit for the highest examinations in the Civil Service, were subject to the marriage bar, and were restricted to working in certain factories. Their sphere of activity was the home, the private sphere and therein, it was claimed, lay their responsibility, their duty and their contribution to the State.'[10] Women's position in Southern Ireland hardly changed in the thirty years following the adoption of the 1937 Constitution. Motherhood was idealised in post-independence Ireland; the unmarried mother was not regarded as a legitimate mother.

'NO WAY OF KNOWING JUST WHAT PROPORTION OF INFANTICIDES WERE BROUGHT TO JUSTICE'

Writing in *Holiday* in December 1949, Frank O'Connor claimed that 'infanticide in Ireland is appallingly common.'[11] Twenty years previously in October 1928 at a trial in Cork Circuit Court Judge Kenny had referred to infanticide as a national industry.[12] As Donovan noted in his study of infanticide and juries in France, the statistics for infanticide in all periods have one problem in common: 'there is no way of knowing just what proportion of infanticides were brought to justice'.[13] It is possible that many single women who killed or concealed their illegitimate newborns in Ireland also 'got through the official net', as McLoughlin put it.[14] The recorded police figures for the murder of infants and concealment of birth probably represented only a minority of those crimes that were committed annually in Ireland. Several women in the case files examined had committed infanticide on more than one occasion and managed to escape detection before being apprehended after reoffending.

A number of infanticide cases may have gone undetected during the War of Independence and Civil War period.[15] It is clear from files held at the National Archives, Kew that in many instances where the bodies of newborn infants were found in suspicious circumstances, there were no suspects and a number of infanticide cases were not prosecuted.[16] Serious delays in bringing cases to trial seem to have continued into the post-independence period; some infanticide cases were not tried for a considerable length of time.

Between 1900 and 1919, an average of fourteen cases per annum across Ireland where infants aged one year and under were murdered were recorded by the police.[17] The average number of concealment of birth cases known to the police was consistently higher than figures for the murder of infants. Published crime statistics are not available for the years 1920 to 1926. However, McAvoy's research on infanticide has shown that the Annual Reports of the Registrar General which were prepared on a Twenty-Six County basis can provide some information on the level of infanticide during this gap period. 'The 1923 report registered 9 cases; the 1924 report, 16 cases; the 1925 report 9 cases; and the 1926 report 20 cases.'[18] There were nineteen cases where infants aged one year and under were known to the gardaí in the Irish Free State in 1927, ten in 1928 and thirteen in 1929.[19] The averages for the ten-year periods 1930–1939 and 1940–1949 were lower. In 1950, six cases where infants aged one year and under were murdered were known to the gardaí, and three infanticide cases were listed as being known to gardaí that year. Statistics on concealment of birth indicate that more than 850 cases of concealment of birth were known to the gardaí between 1927 and 1950.[20] The majority of defendants in these cases would, in all likelihood, have been unmarried women. Concealment of birth offences recorded as being known to the gardaí were higher for the Twenty-Six Counties from 1927 to 1950 than was the case from 1900 to 1919. An average of twenty-three concealment of birth cases per year were recorded as being known to the police between 1900 and 1909. The average dropped slightly in the following decade to nineteen cases per year, but forty-one cases were recorded in 1927 and forty-nine in 1928, while in 1929 there were fifty concealment of birth cases. Between 1930 and 1939 there was an average of forty cases, with a decline to thirty-two during the 1940s. Only two such cases were recorded as being known to the gardaí in 1950. As statistics on the numbers of infanticide and concealment of birth cases that were known to the police in Northern Ireland between 1920 and 1950 are not currently available it is not possible to compare rates of infanticide North and South between 1920 and 1950.

TABLE 1. NUMBER OF MURDER AND CONCEALMENT OF BIRTH CASES KNOWN TO
THE POLICE IN IRELAND, 1900–19

Year	Murder of infants < 1 year	Concealment
1900–04	81	181
1905–09	61	155
1910–14	58	131
1915–19	80	166

McAvoy has considered the possibility that the 1935 ban on contraceptives and travel restrictions during the Second World War may have led to an upsurge in infanticide cases in the Twenty-Six County state. However, her research has shown that there was no increase in the numbers of infanticide cases known to the gardaí during the war years, when travel restrictions may have prevented women from going to Britain in order to abort unwanted pregnancies. As the vast majority of single women in this sample were on low incomes it is doubtful whether they would have been able to cover the costs involved in travelling to Britain and accessing abortionists there. The assumption here is that many single women charged with the murder of their infants would have been unfamiliar with contraceptives and that the 1935 ban would arguably have had little impact on their lives or lifestyle choices.

There has been a great deal of interest in Ireland in recent years, both from the general public and academics, in the fate of Irish women who gave birth outside wedlock in the twentieth century. A number of survivor advocacy groups such as Justice for Magdalenes, a group seeking justice for women who were incarcerated in Ireland's Magdalen Laundries and the Bethany Survivors Group, who are campaigning to have the Bethany Home included in the Residential Institions Redress Scheme, have come to prominence later. The Bethany Home, associated with the Church of Ireland and in operation from 1922 to 1972 was a combined

TABLE 2. MURDER AND CONCEALMENT OF BIRTH CASES KNOWN
TO AN GARDA SÍOCHÁNA, 1927–50

Year	Murder of infants	Concealment of birth
1927–29	42	140
1930–34	35	220
1935–39	31	175
1940–44	12	177
1945–49	15	144
1950	6	2
Total	141	858

maternity home for unmarried mothers, a children's home and place of detention for women convicted of crimes, including infanticide. Media attention, for the most part, has tended to focus on women who were sent to Magdalen convents. Only a partial picture of single maternity in Ireland during the first half of the twentieth century can be said to exist. There are substantial gaps in our knowledge of unmarried motherhood, particularly in terms of the history of single mothers who were admitted to religious-run institutions. Little is known about unmarried women who committed infanticide, although many were incarcerated in religious institutions. A large part of the history of unmarried mothers in Ireland remains unrecorded, as the records of Magdalen asylums run by Catholic religious orders are currently inaccessible to researchers. From 1922 onwards, many single women convicted of the manslaughter or concealment of birth of their illegitimate infants were incarcerated in religious-run institutions rather than in prisons. Without access to the records of convents where such women were detained, their history remains incomplete. However, the judicial records examined here show that many unmarried women convicted of the murder or concealment of birth of their illegitimate infants at the Central Criminal Court, Dublin in the post-independence period were sent to Magdalen convents. Single women convicted at the Assizes before independence were more likely to have been sent to prison than to a religious-run institution. A small number of trial records contain correspondence between probation officers and Magdalen convents and between the convents and the courts. The available evidence makes clear that a very small number of women objected to being detained in convents and sought to be transferred to prison. The trial records do not, however, provide information on how the majority responded to being detained in Magdalen convents. This monograph will add considerably to existing knowledge of female criminal behaviour in Ireland during the first half of the twentieth century.

This study analyses the crime of infanticide on the island of Ireland over a fifty-year period from 1900 to 1920. Existing studies of infanticide in Ireland have concentrated on the period after independence and have been limited to the Twenty-Six County state. The longer time frame allows for a greater understanding of patterns and changes in Irish infanticide cases. Change and continuity in Ireland after independence, particularly in terms of sentencing patterns, can be more fully understood. Although infanticide trials in the South have been the subject of scholarly inquiry in recent years, there have been no detailed studies of unmarried mothers and infanticide in Ulster to date, even though there is a considerable body of archival material on the subject. The records of infanticide trials in Northern Ireland from 1920 onwards provide an interesting comparison with the Twenty-Six County state. Legislation differed in the two jurisdictions as did sentencing patterns. However, the manner in which single, working-class women dealt with an unplanned pregnancy was similar in both jurisdictions.

The experiences of the unmarried women who feature in the records of infanticide cases that came before the courts in Ireland between 1900 and 1950 will form the keystone of this study. The records of infanticide trials can provide a great deal of insight into the lives of single, mainly working-class women during the first half of the twentieth century. The judicial files often provide information about defendants' living conditions and occupation along with their interactions with their employers, neighbours and doctors. Some files also offer insight into defendants' relationships with their kin and the father of the deceased infant. The women who feature in the judicial files examined rejected motherhood for various reasons. Paradoxically, unmarried Irish women who refused to become mothers and were charged with the murder of their illegitimate infants during the period can contribute enormously to our understanding of single motherhood in Ireland. Trial records give the historian access to the range of emotions experienced by a single mother who attempted to conceal her pregnancy for nine months and to her panicked reactions after the birth. The records of institutions or charitable organisations that dealt with unmarried mothers in the same period rarely allow us access to the words of the single mother herself.

The single women who stood trial for the murder of their illegitimate infants in the years between 1900 and 1950 are clearly a very small minority of all single Irish mothers of this period and are somewhat atypical, as most single mothers at the time did not, of course, kill their newborn infants or conceal their births. Family size was large during the first half of the twentieth century and in 1911 36% of married women had seven children or more. In this period Irish babies born in urban areas were twice as likely to die as those born in rural areas. Class, along with geography, was also an important factor in infant mortality: 'A baby born into the family of a labourer was seventeen times more likely to die within a year than the child of a professional.'[21] In the early twentieth century maternal mortality was still a problem. As Clear has noted 'maternal mortality, like infant mortality, was worst among those whose resistance was low – the badly-fed.'[22] It is, nonetheless, worthwhile examining the experiences of these women insofar as the records allow, as their experiences have a significant amount in common with single mothers in general. All entering single motherhood would have experienced many of the same fears, anxieties and concerns as the few who chose to deal with the prospect of single motherhood in a drastic way.

Single motherhood was clearly a feature of Irish life during the first half of the twentieth century, but Irish society was deeply intolerant of unmarried mothers and their illegitimate children. Catholic Ireland castigated single mothers. Nor were uncharitable attitudes confined to Irish Catholics. The records of infanticide cases tried in Northern Ireland suggest that Irish Protestants were no less forgiving. The experience of single motherhood was clearly a huge ordeal for many women who found themselves pregnant and unmarried during the first half of the twentieth century, yet this aspect of the issue was rarely acknowledged in government reports on unmarried motherhood or in the sermons of Irish bishops, where they were viewed as financial burdens and a national embarrassment. The economic and social circumstances of individual women who became pregnant outside wedlock were ignored by most commentators. Referring to the ' "It's always the girl's fault any way" attitude' then prevalent throughout the country, the author of the article in *The Bell* in June 1941 argued that Irish people tended to place the whole blame on the unmarried women who became pregnant.[23] Indeed, most commentators at the time seem to have felt that the problem lay with the women themselves, and rescue workers and others concerned with the problem of single motherhood focused their attention to an extraordinary degree on unmarried mothers and their moral or mental weaknesses. As Luddy has observed, in post-independence Ireland 'unmarried mothers, the "amateur" and the prostitute became the focus of intense scrutiny, with particular emphasis on how these women could be made to conform to a stricter sexual code'.[24]

As Maguire noted, 'few legislative initiatives prior to the 1960s specifically addressed unmarried mothers and their children'.[25] Adoption was
not legalised in Ireland until 1952. Many single Irish women who became
pregnant during the first half of the twentieth century made their way to
the capital, seeking anonymity and sometimes help from Dublin's small
network of rescue societies. There was a class dimension to single motherhood in that, as Earner-Byrne has noted, single expectant women from
middle-class backgrounds were admitted to the special Mother and Baby
homes, while working-class women generally had little option but to enter
a county home.[26] Magdalen asylums generally accepted poorer women
or unmarried women who had experienced more than one pregnancy.
Both Earner-Byrne and Garrett have highlighted the fact that unmarried
mothers in the Mother and Baby homes in Ireland were required to spend
longer amounts of time in the institutions than were single mothers
in Britain.

Unmarried Protestant women could seek assistance in the Bethany
Home or the Leeson Street Magdalen Asylum. By the early 1920s the
policies and practices of the Leeson Street Magdalen Asylum, an institution in Dublin for unmarried Protestant mothers and their babies, were far
more progressive than institutions run for single mothers by Catholic nuns
in Ireland. Women in the former were actively encouraged to leave the
Leeson Street Magdalen Asylum to rebuild their lives and to find work.
Indeed, from 1933 onwards unmarried mothers were only required to
remain in the home for a period of six months after the birth of their
babies.[27] This contrasts sharply with the manner in which many Catholic
institutions were run. Some religious orders seem to have discouraged
women from leaving their institutions and there is evidence in the records
of infanticide trials to suggest that many tried to detain convicted unmarried mothers for as long as possible. From the early 1920s, unmarried
mothers and their babies were kept together in the Leeson Street home for
a number of months and mothers were encouraged to look after their
babies. This was generally not encouraged in Catholic homes. Unmarried
mothers assisted by St Patrick's Guild, a Catholic organisation, were sep-
arated from their infants 'as soon as is practicable'.[28] With the exception
of the Regina Coeli hostel, most of the Catholic institutions that dealt
with single expectant women in Ireland during the first half of the twentieth century seem to have had a narrow, punitive outlook. Kennedy has
drawn attention to the fact that the opening of the lay-run Regina Coeli
hostel in Dublin in 1930 marked a break with the way single mothers and
their children had previously been dealt with by Catholic organisations in

Ireland.[29] However, existing homes run by female Catholic religious orders did not, unlike homes that catered for unmarried Protestant mothers, reform or remodel themselves to any great extent during the course of the first half of the twentieth century. As Smith has noted, few people interested in the welfare of unmarried mothers and their children in Ireland during the 1930s were able to imagine responses to the issue that did not involve institutionalisation.[30]

Single mothers also had the option of finding a foster mother who would raise their infant for the first few years of its life. However, the evidence in the case files examined suggests that such arrangements often fell through and that many working-class women experienced difficulty in meeting the payments to the foster mother. It is worth referring to the case of Mary Margaret H. (not included in the samples studied, as the illegitimate child in question was two-and-a-half years old when he was killed by his mother on an unknown date between 21 March and 1 April 1945) as it provides a clear illustration of the economic and social pressures brought to bear on single mothers during the period under review. Mary Margaret was employed as a domestic servant. She paid a foster mother to look after her son but found it difficult to make the payments to her. She told gardaí that the foster mother was 'pressing [her] for money and [she] was afraid of them all at home and everything'. In her statement she explained that 'the people at home knew nothing about the child and [she] couldn't tell them'.[31] Infants who were boarded-out (fostered) in early-twentieth-century Ireland also had a high mortality rate and were not always well cared for.

Maguire has contested the notion that most illegitimate children were institutionalised, boarded out or adopted in mid-twentieth-century Ireland. Her analysis of public assistance records has shown that, on occasion, unmarried mothers were successful in petitioning the local authorities for home assistance, enabling them to raise their children themselves. Maguire's findings show that it was sometimes possible for a small number of perseverant single mothers to bring their children up themselves with state assistance. According to Maguire, a significant number of unmarried mothers who gave birth in Mother and Baby homes took their children with them when they were discharged. The suggestion here is that, contrary to popular belief, many illegitimate children were raised in the birth mother's parental home. In fact, little is known about the fates of these children. Many infants who were discharged from Mother and Baby homes with their mothers may have been boarded out or adopted soon afterwards. Given the high levels of mortality for illegitimate infants at the time many may not have lived past their first year.

Unmarried women who attempted to raise their children themselves encountered all sorts of obstacles. A report in the *Irish Reports* on the case of husband and wife Elizabeth and Antonio T., who demanded custody of Elizabeth's 7-year-old son from her parents in 1943, underscored the difficulties single women faced, both in terms of attempting to raise an illegitimate infant on their own and being granted custody of their children. In 1936, while she was unmarried and living in Glasgow, Elizabeth T. gave birth to a son. When he was six weeks old, Elizabeth brought her infant son to her parents' home in Co. Louth. She had no home of her own at the time and, as an employee of a fish and chip shop, would probably have found it difficult to raise a child on her own. The court was satisfied that Elizabeth T. had always taken a 'very real interest in her child'.[32] She sent her elderly parents 'both money and clothes for the child and in so far as her circumstances permitted has provided largely for the means whereby he has hitherto been maintained'.[33] However, the court ruled in favour of the boy's grandparents as the judges felt that 'his moral and religious welfare would be jeopardised if he were sent to live with persons whose way of life was contrary to the teachings of their Church and whose conduct was regarded by their clergy with disapproval'.[34] Antonio T. had divorced his wife, and the marriage between Antonio and Elizabeth, which took place in a registry office in Scotland, was not recognized by the Catholic Church. Mr Justice P. Maguire doubted whether Elizabeth and Antonio T.'s marriage was stable and considered that it would be detrimental to the boy's morals and religious belief if he were 'removed from the moral atmosphere in which he has been reared to a home in which the conduct of his mother is regarded by her own clergy with disapproval'.[35] While Mr Justice Kevin Haugh was favourably impressed with Elizabeth T. as a witness and was satisfied that 'motherly feelings alone have prompted her to take these proceedings',[36] he was of the opinion that her son would 'receive little or no Catholic training' in their home in Glasgow.[37] He felt that they would be unable to ensure that the boy attended his sacramental duties when they themselves were unable to do so, and he concluded that the welfare of Elizabeth T.'s son would be better served by leaving him in the care of his grandparents. The court's decision may have permanently deprived Elizabeth of all access to her son. Her lifestyle, which went against the teachings of the Catholic Church, seems to have prejudiced her in the eyes of the court. The case highlights the fact that the odds were stacked against unmarried women who gave birth outside wedlock in Ireland in this period. The teachings of the Catholic Church clearly influenced the judges' decision in this case, thus demonstrating the way in which Catholic morality permeated Irish society. The infanticide cases examined indicate that some unmarried women did raise their children in their parents' home, but these cases constituted a very small minority.

'IT WAS UNFORTUNATE THAT THE WOMAN HAVING GOT THE ORDER WAS UNABLE TO GET THE MONEY.'

Not only were there few options open to the unmarried mother in terms of welfare provision in early twentieth-century Ireland but until 1930 the unmarried mother was unable to seek maintenance from the infant's father in her own right. Legislation that enabled single mothers to sue the fathers of their infants for maintenance was not introduced in the Twenty-Six Counties until 1930 with the passing of the Illegitimate Children (Affiliation Orders) Act. As McAvoy has noted, prior to the passing of that act, women were unable to seek maintenance in their own right.[38] The only alternatives available to them in seeking maintenance were either for their employers or for parents to bring a civil action for seduction by claiming loss of the woman's services as a result of her pregnancy, or if the woman's child was 'supported on the poor rate, the poor law guardians could initiate proceedings against the father, but obtaining a decree involved cross-examination of the mother and corroboration of her evidence'.[39] Reports on Affiliations Orders cases in the provincial press demonstrate that determined and resourceful single mothers used the new legislation to their own advantage and a small number of them succeeded in forcing the putative fathers of their children to face up to their responsibilities. For instance, in June 1936 the *Connacht Tribune* reported that James L. was ordered to pay Mary B. five shillings per week from May 1935 under the Illegitimate Children (Affiliation Orders) Act, 1930.[40] However, few single women charged with infanticide in Ireland at this time seem to have sought maintenance from the fathers of their illegitimate infants. This may have been because they were aware of the difficulties involved in pursuing such a course of action. In the words of a solicitor who had dealt with 'a number of applications for affiliation orders', the bill passed in the Irish Free State in 1930 often 'involves considerable time and work with no outcome whatsoever'.[41] The odds were very much stacked against women who gave birth outside wedlock in Ireland during the first half of the twentieth century. It is hardly surprising that women convicted of infanticide felt that they there very few options open to them.

Success rates in maintenance cases involving single mothers in Northern Ireland may have been slightly higher. The case sheets of the solicitor to the Belfast Poor Law Guardians indicate that in eleven out of eighteen cases between 1920 and 1923 the Belfast Poor Law Guardians were successful in recovering the amount due for maintenance. Nonetheless, as the following example demonstrates, it remained difficult for single Irish women to successfully sue for maintenance on their own behalf from 1930 onwards. At the district court in Galway in 1936, Patrick C. had been ordered to pay Mary M. twelve pounds and four shillings in monthly instalments for the maintenance of their illegitimate child. However, a judge in Galway circuit court reversed the order of the district justice once he was satisfied that Patrick C. was unable to pay the debt he owed Mary M. 'It was unfortunate', the judge remarked 'that the woman having got the order was unable to get the money.'[42] Given the low success rate for women who brought a case against the putative fathers of their infants under the terms of the new legislation, this was perhaps a more typical case. It highlights the difficulties single women encountered and the financial hardship they faced as lone parents, as well as the lack of will on the part of the authorities to compel men to face up to their financial responsibilities.

STUDIES ON SINGLE MOTHERHOOD IN IRELAND

The past two decades have seen an increasing number of publications on the history of single mothers in Ireland during the first half of the twentieth century. Much of the literature on unmarried motherhood in Ireland between 1900 and 1950 has focused on official responses to it. A smaller portion of the research on unmarried motherhood in Ireland during the first half of the twentieth century concerns the children of single women. A number of historians have discussed mortality rates among illegitimate infants in independent Ireland and the way in which the government responded to the disparity in deaths between legitimate and illegitimate infants. Historians who have explored single motherhood in post-independence Ireland have made great use of government sources such as the annual reports of the Department of Local Government and Public Health, the *Report of the Committee on Evil Literature* (1927), the *Report of the Commission on the Relief of the Sick and Destitute Poor, Including the*

Insane Poor (1928) and the *Report of the Committee on the Criminal Law Amendment Acts, 1880–1885 and Juvenile Prostitution* (1931). Luddy, McAvoy, Earner-Byrne and Kennedy have all examined legislation introduced in post-independence Ireland in relation to single mothers and their children. Most scholars agree that state policies directed at unmarried mothers and their children in post-independence Ireland were inadequate. Several scholars have investigated the history of some of the institutions that admitted single expectant women from the 1920s. Luddy has noted how these institutions allowed single women and their families to conceal their shame: 'The value of these institutions managed by nuns was that they shielded both the woman and her family from the gaze and scrutiny of the public.'[43] Earner-Byrne has underlined the class dimension to the various institutions that catered for single expectant women; single expectant women from middle-class backgrounds were admitted to the special Mother and Baby homes, while working-class women generally had little option but to enter a county home.[44]

We know much about the ways in which unmarried mothers were perceived in post-independence Ireland.[45] In a key paper, 'Moral Rescue and Unmarried Mothers in Ireland in the 1920s', Luddy discussed the ways in which unmarried mothers were perceived in independent Ireland.[46] She highlighted the fact that 'conflicting representations of unmarried mothers abounded' and has suggested that although 'sophisticated and complex representation of unmarried mothers existed in the Irish Free State' by the end of the 1920s, such discussion did not lead to significant policy changes in terms of the ways in which single mothers and their children were dealt with.[47] Earner-Byrne has argued that in Ireland between 1900 and 1950, 'the prevailing view of unmarried motherhood was that it was illegitimate, unsustainable and morally wrong'.[48] As Earner-Byrne has noted, such negative constructions of single motherhood 'helped to direct and limit the scope of government policy in relation to the unmarried mother and her child'.[49] Indeed, until the 1960s, most unmarried mothers had little option but to enter institutions and to relinquish custody of their children.

The discourse on unmarried mothers in post-independence Ireland was largely constructed by government officials, priests, politicians and rescue workers and concerned itself with categorising unwed mothers and putting forward various ways of dealing with each category. The experiences of individual single mothers rarely featured in this discourse. Unmarried mothers had, of course, also been viewed negatively prior to independence. However, post-independence there seems to have been an increased sense of concern with morality in the Twenty-Six County state and some writers may have published their views on unmarried motherhood in a bid to influence the government in their approach to the issue.

When unmarried mothers were mentioned in the Irish press during the first half of the twentieth century, they were often characterised in negative terms and referred to as 'troublesome'[50] or as 'offenders'.[51] Articles on single mothers in the Irish press often carried headings such as 'A difficult problem. The Unmarried Mother Question'[52] or 'Unmarried Mother Problem'.[53] Like many commentators, 'Sagart',[54] writing in 1922, viewed unmarried mothers as offenders and as sinners, and discussed their 'degrees of guilt'.[55] Glynn, in 1921, argued that the unmarried mothers sinned against moral law and natural law in 'bringing a child into the world which will bear a brand on it all its life'.[56] 'Girl-mothers' were regarded by many in Ireland during the first half of the twentieth century as 'people who don't deserve respect' and as untrustworthy individuals whose word could not be necessarily relied on in a court of law.[57] Judge Shannon warned the jurors in an abortion case that was tried in February 1937 that Margaret B. was 'a witness to be looked upon with the very greatest possible suspicion' – as she was a single woman who had had three pregnancies.[58] Several scholars have drawn attention to the fact that the language of crime was used extensively to describe unmarried mothers. Kennedy has noted how 'the language used about unmarried mothers during the first half of the twentieth century in Ireland was marked by the colours of crime and sin'.[59] She has highlighted the fact that phrases such as 'rehabilitation of the mother' and 'girls who have fallen again' were used repeatedly in government reports.[60] O'Sullivan and Raftery have also noted the fact that 'the language of criminality was deliberately invoked' in discussions of unmarried mothers, 'highlighting the perception of such women as "criminal" '.[61] In this period unmarried mothers were viewed as having committed a moral crime and as a result were in need of a specific type of spiritual rehabilitation.

Several scholars have recently focused their attentions on single pregnant Irish women who left Ireland for Britain in the post-independence period, and specifically on the emergence of a scheme set up during the 1930s to repatriate single Irish mothers in Britain. Earner-Byrne's research has shown that 'Irish expectant single mothers emigrated to Britain in significant numbers during the twentieth century.'[62] She has identified social hostility to their plight as one of the main factors for the high levels of prenatal emigration among single expectant Irish women in post-independence Ireland. Social services for unmarried women and their children were highly inadequate in Ireland and many women were keen to secure anonymity, 'less punitive care, and free legal adoption' in Britain.[63] Earner-Byrne's research has detailed how the Irish government finally took action in the late 1930s to reverse this trend by sanctioning an assisted repatriation scheme for unmarried Irish mothers in Britain. Garrett has researched the activities of the Child Protection and Rescue Society of Ireland, an organisation that cooperated with English agencies who helped repatriate Irish women from the late 1930s onwards. In examining the reasons that prompted so many single expectant women to leave Ireland for Britain, Garrett also argued that 'the threat of a type of incarceration in semi-penal institutions' was probably one of the main reasons why large numbers of unmarried pregnant women emigrated.[64] He has suggested that some single expectant Irish women may have decided to give birth in England and have their children cared for there because they were aware of the numbers of illegitimate children who died in institutional care in Ireland. Lambert's research has shown that women's fear of shame and stigma was the key motivating factor. In her essay based on the oral evidence of forty Irish women who lived in Lancashire between 1922 and 1960, Lambert referred briefly to the fact that unmarried pregnant Irish women were often 'forced to emigrate rather than bring shame upon their families at home'.[65] Some women in her study concealed their pregnancies from family members, while others received assistance from relatives to emigrate. While poverty and fear of losing employment emerge as important motivating factors in Irish infanticide cases, the desire to avoid the shame and stigma associated with single motherhood loomed large in unmarried pregnant women's minds.

While the history of unmarried mothers and infanticide remains an under-researched area, a number of studies that focus on infanticide in post-independence Ireland have been carried out in recent years. Some studies, such as Ryan's, have focused on newspaper representations of infanticide cases in the 1920s and 1930s, while others have examined the crime in the context of attempts by both church and state to control female sexuality. Ryan has contributed to the research on infanticide in Ireland during the 1920s and the 1930s by studying representations of Irish women and infanticide in both the provincial and the national press.[66] Ryan has argued that while infanticide was regularly reported in Irish newspapers, reports were generally limited to a brief synopsis of events and offered no discussion about unmarried motherhood in Irish society. Ryan's work on infanticide is narrow in scope and does not engage with the archival material available. McAvoy's pioneering doctoral work on infanticide examined the felony from the point of view of the newly independent southern Irish state and its efforts to regulate female sexuality. McAvoy provided a detailed analysis of infant murder and concealment of birth statistics, the law and infanticide, as well as sentencing practices in such cases. McAvoy's research involved close readings of cases tried at the Central Criminal Court and at district court level between 1922 and 1949. She queried whether a strict code of sexual morality operated at all social levels in post-independence Ireland and drew attention to the importance of neighbourhood surveillance in policing the sexual behaviour of young unmarried women.[67]

Maguire's study of childhood in post-independence Ireland explores state provision for neglected and impoverished children, as well as provision for illegitimate children in Ireland from the 1920s to 1960. As well as exposing the gap between republican rhetoric on the state's responsibility to the nation's children and social policies implemented in post-independence Ireland, and exploring the struggles of poor parents, both married and single, to raise their children on low incomes and in substandard housing, Maguire also examined a large body of infanticide cases tried in the Central Criminal Court, as well cases tried in the lower courts.

Maguire's discussion of the judicial records adds to understandings of the ways in which the courts dealt with women tried for the murder or concealment of birth of infants born out of wedlock or as a result of extra marital affairs. The passage of the Infanticide Act (1949) is discussed at length and Maguire highlights the Irish Catholic Church's apparent lack of concern with the fates of illegitimate newborns. Maguire argues that the frequency with which infanticide occurred and the manner in which the courts dealt with the crime suggest that respect for life did not apply equally to all individuals in independent Ireland. In fact, this had also been evident in the two decades prior to independence.

Irish sexual culture is an important component of this study which calls into question the notion of the passive unmarried mother who was seduced and abandoned. Maguire's work on infanticide has also contributed to understandings of Irish sexual culture. Maguire rightly asserts that many Irish women were active agents in the sexual liaisons that resulted in pregnancy outside wedlock. Single women who became pregnant were not always, as Maguire argues, the victims of male seduction or sexual aggression. Some had multiple sexual partners. In Chapter 3, I argue that in many instances sex took place in the context of a relationship that seemed stable and may have been on the road to marriage. However, Maguire highlights the small number of cases where women had multiple sexual partners, without providing a discussion of cases involving women in long-term relationships. Cases where the defendants had themselves been the victims of rape, incest or abuse are also overlooked. Maguire takes no account of the circumstances in which statements were made, although evidence submitted by female defendants in infanticide cases was undoubtedly shaped by the gardaí questioning them. The fact that female suspects may well have been pressurised by their male interrogators to disclose information about their sexual encounters cannot be discounted. Few of these women would have been aware of their legal rights. Most would have been alone when questioned and would have been unable to access legal advice.

Maguire argues that 'infanticide should not be viewed only as the act of desperate women confronted with an unwed pregnancy in a society that placed a high premium on premarital celibacy and stigmatised unmarried mothers and their children'.[68] My research shows that infanticide was committed mainly by unmarried domestic servants in their late teens to mid-twenties. It must be viewed, first and foremost, within the context of the way unwed mothers were viewed in mid-twentieth century Ireland. 'Women who committed infanticide generally put the fate of their newborn children low down in their list of priorities.'[69] The fate of their newborn infants was low down in the list of many single women's priorities presumably because the options for poor unmarried expectant women in mid-twentieth-century Ireland were so limited. Material circumstances militated against the unmarried mother. The sense of shame attached to premarital conception should not be underestimated. While Maguire concedes that there was a certain element of desperation inherent in some infanticide cases, the circumstances that prompted unmarried women to take the lives of their newborn infants are not fully explored. Instead, Maguire seems at pains to prove that many women were callous and showed a patent disregard for the lives of their newborns. Such women, according to Maguire, were not victims. Maguire argues that only a small percentage of women fitted the stereotype of the infanticidal woman as young, unmarried, seduced and abandoned, driven to infanticide by shame and desperation. I would argue that most single women who stood trial at the Central Criminal Court between 1922 and 1950 fitted the stereotype and that although most may not have been seduced and abandoned, some certainly were. Most were quite young. The average age of unmarried women tried at the Central Criminal Court between 1922 and 1950 was 24. Three women were 17 when they went to trial. The vast majority were from working-class backgrounds. Some were extremely poor. Most were employed as domestic servants. Few would have received much formal education. Some were illiterate; several were inarticulate. Maguire does not refer to the women who attempted suicide shortly after taking the lives of their newborn infants, or of the mental anguish and physical suffering many experienced.

'EXTRACTED FROM HER BY INDUCEMENT'

Existing studies on single motherhood have concentrated on represent-ations of unmarried mothers in contemporary discourse, and on the ways in which both church and state responded to the 'unmarried mother question'. This study provides a detailed analysis of the diverse experi-ences of unmarried mothers who faced criminal charges because they were suspected of having committed infanticide. Although statistics relating to female perpetrators of serious forms of crime will be interro-gated, the history of single women who killed their illegitimate infants cannot be understood through official numbers alone. The methodology employed involves a detailed case-by-case analysis of the records of over 300 infanticide cases tried in Ireland, both North and South, during the first half of the twentieth century. Bechtold and Cooper Graves have noted that case-study research methodology offers a number of advan-tages to researchers on infanticide. Case studies, they have argued, 'can offer multiple perspectives, for example, by giving voice to those who have the least power, in this case primarily the infanticidal mother, or by fostering understanding of the role of specific institutions, locations or persons associated with the act of infanticide'.[70] They have also high-lighted the fact that case studies of infanticide 'typically describes the real-life context in which the act of infanticide took place'.[71] I would argue, as Bechtold and Cooper Graves have, that infanticide cannot simply be understood through an analysis of official figures alone, 'because its causes are multifaceted.'[72] The case studies examined give insight into the particular circumstances of individual Irish women, high-lighting their poverty, their isolation, their fears and the role played by family members and the wider community.

This study draws upon the judicial records of over 300 infanticide cases tried at the higher courts in Ireland (Assizes and Central Criminal Court) between 1900 and 1950. Prior to independence in the Twenty-Six County state in 1922 and the partition of Northern Ireland in 1920, serious criminal cases, including the murder of infants aged under one year (infanticide), were dealt with at the Assizes in each county. The Assizes were abolished in the Twenty-Six County state in 1924 with the passing of the Courts of Justice Act but remained in place in Northern Ireland. After independence in the Twenty-Six County state murder of infant cases were tried at the Central Criminal Court in Dublin. Appeals against verdict or sentence were heard by the Court of Criminal Appeal in the Twenty-Six County State. Only a very small number of infanticide cases went before the Court of Criminal Appeal after being tried at the Central Criminal Court.

Most Assize and Central Criminal Court files contain the defendant's statement and depositions of the police officers investigating the case and witnesses who gave evidence along with coroner's reports. Some files also include reports from medical officers who examined the defendants in prison, correspondence from the defendants' solicitors to the court and correspondence between the probation officer and the court. A number of Central Criminal Court files also contain photographs of the infant's body, photographs of the scene of the crime, maps of the area where the crime was committed and plans of the homes where the crime was committed. Crown Books (Trials Record Books in the Twenty-Six County State from 1922 onwards) were also used. They contain brief entries of cases heard and note the plea, verdict and sentence. Court of Criminal Appeal files for the Twenty-Six County state provide more detail than most, as they often included the transcript of the hearing. Three such transcripts were available for the post-independence cohort of cases.

The term 'infanticide' is employed throughout, even though in terms of legislation there was no separate charge of infanticide in Northern Ireland until 1922, and infanticide legislation was only passed in the Twenty-Six County state in 1949. However, the murder of infants was commonly referred to as infanticide during the period; the term 'infanticide' was also often used in newspaper reports on the murder of infants. Until 1949 the deliberate killing of a fully delivered infant was murder and carried a mandatory death penalty under Section 1 of the 1861 Offences Against the Person Act. McAvoy has noted that 'under Section 1 of the 1861 Offences Against the Person Act, a murder conviction carried a mandatory death penalty unless a plea of insanity was accepted, or the accused was under sixteen years of age'.[73] One of the main differences between infanticide cases that were tried in Northern Ireland between 1922 and 1950 and those that were tried in the Twenty-Six Counties was clearly the legislative context. The English infanticide acts of 1922 and 1938, which also applied to Northern Ireland, reduced infanticide to a non-capital offence.

An Act of 1803 created the offence of concealment of birth which was punishable by up to two years in prison. As McAvoy has observed, women were generally charged with concealment of birth rather than murder if 'there was insufficient evidence to prove either murder or manslaughter' or in cases 'where post-mortem evidence was insufficient to sustain a murder or manslaughter charge, but where a clear attempt was made to secretly dispose of the body of an infant in order to hide the fact that its mother had given birth'.[74] Concealment of birth was a misdemeanour, not a felony. Women who stood trial at the assizes prior to 1922 and at the Central Criminal Court, Dublin, from 1922 onwards were usually charged with both murder and concealment of birth. This meant that women could be convicted on a lesser charge of concealment of birth. Juries could also return a manslaughter verdict in cases where individuals stood trial for the murder of infants. Only a small number of cases prosecuted in the Central Criminal Court between 1922 and 1950 actually resulted in murder convictions. In each instance the death sentence was commuted to penal servitude for life.

There are many historical actors in this study; the fathers of the deceased infants who appear in only a minority of cases; the landladies and employers who were often the first to come across the infant's body; the family members who collaborated with the unwed birth mother; the doctors and nurses who treated female defendants prior to their arrest or behind prison walls; the policemen responsible for questioning and charging the defendants in the cases examined, and the legal professionals encountered in the courtroom. It would appear that, on occasion, relatives of the birth mother were compelled to give evidence against her. In some instances, defendants made very brief statements; others were more detailed, and a smaller proportion of defendants made several statements – in many instances this involved the retraction or amendment of the original statement. Most of the files examined included a coroner's report, the defendant's statement and depositions from employers, doctors, and family members if the defendant was resident in the family home. A coroner is an independent official with legal responsibility for the investigation of sudden and unexplained deaths. This may require a post-mortem examination and inquest.

The voice of the unmarried mother that emerges from the statements taken by the gardaí and in the transcripts of trials is one that is controlled to varying degrees by the investigator and the prosecutor. Women suspected of committing infanticide were probed by the police for information; some may have been forced to disclose details of the sexual relationship they had had with the father of the infant. As Smith has noted, 'these statements, in the main, were transcribed by the local Garda sergeant or detective and signed by the accused. There is no way to determine the level of mediation, advice, or coercion that may have taken place in the interview and transcription process.'[75] Some files consist of conflicting statements and contradictory narratives and can, therefore, be read in a number of ways. A small number of women made more than one statement; in most cases the initial statement was false and presumably after further interrogation suspects retracted the first account. Such statements indicate that some women attempted to fabricate stories in order to account for their movements. In most cases the false version of events was ill-planned and defendants soon had to retract such statements. When they were put under pressure by the authorities defendants, who were often poorly educated and unaware of their rights, soon confessed. Catherine A. gave birth in her parent's Co. Wexford home one month after her marriage to the infant's father. Her infant was strangled sometime in late March or early April 1929; pressure had been applied to the neonate's windpipe. Initially, Catherine told the superintendent who questioned her about the death of her newborn that her husband had buried the infant's body. She later retracted her initial statement and told gardaí that 'that statement was not true as I buried it myself. I buried the child in the garden at the back of our house.'[76] Despite the fact that she was married when her baby was born, Catherine's actions match those of countless unmarried defendants in the case files in that she attempted to hide all knowledge of her pregnancy from her family. Catherine said that she did not call for her mother after giving birth alone in her bedroom as she did not want to tell her. She buried the baby on a Sunday morning when her family were at Mass.

Other cases are more straightforward. Indeed, the complexities and contradictions contained in the judicial records of infanticide cases serve to highlight the level of stress and anxiety experienced by unmarried mothers and by those in whom they confided. This could sometimes produce confused responses in suspects' evidence. Women accused of infanticide were under severe psychological pressure when arrested and asked to give statements. Arrests were generally made shortly after the women had given birth, which in most cases had been without medical assistance and followed months of concealing their pregnancies from family, friends and employers. The doctor who examined the defendant in a 1936 Co. Meath case said that when he saw 22-year-old servant Mary S., who had given birth unassisted in her employer's home, 'she was in a very confused condition and not really mentally capable of making any reliable statement'.[77] Most single women confessed quickly; few seem to have made any plans as to the disposal of the body or thought through their actions in advance.

Some women were clearly intimidated or induced into making compromising statements. In some instances the woman's statement was not accepted as evidence in court; this could lead to the woman's acquittal. As D'Cruze and Jackson have noted, 'whilst we must be aware of processes of filtering and distortion, these materials nevertheless offer us a unique connection with the historical past, linking us to the lives and viewpoints of the poorest members of society (in some cases the illiterate)'.[78] Jackson's line of reasoning in relation to sources for the study of the social history of infanticide in mid-nineteenth-century England is similar. He has asserted that 'the narratives contained in depositions were clearly constrained by the law: their form and content were strongly influenced by the interests of the local official and his clerk and they were produced to conform to procedural guidelines and statutory directions'.[79] He has argued that 'in spite of these limitations, depositions can provide invaluable historical information about the generation of suspicions locally, about the motives for prosecution, about the manner in which suspects were interrogated and examined, and about the ways in which evidence of murder was accumulated and evaluated by coroners, magistrates and medical witnesses'.[80] This is also evident in the records of infanticide cases tried in Ireland during the first half of the twentieth century. The structure of depositions and statements submitted by defendants and their relatives, employers and neighbours and the manner in which suspects were interrogated will be referred to in the samples examined throughout the present study, in so far as the records allow. Even allowing for the coercive environment of disclosure, the records of infanticide cases remain an invaluable source. Few women who experienced single motherhood during the first half of thetwentieth century left any records of their own and although they feature in the records of charitable groups, such records often reveal more about the ethos of individual organisations than the actual experiences of single expectant Irish women. The voices of unmarried women who responded to the predicament in which they found themselves by committing a serious crime are more than adequately captured in the judicial records examined in this study.

To date, most studies on infanticide in Ireland have been primarily concerned with the period from 1922 to 1950. Relatively little attention has been paid to the experiences of unwed mothers who were charged with the murder or concealment of birth of their infants during the first two decades of the century. This study covers the period from 1900 to 1950. Trial records are examined on an all-island basis up to independence and from 1920/22 the six counties of Northern Ireland and the Twenty-Six County southern state are treated separately. The pre-independence sample is based on the records of ninety-five murder and concealment of birth cases involving single women that came before the assizes in twelve counties between 1900 and 1921. It was decided to limit the sample for this study and to study the assize records for murder and concealment of birth cases in what it is hoped is a representative spread of counties: Dublin city and county, Co. Carlow, Co. Louth, Cork city and county, Limerick city and county, Co. Clare, Co. Leitrim, Galway city and county, Co. Donegal, Co. Down, Co. Armagh and Belfast city. The sample includes ten convict reference files of unmarried women charged with the murder or the concealment of birth of their newborn infants. Convict Reference Files include letters from prisoners who petitioned the Lord Lieutenant to have their sentences commuted. The files also contain information from prisoners' trials.

The Twenty-Six County state sample (also referred to as the post-independence sample) consists of a total of four cases heard at the Court of Criminal Appeal and the records of 191 cases tried at the Central Criminal Court between 1922 and 1950. The unmarried birth mother was not a defendant in twelve cases. Instead, the infant's father or one or more of the birth mother's relatives were tried. This study includes an analysis of such cases.

This study examines the records of infanticide cases that were tried in Ireland over a longer time span, from 1900 to 1950, so that the manner in which the crime of infanticide was dealt with both before and after independence can be more fully appreciated. Comparative studies of the history of infanticide in Northern Ireland and the Twenty-Six Counties are non-existent. This study is the first to offer a comparative study of single mothers and infanticide in the 'Two Irelands'. Assize records are used for cases tried in Northern Ireland. The northern sample consists of a total of thirty-eight cases, involving thirty-nine defendants from Belfast city and counties Down, Armagh and Tyrone.[81] My research is based on

the records of three inquests and thirty-five trials. Two women in the
northern sample were originally from Éire but they had lived and worked
in Northern Ireland for some time before they were arrested and charged.
The majority of infanticide cases in the Northern sample were tried in
Belfast.[82] This study constitutes a beginning in charting the history of
single mothers and infanticide in Northern Ireland, but until the records
of criminal statistics are made available to researchers, and a study that
encompasses the six counties of Northern Ireland is undertaken, only a
partial picture of the history of the crime of infanticide in Northern
Ireland can be said to exist.

The records of infanticide trials are open to researchers in the
National Archives of Ireland for the period under review while a hundred
year rule applies in the Public Record Office of Northern Ireland and
those who wish to access the court records must apply for permission to
do so. As infanticide cases in the Public Record Office of Northern Ireland
are subject to a one hundred year rule, I am unable to refer to specific
places where suspected cases of infanticide occurred or to identify defendants by name. Defendants in cases held in the Public Record Office of
Northern Ireland are referred to using their initials, whereas in cases
held in the National Archives of Ireland defendants are referred to by
their first names and the initial of their surnames. The full names of
individuals in cases quoted in this chapter are available in the original
material. Most infanticide cases examined were reported in the press and
are therefore, in the public domain. However, given the sensitive nature
of such material I have decided to anonymise defendants who feature in
the case files. Newspaper reports on infanticide trials were used selec-
tively in order to provide further detail about certain cases and to explore
the manner in which cases involving women who rejected unmarried
motherhood were reported at the time. A small number of married
women have been included in the samples studied, either because they
married in the late stages of pregnancy or because they had lived apart
from their husbands for a considerable length of time and another man
was responsible for the pregnancy; their motives and actions mirrored
those of unmarried defendants in the case files.

SINGLE MOTHERS AND INFANTICIDE

This study takes a thematic approach to the history of single mothers and
infanticide. In the following pages I will look at the lives of the
unmarried female defendants who featured in the case files studied. I will

explore their class background, occupational status and living conditions. This study also examines why so many domestic servants were prosecuted for the murder or concealment of birth of their newborn infants, and considers what motivated Irish women to take the lives of their newborn infants in this period. The ways in which Irish families responded to out-of-wedlock pregnancy during the period under review will also be explored. While some single expectant women found allies in their relatives, others feared how family members would react. There were many instances where family members of unmarried women who gave birth were the sole defendants or co-defendants in infanticide cases tried in Ireland. This study assesses the role played by the birth mothers' relatives in suspected cases of infanticide. Their motives will be explored. This study is also concerned with the gendering of responses to pregnancy outside marriage. Were female relatives more likely to have collaborated with their unmarried sisters or daughters than male family members? While the emphasis in this study is, for the most part, on the single expectant women in the case files, it does not focus exclusively on the female defendants. This study is also concerned with men as unmarried fathers, lovers and co-conspirators. The fathers of the illegitimate infants whose deaths were being investigated occasionally appeared as defendants in infanticide cases, and this study will pay particular attention to their experiences and to the kinds of relationships they had with the unmarried birth mothers who feature in the trial records. In so doing, this study will reveal aspects of Irish sexual behaviour and family relationships in the first half of the twentieth century that are normally not documented.

Unplanned pregnancy had profound and, in some instances, tragic effects on the lives of men and women during this period. In March 1935 the *Irish Times* carried a report on an inquest into the death of a 22-year-old man whose body had been found in Carlingford, Co. Louth, on 23 February. After hearing the evidence of several witnesses, the jury concluded that the man's death had been due to suicide by drowning. The report on the tragic incident brought to light the personal dilemmas that unmarried couples had to contend with when faced with an unplanned pregnancy in Ireland during the first half of the twentieth century. The deceased man's girlfriend, who was six months pregnant when the inquest was held, was a key witness. When called on to give evidence, Annie M. explained that 'she had been keeping company with [John] P. since April of 1934 and he was responsible for her condition'.[83] John P.'s suicide seems to have been linked to his girlfriend's pregnancy. The evidence submitted by his girlfriend and his brother George suggested that John felt torn between the demands of his family and his girlfriend's insistence that he marry her. When questioned, George P. admitted that he, along with his mother and brother Thomas, was very displeased with John's relationship with Annie M. During the inquest John P.'s mother recalled how she had told her son 'not to stand in that girl's luck – to let her go her way, and for him to go his way, owing to their differences in religion'.[84] Annie was also aware that John's family had not approved of their relationship. She stated that John had told her once that 'his people objected to his keeping company with her'.[85]

Annie had urged John to marry her when she discovered that she was pregnant. Like most unmarried women who became pregnant out of wedlock during the period, Annie appeared to have been anxious to avoid the shame and stigma of an extramarital pregnancy. She told John that if he did not marry her, her family would turn her out of their home. She might have also been afraid that she would lose her job. On 22 February 1935, John told Annie that he was expecting to receive money at Christmas and said he would marry her then. John was distraught the last time he met Annie, on the night he committed suicide, and had repeatedly cried before leaving her employer's house where they had had tea and biscuits together. The *Irish Times* report on John P.'s death offers a brief glimpse into the private lives of an unmarried couple who found themselves forced to deal with an unplanned pregnancy at a time when unmarried mothers and their illegitimate children were stigmatised and marginalised in Irish society. The tragic outcome in this case, with its denominational undertones, contrasts sharply with the negative and stereotyped constructions of unmarried mothers prevalent in Ireland between 1900 and 1950.

This study considers the ways in which suspected cases of infanticide came to light. Investigations into suspected cases of infanticide involving unmarried women were often initiated prior to the discovery of a body. Gossip played an important role in the detection of infanticide in Ireland during the period under review. Often rumour and hearsay seem to have alerted the authorities to cases that might otherwise have gone undetected. This raises important questions about the surreptitious surveillance of single women in small towns and rural areas. Sentencing practices are also scrutinized. Of particular interest is the manner in which single women convicted of manslaughter or concealment of birth were dealt with in pre- and post-independence Ireland. Sentencing patterns in Northern Ireland and the Twenty-Six County state will also be compared. Throughout the period under review, juries were reluctant to convict single women of the murder of their infants; a minority of women were convicted of murder and sentenced to death, but the sentences were commuted to life imprisonment. In post-independence Ireland, convents were increasingly used as an alternative to prison for unmarried women who had become pregnant outside marriage and taken their infants' lives.

This study tells the story of several hundred Irish women who carried a pregnancy to term during the first half of the twentieth century, denying their condition to everyone they knew, maybe even refusing to admit it to themselves. Most gave birth alone without assistance, some outdoors, others in their bedrooms in the family home or in the workplace. Having delivered in circumstances that must have been fraught, their first concern was to silence the infant's cries and destroy all evidence of pregnancy outside marriage. Many were anxious to return to their daily duties in the workplace or in the home straight away. A large proportion of these women were sent to religious run Catholic institutions, particularly in independent Ireland. It is not known how long they spent in Magdalen convents. The history of infanticide in Ireland during the first half of the twentieth century is also a history of class. Defendants in the case records examined were, for the most part, poor uneducated women who rarely feature in histories of the period. Their experiences of a society that was hostile to unmarried mothers, explored in the chapters that follow, add to our understanding of Irish social and gender history in the twentieth century.

Infanticide cases reveal a society that was, on the whole, deeply intolerant of pregnancy outside marriage. It shows us that within rural Irish communities the police actively pursued rumours about women who became pregnant outside wedlock; they initiated investigations into suspected cases of infanticide before a body was found because they were aware that an unmarried woman in the community had given birth in secret. Sexually active working-class women were monitored. Advice or assistance was rarely offered to the women who feature in the case files but they were the subject of gossip in small towns and rural areas. Yet the trial records also show that in some instances families were willing to tolerate one pregnancy outside marriage. The relatives of some pregnant women rallied around them and helped them during childbirth and afterwards by killing the infant or disposing of its body. Priests rarely appear in individual case files but no doubt many helped to create a mindset that was hardened towards single mothers. Although the Catholic Church's influence is felt in terms of attitudes towards unmarried motherhood it is also clear that many unmarried Irish men and women ignored church teachings and sought sexual relationships outside marriage.

This study is the first to foreground the experiences of the unmarried women who stood trial for the murder or concealment of birth of their illegitimate infants in Ireland during the first half of the twentieth century. It explores their living and working conditions, their relationships with their kin as well as their intimate relationships with the fathers of their infants and offers insights into their experience of interrogation, trial and sentencing. By drawing on the judicial records of over 300 trials this study provides new perspectives on the experience of pregnancy outside marriage in Ireland.

NOTES

1. *Clare Champion*, 25 Nov. 1933.
2. National Archives of Ireland [hereafter NAI], Central Criminal Court [hereafter CCC], IC 95 71, Dublin, 1932.
3. NAI, CCC, Co. Limerick, 1935.
4. *Irish Independent*, 16 Feb. 1931.
5. L. Ryan, 'The Press, Police and Prosecution: Perspectives on Infanticide in the 1920s' in A. Hayes and D. Urquhart, (eds), *Irish Women's History* (Dublin: Irish Academic Press, 2004), p.149.
6. NAI, CCA, 13/1935.
7. NAI, CCC, IC 94 54, Co. Clare, 1930.
8. D. Ferriter, *The Transformation of Ireland 1900–2000* (London: Profile, 2005), p.286.
9. Owens, R. Cullen, *A Social History of Women in Ireland 1870–1970* (Dublin: Gill and Macmillan, 2005), p.252.
10. Valiulis, M., 'Virtuous Mothers and Dutiful Wives: The Politics of Sexuality in the Irish Free State', in M. G. Valiulis (ed.), *Gender and Power in Irish History* (Dublin: Irish Academic Press, 2009), p.101.
11. O'Connor, F., 'Ireland' in *Holiday*, Dec. 1949, p.40.
12. *Irish Times*, 3 Oct. 1928.
13. J.M. Donovan, 'Infanticide and the Juries in France, 1825–1913', *Journal of Family History*, 16, 2 (1991), p.159.
14. D. McLoughlin (ed.), 'Infanticide in Nineteenth-Century Ireland' in A. Bourke et al., (eds), *The Field Day Anthology of Irish Writing: Irish Women's Writing and Traditions, Vol. IV,* (Cork: Cork University Press, 2005), p.915.
15. Further information about infants who died in suspicious circumstances between November 1920 and December 1921 is contained in War Office files, WO 35/161A and WO 35/161B, which are held at the National Archives, Kew.
16. Between November 1920 and December 1921 courts of inquiry held by military personnel replaced inquests. There were thirty-seven cases where the body of a newborn infant was found in suspicious circumstances. Inquiries were held to investigate the deaths of eighteen female infants and seventeen male infants. A further two cases were the sex of the infant was not determined were also investigated. Thirteen infants died due to neglect at birth or lack of skilled attention. In a number of cases the umbilical cord was still attached to the infants' bodies. Many of the mothers of these infants may well have been unmarried. They would probably have given birth alone and in secret and would not have re-

ceived any skilled attention. Most of the other infants had been drowned, exposed or suffocated and some had clearly met with violent deaths. Enquiries were made in several cases but no suspects were found. There was a definite suspect in only one case in the War Office files.

17. Information on the number of crimes known to the police in Ireland between 1900 and 1919 was obtained in the annual parliamentary reports on Judicial Statistics of Ireland. See *General Index to the Bills, Reports and Papers Printed by Order of the House of Commons and to the Reports and Papers Presented by Command 1900 to 1948—49*, (London: HMSO, 1960), pp.381–383.

18. S. McAvoy (Larmour), 'Aspects of the State and Female Sexuality in the Irish Free State, 1922–1949' (Ph.D thesis, University College, Cork, 1998), p.279.

19. Information on the number of crimes known to the gardaí in the Twenty-Six Counties from 1927 onwards was obtained in I. O'Donnell, E. O'Sullivan and D. Healy (eds), *Crime and Punishment in Ireland 1922 - 2003: A Statistical Sourcebook*, pp.2–11.

20. Ibid.

21. Hill, M. and Lynch, J., UCC Multitext Project in Irish History, at http://multitext.ucc.ie/d/Ireland_society_economy_1870–1914 (accessed 5 July 2011)

22. Clear, C., *Social Change and Everyday Life in Ireland, 1850–1922* (Manchester: Manchester University Press, 2007), p.99.

23. M.P.R.H., 'Illegitimate: being a discourse on the problems of unmarried mothers and their offspring', *The Bell*, 2, 3, (1941), p.80.

24. M. Luddy, *Prostitution and Irish Society, 1800–1940* (Cambridge: Cambridge University Press, 2007), p.16.

25. M. J. Maguire, 'The Myth of Catholic Ireland: Unmarried Motherhood, Infanticide and Illegitimacy in the Twentieth Century' (Ph.D thesis, American University, Washington D.C., 2000), p.54.

26. L. Earner-Byrne, 'The Boat to England: An Analysis of the official reactions to the Emigration of Single Expectant Irishwomen to Britain, 1922 –1972', *Irish Economic and Social History*, XXX, (2003), p.57.

27. Representative Church Body Library, Governesses' Minute Book for the Leeson Street Magdalen Asylum, 1928–1934.

28. Dublin Diocesan Archives [hereafter D.D.A.], St Patrick's Guild, Archbishop Byrne Papers, Lay Organisations 2.

29. F. Kennedy, *Cottage to Crèche: Family Change in Ireland*, (Dublin: Institute of Public Administration, 2001), p.62.

30. J. Smith, "The Politics of Sexual Knowledge: The Origins of Ireland's Containment Culture and 'The Carrigan Report' (1931)", *The Journal of the History of Sexuality*, 13, 2, (2004), p.212.

31. NAI, CCC, Co. Limerick, 1945.

32. *The Irish Reports*, (1944), 'In the matter of William Dominic M. T., an infant, and in the matter of the Courts of Justice Act, 1924 (I),' p.511.

33. Ibid.

34. Ibid., p.545.

35. Ibid., p.514.

36. Ibid., p.515.

37. Ibid., p.517.

38. S. McAvoy, 'The Regulation of Sexuality in the Irish Free State, 1929–25' in E. Malcolm and G. Jones, (eds), *Medicine, Disease and the State in Ireland, 1650–1940* (Cork: Cork University Press, 1999), p.230.

39. Ibid.

40. *Connacht Tribune*, 13 June 1936.

41. M.P.R.H., 'Illegitimate: Being a Discourse on the Problems', pp.79–80.

42. *Connacht Tribune*, 13 June 1936.

43. M. Luddy, 'Moral Rescue and Unmarried Mothers in Ireland in the 1920s', *Women's Studies*, 30, 6 (2001), p.804.

44. Earner-Byrne, 'The Boat to England', p.69.
45. See M. Luddy, 'Moral Rescue and Unmarried Mothers in Ireland in the 1920s', *Women's Studies*, 30, 6, (2001); L. Ryan, 'Sexualising Emigration: Discourses of Irish Female Emigration in the 1930s', *Women's Studies International Forum*, 25, 1, (2002); E. O'Sullivan and M. Raftery, *Suffer the Little Children: The Inside Story of Ireland's Industrial Schools*, (Dublin: New Island, 1999) and in E. O'Sullivan, '"This otherwise delicate subject": Child Sex Abuse in early Twentieth-Century Ireland' in O'Mahony, Paul (ed.), *Criminal Justice in Ireland* (Dublin: Institute of Public Administration, 2002).
46. Luddy, 'Moral Rescue and Unmarried Mothers'.
47. Ibid., p.798.
48. Earner-Byrne, 'Boat to England', p.69.
49. Ibid.
50. *Clare Champion,* 25 November 1933.
51. Ibid.
52. Ibid.
53. *Irish Times*, 22 January 1926.
54. An anonymous author who used the pseudonoym 'Sagart' in an article in unmarried mothers which was published in the *Irish Ecclesiastical Record* in 1922.
55. 'Sagart', 'How to Deal with the Unmarried Mother', *Irish Ecclesiastical Record*, XX, 20, (1922), p.148.
56. J. Glynn, 'The Unmarried Mother', *Irish Ecclesiastical Record,* 18, (1921), p461.
57. *People* (Wexford), 25 May 1929.
58. NAI, CCA 8/1937.
59. Kennedy, *Cottage to Creche*, p.145.
60. Ibid.
61. E. O'Sullivan and M. Raftery, *Suffer the Little Children: The Inside Story of Ireland's Industrial Schools* (Dublin: New Island, 1999), p.73.
62. L. Earner-Byrne, 'Moral Repatriation': The response to Irish unmarried mothers in Britain, 1920s – 1960s' in P.J. Duffy, (ed.), *To and From Ireland: Planned Migration Schemes c. 1600–2000* (Dublin: Geography Publications, 2004), p.155.
63. Ibid., p.156.
64. P.M. Garrett, 'The abnormal flight: The migration and repatriation of Irish unmarried mothers', *Social History*, 25, 3, (2000), p.336.
65. S. Lambert, 'Irish Women's Emigration to England, 1922–60: The Lengthening of Family Ties' in A. Hayes and D. Urquhart (eds), *Irish Women's History*, p.157.
66. L. Ryan, 'The Press, Police and Prosecution: Perspectives on Infanticide in the 1920s' in A. Hayes and D. Urquhart, (eds), *Irish Women's History*, and L. Ryan, *Gender, Identity and the Irish Press 1922–1937: Embodying the Nation*, (Lampeter: Edwin Mellen, 2002).
67. McAvoy (Larmour), 'Aspects of the State and Female Sexuality in the Irish Free State, 1922–1949' (PhD thesis, University College, Cork, 1998).
68. M.J. Maguire, *Precarious Childhood in Post Independence Ireland*, p.203.
69. Ibid., p.202.
70. B. Bechtold and D. Cooper Graves, (eds) *Killing Infants: Studies in the Worldwide Practice of Infanticide* (Lampeter: Edwin Mellen, 2006), p.195.
71. Ibid.
72. Ibid., p.197.
73. McAvoy (Larmour), 'Aspects of the State', p.276.
74. Ibid., p.292.
75. J. M. Smith, *Ireland's Magdalen Laundries and the Nation's Architecture of Containment* (Manchester: Manchester University Press, 2008), p.60.
76. NAI, CCC, IC 94 75, Co. Wexford, 1929.
77. NAI, CCC, ID 56 30, Co. Meath, 1936.
78. S. D'Cruze, and L.A. Jackson, *Women, Crime and Justice in England since 1660* (London: Palgrave Macmillan, 2009), p.12.
79. M. Jackson, 'Fiction in the Archives? Sources for the Social History of Infanticide', *Archives,* 27, 107, (2002), p.181.

80. Ibid.
81. The records of infanticide cases held in the Public Record Office of Northern Ireland are currently subject to a one hundred year rule. I applied for permission from the Northern Ireland Courts Service through the Public Record Office of Northern Ireland to see catalogued infanticide and concealment of birth files. Infanticide and concealment of birth files are catalogued for Belfast city, Co. Down, Co. Antrim and Co. Armagh. Infanticide and concealment of birth files have not yet been catalogued for Co. Londonderry, Co. Fermanagh or Co. Tyrone. I was, however, granted permission to see the records for some cases tried at the Co. Tyrone Assizes.
82. Ten cases of murder, one case of infanticide and eight cases of concealment of birth in this sample went before the courts in Belfast. Three cases of murder and one case of infanticide in this sample went before the courts in Co. Down. In four additional cases tried in Co. Down it was not clear if charges were brought against single women suspected of killing their infants. One case of murder and one case of infanticide in this sample went before the courts in Co. Armagh during the period under review. Five cases of murder, three cases of infanticide and one case of concealment of birth in this sample were tried in Co. Tyrone.
83. *Irish Times*, 23 March 1935.
84. Ibid.
85. Ibid.

CHAPTER ONE

'Girl Murderers':
Unmarried Mothers and Infanticide

At a quarter to eight in the evening of Saturday 15 February 1941, Mrs. Ethel F. of Terenure, in the city of Dublin, heard loud moaning coming from the servant's room. Ethel ran upstairs right away. She managed to open the door a little before her servant, 21-year-old Mary M., prevented her from opening it fully. Mary, who had taken to bed at five o'clock that afternoon, asked her employer not to enter the bedroom. 'Please don't come in madam', she pleaded.[1] From where she stood, Ethel could see that Mary's legs were covered with blood. Her hands and arms were also covered with blood. Ethel then ran downstairs and, having consulted with her mother Louisa, who was also in the house at the time, she telephoned for an ambulance.

Ethel's mother said that when she saw Mary on 15 February 'she was clad only in an undergarment' and 'was steeped in blood up to her elbows. There was blood on her legs. The carpet, bed and walls of the room were covered with blood.'[2] Mrs B. asked Mary what was the matter, was she going to have a baby, and Mary said: 'On my word of honour madam, no. Please don't send me away.'[3] Women in these circumstances frequently denied that they were pregnant when confronted about it.

To begin with, Mary's employer may not have suspected that her young employee had given birth secretly and unassisted in her bedroom. In her deposition, Ethel F. stated that when she first went upstairs to Mary's room at a quarter to eight, she did not have any idea what the matter was with Mary, nor did she hear or see any sign of a baby in the room. Once she had phoned for an ambulance, Mary M.'s mistress returned to her servant's room. On that occasion Ethel saw Mary kneeling on the floor, washing her hands in a bucket of hot water. Ethel said that she thought Mary was wearing a black dress by then. There was blood on the mattress of Mary's bed, on the walls and on the carpet. While she may not have initially suspected that her servant had given birth in the upstairs bedroom, this time Mary's mistress' suspicions were aroused. Ethel entered the room and asked Mary what on earth was wrong with her, was she expecting a baby? Mary continued to deny what had happened and said 'I swear I'm not madam.'[4] Ethel asked Mary to hurry dressing, telling her employee that she had phoned an ambulance to take her to hospital and that she would help her. Although Mary begged her employer not to send her away, Ethel insisted that she go and receive medical attention. At the end of her deposition Ethel declared that the accused was most respectful and honest.

When ambulance driver Thomas Meyler arrived at the house he spoke to Ethel and Louisa and then went upstairs. At the time, Mary was standing just inside the door to her bedroom. He recalled seeing Mary 'dressed in a frock with stockings on but no shoes. She seemed as if she just got out of bed.'[5] Thomas asked Mary if she was a maternity case. Once again Mary denied that she had just given birth. The driver persisted and asked her how blood got around the place, on the carpet and bed, but Mary made no reply. He then took her to the Coombe hospital, a maternity hospital, despite her repeated denials. Soon afterwards, staff at the Coombe hospital found the body of Mary's new-born infant in the chocolate-coloured attaché case she had brought with her. The doctor who examined the infant's body stated that the baby's arms were broken between elbow and shoulder. 'There was a purple brown mark in front of its neck.'[6] The state pathologist came to the conclusion that Mary had strangled the infant with her hands. He believed that the fractures to the infant's arms were caused by violence. It was, he felt, very unlikely that the injuries were caused during self-delivery.

Mary M., like many single women who feature in the records of Central Criminal Court files between 1922 and 1950, was charged with the murder of her unnamed infant of which she had recently been delivered. Mary was convicted of manslaughter, and although she was sentenced to two years' imprisonment with hard labour, the sentence was not imposed as Mary agreed to enter into a recognizance and to spend two years in the High Park Convent, run by the Sisters of Our Lady of Charity, in Drumcondra on Dublin's north side. Many single women in post-independence Ireland, as Chapter 5 makes clear, met with the same fate.

Mary's experience of childbirth seems to have been broadly similar to that of most single women who stood trial for infanticide in Ireland during the first half of the twentieth century, in that she delivered secretly and without assistance in a bedroom in her employer's home, having attempted to conceal her pregnancy from everyone she knew, perhaps even denying it to herself for many months. Presumably Mary would have experienced feelings of panic and fear along with physical pain that February morning in 1941. Nonetheless, she, like most of the defendants in the cases examined, was determined to cover it up and to conceal all signs of infant life and of labour. Mary must have managed to stifle most of her cries during the birth. Those present in the house at the time only heard her final cries. Although Mary had haemorrhaged she still managed to find the physical strength to take her infant daughter's life. Mary had strangled her infant daughter with her hands. Soon after undergoing an experience that must surely have been both physically and mentally traumatic, Mary had to deal with her mistress's questions and to deny her entry to her bedroom. She then washed and dressed, put the infant's body in her attaché case and waited for the ambulance to arrive.

Between 1900 and 1950, countless employers in Ireland came across similar scenes. The everyday domestic spaces they inhabited became crime scenes for a short period of time. Such incidents would undoubtedly have been shocking, if not traumatic, for parents, siblings and employers as well. Mary M.'s employer Ethel and her mother Louisa must have been in shock after the incident that unfolded in their household. Ethel had herself given birth a short time previously but as a married middle-class woman her experience of childbirth would have been far removed from Mary's. It is clear from the evidence of Maria H.'s employer that the discovery of an infant's body in the household was often a frightening and disconcerting experience. When Maria called her employer into her bedroom on 17 October 1910, her employer saw 'half the head of a baby at the foot of the bed'.[7] Arabella Ferguson said that she sent for the district nurse at once but 'did nothing for the child, or the mother except to put a blanket over the mother'.[8] She said that she was very nervous and did not know what to do.

Why is it that unmarried women like Mary M. turn up again and again in the records of Irish infanticide trials? This chapter endeavours to compile a profile of the unmarried women who feature in the trial records during the first half of the twentieth century. This chapter will also attempt to shed some light on the link between single servants and the crime of infanticide during the first half of the twentieth century. Although there is a strong emphasis on domestic servants who committed infanticide, this chapter will also analyse the experiences of defendants who were not employed as servants. Infanticide is a crime

that is generally associated with poor, single women. The vast majority of single women charged with murder or concealment of birth in
Ireland between 1900 and 1950 were from the lower socio-economic
layers of Irish society. Poverty was clearly a factor in many infanticide
cases involving single women, and it will be explored. Many defendants were employed as servants. Hearn's work on domestic service
has shed a great deal of light on the working conditions of domestic
servants in Dublin between 1880 and 1922. The judicial records of
infanticide trials add another dimension to the experience of domestic
service in Ireland during the first half of the twentieth century. Much
can be gleaned from the records of the trials about the living and working conditions of domestic servants, and of poor women who carried
out domestic chores in their parents' homes. For instance, while servants
would generally have slept in areas apart from their employers, Mary
C., who was employed as a domestic servant by a Co. Wexford farmer
in 1928, slept in the same bed as her employer, his son and daughter.[9]
By documenting servants' experiences of secretly giving birth in the
workplace and taking the life of the illegitimate newborn soon afterwards, the court records illustrate how both servant and employer
responded to an unfolding crisis. The nature of their relationship is
exposed at a moment of crisis in the trial records. Some employers
reacted with compassion; others dismissed their employees as soon as
they learned that the woman was pregnant or had given birth. The
records illustrate the extent to which single women in service in this
period were deprived of the right to privacy. Suspicious employers could
go through their servants' belongings without requesting permission to
do so. Case records also shed some light on how unmarried women
coped with the pressure of concealing a pregnancy and of giving birth
alone, and reveal that some women who were suspected of having killed
or concealed the birth of their illegitimate infants attempted to commit
suicide. This chapter will consider whether domestic servants were more
likely to commit infanticide than women from other occupational backgrounds, or whether servants were more likely to get caught. It will
also explore employers' responses to out-of-wedlock pregnancy, while
the reaction of defendants' family members is detailed in Chapter 2.

A PROFILE OF SINGLE WOMEN CHARGED WITH INFANTICIDE

Richter's research on infanticide in Imperial Germany has shown that
the profile of the typical ' "reproductive criminal" is remarkably

clear'.[10] The 'type' is also clear in the Irish infanticide cases under review. In fact, the typical defendant changed little during the period from 1900 to 1950. Most single women charged with infanticide in Ireland shared the same basic characteristics. The typical unmarried woman who stood trial for the murder or for concealment of birth of her infant was in her mid-twenties and was employed as a domestic servant. Single women charged with infanticide in Ireland between 1900 and 1950 were often referred to as 'girls' in official documents and in newspaper reports on the infanticide cases that came before the courts. In a letter to the Secretary of the Department of Justice dated 28 March 1941, a senior civil servant noted that 'it is almost without exception that the accused' in Irish infanticide cases 'are young girls'.[11] In fact, most single women in the case files examined had reached the age of majority. The use of the term 'girl' to describe adult women suggests that unmarried women in their early to mid-twenties were regarded, by some, as being dependant on their fathers. It is unlikely that a male of the same age would have been referred to as a 'boy'. J.M. was in fact 24 when she was charged with the murder of her illegitimate daughter but a report in the *Irish News* referred to her as a 'girl murderer'.[12] In some instances single women charged with infanticide had not yet reached adulthood and the term 'girl' was applicable. However, in other instances reporters may have referred to single women suspected of killing their infants as 'girls' in order to create a more sensational story or to portray them in a sympathetic light.

I.C. was 16 years of age when she gave birth in Belfast in November 1913. When her mother was tried for the murder of her daughter's illegitimate infant in November 1938, Mary Anne S. was described by gardaí as a girl of about 18 years of age. However, during the course of the investigation it emerged that 'at the time of the carnal knowledge Mary Anne S. was under the age of 17 years', the age of consent.[13] The putative father of her illegitimate newborn was arrested in August 1938 and charged with unlawful carnal knowledge.[14] While Mary Anne S. and I.C. were the youngest unmarried birth mothers in the infanticide cases studied, they were not the youngest defendants. Neither woman stood trial. I.C. died soon after giving birth in a maternity hospital in Belfast in November 1913. Her mother and grandmother were charged with concealing the body of her newborn son in a drain in a field to the rear of their home. Mary Anne's mother assisted her in the delivery of her illegitimate daughter in their home and later put the infant in a deep hole of water. Mary Anne saw her mother removing her newborn infant but does not seem to have objected to her actions. Mary Anne's mother was convicted of murder and sentenced to death.

The youngest defendant in the pre-independence sample was 18-year-old Eliza M. The oldest, Winifred B., was 39 years of age when she stood trial for the murder of her female infant at the Co. Limerick Summer Assizes in 1911. The three youngest defendants in the Twenty-Six Counties sample were 17 years of age when they stood trial, while the two youngest defendants in the northern sample were 19 years of age when they stood trial. The age of the defendant was not always recorded in the case files. However, the information available indicates that the average age of unmarried female defendants in all three samples was 24.

Where did the unmarried women who feature in the judicial records of infanticide trials during the first half of the twentieth century come from? The vast majority of single women tried for the murder or concealment of birth of their illegitimate infants in the Twenty-Six County state between 1922 and 1950 were from small towns or rural areas. A total of fourteen Central Criminal Court cases involving single women occurred in Dublin city between 1922 and 1950. A number of the women charged with the murder or concealment of birth of their illegitimate infants in Dublin city were not originally from Dublin but had migrated there from other parts of the country in search of work. There were two cases in Cork city and two in Limerick city. No infanticide cases in this sample were discovered for Galway city. Cities such as Dublin, Cork, Galway and Limerick only account for eighteen out of a total of 195 cases, indicating that in post-independence Ireland reported infanticide was largely a rural phenomenon. It may have been the case that rates of detection of infanticide were higher in rural areas because tight-knit communities observed the sexual behaviour of young women more closely than in the cities. It is not possible therefore, to discuss the geographic spread for pre-independence Ireland and the northern state with certainty, but the pattern in these cohorts of cases seems to be similar to that of the Twenty-Six Counties, in that most women convicted of infanticide were from small towns and rural areas. Between 1900 and 1919 the highest number of infant murder and concealment of birth cases occurred in urban areas. A total of 106 cases (11.7 per cent) occurred in Belfast, while eighty-six (9.5 per cent) occurred in the Dublin Metropolitan Police District area. Although they account for 21 per cent of all recorded cases for that period, infanticide was still a predominately rural crime. There is a strong Belfast bias in the northern sample, with nineteen Belfast cases, nine Tyrone cases, eight Down cases and only two Armagh cases. No overall county-by-county breakdown was available for Northern Ireland between 1920 and 1950 and, as access to the files was restricted, the number of cases examined per county may not accurately reflect the number of recorded cases in those four counties.

Unmarried women charged with infanticide in Ireland during the first half of the twentieth century were typically employed as domestic servants. This also held true for women in the northern sample, where, given its Belfast bias, they may have been expected to have been employed in other sectors of the economy. The occupations of the birth mothers were recorded in a total of 102 cases in the southern post-1922 sample. The uniformity within the sample in terms of occupation is striking. Ninety-two women worked as domestic servants. Rebecca A. was the only defendant employed in a factory in the southern sample. One woman worked as a kitchen helper in a hotel, one woman was employed as a cook and two women worked as maids in hotels. One woman was an inmate worker in a union hospital; another was employed as an attendant in a mental hospital. Margaret S. worked as a dressmaker and two women were employed as shop assistants. Many women who were not gainfully employed would have worked on their parents' farms and in the home. A.R., aged 36, lived with her father in Co. Down and was 'keeping house for him'.[15] Although Mary M. worked on her family's farm, it is not known whether she received any cash payment for her labour.[16] Twenty-three-year-old Mary R. told police that she was a domestic servant, she had been out of work for two years. For two years Mary 'remained at home helping [her] mother in house duties'.[17]

Those tried before 1922 were, in the vast majority, employed as domestic servants. Thirty-nine women worked as domestic servants; two women were employed as maids in hotels, while three women were employed as cooks. One woman was employed in a laundry, one woman worked in a factory and another listed her occupation as weaver. Two of the three women were from Belfast, the third was from Co. Dublin. Two women worked as shop assistants and one woman was employed as a 'wardswoman' in a workhouse. Although single working-class women in Northern Ireland appear to have had more opportunities in terms of occupation than their southern counterparts, the regional contrast is less striking than might be expected, and again domestic servants predominate in the Six County state.

'THE PARENTS OF THIS GIRL BELONG TO A VERY
POOR LABOURING CLASS.'

In a report to the Under-Secretary, Mary M.'s family were described as being 'of the labouring class'.[18] Mary M., aged 26, was convicted of the concealment of birth of her illegitimate newborn in July 1916. At the time, Mary was living with her mother in Co. Galway. Most single women charged with infanticide or concealment of birth in Ireland during the first half of the twentieth century were from working-class backgrounds. Like 21-year-old Deborah S., they were, for the most part, the daughters of men who worked as labourers or who were described as being from the labouring class. This did not necessarily imply poverty. While it was noted that Bridget R.'s father was a labourer, the family were, according to Sergeant Duffy, 'comfortable and in good circumstances for people of the class'.[19] However, not all women in this sample were in good circumstances. Many single Irish women charged with murder or concealment of birth in this period came from extremely poor backgrounds. According to Margaret R.'s solicitor, her parents 'belong[ed] to a very poor labouring class' and were unable to make any contribution towards the legal costs of her trial in the Central Criminal Court, Dublin in February 1926.[20] When the Superintendent of the Garda Síochána in Monaghan reported to the registrar of the Court of Criminal Appeal on the family history and circumstances of Mary S., he sketched out their economic status: Mary S. and her children lived in 'a small corrugated iron-roofed house;'[21] a number of rooms were described as 'barely habitable'.[22] She received financial assistance from the County Monaghan Protestant Orphan Aid Society.

Like many other women charged with infanticide, 23-old Mary R. lived with her parents and siblings, in a labourer's cottage in Co. Cavan.[23] Most defendants who resided in their parents' home at the time of arrest lived in cramped living conditions in small cottages where several adults often shared the same bed. Inspector Patrick Mitchell stationed at Killaloe, Co. Clare, saw the room Mary H. slept in when he took a statement from her in June 1923. Mary was charged with concealment of birth. Inspector Mitchell said that it appeared to be a small room; Mary's parents also slept in the same room. Mary's father described himself as a labouring man, and neither of her parents was literate. In her deposition, Mary M., who stood trial for the conceal-ment of birth of her daughter's illegitimate infant in 1901, said that she shared a bed with her daughter Bridget and another woman.

Katherine N., aged 18, her two sisters and her parents all slept in the same bedroom in their Co. Cork home.[24]

Margaret, her cousin and mother all shared the same bed. Margaret's brother Patrick slept in another bed in the same room. The living arrangements of Margaret F.'s Co. Clare labouring family were typical of the period. Maria O. and her brother John lived in a house that contained only two small rooms near Ahascragh, Co. Galway.[25] According to police evidence the bedroom measured about nine feet square and the kitchen measured approximately ten feet square. These cottages were not always well maintained. The doctor who examined Margaret F., charged with murder and concealment of birth in June 1943, said that 'the conditions in [her] house were very filthy, with dust and dirt'.[26] He also stated that 'there was no proper bed in the house'.[27] A number of Central Criminal Court infanticide files include the plans of the houses in which the defendants lived or worked, and several files also contain photographs of houses, bedrooms and the areas in which infants' bodies were discovered. Many of the women who feature in the trial records examined were from large families. Bridget M., aged 18, was the eldest of a large Limerick family. (In his deposition Sergeant Peter Higgins said that 'there is a very large family'. He did not specify how many siblings Bridget had.[28]) Personal space and privacy must have been very limited in small labourers' cottages. This meant that if an unmarried woman gave birth in the family home it was likely that her relatives would realise what had happened despite her best efforts to conceal it; some family members denied having been present during the birth in order to avoid being regarded as suspects in the case.

It is possible that women in the northern sample, particularly those from Belfast, were more likely than their southern counterparts to have been the daughters of skilled workers. However, this is far from certain, as the occupation of the defendants' father was rarely recorded. S.W.'s bail was paid by a male with the same surname, presumably her father. He was a boilermaker. J.E.'s bail was paid by a man who worked as a master printer; it is quite likely that this man was a male relative. J.E. lived with her mother and sisters. Her father was not mentioned in their evidence and it is possible that he was deceased. Given that a number of defendants in the northern sample lived in Belfast with their families, it seems likely that their fathers would have been employed in the city's factories.

J.M. was not a native of Belfast and she may not have had any friends or family to rely on. She became dependent on the public welfare system once she had given birth in April 1927. It is unclear whether she had been able to find work since her daughter's birth but it appears unlikely. Unmarried domestic servant J.M., who was 24 years old, attempted to admit her fifteen-month-old daughter to the workhouse in April 1928 but apparently became frustrated when she was in the process of doing so. According to one witness, J.M. grew 'fed up' and seems to have contemplated drowning both herself and her child.[29] When she was charged, J.M. told District Inspector Hamilton that 'the baby was crying and she was hungry'.[30] She said that she had no money and that at the time she thought there was no other way than to take her daughter's life. J.M. admitted that she smothered her baby with her hand and put the baby's body under her bed. A report on the case in the *Irish News* quoted the defence's speech to the jury. Mr Marrinan referred to the case as 'a sorrowful story of a young woman faced with poverty, and perhaps with a slow lingering death for her child'.[31] He claimed that J.M. had had nothing to eat at the time of her infant's death, 'her only sustenance being perhaps a drink of water'.[32] He also alleged that J.M. was 'a wreck in our social system'.[33]

While few women charged with infanticide in Northern Ireland seem to have been quite as impoverished as J.M., newspaper reports of cases where the mothers of illegitimate children in Northern Ireland were charged with abandonment indicate that the unmarried mothers of young infants often felt unable to cope financially with raising a child single-handedly. Newspapers often published reports about infants that had been abandoned by their mothers during the period under review. In many cases, unmarried mothers seem to have been reluctant to seek help from friends or relatives because they wanted to conceal the fact that they had given birth. In July 1930, E.C. abandoned her infant near a viaduct outside Newry. A letter was found next to the baby. E.C. asked if 'some kind person' would 'take [her] wee son'.[34] She explained that she was 'weary of begging and starving', that her son was 'crying for milk' and that she was unable to take care of him because she had no money.[35] It is also probable that single women like A.M., who had already given birth and were struggling to support their firstborn infants, may have felt unable to cope with the birth of a second infant.[36]

Examples of defendants' poverty and difficult circumstances proliferate in the trial records examined here. It is only possible to highlight a small number of cases. Some of the single women who feature in the trial records may have refused to be hospitalised because they were unable to afford appropriate clothing either for themselves or the infant. Mary W.'s doctor gave her a certificate for Thomastown County Home in February 1944 so she could have the baby there, but in her statement her sister Catherine explained that Mary did not go to the Union 'because she has no clothes for herself or the child'.[37]

Although the vast majority of single women were from poor backgrounds, there were, of course, some exceptions. For instance, Agnes M. was described as being 'a tall well dressed girl wearing a broad hat'.[38] Her family may have been in reasonably prosperous circumstances, as Agnes was able to afford to stay in a boarding house in Dublin for six weeks and to travel from Dublin to Killaloe by train with her newborn infant in September 1912. Agnes received a well-written letter in an elegant hand from her mother while she was in Dublin. The letter indicates that Agnes's family may have been well educated, and probably middle class rather than working class. Edith A. was tried for the murder of her unnamed female child at the Central Criminal Court in October 1937. Edith's father had a farm that consisted of about ninety-two acres, and the family, who were Church of Ireland, lived in a large two-storied house. According to the rector of St Anne's in Ballyshannon, Edith's parents were respectable parishioners. He considered that their home 'is a fit one for not only Edith A. but for any person to live in'.[39]

'A PERSON OF NO MEANS'

Poverty certainly seems to have been an important factor in many infanticide cases tried in Ireland during the first half of the twentieth century. It confirms Richter's findings for Germany – that 'infanticide was primarily an outcome of poverty'.[40] Given the economic circumstances of most of the unmarried women who stood trial for infanticide, it seems likely that few of them were able to afford the costs of having a solicitor or a barrister to represent them in court. Information as to whether women in this sample were defended or undefended in court is available for eleven cases in the pre-independence sample. Eight women were defended in court, while three women were listed as undefended. Women who were unable to afford legal representation would clearly have been at a disadvantage when their case went to trial, and it was the practice for some to be assigned legal representation. It is possible that many more women were assigned legal representation, but this was not recorded in the relevant files. Some women who did not have legal representation in court cross-examined witnesses themselves. At the trial for the murder of her illegitimate son in December 1901, Bridget N. appears to have cross-examined witnesses for the Crown. Bridget M. also interrogated several Crown witnesses during the trial for the murder of her illegitimate son at the Co. Donegal Winter Assizes of 1900. Only cursory references to legal costs appear in some of the records of northern infanticide cases. It is clear from the information recorded in the Crown Books that a number of women in the northern sample (at least four) were assigned legal representation. Another three women had legal counsel, but as it was not assigned to them, the women or their families must have been able to cover the costs of legal representation. At least another three were not professionally represented in court. This figure is likely to have been higher as a defendant's legal representation or lack thereof may not always have been noted in the relevant Crown Books and it seems likely that many single women who had been employed as domestic servants would have been unable to cover their legal costs. Also, as in the case of a father and daughter from Co. Down, who were charged with the murder and concealment of birth of a new-born infant in May 1931, many women in the northern sample would not have been professionally represented in court.[41]

More information about legal representation is available in the post-independence Twenty-Six County sample. Women and men charged with the murder of illegitimate infants in the Irish Free State were often unable to meet the legal costs that were incurred in going to court. In a 1943 Co. Meath case, John E., the father of a woman who was pregnant before she married, was convicted of the murder of her infant. John E.'s solicitors wrote to the registrar at the Central Criminal Court to request a copy of the depositions free of charge. In the letter his solicitors described John E. as 'a man of very slender means, residing on a farm of about 20 acres'.[42] They explained that 'it is more than difficult for the accused to raise any funds beyond the minimum required to meet the actual costs of the defence'.[43] In a 1943 Co. Galway case, Mary Kate M., a single woman, and John M.G., a married man, were tried for the murder of their infant. Mary Kate experienced difficulty in meeting the legal costs. Her solicitors wrote to the county registrar at Green Street Courthouse in September 1943 to request a copy of the depositions free of charge. Although Mary Kate worked on the family farm, she was not gainfully employed and her solicitors described her as 'a person of no means'[44] who was 'unable to retain Counsels and Solicitors'.[45] According to a Tipperary solicitor, 24-year-old Kathleen L. was destitute. Neither Kathleen nor her parents had any 'means whatsoever by which they could pay [his] fees'.[46] Letters from solicitors regarding financial difficulties faced by their clients appear in only five of the cases included in this study. However, at least 118 further defendants were granted some form of legal aid.

'OF LOW MENTAL CALIBRE'

Although only one woman in the pre-independence sample appears to have been illiterate, few women in any of the samples studied here would have received much formal education. A number of women charged with infanticide had difficulty expressing themselves. At least four single women and the relatives of several women in the Twenty-Six Counties sample were illiterate. Petitions filed by prisoners in the pre-independence samples underscore the fact that they were unaccustomed to expressing themselves formally in writing. Margaret P. was convicted of the manslaughter of her illegitimate infant in July 1906 and sentenced to serve twelve months in prison. Writing to the Lord Lieutenant, she told him that 'it was not very nice to give me such a large time here such a long time in prison'.[47] In her petition, Bridget R. stated that if the Lord Lieutenant took pity on her 'and could see [his] way to take something off [her] time [she] would be very thankful to [him] and [she] will promise never to come back to prison again for [she] [is] very sorry for bringing such disgrace on [her] people as there was never anything against any belonging to [her] till this misfortune befell [herself] but [her] mother and father is forgiving [her] and taking [her] home under their care'.[48] The letters, notes and petitions in these files are replete with grammatical and spelling errors. Some writers were clearly unfamiliar with official legal terminology. Julia S.'s father referred to her crime as 'a charge of Infancy'.[49]

Lack of education placed unmarried mothers at a serious disadvantage both during the pre-trial process and in the courtroom. Coupled with the physical and psychological strain of giving birth alone, it is hardly surprising that the statements of unmarried mothers charged with the murder of their newborn infants or with concealment of birth sometimes appear quite confused. The doctor who examined Mary S., a 22-year-old unmarried woman who gave birth unassisted in her employer's home in February 1936, said that when he saw her, 'she was in a very confused condition and not really mentally capable of making any reliable statement'.[50]

Judges, barristers and doctors sometimes commented on the level of intelligence of women charged with infanticide. The medical officers who examined Mary C. in Sligo Prison in May 1947 stated that she 'appeared to show a high degree of intelligence for her education'.[51] Mary apparently answered all their questions freely and logically. There were few instances where doctors who came into contact with women suspected of having killed their infants commented favourably on their intellect. More often, however, unmarried mothers suspected of committing infanticide were often perceived as stupid, ignorant or mentally defective. In a report written on 14 June 1929, a medical officer stated that Deborah S. was 'of low mental calibre'.[52] The medical officer who examined Mary M. in Mountjoy Prison in September 1948 reported that he 'found her childish in manner' and that while she had attended school until she was 13 years old, 'she shows a very low standard of education and is unable to do simple calculations'.[53] She never read newspapers or books and took no interest in general affairs. Mary was also 'completely ignorant of the dangers connected with child birth and also with some of the essential physical facts', and the medical officer concluded that she was both mentally immature and mentally defective.[54] The doctor who examined Mary M. in September 1940 said that 'in [his] opinion the girl is barely normal'.[55] In his report on Mary M. the prison medical officer noted that, while she was fit to plead, 'the mentality of this prisoner is low'.[56] Dr Thomas McDonagh said he thought that Jane M., convicted of the murder of her unnamed female infant in November 1945, was 'sub-normal in intelligence'.[57] The extract from the medical officer's journal in Mary M.'s file dated 28 June 1949 stated that 'she is a simple minded type and one easily swayed by others'.[58] The medical officer who examined Frances B. in Mountjoy Prison in November 1949 noted that she was 'dull' and 'slow in replying to questions'.[59]

Mary M., the 21-year-old domestic servant we met at the start of the chapter, was tried at the Central Criminal Court for the murder of her unnamed female infant in April 1941. Dr James Maher spoke to Mary when she was admitted to the Coombe Hospital. In his deposition he noted that Mary was not inclined to speak at the time. He also added that 'from her attitude to the questions I thought she was a bit dull mentally'.[60] This patronising attitude by well-educated, affluent doctors may have been rooted in class bias. Insensitive remarks made by doctors reveal a lack of sympathy and understanding and suggest that some may have been ill-equipped to deal with women who may have committed infanticide. However, remarks made with regard to the intellectual ability of these women may have, in some instances, been calculated to work in the woman's favour. Elizabeth H. was sentenced to death at the Central Criminal Court in December 1927 for the murder of her infant. She was described by the trial judge, Mr Justice Johnston, as 'a person of weak intellect'.[61] He 'strongly endorsed' the jury's recommendation of the prisoner to mercy as he 'was of opinion that she was a person of low intellect and that her intellect was further clouded by the distressing circumstances attending the birth of the child'.[62] It is apparent that Mr Justice Johnston did not want to see Elizabeth H. executed. His remarks on her intellect indicate that he felt that she was not fully responsible for her actions. This may have provided the authorities with a pretext to pardon her.

Terms such as 'weak intellect' and 'feeble-minded' appear to have been poorly defined during the period under review and in some cases may have been liberally applied to single women charged with the murder or concealment of birth of their newborn infants.[63] Dr Hackett, the medical officer in Mountjoy Prison, was of the opinion that Bridget R. was 'not mentally strong'.[64] However, there is no further evidence in the file to explain how or why Hackett concluded that Bridget was not mentally strong. It is not known to what extent Bridget's apparent mental weakness affected her judgement and behaviour. In a letter to the Under-Secretary, the judge who tried Hannah A. for the murder of her illegitimate daughter said that she appeared 'to be a woman who did not realise the crime she committed and to be of weak intellect'.[65] Hannah was convicted of murder and sentenced to death at the Limerick Summer Assizes in July 1910 but both judge and jury strongly recommended leniency. There is no further detail in Hannah's file about her weak intellect and it is possible that accounts about her intellectual ability may have been exaggerated, thereby providing both judge and jury with a convenient excuse to suspend the death sentence that was passed on her.

Two single women charged with the murder or concealment of birth of their illegitimate infants between 1922 and 1950 were considered to be mental defectives. Edith A., according to the medical officers who examined her in Mountjoy Prison in November 1937, was mentally defective. They came to the conclusion that she was unfit to plead. In a letter to prison authorities, the rector in Edith's parish stated that she had always been mentally defective and 'though she went to school regularly for a good many years could never learn anything and is almost or quite unable to read or write'.[66] In his deposition Edith's father said that he did not think she was capable of taking care of herself. He also stated that she had never been 'normal'. Edith's stepmother was of the opinion that Edith was not accountable for what she did. She also maintained that Edith was not normal. The medical officer who examined Margaret F. in Sligo Prison concluded that she was a mental defective. She was found insane at her trial in December 1943.

In some instances, neighbours, relatives and members of the local police force, rather than medical professionals, offered their opinions about a woman's intellect, but the judicial authorities did not always agree with their assessments. Julia S., who was 22 years old, stood trial for the murder of her infant daughter at the Munster Winter Assizes in December 1915. Julia 'appears to have been locally regarded as of weak intellect'.[67] Julia's neighbour, Kate Murphy, said that she had known 'this girl always' and did not think Julia was 'quite right in the head'.[68] Sergeant James Butler said that he had known Julia for the past sixteen or seventeen years. He believed that she was 'of very weak intellect'.[69] A report from the Royal Irish Constabulary (RIC) inspector for Co. Kerry stated that Julia was both 'a person of weak intellect and loose morals'.[70] However, the judge who tried her case felt that the claims about her intellect were exaggerated. At the Cork Winter Assizes her legal representatives pleaded for a mitigation of the sentence handed down to her on the grounds that she was 'not strong of intellect'.[71] The judge said that he was sending her to prison 'for her own good as she would receive good medical attendance there'.[72] A link was made in Julia S.'s case between weak intellect and promiscuity. This was not uncommon at the time. It was often assumed in the nineteenth and early twentieth centuries that mentally defective or 'feeble-minded' women were generally promiscuous and were vulnerable to unscrupulous men. Jackson has shown that those concerned with mental deficiency in Victorian and Edwardian England argued that as feeble-minded women lacked willpower and were often unable to fend for themselves, they drifted into crime and vagrancy. 'More crucially, their supposedly natural bestiality and lack of self-control predisposed them to sexual promiscuity. This behaviour, it was feared, would not only propagate their own degenerate stock but also taint the normal healthy inheritance of those with whom they mixed.'[73]

Mental deficiency was often invoked to explain single motherhood in Ireland. A report issued by St Patrick's Guild in the early 1920s averred that approximately 15 per cent of the single mothers it dealt with were mentally deficient and 'quite 50% a little abnormal'.[74] In their joint evidence to the Poor Law Commission, Mrs Noel Guinness, a member of the Dublin Board of Guardians until its dissolution, and the Hon. Ethel MacNaghten, a member of the Belfast Board of Guardians, went as far as to suggest that every unmarried expectant women who sought admission to a maternity home under the local authority should be 'examined by a mental specialist with a view to deciding whether or not, after the birth of a child, she was a fit person to take up normal life again, or whether she should be the subject of special care and control'.[75] Joseph Glynn argued in 1921 that at a time when 'scientific vice is widespread, it is only the frail, ignorant girl, often mentally deficient, and always weak-willed, who finds herself pregnant'.[76] In a letter to the Clare Board of Health, Dr Fogarty, the Bishop of Killaloe, stated that 'a great many' single mothers were of 'the feeble or weak minded sort'.[77] These women, he argued, 'will never be able to take care of themselves and are easy victims to the wrecker'.[78] He suggested that they should be collected into institutions run by nuns. Rather than holding the men who allegedly took advantage of vulnerable women accountable, or attempting to educate these women about human sexuality, the bishop clearly felt that these women should be institutionalised. According to the bishop, as long as these women 'remain in such institutions they are quite happy and inoffensive'.[79] Devane also favoured committing unmarried 'semi-imbecile' and 'mentally deficient' women who had had illegitimate infants to Good Shepherd Homes.[80] He argued that as they were unable to protect themselves and were 'irresponsible', they often drifted into prostitution after a first lapse.[81] Luddy has noted how 'repeated pregnancy outside marriage was to become closely identified with mental deficiency'.[82] She has also highlighted the fact that in Ireland there was little understanding of mental deficiency in the late nineteenth and early twentieth centuries. Although written evidence relating to doctors'assessments of women's mental fitness in the records of infanticide trials is scant, it would appear from the material available that single women's moral conduct and supposed lack of self-control were certainly taken into consideration.

'A PERSON OF ... LOOSE MORALS'

In a report written about Bridget R., who was convicted of concealment of birth in March 1912, an RIC sergeant stationed in Enniskerry, Co. Wicklow, stated that 'the standard of morality among the people of her class here is, unfortunately, very low'.[83] He felt that it required 'legal punishment to remind such people that the action of this girl, or others who might act similarly, is wrong'.[84] In Ireland, poor, working-class women may not have been as influenced by church teaching or by the notions relating to respectability and appropriate feminine behaviour held by their middle-class counterparts. As Weeks has pointed out in discussing English patterns, ' "chastity" may not have had the same social meaning for a working-class girl, accustomed to different courtship and marriage patterns, as for a middle-class young lady'.[85] Infanticide was clearly an ongoing problem in Ireland, both North and South. However, greater concern may have been expressed about its prevalence in independent Ireland, given the particular moral climate of the 1920s and 1930s. Judges who tried infanticide cases during the period under review frequently remarked on the prevalence of infanticide in post-independence Ireland. In a 1929 Co. Wexford case, 'Mr Justice O'Byrne said that child murder had, unhappily, become very prevalent in the country.'[86] The State Solicitor also referred to 'the very regrettable frequency with which these cases are turning up'.[87] Julia S. was tried for the murder of her infant daughter at the Cork Winter Assizes in December 1915. She does not seem to have been influenced by Catholic teaching on sexuality or middle-class notions of female respectability. Julia was regarded by members of the community in which she lived in Castleisland, Co. Kerry, as a woman of 'loose morals'.[88] Julia, who was 22 years old, was unmarried but had given birth twice. Indeed, many women in the pre-independence sample would not have conformed to Catholic, middle-class ideals of femininity and respectability. This is a phenomenon also evident in other samples.

A very small proportion of single women who stood trial for infanticide were illegitimate. In her deposition Annie T.'s mother confirmed that her 24-year-old daughter, who was charged with the murder of her illegitimate male child in October 1917, was illegitimate.[89] Annie T. had already given birth to an illegitimate child. Annie and her mother may have been regarded with suspicion and looked down upon by other members of their community in Balbriggan, Co. Dublin. Rumours had been circulating about Annie's pregnancy prior to her arrest. In her evidence Kate K. explained that she was 'an illegitimate' and did not 'know who was [her] father'.[90] In a 1931 Co. Kilkenny case, Mary K.'s mother informed the gardaí that her daughter was an illegitimate child.[91] Illegitimacy occurred more frequently than most commentators would have cared to admit at the time and the case files show that some women, like Annie T.'s mother, managed to raise a child born outside wedlock and to remarry, in spite of the stigma attached to single mother-hood.

Indeed, in some Twenty-Six Counties cases there is evidence to suggest that even before they were arrested, women charged with infanticide had become marginalised within their own communities. This seems to have been due in part to their extreme poverty, but in greater measure, perhaps, because other members of the community disapproved of their moral behaviour. According to the gardaí in Monaghan, Mary S. 'had the reputation of being of loose moral character'.[92] This seems to have affected their handling of the case; they seemed to have little sympathy for Mary S. and her 17-year-old daughter. Prior to her marriage, Mary S., 'who was then employed as a domestic servant, gave birth to an illegitimate child'. According to the garda report on the defendant and her family, it was freely stated in the locality that Mary's husband was not the father of some of the younger members of her family. Following his death, several men, 'whose relations with Mrs S. from the moral aspect were suspect, frequented the house. Of these one is reputed to be the father of several of the children and one of another of them.' As a result Mary S.'s family 'were largely shunned by their neighbours'.[93] Perhaps even more damning, in the eyes of the police, was that Mary S. 'did not appear to worry in the least as to the views, or opinions, regarding her which were held by her neighbours'. In a further garda report on the case, discussed by members of the government at a Cabinet meeting in December 1938, the author referred disapprovingly to the 'apparent simplicity' with which 16-year-old Mary Anne S. was seduced and to the 'unrepentant attitude and youth of the seducer'. This, its author noted, was 'an interesting commentary of itself of the type of people involved'.[94] Mary Anne S. did not conform to the stereotyped image of a vulnerable, wronged fallen woman. The putative father of her infant claimed that she was sexually experienced. There was also much difficulty with Mary Anne at the District Court, where she apparently did not want to give evidence at all. The gardaí clearly disapproved of the character and reputation of Mary Anne's family and felt that 'the ruthless disposal of the infant can hardly be attributed to those motives which might in other cases be responsible, namely, the anxiety to protect the family from the shame attaching to such a misfortune'.[95]

Unmarried Co. Limerick mother of three, Kate K. led a lifestyle that would have earned her the disapproval of her neighbours. In her statement she told the gardaí that she had 'three illegitimate children living, two boys and one girl'.[96] She lived with her mother and had never known her father. This kind of exclusion or isolation may help explain the high rates of conviction for infanticide among the very poor in Irish society. If women like Mary S. were shunned by the community and considered morally suspect, it is hardly surprising that people would have reported her single daughter's pregnancy to the authorities. The existence of women like Kate K. and Mary S., albeit on the fringes of the communities in which they lived, shows that some Irish families were more accepting of children born outside wedlock than has often been assumed. Hanna L., whose mother had been single when Hanna was born in her grandmother's Co. Cork cottage in 1909, had been raised by her grandparents. At the age of 18, and unmarried, she also gave birth in her grandmother's cottage.[97]

When Sergeant Cornelius Horgan arrested 19-year-old domestic servant Mary T., alias Patricia O., on 23 February 1935 and charged her with murder and concealment of birth, she responded by saying 'it is my first offence sir'.[98] For most of the unmarried women who feature in the trial records of Irish infanticide cases, it was their first – and quite possibly their only – brush with the law. Nonetheless, a small proportion of infanticidal women already had a criminal record, usually for minor offences such as petty theft or drunkenness. Anne L. had been charged with being drunk and disorderly seven months before she was charged with concealing the births of her twin infants in Dublin in August 1900.[99] Co. Roscommon sisters Elizabeth and Rose E. had been convicted of the larceny of three turkeys at Roscommon District Court less than a year prior to their trial for the murder of Elizabeth's illegitimate daughter in October 1934.

Mary C. was convicted of soliciting at Dublin District Court in October 1940, three years before she was charged with the murder of her illegitimate infant.

'NO ONE TO LOOK AFTER IT'

As Kiernan, Land and Lewis noted in their study of lone motherhood in twentieth-century Britain, 'at the turn of the century the options for single, pregnant women were few'.[100] The options for unmarried expectant women in Ireland during the first half of the twentieth century would also have been very limited, particularly if the women were poor. It was difficult for unmarried women in Ireland to compel the putative fathers of their infants to pay maintenance costs during the period under review. The case notes of the solicitor to the Belfast Poor Law Guardians in affiliation proceedings give some indication of the difficulties single mothers faced in attempting to bring proceedings against the putative fathers of their infants for maintenance. In March 1922, Hugh Harper communicated with the putative father of Nellie M.'s infant on her behalf and requested payment for the amount due for relief. However, the man in question denied paternity. According to the solicitor, 'proceedings were instituted but were returned unserved as defendant had removed and his whereabouts were unknown to Nellie M'.[101] Several men left the area where they had been living, once they learned that a woman with whom they had been involved intended to sue them for maintenance costs. Other women were unsuccessful in bringing proceedings against the putative fathers of their infants, because they could not provide sufficient evidence to prove paternity. A 1928 Department of Justice memorandum on illegitimate children acknowledged the difficulties single mothers faced prior to the passing of the Affiliations Order Act in the Twenty-Six County state: 'It can be readily appreciated that girls of the domestic service class who get into difficulty find themselves in a position of great hardship trying to earn their living and to maintain an illegitimate child away from their ordinary place of work.'[102] The author of the report also drew a link between the difficulties involved for women in obtaining affiliation orders and infanticide, implying that the crime of infanticide may decline if it were easier for women to obtain affiliation orders and thus a weekly contribution from the child's father. It remained difficult for women to obtain a successful outcome after the passing of new legislation.

Most single women would have found it extremely difficult to raise an infant on their own limited means and most would have been anxious to avoid the shame associated with single motherhood. Many felt that as poor single women they had very few options. In her study of infanticide in Chicago between 1870 and 1930, Oberman noted that while 'a determined and resourceful pregnant woman could have identified an abortionist and borrowed the money needed to secure an illegal abortion ... a more passive or socially isolated woman might have desired an abortion but have been unable to locate or afford one'.[103] Poor, single women living in rural areas of Ireland without the know-ledge or financial means to seek an abortion and without partners to provide them with money or to make contact with abortionists on their behalf may have been more inclined to commit infanticide.

While most single women seem to have killed their infants and disposed of the bodies almost immediately after giving birth, a small number of women struggled to find a way of dealing with an illegitimate infant before taking the baby's life. Johanna W., who was 30 years old, gave birth to a son in her cousin's Co. Limerick home soon after returning home from England in October 1943. She was attended at the birth by a doctor and a nurse, and her son was christened. Initially Johanna left her son with a foster mother. However, the arrangement broke down and Johanna then left her infant son with another woman who kept him for just a month before returning him to his mother in March 1945. Johanna did not return to her parents' home with her son. Instead she tied a handkerchief around her son's neck, choking him. In her evidence Johanna explained that she 'would not have done that to the child but for [she] had no one to look after it'.[104] In May 1937, L.M. wrote to ask a couple, from whom she had rented a room shortly before she went to a Co. Down workhouse to give birth, if they would come to take her out and if they would then look after her newborn infant.[105] However, they declined to assist L.M. and she suffocated her infant soon after she was discharged from hospital. C.K. lost her job as a domestic servant in Co. Tyrone because her employer noticed that she was pregnant.[106] Following the birth of her baby in March 1926, C.K. appears to have tried to find a foster mother who would look after her infant. She wrote a letter to a woman from the workhouse hospital, asking her to take in her baby. However, as she was unemployed, C.K. does not seem to have had enough money to pay the woman nor does she seem to have sought help elsewhere. When she was discharged from the workhouse hospital C.K. was seen wandering the roads with an infant. Her experience mirrors that of a number of defendants in the samples examined. Some women seem to have struggled for some time to pay a foster mother to mind their infant. In some instances, poorly paid women who were unable to maintain such payments eventually took their infants' lives. Mary O. gave her illegitimate daughter to a foster mother in Kilrush, Co. Clare, a number of weeks after its birth, but she had difficulty in making regular payments to the woman and as the latter 'had not received any remuneration up to 1-3-17 she on that date handed back the child to Mary O'.[107] The baby died soon after. At first Mary O. said that the baby died in her arms when she was walking back from the foster mother's home, but she later admitted putting the baby's body in a bog trench. It was later found that death was due to suffocation. With no state assistance apart from the workhouse, which for many would have been an unattractive option, very few options were available for single mothers like Mary O. without family support during the first two decades of the twentieth century.

DOMESTIC SERVANTS AND INFANTICIDE

The cases examined in this study show that between 1900 and 1950, single working-class women were far more likely to have been charged with murder or concealment of birth than women from other class backgrounds. Domestic servants were more likely than working-class women of other occupations to kill their illegitimate newborns. How can the correlation between class and infanticide, and, more specifically, between domestic service and infanticide, be explained? As a large proportion of gainfully employed women worked as domestic servants it is hardly surprising that so many would feature in the records of infanticide trials. Half of the single women charged with the murder or concealment of birth of their illegitimate infants in the Irish Free State in 1925 and 1926 in Ryan's sample were employed as domestic servants.[108] She has argued that the high rate of infanticide by unmarried domestic servants can be attributed to the nature of their work: 'after all an illegitimate child could cost them not only their employment, but also the roof over their heads, leaving them at the mercy of the workhouse'.[109] Studies of infanticide in Canada and Britain have reached similar conclusions. In her study of infanticide in twentieth-century Canada, Kramar has argued that 'since the loss of a servant girl's reputation had catastrophic economic and social consequences, it seems reasonable to infer that domestic servants were more likely than were single women employed in other occupations to conceal pregnancy and to commit maternal neonaticide'.[110] Similarly, in his study of infanticide in Britain between 1800 and 1939, Rose has argued that single women employed as domestic servants were 'particularly vulnerable if they became pregnant, as it would mean instant dismissal without references; for this reason they figure so prominently in the story of infanticide; a factory worker could deposit her baby with a daily minder, and her employer need not know, less care'.[111] According to D'Cruze and Jackson, in England 'single women often had reasons to do with paid work – either the impossibility of earning a living sufficient to keep a child or the fear of losing their employment if they were found to be pregnant'.[112] And according to Hearn, 'a reference was absolutely essential when a servant was seeking work'.[113] Servants may have been motivated to kill their illegitimate newborns because they feared that immediate loss of employment would result if their employers learned that they were pregnant. Their fears were often justified. According to Hearn, 'a pregnant servant could expect very little sympathy from her mistress, or indeed from her parents'.[114] This is clear in many of the cases examined. Hearn has noted that when 'girls seduced by masters, members of his family or others became pregnant, they were often dismissed instantly without a character and literally put out on the street'.[115] At least one single expectant woman in the northern sample lost her job because she was pregnant. C.K. was charged with infanticide at the Omagh Winter Assizes in July 1926. She had been employed as a servant but lost her job because of her pregnancy.[116] Several women in the other samples examined were also dismissed. Hannah A. worked as a wards-woman in Newcastle West workhouse. When the matron in the workhouse heard that Hannah was pregnant, she spoke to her about it and told her she would have to leave.[117] She kept Hannah on only until she found a replacement. Margaret D. said that after she had given birth on 21 September 1909, her employer 'hunted [her] out of the house in the morning and left [her] walking into Newcastle workhouse'.[118] Margaret said that she was 'bad with pain and weakness' after the birth and was 'very bad on the road', but that her employers offered her no assistance.[119] She claimed that she would have died 'only the people were good on the road'.[120]

'THE LAST PERSON I WOULD EXPECT TO DO THE CRIME SHE IS CHARGED WITH'

Some employers were more sympathetic to the plight of their unmarried, pregnant servants. When Eliza M.'s employer Harriet H. saw that her servant was haemorrhaging during the night of 23 October 1919, Harriet immediately 'attended upon her'.[121] She put Eliza to bed and got her a hot-water bottle. Eliza spent the following day in bed. When Harriet realised that her servant had given birth she sent for Eliza's mother. Bridget K. had worked in a Co. Monaghan household for three years prior to her arrest for the murder of her infant son in August 1938. Her employer continued to take an interest in her after her trial and conviction of manslaughter. She was also listed as a witness for the defence and attended Bridget's trial. Following Bridget's conviction, her mistress and her parents had Bridget's solicitors contact the court authorities as they were 'most anxious to know the nature of the Order and also the address of the Institution in which the girl is'.[122]

Some employers, when asked about their employee's characters, made positive comments about their servants. In her evidence, Kate N.'s employer said that Kate had a good character and worked well. Kate had been in her employment in Corofin, Co. Clare, for three years at the time of her arrest in December 1919.[123] Similarly, Catherine O.'s employer said that he had always regarded her as 'a quiet respectable modest girl'.[124] Catherine O. was arrested on suspicion of murdering her newborn infant in September 1902. A.M.'s Belfast employer said that she was 'an excellent servant'.[125] Mary F. was employed as a domestic servant in Dundalk, Co. Louth. Her employer gave evidence as to Mary's character in court. He stated that he never noticed Mary's condition and said that he 'always found Mary F. absolutely honourable, reliable and capable and the last person I would expect to do the crime she is charged with'.[126] Margaret M. was employed as a servant by a Co. Limerick farmer. In his evidence he stated that he 'found the girl a good worker'.[127] Mary C. was convicted of the manslaughter of her newborn infant at the Central Criminal Court, Dublin, in October 1941. Shortly before her trial, Mary's employer, who lived at Belgrave Square in Rathmines, Dublin, wrote to the Chief State Solicitor's Office to suggest that Mary return to her service on probation. Mary's mistress said that she would ensure that Mary 'went to her religious duties' and would also have her enrolled on an evening course in the technical school. Mary's employer said that she was interested in her servant's fate even though she has only lived with her for a short time as a general servant. Although Mary's employer was 'horrified' when she discovered what Mary had done, she felt that Mary had 'committed the crime in a state of frenzy' and was essentially 'good'. She had visited Mary in prison (Mary had apparently begged her to do so). Mary's employer felt that 'in many cases when sent to a penitentiary these girls come out worse than before going there'.[128] It is unlikely that Mary's employer's suggestion was acted upon. Mary probably spent twelve months in the Henrietta Street Convent in Dublin. It challenges Hearn's assertion that 'a pregnant servant could expect very little sympathy from her mistress, or indeed from her parents'.[129] Not all employers were devoid of compassion and sympathy.

Working-class women seem to have been exposed to a greater degree of scrutiny than women of other class backgrounds during the period under review. As D'Cruze and Jackson have observed, 'women's behaviours were closely monitored and regulated across a range of sites, including the private worlds of household and family, or through the related spaces of the workplace'.[130] It was also much more likely that servants who gave birth secretly and hid the infant's body would have been discovered by their employers, as they generally lived in the same household. Unmarried, pregnant domestic servants were, as McAvoy has pointed out, 'particularly vulnerable to discovery'.[131] They generally lived in their employer's household and would have had little privacy. Servants who lived in their employer's household were under close surveillance. Working-class women were probably more likely to have been discovered by their employers if they worked as domestic servants or by their landladies if they lived in rented rooms. As Hearn has noted in her study of the lives of domestic servants in Dublin in the late nineteenth and early twentieth centuries, 'servants spent twenty-four hours a day in their workplace and were generally in constant daily contact with their mistresses'.[132] The employers of unmarried pregnant servants often noticed the change in their physical appearance and many suspected that their employees were pregnant. In his deposition Matthew K. said that 'from the day' Mary H. 'came into [his] employment [he] noticed the stomach was high with her'.[133] Some employers confronted their employees and referred to their concerns, but the women generally denied that they were pregnant and lied about the reason for the change in their appearance. When M.S.'s Belfast employer noticed that 'she was a bit stout' in the spring of 1917 and inquired about her condition, M.S. told her that 'she never wore corsets and that was the explanation of her figure'.[134] Susan M.'s Co. Limerick employer was suspicious about her condition and asked her what was wrong with her, but Susan lied and told her that 'she was not regular for the past four months' when her employer noticed 'blood about the room on the floor'.[135] Both Bridget L. and her mother Mary lied about Bridget's pregnancy when they were questioned by the police in July 1901. Bridget denied that she had been recently confined and told the Head Constable of Rathmullen that 'she had been suffering from bile on her stomach and that her sickness had ceased but on Sunday the 23rd June 1901 her sickness came on and that the swelling that she previously had left her'.[136] Bridget's mother also denied that her daughter had been 'in the family way'.[137] She claimed that Bridget had been 'suffering from bile in the stomach and that her usual sickness stopped and that on Sunday night it came on'.[138]

Some single women appear to have been practically homeless in the latter stages of pregnancy, presumably dismissed from their jobs or turned out from their parents' homes. Mary T., aged 19, left her position as a domestic servant in Co. Waterford in the final stages of her pregnancy. She gave birth alone in a disused house on the back road between Carrick-on-Suir and Clonmel, on a date unknown between mid-January and mid-February 1935. Mary told gardaí that she killed 'the child as [she] had nowhere to go or nowhere to take it'. Mary remained in the derelict house 'with the dead child' the night after giving birth. At about 8 a.m. next morning she put a blue knitted jumper on the infant's body and hid it under bushes in the corner of a graveyard close by.[139] The case records do not reveal Mary's movements from then on. She may well have sought work in the area. Norah M.'s brother stated that his sister had no fixed place of residence when she gave birth in March 1912 but went from one friend's house to another.[140] Single expectant women attempted to escape the notice of family, neighbours and friends during the latter stages of pregnancy. Some women rented rooms in areas where they were not known. M.H. rented a room in Lurgan shortly before she was due to give birth in March 1920. She may not have wanted people to notice her condition, as she spent most of her time in bed. Her landlady told the police that 'since she came to [her] she was in the habit of lying long every morning'.[141] Bridget N.'s Co. Limerick employer dismissed her in September 1901 because he suspected that she was pregnant.[142] Bridget gave birth in the workhouse but had nowhere to go when she was discharged; she seems to have slept outdoors for some time afterwards.

Ryan has suggested that there was a class dimension to the infanticide cases reported in the Irish press; she has argued that the women who were charged and tried were either domestic servants or poor women who lived in rural areas. Unmarried middle-class women, according to Ryan, would have had more options available to them at the time: it would have been easier for them to arrange a private adoption. Ryan has also argued that 'respectable' middle-class women would have been less likely to have been suspected of 'any unsavoury activity' in the first place.[143] The births of illegitimate children to middle-class women may have gone undetected, as more affluent women would have been able to afford to pay for private maternity care or abortions. According to Detective Inspector Martin O'Neill, Dublin-based abortionists Christopher Williams and Mary Moloney were 'visited at their various addresses by girls particularly of the better class type from the country and city'.[144] Given that Williams and Maloney usually charged between twenty-five and thirty-five pounds, it is hardly surprising that their clients may have been 'of the better class type'.[145] The women who feature in the trial records examined would not have had the means to pay those willing to perform illegal abortions.

Mary Anne Cadden was one of most notorious abortionists in mid-twentieth-century Ireland. She qualified as a midwife in 1926 and set up a nursing home in Rathmines, a Dublin suburb. The records of Mary Anne Cadden's trial for child abandonment and for obtaining money by false pretences in April 1939 provide a rare glimpse into the manner in which single women from wealthier backgrounds dealt with an unplanned pregnancy. The relatives of two unmarried women who were due to give birth in the private nursing home run by Nurse Cadden in Rathmines paid her fifty pounds in March 1938 to have the babies adopted by a community of nuns. The gardaí suspected that Cadden had kept the money and abandoned the infants. The unmarried mothers and their relatives who paid Cadden her fee to arrange the adoption gave depositions. Both the unmarried women who had given birth in Cadden's private nursing home explained that they had been anxious to avoid publicity and scandal, and as their relatives provided them with money to pay for private medical care they were able to keep the birth of their infants a secret from family and friends. Annie H. told the gardaí that she only saw her baby once and 'never wanted to see it again'.[146] Annie's aunt said that she wanted to have the baby adopted so that the 'shame' would 'be buried as quickly as possible'.[147] Mary Kate C.'s brother covered the cost of her stay in Cadden's nursing home and he also paid Cadden fifty pounds to have his sister's baby adopted. Mary Kate was also anxious to get rid of her baby. She said that she 'did not want to see the child again ... [She] wanted to forget all about [her] shame and [she] did not want the people in the County to know anything about it.'[148] Many unmarried middle-class women who became pregnant in Ireland during the first half of the twentieth century may have given birth in private nursing homes and arranged to have their babies privately adopted. However, records of these kinds of cases rarely surface.

'SHE WENT UPSTAIRS ABOUT 10 O'CLOCK AND CAME BACK DOWN AGAIN IN A FEW MINUTES WITH AN ARMFUL OF BLOODSTAINED CLOTHES'

There are numerous examples in the case files of employers who discovered that their servants had given birth and attempted to conceal the infant's body in their household. It would have been extremely difficult for domestic servants both to give birth in their employer's home and to dispose of the infant's body without being detected. Mary C., a domestic servant employed in a County Donegal household, informed her employer's sister, Charlotte Clyde, that she felt ill in mid-October 1919. Mary spent some time in bed. Charlotte Clyde told police that when her employee had recovered and returned to her duties she noticed that her appearance had changed. Mary 'looked slighter than she had been'.[149] Her suspicions aroused, Charlotte entered Mary's bedroom and spotted a bag hanging on the wall. Charlotte thought that the bag looked bulky; she caught hold of it and discovered that it was quite heavy. Mary had wrapped her baby's body in an old serge skirt and hidden it in the bag. Charlotte alerted the police and an inquest was held.

It was often, though certainly not always, other women in the cases examined who first spotted physical signs that indicated that a woman may have recently given birth. Annie M. gave birth in her employer's Co. Limerick home in March 1932. Her employer's wife became suspicious about the nature of Annie's illness when she went to her servant's bedroom to give her a cup of tea and noticed that Annie's hands were 'all messed with blood'.[150] Mary K. was also employed as a servant on a Co. Limerick farm and, like Annie M., her employer's wife's suspicions were raised when she noticed that Mary's legs were stained with blood shortly after she gave birth in February 1931.[151]

A 1924 Co. Down infanticide case illustrates how difficult it was for domestic servants both to give birth in an employer's household and to dispose of the infant's body without being detected. While the woman in question managed to give birth without arousing her employer's suspicions, she unwittingly drew attention to what had occurred by carrying her bloodstained sheets openly through the house. A.B.'s servant K.C. spent two days in bed in early January 1924. She complained of having a pain in her side. On Tuesday morning K.C.'s mistress saw her go downstairs with 'an armful of bloodstained clothes'. She said she was going to wash them. A.B. 'then went upstairs as [she] was becoming suspicious'.[152] She found a cardboard box parcelled up in one of the drawers in K.C.'s room. When she opened the box she saw that it contained the body of a newborn infant. A.B. immediately confronted K.C. and K.C. admitted that she had given birth to a child. She claimed it was dead when born. A.B. sent her servant to bed and called for a doctor. Even when servants managed to give birth undetected, they often disposed of the infant's body in a flimsy manner, sometimes even leaving it in their employer's home where the decomposing body would inevitably attract attention. As Marland noted in relation to women who committed infanticide in Warwickshire in the 1850s and 1860s, 'the single mother was also more likely to conceal her birth, but often in a very flimsy, distracted way, hiding the child under the bed, in a box or in piles of clothes, or abandoning it in the privy, the scene of many Warwickshire births'.[153] This is also evident in the records of Irish infanticide trials. Although Bridget R.'s employer said she 'did not notice anything wrong with the accused except her perhaps looking unwell', soon after Bridget left her employment in November 1911, Emily Scannell noticed 'a disagreeable smell in the basement'.[154] Having discussed the matter with her husband, Emily examined Bridget's bed and found large bloodstains. Emily's husband then found a parcel containing an infant's body approximately eight yards from the bedroom in the basement that Bridget had occupied.

<h3 style="text-align:center">'A PREY TO EVIL DOERS'</h3>

There was a strong correlation between domestic servants and unmarried mothers in Ireland throughout the fifty-year period examined. This correlation became a cause for concern in the Twenty-Six County state after independence and was commented on by a number of witnesses to the Carrigan Committee. At the seventh meeting of the Carrigan Committee, Irish Women Workers Union representatives informed the Carrigan Committee that 'unmarried mothers are mostly domestic servants'.[155] Many of the servants who stood trial for murder or concealment of birth were women who would have left home in their mid-to-late teens to work as domestic servants, and would therefore have been free from parental supervision at a relatively early age. As employers did not always monitor their servants' behaviour closely, many domestic servants may well have enjoyed a greater degree of independence than most of their peers. This may help explain why domestic servants are over-represented in the records of infanticide trials. District Court Justice Dermot Gleeson also drew a link between domestic servants and single motherhood. He was of the opinion that a lack of proper education contributed to the downfall of many girls. He argued that their lack of knowledge of 'physical facts' meant that young domestic servants became 'a prey to evil doers'.[156] Similarly, a

Co. Roscommon priest noted that girls usually went into service at 14 years of age and because of their inexperience and ignorance were 'frequently led astray'.[157] In her study of domestic service in Dublin between 1880 and 1922, Hearn noted that most young girls who went into service at the age of 14 would have 'been innocent of the "facts of life" '.[158] She has suggested that as servants were 'often lonely, deprived of the companionship of members of the opposite sex', they were particularly vulnerable and 'employers and their friends frequently took advantage of this situation'.[159] Many groups and individuals concerned with the welfare of young Irish domestic servants insisted that they were innocent and frequently taken advantage of. Such statements clearly need to be treated with caution. Assumptions about the purity of young Irish women may well have been exaggerated. Some of the servants who feature in the trial records examined had been pregnant more than once and a small proportion had committed infanticide before. Nonetheless, many servants seem to have been poorly informed about sex, pregnancy and childbirth. This is discussed at length in Chapter 3.

When single women tried for infanticide in Ireland realised that they were pregnant (and many women claimed that they did not realise they were pregnant until the pregnancy was quite advanced), they did their utmost to conceal it from everyone they knew. Very few women confided in anyone about the pregnancy. In her study of infanticide cases in Upper Bavaria between 1848 and 1919, Schulte argued that 'a secret pregnancy and the birth, which almost all of the women who committed infanticide endured alone, were a tremendous exertion and demanded complete reserve in the face of questions'.[160] Most single women in the cases sampled generally denied that they were pregnant if friends, relatives or employers inquired. When she was arrested in January 1935, Margaret D. told gardaí that she had managed to hide her pregnancy from her mother by wearing loose-fitting clothes:

> I had an old loose bib on me here around the house and my mother could not notice me. She never knew anything about it. I tried to hide it from her. I used remain in bed and she used make me get up and then I used remain sitting down on the chair so that she could not see me.[161]

When R.G.'s Co. Tyrone employer suspected that she was pregnant and questioned her about it, R.G. lied and told her employer that she had always been stout.[162] Single pregnant women who lived with their parents also felt that they had to tell lies in order to hide their condition

and to account for any absences from the family home during their confinement. Margaret M. left home to give birth in the Limerick union
hospital in August 1910. She told her father that she 'had been in
hospital for three weeks with a sore hand'.[163]

Schulte has argued that some women who repeatedly denied that
they were pregnant when questioned by employers and co-workers 'did
at least manage to create a measure of uncertainty about their condition
through their assertions and explanations'.[164] She has also suggested
that by denying that they were pregnant, women who committed
infanticide were not just seeking to allay suspicion so that they could
retain their jobs, but that 'their roots went deeper and were not directly
connected with the credibility that the maids wished to give their
assurances'.[165] She has argued that by denying the child they were
carrying, women who committed infanticide were also 'depriving it of
any identity in the eyes of the outside world and, most importantly,
in their own eyes: The child remains a piece of nature, without a
history.'[166] It is possible that some women in the Irish cases sampled
may also have denied the existence of the child they were carrying both
to themselves and to people who questioned them about their condition.
Several women described the acute sense of distress they experienced
when they realised that the infant was alive, and because they had not
prepared for such an outcome, they generally strangled or suffocated
the infant almost immediately. Bridget C. initially told gardaí that 'the
child was dead when it was born' in her Co. Longford home in January
1939. However, she later admitted that the baby had been alive. She
explained that she was distressed when she realised that the infant was
alive. 'I will tell you the truth. I was very upset the child was born alive.
I held it in my hands for about half an hour and I think it died with the
cold. I was so upset I was not sure if it was dead when I put it in the
haycock.'[167]

After the birth, many women continued to deny that they had been
pregnant. Some women refused medical attention, even when they
were clearly in need of assistance, in order to conceal the fact that they
had given birth. A.M. gave birth in her room in the house in Belfast
where she worked as a nursemaid in September 1930. Her employer
said she noticed that 'her bed was in a bad condition' and offered to
fetch a doctor, but A.M. maintained that she was all right and said she
'had often been like that before'.[168] When M.B.'s Belfast employer questioned her about being unwell in November 1930, she said 'it [was]
just [her] usual illness'.[169] Bridget C.'s employer saw that her servant

was in great pain on 27 January 1941 and wanted to send for a doctor. Bridget told her that she was fine and tried to allay her employer's suspicions about her pain and blood loss by telling her that 'she had not got her monthly occurrence since she came to our house and that all came in one lump now'.[170] At the time there was blood on the floor where Bridget had been sitting. The doctor arrived soon afterwards and Bridget was charged with the murder of her unnamed male infant.

Many women in the cases sampled would have worked long hours as domestic servants and performed demanding physical work while they were in the late stages of pregnancy. Teresa M. haemorrhaged a number of times in the later stages of her pregnancy but she 'did [her] work all along' on her father's farm in Co. Offaly 'and made no complaint'.[171] As Schulte noted in her Bavarian study, unmarried pregnant servants often 'performed the full quota of work expected of them until the moment of labour and then carried on as if nothing had happened'.[172] Many Irish women also carried on as if nothing had happened. A number of women resumed their normal daily chores in the households where they were employed as domestic servants only hours after giving birth alone. Lizzie K. gave birth in her employer's Co. Limerick home between 11 p.m. and midnight on 23 April 1909. Lizzie remained in bed until six o'clock the following morning. She got up then and 'milked the cows, fed the calves and everything and small jobs around'.[173] Margaret F. gave birth in a field at the back of her mother's house in Co. Clare in June 1930. In her evidence, Margaret's cousin Bridget recalled how shortly after giving birth unassisted outdoors, Margaret had brought in the goats herself; 'they would not come for [Bridget]'. Margaret did not go back to bed to rest that day and she got up the following day as usual. I.L. told the police that following the birth of her infant she 'carried on at [her] work ever since as [she] did not want anybody to know'.[174] I.L. was employed as a servant in a Belfast household.

Performing physical work throughout the pregnancy and giving birth unassisted clearly took its toll on many defendants in the case records examined. S.C., like many other women charged with the murder or concealment of birth of their infants, was very weak and in need of medical attention after giving birth without any support or assistance in Belfast in May 1920. Sergeant William Hackett had to assist S.C. downstairs and lay her on a couch. He said that she was 'apparently very weak and sick'.[175] He did not arrest or charge her immediately 'owing to her condition'.[176] In her statement, S.C. explained that 'no person did anything for [her]' until the police arrived.[177] She said that she had been in bed for over a day without any assistance and she claimed that she was nearly dead. S.C.'s version of events may sound melodramatic. It seems unlikely that she was close to death following the birth of her infant and she probably went on to make a full recovery. However, S.C. may well have felt that her life was endangered and her words highlight the fact that secretive, unassisted births must have been a frightening experience for many single women.

This chapter has attempted to construct, in as far as the sources allow, a profile of Ireland's 'girl murderers' – unmarried women who stood trial for the murder of their infants during the first half of the twentieth century. The lives of many of the women who feature in the case files were marked by poverty and hardship; often the daughters of labourers, these women were afforded very few educational opportunities. Their employment opportunities were likewise restricted. Most of the gainfully employed women in the cases examined worked as domestic servants. The defendants in the cases examined enjoyed very little privacy. The servants among them were constantly monitored in the workplace; women who lived in the family home had to make do with cramped living quarters. Their living arrangements at work and at home meant that, in most cases, it was unlikely that a birth would remain unnoticed. The experiences of unmarried pregnant women living on either side of the border after 1920 were remarkably similar. Poor, unmarried women in Ireland, North and South, felt compelled to commit infanticide for very similar reasons and despite the differences in terms of legislation between the two jurisdictions, the overall picture is much the same.

The trial records afford us a glimpse of their experiences of unassisted childbirth. Often, the defendants themselves said very little about the experience of giving birth unassisted. It is clear that in many cases the physical and emotional strain of giving birth outside wedlock took a heavy toll on single women; this was frequently alluded to in the depositions of employers, family members and medical professionals. Some women claimed that they were unable to recall what had happened immediately after giving birth. Joan C. was charged with the murder of her unnamed male infant in March 1944. When Dr William O'Connor examined the baby's body he found a knotted cloth tied around the infant's neck. Part of the infant's gum was torn. The doctor concluded that the baby had been strangled and that death was caused by asphyxia. In her statement Joan C. said that she did not recall tying a cloth around the infant's neck and claimed that if she had done so it had not been intentional. Joan insisted that she was suffering from a loss of memory and could not remember what had happened or what she had done. 'I don't remember putting any cloths around the child except my coat ... I don't remember being brought to Tralee hospital.'[178] It is clear from the depositional evidence of Joan's sister and father that they were alarmed by her behaviour. Mary C. gave a very vivid description of her sister Joan shortly after she had given birth. 'She appeared to be convulsed. She was tearing the bedclothes. She was working her hands. As a result of that convulsed condition I brought in her father and he had to hold her in bed.'[179] Joan C.'s behaviour is one of the more extreme examples of mental disturbance that manifested itself in single mothers accused of infanticide.

The women who feature in the trial records examined were, for the most part, ordinary Irish women, who, by becoming pregnant outside wedlock, felt under immense pressure to conceal all signs of pregnancy and birth and took their infants' lives. It was a response repeated countless times in Ireland between 1900 and 1950. When Margaret D. was arrested and charged with the murder of her infant daughter in January 1935 she told gardaí that she did not know what she was doing at the time and 'was sorry a minute after'.[180] Other women may have regretted their actions, as Margaret seems to have done, while some, like Nora K., became depressed and despondent subsequently. When Nora K. was arrested in August 1925 for the murder of her seven-week-old daughter she told gardaí that the infant died in her arms. She then stated that she didn't care 'what happens [to her]'. Guard Patrick O'Leary noted that Nora seemed 'very depressed and put about and was crying'.[181] Maguire argues that 'infanticide should not be viewed only as the act of desperate women confronted with an unwed pregnancy in a society that placed a high premium on premarital celibacy and stigmatised unmarried mothers and their children'.[182] Maguire argues that only a small percentage of women fitted the stereotype of the infanticidal woman as young, unmarried, seduced and abandoned, driven to infanticide by shame and desperation. According to Maguire, 'many defendants were, in fact, criminally or maliciously motivated'.[183] Such women, according to Maguire, were not victims. Moreover, she suggests that 'infanticide can be seen as little more than a form of birth control for women who wanted to engage in sexual activities without having to care for the offspring that might result'.[184] It is not possible to determine what percentage of women were maliciously motivated, based on the available evidence. However, infanticide seems to have been used as a form of birth control in only a very small number of cases. There are more instances of women's physical and mental suffering, of women who felt alone, marginalised and vulnerable in the trial records than there are of women who callously disposed of their illegitimate infants and used infanticide as a means of controlling their fertility.

NOTES

1. National Archives of Ireland [hereafter NAI], Central Criminal Court [hereafter CCC], Dublin, 1941.
2. Ibid.
3. Ibid.
4. Ibid.
5. Ibid.
6. Ibid.
7. NAI, Dublin, Crown Files at Commission, Leinster Winter Assizes, 1910.
8. Ibid.
9. NAI, CCC, Co. Wexford, 1928.
10. J.S. Richter, 'Infanticide, Child Abandonment, and Abortion in Imperial Germany', *Journal of Interdisciplinary History*, 28, 4 (1998), p.513.
11. NAI, Department of the Attorney General, 2000/10/2921.
12. *Irish News*, 21 July 1928.
13. NAI, Department of the Taoiseach, S11040.
14. NAI, Department of the Taoiseach, S11040. The case against the putative father aged 16 years and 10 months later collapsed. Mary Anne's evidence was deemed unreliable.
15. Public Record Office of Northern Ireland [hereafter PRONI], DOW1/2B/38/7.
16. NAI, CCC, Co. Kilkenny, 1948.
17. NAI, CCC, Co. Cavan, 1940.
18. NAI, Convict Reference File [hereafter CRF] M 37/1916.
19. NAI, CRF R 26/1912.
20. NAI, CCC, Co. Wicklow, 1926.
21. NAI, Court of Criminal Appeal [hereafter CCA], 36/1938.
22. Ibid.
23. NAI, CCC, Co. Cavan, 1940.
24. NAI, CCC, Co. Cork, 1948.
25. NAI, Co. Galway, Crown Files at Assizes, 1905–06.
26. NAI, CCC, Co. Mayo, 1943.
27. Ibid.
28. NAI, CCC, Co. Limerick, 1932.
29. *Irish News*, 21 July 1928.
30. Ibid.
31. Ibid.
32. Ibid.
33. Ibid.
34. *Irish News*, 14 August 1930.
35. Ibid.
36. PRONI, BELF/1/1/2/97/5, 1931.
37. NAI, Co. Kilkenny, 1944.
38. NAI, Co. Clare, Crown Files at Assizes, 1912.
39. NAI, CCC, Co. Donegal, 1937.

40. Richter, 'Infanticide', p.533.
41. *Irish News*, 25 May 1931.
42. NAI, CCC, Co. Meath, 1944.
43. Ibid.
44. NAI, CCC, Co. Galway, 1943.
45. Ibid.
46. NAI, CCC, Co. Limerick, 1942.
47. NAI, CRF/1906/P17.
48. NAI, CRF R 26/1912.
49. NAI, CRF S 2/1916.
50. NAI, CCC, Co. Meath, 1936.
51. NAI, CCC, Co. Donegal, 1947.
52. NAI, Department of the Taoiseach, S 5886.
53. NAI, CCC, Co. Kilkenny, 1948.
54. Ibid.
55. NAI, CCC, Co. Donegal, 1940.
56. NAI, CCC, Dublin, 1941.
57. NAI, CCC, Co. Sligo, 1945.
58. NAI, CCC, Co. Tipperary, 1949.
59. NAI, CCC, Co. Sligo, 1949.
60. NAI, CCC, Dublin, 1941.
61. NAI, Department of the Taoiseach, S 5571.
62. NAI, Department of the Taoiseach, S7788A.
63. A Department of Taoiseach file containing different memorandums relating to the Carrigan Committee defined an idiot as 'a person so defective in mind from birth or early age as to be unable to guard herself against common physical dangers'. The term 'imbecile' applied to a 'person in whose case there exists from birth or early age mental defectiveness not amounting to idiocy, yet so pronounced as to render her incapable of managing herself or her affairs or earning her means of livelihood', while the term 'feebleminded' referred to 'a person in whose case there exists from birth or early age mental defectiveness not amounting to imbecility, yet so pronounced that she requires care, supervision and control for her own protection or the protection of others'. (NAI, Department of the Taoiseach, S6489A.)
64. NAI, CRF R 26/1912.
65. NAI, CRF/1911/A 11.
66. NAI, CCC, Co. Donegal, 1937.
67. NAI, CRF S 2/1916.
68. Ibid.
69. Ibid.
70. Ibid.
71. Ibid.
72. Ibid.
73. M. Jackson, *The Borderlands of Imbecility: Medicine, Society and the Fabrication of the Feeble Mind in Late Victorian and Edwardian England* (Manchester: Manchester University Press, 2000), p.106.
74. NAI, Department of Justice, 90/4/6, Letter dated January 1927 from Miss Cruice, Hon. Secretary of St Patrick's Guild to all the Irish bishops.
75. *Irish Times*, 22 January 1926.
76. J. Glynn, 'The Unmarried Mother', *Irish Ecclesiastical Record*, 18 (1921), p.463.
77. *Clare Champion*, 25 November 1933.
78. Ibid.
79. Ibid.
80. R.S. Devane, 'The Unmarried Mother: Some Legal Aspects of the Problem. II – The Legal Position of the Unmarried Mother in the Irish Free State', *Irish Ecclesiastical Record*, 23 (1924), p.183.
81. Ibid.
82. M. Luddy, *Prostitution and Irish Society, 1800–1940* (Cambridge: Cambridge University Press, 2007), p.117.

83. NAI, CRF R 26/1912. Bridget R. stood trial for concealing the birth of her illegitimate infant in March 1912.
84. Ibid.
85. J. Weeks, *Sex, Politics and Society: The Regulation of Sexuality since 1800* (London: Longman, 1989), p.61.
86. *The People* (Wexford), 29 June 1929.
87. *The People* (Wexford), 11 May 1929.
88. NAI, CRF S 2/1916.
89. NAI, Leinster Winter Assizes, December 1917.
90. NAI, CCC, Co. Limerick, 1935.
91. NAI, CCC, Co. Kilkenny, 1931.
92. NAI, Court of Criminal Appeal [hereafter CCA], 36/1938. Letter from Oifig an Choimisineara to the Registrar, Court of Criminal Appeal, Dublin.
93. Ibid.
94. NAI, Department of the Taoiseach, S11040.
95. Ibid.
96. NAI, CCC, Co. Limerick, 1935.
97. NAI, CCA 30/28.
98. NAI, CCC, Co. Waterford, 1935.
99. NAI, Dublin, Crown Files at Quarter Sessions, 1900.
100. K. Kiernan, H. Land and J. Lewis (eds), *Lone Motherhood in Twentieth-Century Britain: From Footnote to Front Page* (Oxford: Clarendon, 1998), p.98.
101. PRONI, HA5/1366.
102. NAI, Department of Justice, 9/19.
103. M. Oberman, 'Understanding Infanticide in Context: Mothers who Kill, 1870–1930 and Today', *Journal of Criminal Law and Criminology*, 92, 3 & 4 (2002), p.721.
104. NAI, CCC, Co. Limerick, 1945.
105. PRONI, DOW/2B/44/5, 1937.
106. PRONI, TYR1/2B/35, 1926.
107. NAI, Co. Clare, Crown Files at Assizes, 1917.
108. L. Ryan, 'The Press, Police and Prosecution: Perspectives on Infanticide in the 1920s', in A. Hayes and D. Urquhart (eds), *Irish Women's History* (Dublin: Irish Academic Press, 2004), p.142.
109. Ibid.
110. K. Johnson Kramar, *Unwilling Mothers, Unwanted Babies: Infanticide in Canada* (Vancouver, BC: University of British Columbia Press, 2006), pp.26–7.
111. L. Rose, *The Massacre of the Innocents: Infanticide in Britain 1800–1939* (London: Routledge, 1986), p.19.
112. S. D'Cruze and L.A. Jackson, *Women, Crime and Justice in England since 1660* (London: Palgrave Macmillan, 2009), p.82.
113. M. Hearn, 'Life for Domestic Servants in Dublin, 1880–1920', in M. Luddy and C. Murphy (eds), *Women Surviving: Studies in Irish Women's History in the 19th and 20th Centuries* (Swords: Littlehampton, 1990), p.167.
114. Ibid.
116. Ibid.
116. PRONI, TYR1/2B/35, 1926.
117. NAI, Co. Limerick, Crown Files at Assizes, 1910.
118. NAI, Crown files at Assizes, Limerick City and County 1908–10.
119. Ibid.
120. Ibid.
121. NAI, Dublin Crown files at Commission, City and County, Leinster Winter Assizes 1919.
122. NAI, CCC, ID 60 62, Co. Monaghan, 1938.
123. NAI, Co. Clare Spring Assizes, 1920.
124. NAI, Co. Louth, Crown Files at Assizes, 1900–05.
125. PRONI, BELF/1/2/2/40/68, 1930.
126. NAI, CCC, Co. Louth, 1934.

127. NAI, CCC, Co. Limerick, 1937.
128. NAI, CCC, Co. Meath, 1941.
129. Hearn, 'Life for Domestic Servants', p.167.
130. D'Cruze and Jackson, *Women, Crime and Justice*, p.1.
131. S. McAvoy (Larmour), 'Aspects of the State and Female Sexuality in the Irish Free State, 1922–1949' (PhD thesis, University College, Cork, 1998), p.307.
132. Hearn, 'Life for Domestic Servants', p.166.
133. NAI, Limerick City & County, Crown Files at Assizes, 1904–05.
134. PRONI, BELF/1/1/2/53/7, 1917.
135. NAI, Co. Limerick, Crown Files at Assizes, 1915.
136. NAI, Co. Donegal, Crown Files at Assizes, 1900–02.
137. Ibid.
138. Ibid.
139. NAI, CCC, Co. Waterford, 1935.
140. NAI, Co. Clare, Crown Files at Assizes, 1912.
141. PRONI, ARM1/2D/14/5, 1920.
142. NAI, Co. Limerick, Crown Files at Assizes, 1901–02.
143. Ryan, 'Press, Police and Prosecution', p.145.
144. *Irish Times*, 30 October 1943.
145. Ibid.
146. NAI, CCC, Dublin, 1939.
147. Ibid.
148. Ibid.
149. NAI, Co. Donegal, Crown Files at Assizes, 1919–21.
150. NAI, CCC, Co. Limerick, 1932.
151. NAI, CCC, Co. Limerick, 1931.
152. PRONI, DOW1/2B/31/5, 1924.
153. H. Marland, 'Getting Away with Murder? Puerperal Insanity, Infanticide and the Defence Plea', in M. Jackson (ed.), *Infanticide: Historical Perspectives on Child Murder and Concealment, 1550–2000* (Aldershot: Ashgate, 2002), p.183.
154. NAI, CRF, R 26/1912.
155. NAI, Department of Justice, 90/4, Minutes of Evidence, the Carrigan Committee.
156. Ibid.
157. Ibid.
158. M. Hearn, *Below Stairs: Domestic Service Remembered in Dublin and Beyond 1880–1922* (Dublin: Lilliput, 1993), p.96.
159. Ibid.
160. R. Schulte, *The Village in Court: Arson, Infanticide, and Poaching in the Court Records of Upper Bavaria, 1848–1910* (Cambridge: Cambridge University Press, 1994), p.102.
161. NAI, CCC, Co. Limerick, 1935.
162. PRONI, TYR1/2B/35, 1925.
163. NAI, Co. Limerick, Crown Files at Assizes, 1910.
164. Schulte, *Village in Court*, p.104.
165. Ibid.
166. Ibid.
167. NAI, CCC, Co. Longford, 1939.
168. PRONI, BELF/1/2/2/40/68, 1930.
169. PRONI, BELF/1/1/2/95/6, 1931.
170. NAI, CCC, Co. Galway, 1941.
171. NAI, CCC, Co. Offaly, 1934.
172. Schulte, *Village in Court*, p.102.
173. NAI, Crown Files at Assizes, City and County of Limerick, 1908–10.
174. PRONI, BELF/1/1/2/80/6, 1926.
175. PRONI, BELF/1/1/2/62/5, 1920.
176. Ibid.
177. Ibid.

178. NAI, CCC, Co. Kerry, 1944.
179. Ibid.
180. NAI, CCC, Co. Limerick, 1935.
181. NAI, CCC, Co. Tipperary, 1925.
182. M.J. Maguire, *Precarious Childhood in Post-Independence Ireland*, p.203.
183. Ibid., p.202.
184. Ibid., p.203.

CHAPTER TWO

'Done to death by father or relatives': Irish Families and Infanticide Cases

In a Lenten pastoral published in February 1929, Dr Collier, the Bishop of Ossory, made several references to the crime of infanticide. An article entitled 'The Infanticide Scandal', which quoted extensively from the bishop's pastoral, appeared in the *Irish Catholic* on 16 February 1929.[1] In his pastoral, Dr Collier lamented the fact that illegitimate newborns were often murdered in circumstances which he described as 'callous and revolting'.[2] He also noted that 'in some cases the unfortunate illegitimate child was done to death by father or relatives'.[3] The bishop stated that the teaching of the Catholic Church was clear and simple. 'The newborn child has an inalienable right to life, quite as much as a grown boy or girl, man or woman, and no difference can be recognised in the murder of the one or the other.'[4] Judges who presided over infanticide trials in Ireland during the period under review regularly reminded juries that the life of a child, even an illegitimate child, was 'just as sacred in the eyes of our law as the life of any adult person'.[5] However, it is clear from the records of infanticide trials that many Irish people drew a distinction between the lives of illegitimate infants and those born to married couples, and chose to ignore Catholic teaching. There were many instances where relatives of unmarried women who gave birth were the sole defendants or co-defendants in infanticide cases tried in Ireland between 1900 and 1950. In a small number of cases some co-resident family members, including relatives through marriage, were charged with a range of offences relating to the death of an illegitimate infant. Although illegitimate infants were 'done to death' by their fathers in a small number of cases that were tried in Irish courts during the first half of the twentieth century, this chapter will focus on cases where infants were murdered or suspected of having been murdered by relatives of the birth mother. The central issue is to explore how Irish families responded to out-of-wedlock pregnancy during the period under review. While some single expectant women found allies in their relatives,

others feared how family members would react. Examining the
motives of the relatives of single mothers who played a part in the
deaths of illegitimate infants reveals that unmarried motherhood was
severely frowned upon in Ireland. It led the relatives of some single
pregnant women to assist their female kin in destroying the evidence
of extramarital conception in order to protect the family's honour and
moral reputation in the wider community. Gender was an important
factor in terms of relatives' responses to extramarital pregnancy.
Female relatives were more likely to have assisted their female kin than
male family members. Within the wider community there seems to
have been a level of curiosity about infanticide trials involving family
members that was often absent from reports on single women charged
with infanticide. For instance, during the trial of a brother and sister
at a special court in May 1936 for the murder of an unnamed female
infant, the reporter for the *Connacht Tribune* noted that although 'the
public were excluded ... a large crowd assembled outside the courthouse and remained there for hours'.[6] Cases involving siblings often attracted more interest than cases involving a lone female defendant.
The public may have been interested in learning about the tensions
that arose within families when an unmarried female became pregnant
and the family drama that would be replayed in the courtroom.

According to D'Cruze and Jackson, in England infanticide tended
to be the action of isolated women from the mid-seventeenth century
onwards.[7] However, in their study of infanticide in Cheshire between
1650 and 1800, Dickinson and Sharpe found 'scattered but intriguing
evidence of friends and family rallying to help the mother through
childbirth, and to assist in concealing the dead child subsequently'.[8]
Their research has shown that accessories to the crime of infanticide
were generally relatives. Relatives, they noted, were the people who
would naturally be called on in a crisis.[9] Their observations are also
applicable to early-twentieth-century Ireland. In his study of women
accused of murdering their newborn children in England in the
eighteenth century, Jackson referred to several cases where the relatives of the birth mother (usually mothers of the accused women) were
tried along with her for the murder of a newborn infant or concealment of birth. According to Jackson, 'the people most likely to be
indicted as accomplices, if present at the birth, were the suspect's
mother and the child's father'.[10] Studies of infanticide in twentieth-
century Ireland have not examined in much depth the role that relatives
played. Ryan has noted that while 'the image of the single young

woman alone in the dock is the dominant representation of suspects in newspaper accounts of infanticide trials, there were some notable exceptions. Interestingly, these cases usually involved other family members, both male and female.'[11] Ryan's study of newspaper accounts of infanticide trials is quite narrow in scope; it concentrates on four years only: 1925, 1926, 1928 and 1936. Moreover, her work does not explore the significance of the involvement of relatives of the birth mothers in infanticide cases. In general, little attention has been paid to the role relatives played in historical studies of infanticide. A reasonably high level of family involvement in infanticide cases involving single mothers may have been unique to southern Ireland during the period under review. It was not matched in the northern sample. The relatives of the birth mother in infanticide cases prosecuted in other jurisdictions appear to have been less likely to collaborate with their female kin in committing infanticide, and they may have been less likely to have been regarded as suspects by the law enforcement authorities.

A significant proportion of the birth mothers in cases tried in the Twenty-Six Counties area between 1900 and 1950 lived in their parents' homes and this may help explain why relatives in southern Irish infanticide cases were likely to have collaborated in the killing of an illegitimate newborn. Almost all the birth mothers in cases where charges were brought against their relatives lived with those family members tried for the murder or concealment of birth of an illegitimate infant. They shared cramped living quarters, and relatives of the birth mother were often present when the infant was delivered. The records of infanticide cases tried in Ireland between 1900 and 1950 shed some light both on the extent to which families tried to conceal the birth of illegitimate children and the brutal ways in which they took the lives of infants born out of wedlock. The records of infanticide cases frequently reveal a great deal about family dynamics. The evidence of single mothers and the depositions of their relatives charged with infanticide in Ireland provide a considerable degree of insight into the lives of working-class families. Micro-level case analysis of infanticide trials where relatives of unmarried mothers were charged with murder or concealment of birth reveals how family members responded to extramarital pregnancy and how the birth of an illegitimate infant was dealt with at a family level. The perspective of those closely related to the birth mother is captured in almost one third of the cases in the pre-independence sample and in the Twenty-Six Counties sample. One or more relatives of the birth mother gave depositions in thirty cases in the pre-independence sample (32 per cent) and in sixty-five cases in the Twenty-Six Counties sample (33 per cent). It was not unusual for more than one member of the same family to provide statements, and in some instances relatives who gave depositions were also charged with the murder or concealment of birth of the infant whose death was being investigated. The evidence of relatives of the birth mother must be treated with caution. In some instances it was contested or contradicted by the birth mother. This is understandable, given the circumstances in which many families found themselves. Most relatives of the unmarried mothers in this sample would naturally have felt under pressure when the police questioned them. The relatives of some women may well have lied and denied playing any part in the crime, even if they had provided their female relatives with some form of assistance. When she was questioned by police in June 1903, Kate M.'s sister Margaret said that she never knew if her sister was in the family way.[12] She insisted that she 'knew nothing and did not bother [herself] about [Kate]'.[13] She also denied that her sister had given birth in their mother's house, although their next-door neighbour claimed she had heard a great deal of noise in their house on the night Kate gave birth. Kate stood trial for the murder and concealment of birth of her newborn infant at the Munster Winter Assizes of 1903. Charges were not brought against her sister Margaret.

'TOTALLY UNAWARE SHE WAS IN A PREGNANT CONDITION'

When questioned by the police, relatives of single pregnant women in the cases sampled generally insisted that they were not aware that the birth mother was pregnant. It seems improbable that family members who lived in the same household and sometimes even shared a bed with the birth mother would not have suspected pregnancy, yet relatives often strenuously denied all knowledge of the pregnancy and/or birth until the last. Some finally admitted they had known about the pregnancy after persistent police questioning. Relatives of the birth mother in the Irish cases sampled may also have denied knowledge of the birth mother's pregnancy for fear of being implicated in the crime. The doctor who gave 20-year-old Mary W. a certificate to give birth in the Thomastown County Home seems to have been exasperated with her older sister Catherine, who claimed not to know that her sister was nine months pregnant. Dr Lane told Catherine that she 'must be stupid not to know that [Mary] was going to have a baby'.[14] Catherine certainly had her suspicions but like many relatives of defendants in the cases sampled she was keen to protect the family's reputation and was probably reluctant to voice her suspicions in public. In her statement Catherine recalled noticing that her sister was getting bigger in mid-February 1944. Mary apparently managed to allay her suspicions. When Catherine 'asked her was there anything wrong meaning was she going to have a baby, [Mary] persuaded [her] that there wasn't'.[15]

The relatives of some women in the cases sampled denied that the birth mother was pregnant in order to protect their female kin from the law enforcement authorities. Mary M. seems to have done her utmost to prevent the police from bringing charges against her daughter, Bridget L. When questioned 'as to the rumour that was through the country with reference to her daughter' on 2 July 1901, Mary M. insisted that her daughter was not pregnant.[16] Mary M. told Constable Richard Shier that 'the cutty[17] was not in the family way'.[18] She also lied and said that Bridget 'was suffering from bile in the stomach and that her usual sickness stopped and that on Sunday night it came on'.[19] Mary explained that she shared a bed with her daughter and insisted that Bridget could not have been pregnant without her noticing it. She also stated that she had 'washed a sheet that was stained this morning and that her daughter could show me the petticoat she was wearing which was also stained with blood'.[20] Mary was clearly trying to imply that Bridget was menstruating and was, therefore, not pregnant. Ultimately, Mary M.'s attempts to allay police suspicions about her daughter were in vain. The infant's body was later located in a field close to Mary M.'s house. Its limbs and head had been severed. Both mother and daughter were arrested and charged with concealment of birth.

The 67-year-old grandmother of the birth mother in a 1928 Co. Cork case insisted that from the time the garda investigation into the death of her granddaughter's newborn began in January 1928 until her trial for murder in November of the same year, she had not known Hannah was pregnant. Hannah L.'s grandmother Mary had thirteen children, and six of her grandchildren were born in her cottage. She admitted assisting at those births. Hannah shared a bed with her grandmother but despite this, Mary L. continued to insist that she had not suspected that her granddaughter was pregnant. Under cross-examination Mary stated that she never noticed any change in Hannah's physical appearance. Mary said that Hannah did not appear to be getting 'stouter'. She explained that she 'didn't expect the like' and that 'the only thing [she] knew about was that [Hannah] was complaining about an ear and tooth ache'.[21] It seems implausible that, as State Counsel Mr Carrigan put it, 'wise woman as you ought to be you never knew that Hanna was in the family way'.[22] Mr Carrigan said it was incredible, utterly incredible, that 'any mother of a family living in the same house with her daughter or granddaughter and sleeping in the same bed could fail to observe the daughter's condition'.[23] The jury clearly agreed with him, as Mary L. was convicted of the murder of her grand-daughter's illegitimate infant.

There are, of course, cases where relatives of the birth mother genuinely seem to have been unaware that a female family member was pregnant, particularly if the woman had been living away from home for some time. Mary Bridget B.'s sister Josephine was the first member of their Co. Leitrim household to learn that her sister had been pregnant and had given birth unassisted in her bedroom. Mary Bridget called her sister into her bedroom on the morning of 18 June 1944. Once Josephine had closed the bedroom door, Mary Bridget told her that 'she was very ill and that she wanted a doctor that she had a baby yesterday'.[24] Josephine, who was visibly upset and in tears, broke the disturbing news to their mother Catherine. In her deposition, Catherine B. quite vividly described the sense of shock she experienced on learning that her daughter had given birth; she also recalled her encounter with her daughter shortly afterwards. Catherine asked her daughter:

> what she had said and in God's name what did she mean by saying she had a baby on yesterday. She faced away to the wall and didn't answer. I repeated the question a second time. She then said 'didn't I tell Josie. Isn't that enough.' I then said is it true what you told Josie and she said it was.[25]

Mary Bridget had been at service and living away for a number of months. She returned home a fortnight before she gave birth and informed her mother that she was unwell and had been suffering from kidney trouble. Neither Mary Bridget's mother nor her sister seem to have suspected that she was pregnant when she returned from service. They may have attributed any weight gain they noticed to her kidney trouble. This case is unlike many others where relatives denied knowledge of an unmarried relative's pregnancy in order to impede a police investigation. Catherine B. sent for a doctor as soon as she discovered what had happened. She cooperated with the doctor and the police and helped locate the infant's body.

The relatives of some single expectant women did suspect that the birth mother was pregnant, in the early stages of the pregnancy, but few family members referred to such suspicions in their evidence. However, in her deposition Ellen D. said she had noticed that her unmarried daughter, 25-year-old domestic servant Mary Anne, was pregnant, sometime between September and October 1935.[26] Mary Anne would have been approximately four months pregnant at the time. Ellen must have questioned Mary Anne about her suspicions because Mary Anne, who worked away from home, lied and told her mother that she had married recently and planned to give birth in Galway.

A CULTURE OF SHAME

When K.F. was apprehended in Belfast in November 1914 she pleaded with the police not to inform her parents about what she had done. She said it would 'break their hearts and disgrace them for life'.[27] Many unmarried women in the cases examined expressed similar sentiments. According to Schulte, 'extramarital pregnancy was not in itself considered a disgrace in nineteenth-century Upper Bavaria ... Illegitimacy in Bavaria was integrated into the social structure of peasant society and did not clash with the requirements and standards of the family as the basic element of farming life.'[28] The parents of single women who gave birth to illegitimate infants in areas such as Upper Bavaria often raised the children in their homes while their daughters continued to work, but this was generally not an option for unmarried women faced with an unplanned pregnancy in Ireland during the period under review. Blaikie's study of north-east Scotland has shown that illegitimacy rates were relatively high in the nineteenth century and that illegitimate children were often raised in their grandparents' homes.[29] However, in Ireland, both North and South, the shame and stigma associated with unmarried motherhood remained a powerful driving force. My research on infanticide cases in Northern Ireland between 1900 and 1950 does not suggest that there was any greater tolerance of illegitimate births in Ulster than in other parts of Ireland.[30] As Hill has put it, 'whether their mothers were rich or poor, children were only welcomed when born within a union legalised by marriage. In a country which placed a high value on chastity and self-restraint, illegitimacy was socially unacceptable.'[31] Almost all single women charged with infanticide in the northern sample had been unwilling to tell family members about their pregnancy. When she was arrested, K.M. said: 'my people know nothing about my condition'.[32] She also said that she 'did not wish to write about it to [her] mother'.[33] Like many others charged with infanticide, E.H. gave birth alone in her bedroom in July 1930.[34] She told police that after the birth she sat up in bed for about half an hour because she did not know what to do next and was too frightened to call down for her mother.

Out-of-wedlock pregnancy would have constituted a serious crisis for most Irish families during the period, and the records of infanticide trials reveal that the relatives of unmarried female defendants responded to the crisis in several different ways. Poverty was also an important motivating factor in infanticide cases. Many women in the case files were extremely poor; another child would have put additional pressure on a family's limited resources. The judicial records show that most Irish families reacted angrily to the news that an unmarried female relative was pregnant. According to Sergeant James Butler, when he arrived at Ellen S.'s house in Castleisland, Co. Kerry, in September 1915 and asked what was the matter, she pointed to her granddaughter Julia S. and said: 'this one here ... has a baby this morning, take her away from me I don't care what you will do with her'.[35] She also told the police that Julia had given birth on a previous occasion. When Austin N. was informed that his unmarried daughter Mary had given birth in March 1927, he 'commenced to cry and clap his hands and went away'.[36] One witness asked Mary's father to return to the house several times but he refused to see his daughter. Garda Superintendent Joseph Devine arrested 18-year-old Hannah L. for the murder of a newborn infant at her grandmother's cottage in January 1928. Superintendent Devine described her grandmother's reaction to the news of her arrest in his evidence. He said that Mary L. 'got into a violent temper' on learning that Hannah had been charged with murder and concealment of birth.[37] He said that she called Hannah names, 'a ruffian and a vagabond and she became quite violent'.[38] He stated that Mary L. 'used that language to her and repeated it over and over again'.[39] Superintendent Devine said he had to intervene and to tell her to stop interfering with the girl and told her not to use that language towards her.[40] When she was questioned in court, Mary L. confirmed Superintendent Devine's version of events. She said that when Hannah told her what she had been charged with, she 'asked her who was the father of it and

[she] hallooed out, and one of the two men [gardaí] said to leave her alone and not to worry [Hannah], that she had trouble enough'.[41] Initially, Mary L.'s reaction to the news that her unmarried grand-daughter had given birth and subsequently killed her infant would appear to have been standard for the period, but the case was more complex than most. Although Hannah originally confessed to murdering her illegitimate infant, she later retracted her confession and claimed that her grandmother had been responsible for the baby's death. Mary L., aged 67, was convicted of murder in November 1928. If Hannah's version of events is to be believed, then Mary L.'s reaction, as described, was fabricated for the benefit of the gardaí present.

Many unmarried women seem to have feared that pregnancy would lead to rejection by their families. In her study of women in twentieth-century Ireland, Hill referred to several instances where unmarried pregnant women were thrown out of their homes. She has argued that social exclusion for women who became pregnant outside marriage was common.[42] The records of Irish infanticide trials show that some single women were indeed turned out of their parents' homes because they were pregnant. Two single expectant women, both from Belfast, were turned out of their parents' homes in the latter stages of pregnancy in 1925 and 1927 respectively, most likely because they were pregnant, and one woman's father inflicted physical violence on her, presumably because he had learned of her condition.[43] In Co. Dublin, Annie T.'s stepfather 'put her out of his house' a day or so after the birth of her first illegitimate child. Annie's life had apparently been endangered on that occasion.[44] Bridget M. spent three weeks in Mary S.'s house in Ballykerrin, Co. Donegal, in June 1900 before she went into the workhouse to give birth. Bridget told Mary S. that 'the reason she came to [her] house was because her own people would not keep her at home'.[45] Bridget also told a nurse in the Milford Union workhouse in Co. Donegal that 'her father had put her out of his house'.[46]

According to D'Cruze and Jackson, 'the emotional and social costs of illegitimacy could be very high' and 'until the availability of oral contraception and changing public opinion on single parenthood in the last fifty years, pregnant unmarried women were placed in very difficult circumstances unless they had supportive and/or affluent kin or friendship networks'.[47] Most of the women in the infanticide cases sampled had neither supportive nor affluent kin or friendship networks. The emotional stress that many single Irish mothers experienced during the period under review is evident in a 1934 Co. Clare case. In March of that year, 19-year-old Teresa M.'s father heard rumours that his daughter was pregnant and confronted her about the matter. Teresa denied that the rumours were true. Her father informed her that if she were pregnant he would cut her throat. Still Teresa insisted that she was not pregnant. Her father then responded rather menacingly by saying that 'he would know when the time comes along and if it was the truth [she] would suffer'.[48] Although a number of women in the cases examined were certainly threatened and intimidated by members of their families, this is only part of the picture. Not all families were unsympathetic. While most unmarried women lied to their parents about their pregnancy and did their utmost to conceal their condition from family members, a small proportion of unmarried women confided in their relatives.

RELATIVES' RESPONSES TO THE BIRTH OF AN ILLEGITIMATE INFANT

The relatives of some women reacted to the discovery that an unmarried female relative had given birth and subsequently taken the baby's life by alerting the authorities. Margaret C.'s sisters Annie and Ellen informed on her.[49] Margaret, aged 19, gave birth alone in her employer's house on a Sunday morning in October 1913 'while the people were at second mass'.[50] Margaret claimed that when she 'came to after the birth' she found that her newborn was dead. She rolled the infant's body up in a piece of cloth and hid it under her bed. Margaret told police that ten days after the birth, on her way to her parents' home, she put the parcel in a drain somewhere between the railway station and their house. Even before Margaret was arrested her sisters and her mother had heard rumours about her pregnancy. Margaret's sisters had already asked her to return home and to go to the doctor with them. As soon as Margaret arrived home one Wednesday evening in October 1913 her mother questioned her about what had occurred. Margaret confessed immediately and her sisters Annie and Ellen then went to the police station to report the matter. E.A.'s mother said that she had known her daughter was pregnant although she did not specify how long she had known about her daughter's condition.[51] When she heard cries from the yard of her Belfast home in February 1910, she sent for a policeman. Margaret D.'s father played a pivotal role in his daughter's arrest in January 1935. He gave a detailed deposition. Patrick B. suspected that his daughter had been pregnant. When he heard that an infant's body had been found in a nearby quarry, Patrick 'interviewed [his] daughter the accused about the matter'.[52] Margaret 'was shy in answering' her father but he persisted, saying 'Tell me the truth and I will get you out of it if I can.'[53] When Margaret admitted that she had left her baby's body in a disused quarry, Patrick contacted the gardaí. Sergeant John McDermott said he arrived at the house on 20 January 1935 at 2.25 a.m., twenty-five minutes after being called out. He recalled that when he arrived, Patrick D. spoke to his daughter and said: 'The sergeant is here now Madge tell the truth.'[54] Margaret made a statement and was then charged with the murder of her unnamed female infant. Patrick also attended his daughter's trial at the Central Criminal Court in Dublin in March 1935 and his presence may well have influenced the outcome. Margaret pleaded guilty to the manslaughter of her female infant. The plea was accepted and Margaret was released and handed over to the care of her father having paid a recognizance of ten pounds.

It is possible that Bridget M.'s brother Thomas informed on her. A garda investigation was instigated prior to the discovery of her infant's body. Bridget claimed that she had not been on good terms with her brother for eight months. She also stated that her brother had warned her that 'he would have the handcuffs on us before long'.[55] Thomas seems to have objected to the way in which Bridget's infant was treated. He said that he told his mother to put the newborn baby in Bridget's bed where it would be warm. Instead the infant was 'put on a potato basket on a flag floor'.[56] Thomas allegedly predicated that the infant would soon die, as 'it could not live from the position it was in on the cold floor'.[57] Thomas's evidence suggests that there was a history of discord in the family and this, along with the events of 25 July, may have prompted him to alert the gardaí. It is, of course, also possible that he distanced himself from his mother and sister during the investigation in order to avoid being charged along with them. The investigation may have been instigated, as in so many other cases, because of rumours that had been circulating in the locality about an unmarried woman's pregnancy.

A long-standing grievance between sisters Hannah C. and Margaret M. may have led to Hannah's arrest in September 1918. During the course of Hannah's trial in July 1919 it emerged that her sister Margaret had been on bad terms with her for some time. This may well have motivated her to report the part Hannah had allegedly played in the death of their younger unmarried sister's infant daughter in October 1918. The barrister who defended Hannah claimed that

Margaret M. had 'showed in the witness box a vindictiveness and
hostile anxiety to put the rope around her sister's neck'.[58] According to
Mr Moloney, Margaret had, 'from trial to trial tried to add a fresh nail
to the coffin of her sister'.[59] In his evidence, Margaret's husband Stephen
confirmed that his wife and her sister Hannah were on unfriendly terms.
He had not spoken to his sister-in-law for a number of years.

In other cases relatives may have unintentionally provided the
police with information that led to the arrest and trial of an unmarried
female family member. E.H.'s father sent for the police when he found
an infant's body in an ash pit near their Belfast home in September
1909.[60] E.H.'s father may not have suspected that his daughter had
given birth to a male infant and hidden its body near the ash pit. Yet,
while E.H.'s father may not have deliberately set out to inform on his
daughter, the relatives of some women in the cases cited did just that.
They may have feared that unless they reported the matter to the
police they would be suspected of some sort of involvement in the
crime. Margaret D.'s father may have thought that by informing the
police he would be able to help his daughter, and in fact her sentence
was comparatively lenient. She was released into her father's custody
rather than being sent to a religious-run institution, which was the fate
that awaited most women in her position. Others, however, may well
have acted out of a sense of anger or vengeance.

Some families shielded their unmarried female relatives and
attempted to protect them from the prying eyes of their neighbours,
and the relatives of a number of women in the cases sampled ran the
risk of arrest by collaborating in the murder or concealment of birth
of their female kin's illegitimate newborn. In October 1922, Margaret
H. sent a letter to her daughter Annie, an unmarried woman who had
given birth in the county home in Monaghan, advising her to smother
her illegitimate infant. These letters were used as exhibits during the
trial of Annie M. and her mother Margaret H. and are included in the
judicial records for the case held in the National Archives of Ireland:

> Annie I am in a worse state nor ever its not hard two [sic] do if
> you would take currage [sic] then turn it over on its face and
> throw yourself across [sic] it yoou [sic] could do that no matter
> whoo [sic] was in the room you now [sic] that you need not come
> home with it you would be ashamed to much any one [sic] and
> the place your [sic] in is the right place if all goes on well you can
> come Monday or Tuesday ...[61]

In her first statement, dated 19 October 1922, Annie explained that she did not dare to 'go home to [her] home with the baby as [her] mother threatened [her] not to take it home'.[62] She insisted that her mother had sent her a letter while she was in the county home 'telling [her] how to do away with the child'.[63] Annie was subsequently charged with the murder of her infant and her mother Margaret was charged with being an accessory both before and after the fact. This case was by no means unusual. Although written evidence documenting the role that relatives of the birth mother played in the death of an illegitimate infant has not survived in any other cases examined, the relatives of a number of defendants stood trial for the murder or concealment of birth of illegitimate infants. Newspaper reports on infanticide cases in the South occasionally carried headings such as 'Murder Charge against a Grandmother'.[64] 'Mother and Daughter Sentenced'[65] and 'Infanticide Alleged against three members of family'.[66] The relatives of sixteen single women in the pre-independence sample (17 per cent of all cases) were charged with the murder or concealment of birth of their illegitimate infants. There were many instances where the family members of unmarried women were the sole defendants or co-defendants in infanticide and concealment of birth cases tried at the Central Criminal Court between 1922 and 1950. Relatives of the birth mother were charged with the murder or concealment of birth of an illegitimate infant in twenty-nine cases in the Twenty-Six Counties sample (15 per cent of all cases). There were several more cases where criminal charges were not brought against relatives of the birth mother although it seemed quite clear that they had assisted her in some way. Relatives of the birth mother were the sole defendants in three infanticide cases in the pre-independence sample and in nine cases in the Twenty-Six Counties sample. By contrast, there was only one case (2.6 per cent) in the northern sample where a relative of the birth mother was charged with infanticide. In that particular case, the man charged was both the woman's father and the father of her infant. J.R., 'a grey-haired farmer about 66 years of age', was charged with the murder of his daughter's female infant and with having had 'carnal knowledge' of his daughter in May 1931.[67]

GENDERED RESPONSES TO THE BIRTH OF AN ILLEGITIMATE INFANT

It is clear from the cases in the pre-independence sample that female relatives were far more likely to have been implicated in infanticide cases than male relatives, and the mothers of single pregnant women were more likely to have collaborated in infanticide cases than any other family member. Three male relatives of the birth mother were charged with the murder or concealment of birth of an illegitimate infant in the pre-independence sample. Charges were brought against fourteen female relatives of the birth mothers. This is also evident in cases tried at the Central Criminal Court, Dublin, between 1922 and 1950. Eight male relatives of the birth mother were charged with the murder or concealment of birth of an illegitimate infant in the Twenty-Six Counties sample, whereas charges were brought against twenty-three female relatives.[68] The mothers of thirteen birth mothers in the Twenty-Six Counties sample were tried. This accounts for almost half of the cases where relatives of the birth mother were charged. From the cases in these samples it would appear that female relatives were generally more sympathetic and understanding of the difficult position in which unmarried pregnant women found themselves. In their statements a number of single women recalled the concern and protective kindness their relatives displayed towards them. For instance, 17-year-old Annie S. told gardaí that her mother took the baby away after the birth in their Co. Monaghan home in July 1938, gave her tea and fixed the bedclothes in the bed.[69] The mothers, sisters and grandmothers of several women assisted them during delivery. Nora C. told the police that her mother was present when she gave birth in May 1903 and attended to her.[70] Sarah Jane B.'s mother told the police that she was present when her daughter gave birth in her Co. Donegal home in January 1910.[71] She also said that she helped Sarah Jane to bed afterwards, washed her baby and put the infant in a cradle.

There are fewer examples of fathers shielding their daughters. Male relatives were far less likely to have been suspected of assisting an unmarried sister or daughter in killing an illegitimate newborn. While Margaret M.'s mother acted compassionately on learning of her daughter's pregnancy, her brother Patrick was not supportive. Mary M. made a detailed deposition in January 1905. She said that she had known that her daughter was pregnant. She confronted Margaret about it and advised her to 'go to some hospital or somewhere to be confined'.[72] Mary M. said she told her daughter to go away for her confinement as she was 'too old to mind her and her brothers were not satisfied that she should stay in the house and be confined in it'.[73] Mary gave Margaret some money and she left her home in Co. Carlow and went to the South Dublin Union hospital. Mary also sent her daughter money by post to cover the cost of her train fare home. Margaret's brother Patrick wrote to her during her stay in the South Dublin Union, reminding her that she had disgraced her mother and instructing her not to bring the infant with her when she returned home. While Mary's mother was supportive her male relatives showed themselves to be far less willing to forgive her sexual transgression. However, accounts like Annie S.'s[74] and Margaret M.'s[75] serve to suggest that unmarried Irish women who became pregnant were not always automatically cast out of the family home. As guardians of family honour some women helped their female relatives to conceal what was considered a shameful event.

CONFIDING IN FEMALE RELATIVES

While most unmarried women in the cases sampled lied to relatives about their pregnancy and did their utmost to conceal their condition from family members, a small proportion of the women confided in their relatives. A number of single women in the pre-independence and Twenty-Six Counties samples admitted confiding in female relatives. Anne L. had clearly confided in her sister Sarah. When she was questioned in August 1900, Sarah told the police that she 'was aware [Anne] was in the family way'.[76] It is hardly surprising that unmarried expectant women would have found a natural ally in close female relatives. There were, however, varying degrees of involvement. While some female relatives were willing to provide some sort of assistance, not all were willing to run the risk of breaking the law. For instance, Katie R., whose sister Christina was charged with the murder of her infant, procured a medical certificate for her sister under a different name so that she could enter the South Dublin Union as a married woman. Christina corresponded with Katie while she was in the South Dublin Union and Katie agreed to go to the South Dublin Union to request the discharge of a woman named Lily Parkinson, as Lily had promised to put Christina's baby in a home: 'I wrote to my sister on a Tuesday to come in to take Lily Parkinson out of the Union as Lily Parkinson had already said that if I got anyone to take her out of the Union when I would be coming out she would take the baby and put it into a home.'[77] Katie assisted her sister in entering the Union and she allegedly helped her sister's acquaintance Lily Parkinson to leave the South Dublin Union, but unlike female relatives in several other cases in this sample, Katie R. was not suspected of having played a part in the death or disappearance of the child.

It is clear from the samples analysed that unmarried pregnant women were far more likely to have confided in female relatives than male family members. The northern sample proves to be an exception to the rule; few defendants in the post-1920 northern cases examined seem to have confided in male or female relatives. Although two women in pre-1920 Belfast infanticide cases had informed their mothers of their pregnancy, neither woman assisted her daughter during childbirth. C.G.'s mother had known that her daughter was pregnant for a fort-night before C.G. gave birth in Belfast in October 1907.[78] In February 1910, E.A.'s mother told police that she had known that her daughter was 'in the family way'. It is not known when E.A. informed her mother that she was pregnant.[79] J.E. claimed not to have confided in her sister even though they lived together in Belfast, and although J.E.'s sister assisted her, this only occurred after the delivery when she found J.E. 'on her hunkers at the chamber' in July 1929.[80] J.B. did her utmost to conceal her pregnancy from her sister and father. When she was sent to the Belfast Union Infirmary in January 1925 she told the master of the hospital that 'neither her mother nor anyone else knew of her condition'.[81] She said that when she heard her sister coming upstairs to see her after she had given birth secretly she was afraid that she would hear the cry of the baby, so she rolled it up in a piece of cloth and put it in a case. J.B.'s father told the police that he was 'totally unaware she was in a pregnant condition'.[82] Her sister also denied knowing that J.B. was pregnant. It is particularly surprising that J.B.'s sister did not suspect her pregnancy as they shared the same bed and worked together in the same factory. It is, of course, possible that J.B.'s sister was aware but that J.B. did not want to implicate her in the crime.

The relatives of fourteen women confessed to killing an illegitimate newborn in the Twenty-Six Counties sample. Catherine W. confessed to killing her sister's baby in February 1944. She said: 'I removed the child a few feet from her and caught its throat with my right hand and squeezed it to kill it so that my father and the people would not know. I kept squeezing its throat for ten or fifteen minutes and it was mak-ing a choking or suffocating noise.'[83] Mary S. said that when she saw her daughter's newborn infant in the yard at the back of their Co. Meath home in December 1934 she 'took it and threw it into the river'.[84] She said she did not know what she was doing at the time.

Catherine M.'s mother initially denied being involved in the death of her daughter's infant son. When they were being questioned, Catherine pleaded with her mother to tell the truth. According to Sergeant Liddane, Rosanna M. 'started to cry again and said "How can I tell it? How can I say I put it in the river?" '.[85] The relatives of seven women in the Twenty-Six Counties sample denied playing any part in the death of an infant, while the relatives of five more single women denied killing infants but admitted that they had assisted the woman in some way.

THE BIRTH MOTHERS' MOTHERS AND INFANTICIDE

Annie T. and her mother Annie M. were both charged with the murder of Annie's illegitimate son in October 1917. The body of Annie's infant was found 'face down wholly immersed in water and mud, one foot deep' in the garden of their home in Balbriggan, Co. Dublin.[86] In her statement, Annie's mother admitted to being the only person present when her daughter's baby was born.[87] She told the police that Annie's baby was 'dead when it was born' and said that about half an hour after the birth she took the infant's body 'to the garden where there is a manhole at the end of the drain and put it into it with an old piece of sacking and covered all up with some sticks and old potato stocks'.[88] Annie T. described how her mother had assisted her when she became 'ill with pains' on 14 October 1917.[89] Annie recalled how 'after the child was born [her] mother carried [her] back into [her] bed'.[90] Annie M. was not the only mother who became embroiled in an infanticide trial during the period under review. The mothers of eight single women in the pre-independence sample (8 per cent) were charged with the murder or concealment of birth of their illegitimate infants, and the grandmothers of two women were charged with concealment of birth (2 per cent). The mothers of thirteen women in the Twenty-Six Counties sample (7 per cent) and one woman's grandmother were charged with murder or concealment of birth (0.5 per cent).[91] A Belfast case, tried in November 1913, involved three generations of women from the same family. Although there were a number of cases in the South where the mothers of single women suspected of infanticide were charged with the murder or concealment of birth of their daughters' illegitimate infants, such charges were not brought against the mothers of unmarried women in the northern sample between 1920 and 1950. Charges were brought against female relatives of the birth mother in just one of eighteen northern cases in the pre-independence sample.

As previously noted, the mothers of several women in the pre-independence and Twenty-Six Counties samples assisted them during childbirth and attended to them afterwards. In some cases the mothers of the birth mother appear to have killed the infant and disposed of its body while their daughters recovered in bed. It is not clear from the available evidence whether the mothers of the birth mothers in this sample who faced prosecution killed their illegitimate grandchildren in order to avoid the shame and stigma of an illegitimate pregnancy in the household, or whether they feared how their husbands or other family members would react if they discovered an unmarried relative had given birth. Nor is it clear whether the mothers of the birth mothers took criminal action out of a sense of kindness and concern for their daughters. Were they anxious to protect their daughters' reputations or were they motivated out of anger and an overwhelming urge to conceal the shame of an illegitimate birth in the household? Relatives who assisted an unmarried mother to kill or conceal the birth of an illegitimate infant obviously experienced a range of emotions, and in most cases sampled such emotions are not clearly articulated. The mothers of some single pregnant women may well have been motivated to kill their daughters' newborn infants because they were afraid of how their husbands would react if they discovered that an unmarried daughter had given birth. Nora M., who was convicted of the concealment of birth of her daughter's infant in November 1933, told gardaí that she 'didn't make any alarm about it then because I was afraid of her father'.[92] Similarly, Johanna M.'s mother Nora said that she did not tell her husband about the birth and was afraid to take the baby into her house in Dungarvan, Co. Waterford, in November 1941. Instead she left the infant in a shed to die.[93] The actions of these women provide a considerable degree of insight into the powerful sense of shame and stigma associated with extramarital sexual activity in Ireland in this period.

'I THOUGHT I WAS DOING A GOOD TURN': THE BIRTH MOTHERS' SISTERS

The sisters of eight unmarried mothers in the Twenty-Six Counties sample (4 per cent) were charged with the murder or concealment of birth of a newborn infant, while the sisters of four single women in the pre-independence sample (4 per cent) were charged with the murder or concealment of birth of their infants. In the pre-independence sample, the birth mother's sisters were co-defendants in three cases, while in another case charges were brought against the birth mother's sister only. The birth mother's sisters were the sole defendants in two cases in the Twenty-Six Counties sample, while the birth mother's sisters were co-defendants along with the birth mother and/or other family members. Charges were not brought against any sisters of the birth mothers in the northern sample. The bond between sisters charged in southern infanticide cases was often particularly striking. Sisters Rose and Elizabeth E. were both sentenced to death for the murder of Elizabeth's baby in March 1935. An official in the Department of Justice noted that Rose E. 'assisted in the killing of [her] sister's child' because of 'her affection for the sister'.[94] Elizabeth confided in her younger sister about six weeks before she was due to give birth. From then on Rose E. seems to have taken charge of the situation. In his charge to the jury, the trial judge said that 'the two accused were acting in concert during the whole time'.[95] Indeed, Rose went to considerable lengths to assist her sister. She accompanied Elizabeth to the county home in Roscommon shortly before Elizabeth was due to give birth. She visited her there on several occasions and told their parents that Elizabeth was suffering from appendicitis and had to undergo an operation in the county home. She also hired a car to bring Elizabeth and her infant daughter home. Following the infant's death, Rose said that she took the baby from Elizabeth's arms and buried it in a nearby field. Despite extensive police searches the infant's body was never found. Elizabeth said that Rose consoled her after the baby's death. 'Indeed many a time we talked about it', Elizabeth recalled. Apparently Elizabeth 'used to be regretting the child' but Rose 'used to tell [her older sister] it was better off'. The 'story' told by Elizabeth and Rose E. was, according to Justice O'Byrne, 'a tissue of false-hoods'[96] but 'no medical evidence was, or could be, tendered to the jury that she died a violent death'.[97] The sisters were both sentenced to death for the murder of Elizabeth's infant daughter but the sentence was later commuted to penal servitude for life. Rose was released on licence on 1 December 1936. It is not known how long Elizabeth spent in prison. Despite the intense pressure of the trial at the Central Criminal Court, followed by an appeal hearing and the death sentence being upheld after the appeal, neither sister changed her version of events. Rose E. remained loyal to her sister throughout the investigation and during the trial. She never revealed where she had buried the baby, despite having been put under considerable pressure by the authorities. While Rose E. did not yield to pressure, Cáit ní C. eventually told gardaí that her older sister Máire killed her newborn infant. Both sisters were questioned separately by gardaí until 1 a.m. in February 1941. Cáit had probably been interrogated for several hours before she incriminated her sister. When she was asked 'Cé agaibh a rinne é?' (Which of you did it?), according to Garda Michael Ó Riada, 'Dúirt si Máire' (She said Máire).[98] 'Thachtaigh sí é lena lámha ar a muinéal.' (She choked it with her hands on its neck.)[99]

Catherine W. described her role in greater detail than any other woman charged with the murder or concealment of birth of a sister's illegitimate infant. Catherine helped deliver her sister's baby in February 1944. She later told gardaí that she cut the umbilical cord with scissors, assisted her sister Mollie indoors after she had given birth in the farmyard, heated milk for her and helped her to bed. Catherine then caught the baby's 'throat with [her] right hand and squeezed it to kill it so that [her] father and the people would not know'.[100] She also said she 'got up early next morning and went out and gathered up the hay that was blood stained and covered it over. After breakfast [her] father went off to work and [she] brought in the blood stained hay and burned it in the fire. [She] gave Mollie her breakfast in bed ... [she] asked her what would [they] do with the child and [they] both decided to take it up in Peter Walsh's field at Dronagh'.[101] The sisters put the infant's body in a cardboard box and buried it in a neighbour's field. Catherine also lied to her sister's doctor, and when Dr Lane inquired about where Mary's baby was born, Catherine told her, as instructed by her sister, that she had given birth in the Regina Coeli hostel in Dublin, a hostel for unmarried mothers and their children. In her statement Mary W. said that she and her sister Catherine discussed her pregnancy just after Mary had received a ticket for admission to the county home from her doctor. The sisters may well have decided in advance of the birth that they would conceal the infant's existence. This was quite risky, given that their doctor was aware that Mary had been pregnant. In May 1944 Catherine and Mary were both charged with the murder of Mary's infant son.

Sadie D.'s sister Mary Kate admitted smothering Sadie's newborn infant when questioned by gardaí in her Co. Roscommon home in September 1947. Sadie, who was unmarried, went to live with her sister and her sister's husband approximately four months before she gave birth. Sadie's sister arranged for her to give birth in a nursing home in Boyle, Co. Roscommon. Mary Kate also arranged for a driver to collect Sadie and her infant from the home after the birth. Mary Kate clearly went to a considerable amount of effort and expense in her efforts to assist her sister. Yet she smothered Sadie's illegitimate infant the night she returned from the home. Mary Kate admitted that she had 'done it' but claimed that she 'did not know what [she] was doing'.[102] Although Mary Kate stated that she did not know why she did it, it is likely that she wanted to protect the family's reputation in the community and to relieve Sadie of an unwelcome burden. Neither sister alluded to motive in their evidence. Mary Kate may have acted on sudden impulse when she took the baby's life in September 1947. After all, she had arranged for Sadie to be confined in a private nursing home, and a number of people outside the immediate family circle were aware that Sadie had given birth. Then again, it is possible that the killing was premeditated and possibly planned by both sisters despite the fact that Sadie had given birth in a nursing home in the local area. A small number of women in the samples examined gave birth in private homes or public hospitals but in most cases they seem to have failed to appreciate that the disappearance of an infant whose birth was registered could lead to an investigation. They may have assumed that the authorities would not inquire into the disappearance of a newborn infant.

Bessie D. also assisted her sister Susan when she gave birth in their father's home in Co. Donegal in June 1926. Bessie was later charged with concealing the birth of her sister Susan's illegitimate newborn. Charges were not brought against Susan. Like Rose E., Bessie had known her sister was pregnant for some time before the birth. In her statement, Bessie claimed that the infant had been born prematurely. She claimed that Susan had miscarried at six months. Although Bessie denied assisting her sister during labour, she told gardaí that following the birth she saw that 'there was no life in [the baby]' so she 'rolled the body up in a white cloth' and that she 'bandaged up [her] sister and took care of her until she was well''[103] Bessie explained that their father buried the infant's body. It is impossible to know from the depositional evidence how women like Susan D. and Sadie D. would have felt about their sisters taking their infants' lives. Their feelings are not articulated in official documents. It is quite possible, however, that unmarried women such as Susan and Sadie would have expressed their desire to be rid of the burden of an illegitimate infant to their sisters and that their sisters acted on their behalf, with their full consent.

In July 1938, 19-year-old Mary M. and her 26-year-old sister Margaret were charged with the murder of Mary's infant son. The sisters were natives of Co. Waterford. They had both been employed as domestic servants in Dublin. Margaret told gardaí that 'we did do it' in July in 1938.[104] The sisters buried the infant in the garden of the household where Margaret had been employed. As neither sister supplied a detailed statement it is not known how long Margaret had been aware of her sister's pregnancy or to what extent she had assisted her. The trial records include a document entitled 'Statement of Miss Mary M. in answer to questions put to her by Inspector Killeen'.[105] Mary's evidence reveals little about the crime, the birth of her son or her sister's role in events. Although Mary answered questions put to her about her 'native place', her employers and dates of employment, she refused to say why she had been an inmate in the Dublin Union, nor did she respond when asked if she had given birth to a baby in the Dublin Union. Inspector Killeen posed a series of questions about her movements from the time of her discharge from the Union but again Mary gave no reply. Mary's sister Margaret collected her sister from hospital and seems to have helped her to conceal the infant's remains in her employer's back garden. A workman found the infant's bones in the garden some time after Margaret had left Dublin.

While the sisters of some women clearly knew about the pregnancy for a considerable amount of time before the birth, this was not always the case. It is not evident whether Cáit ní C. knew about her sister's pregnancy before Máire went into labour in February 1941. Máire informed her sister that she had a pain in her stomach and asked her to fetch her a drink, which Cáit did. But Cáit may have been aware that Máire was suffering from something more than a pain in her stomach, as she went to seek advice from a female neighbour. A 1949 Co. Tipperary case showed that even sisters who seemed to have a close relationship might not have confided in each other about a pregnancy, due to a sense of shame or denial.[106] Sisters Mary and Nan M. were charged with the murder and concealment of the birth of Mary's newborn daughter in March 1949. According to Nan, when Mary went into labour she told her sister that she would be ashamed to tell her what was happening. Eventually Mary admitted that she was going to have a baby and asked Nan not to tell anyone. Unbeknown to Mary, apparently, Nan was herself about five months pregnant at the time. It seems extraordinary that the sisters, who shared a room and were employed as servants in the same boarding school, did not realise that they were both pregnant, or did not confide in each other. Nan did not refer to her own pregnancy in her statement. The medical officer who examined her while she was in custody awaiting trial estimated that she was about eights months pregnant.

Cases where sisters or female cousins collaborated with the birth mother are very similar to instances where the birth mother's mother came to her daughter's aid. Poverty, a desire to avoid the shame and stigma attached to pregnancy outside wedlock and fear of other relatives' reactions recur as motives in cases involving female family members. Margaret H. was charged with the murder of her sister Bridget's newborn infant in July 1905. Margaret may have decided to kill her sister's newborn infant because her sister had died shortly after giving birth. She may have felt that raising an illegitimate infant would have been an unnecessary burden on her and her elderly parents. Like other family members in this sample she may also have been keen to avoid the stigma associated with illegitimacy. Financial considerations may well have been a factor in a 1944 Co. Kilkenny case. Mary W., who was 20 years old, felt that she could not give birth at home because they had 'no sheets or anything'.[107] Mary's sister Catherine told gardaí that her sister did not want to go the county home either, 'because she has no clothes for herself or the child'.[108] Mary's father was a labourer and she was herself unemployed at the time of the birth.

It is not difficult to decipher a motive in a case that was tried at the Co. Limerick Winter Assizes in 1908. Kate H. and her sister Margaret S. were both charged with the murder of Kate's infant son in November 1908. Kate married about four months before she gave birth but her husband was not the infant's father. Kate told the police that when her husband married her he 'had no knowledge that [she] was with child'.[109] Although Kate said that she 'never had any unpleasantness with [her] husband about the child though he knew that he was not the father', it seems likely that the birth of her son caused tension between them and this may have provided both Kate and her sister Margaret with a motive for taking the baby's life.[110] When she was arrested, Margaret said that she thought she was doing her sister a good turn.

While the sisters of some women who gave birth outside marriage may have been prompted to act because of feelings of protectiveness and concern, others may have been motivated to kill or conceal the birth of their illegitimate infants for more selfish reasons. As Lambert put it, 'the strength of the family ideal in Irish society meant that the behaviour of individual members reflected upon the reputation of the whole family'.[111] Earner-Byrne has also commented on this, noting that 'the fear of the loss of one's reputation was based largely on the understanding of the family as a unit: if one member disgraced themselves the rest of the family was tarnished by association. Protection of the family's reputation was perceived as extremely important to the traditional Irish family.'[112] The sisters of some single pregnant women may have been motivated to kill or conceal their sisters' illegitimate infants because they knew that the stigma associated with single motherhood would have had repercussions in their own lives. Their own marriage prospects may have been seriously undermined by their sisters' actions and behaviour. In her statement Mary B. said that she was not 'on good terms' with her brother and his wife.[113] Mary may well have been angry with her brother, James B., for bringing the family name into disrepute because his wife gave birth shortly after their marriage. A newspaper report described their union as a 'hasty marriage by force of circumstances'.[114] James's sister Mary told gardaí that her mother had tried to arrange for the baby to be adopted. She said that 'this was done for my account until I would be suited for'.[115] Mary B. was not suspected of involvement in the death of her brother's daughter but her evidence sheds some light on the negative effects a sibling's conduct could have on a close relative's marriage prospects. In October 1931 Bridget M. was charged with the murder of her newborn infant. According to Sergeant James Kinsella, Bridget's sister reacted angrily to the news of her sister's arrest: 'While the accused was dressing her sister Rita said you have disgraced the whole family, you are no kiddie, you knew what you were doing.'[116]

The bond between sisters charged in infanticide cases is particularly striking in the South, both before and after independence. However, while the sisters and mothers of a single woman who gave birth at home in southern Ireland sometimes came to her assistance and subsequently helped her to kill or conceal the infant's body, this was not a feature of the cases tried in Northern Ireland. The records do not reveal why this was so. If a single woman gave birth in the family home in Northern Ireland her relatives rarely seemed to have been aware of this until after the baby was born and they generally then called for a doctor or the police. Few single women charged with infanticide in the North referred to their sisters in their statements, and the sisters of women charged with infanticide were rarely interviewed by the police. Furthermore, the police do not seem to have suspected the female relatives of single mothers charged with infanticide in the cases under review. M.B. gave birth in her employer's Belfast home in November 1930 and left the body in their coalhouse. She returned to collect the body a few days later and was accompanied by her sister. It seems that M.B.'s sister was unaware of what the bundle in the coalhouse contained. M.B.'s employer was the only other person who knew what had occurred. When M.B.'s mistress asked her if her sister would tell their mother, M.B. replied: 'No. She thinks it's only a bundle of clothing I called for.'[117] Although M.B.'s sister was present when she threw the parcel that contained the infant's body over a hedge, her sister was not considered a suspect in the case and was not questioned by the police. Relatives of the birth mother in northern infanticide cases were apparently less likely to have collaborated with single women who gave birth to illegitimate children in the family home than their southern counterparts, but the records do not reveal why this was so. It is unlikely that policing methods were markedly different in the investigation of infanticide in Northern and Southern Ireland. My research on abortion cases tried in Northern Ireland suggests that female family members were perhaps more likely to have collaborated in backstreet abortions than in infanticide cases.[118]

MALE RELATIVES AND INFANTICIDE CASES

In her study of infanticide in Ireland from 1925 to 1957, Guilbride noted that men were notably absent from the trial records. This is true in certain cases. In a 1930 Co. Dublin case, Superintendent John Hughes did not question the suspect in her brother's presence as he assumed that he had no knowledge of his sister's pregnancy. He explained that he had brought Christina R. into another room when he first questioned her 'as it would be awkward to have [her brother] present and she must have felt very sensitive of having given birth to a child. I did not know that her brother was aware of the fact that she had given birth to a child.'[119] Superintendent Hughes was correct in his assumptions. Christina had not informed her brother about her pregnancy. When Justice O'Byrne asked her if she had gone to her brother's house with her baby when she left the South Dublin Union she explained that she 'would not go down Capel Street at all as [she] did not want [her] brother to know anything about it'.[120] Other defendants, like Bridget M., seem to have been less apprehensive about

male relatives learning about an out-of-wedlock pregnancy. Bridget
M.'s three brothers were present at the birth of her infant in July 1926
and the youngest, 16-year-old Peter, buried Bridget's infant in the garden
of their mother's home in Abbeylara, Co. Longford, in July 1926. The
cause of the infant's death was asphyxia. A wad of brown paper was
found at the entrance to its air passage. Peter, Bridget and their mother
Mary were charged with concealment of birth.[121] Eileen Q. gave birth
in her father's Co. Meath home in November 1943.[122] Although two
of Eileen's siblings and her uncle were also in her parents' home at the
time, Eileen's husband of approximately seven weeks and her father
were the only members of the household aware that she had given
birth. Eileen's husband was with her during the birth; her father
entered their room just after the birth. Delia M.'s brother John heard
his sister screaming the night she gave birth to her third illegitimate infant in his father's two-roomed cottage in Co. Mayo in February 1935.
John also heard her infant's cries in the kitchen that night. Delia later
told John that the baby had died and that their father 'had put
it aside'.[123] Both Delia and her father were charged with the infant's
murder. Many of the women who feature in the trial records lived in
labourers' cottages and a small proportion of defendants in the cases
examined gave birth in their parents' cottages. It seems highly unlikely
that family members living in such close proximity would not have
been aware that a female relative had given birth. Nora C.'s father and
brother were both present when Nora gave birth to her second illegitimate infant sometime between November 1928 and March
1929.[124] Nora's first-born was raised in her father's home. Other men
who came into regular contact with unmarried pregnant women, such as
male co-workers, were often well aware that the woman was pregnant.
Lizzie K. was tried for the murder of her male infant at the Co. Limerick
Summer Assizes in 1909. Lizzie had been employed as a domestic servant,
and her co-worker, Michael Earl, submitted detailed evidence against
her. Soon after he took up his position as a servant in the same Co.
Limerick household, Michael Earl noticed that Lizzie's appearance was
'like one in the family way'.[125] Then, in late April, he noticed that Lizzie
'had got thinner in her appearance'.[126] He also stated that shortly before
he observed the sudden change in her appearance he had 'heard her
moaning' one night 'as if she were suffering from pain'.[127]

Male relatives of unmarried mothers were called on to give
evidence in infanticide cases tried during the first half of the twentieth
century. Some men made detailed statements while others appear to

have had scant knowledge of their female relatives' lives. The nature of the evidence submitted by male relatives varies considerably. As previously recounted, Margaret D.'s father played a pivotal role in his daughter's arrest and made a detailed statement to the gardaí in January 1935.[128] John W., whose daughters were charged with murder and concealment of birth in May 1944, made a very brief statement to the gardaí simply confirming that he recognised the items of clothing his daughter's baby had been wrapped in.[129] As few family members in the northern sample, male or female, provided depositions, it is only to be expected that male relatives submitted evidence in only a small number of cases. Their evidence tended to be brief. In January 1925 J.B.'s father simply confirmed his daughter's age and her single status, and stated that he was 'totally unaware she was in a pregnant condition'.[130] Male family members gave depositions in twelve cases (13 per cent) in the pre-independence sample.[131] In the northern sample, six male relatives of the birth mothers (16 per cent) gave depositions.[132] The male relatives of thirty-one single women (16 per cent) charged with the murder or concealment of birth of their illegitimate infants in the Twenty-Six Counties sample made depositions. In addition, the male relatives of a number of women tried at the Central Criminal Court, Dublin, between 1922 and 1950 gave evidence in defence of their female kin.[133] Although Bridget M.'s father did not make a deposition he was listed as a witness for the defence at her trial for the murder and concealment of birth of her newborn female infant at the Central Criminal Court, Dublin in March 1933. He also paid the sum of money required as part of her recognizance. In fact, the fathers of at least eight unmarried female defendants gave evidence in their daughters' defence when the case went to trial. In some instances the putative father also attended the woman's trial and gave evidence in her defence. The father of Margaret S.'s deceased infant was listed as a witness for the defence at her trial in February 1937. Mary S.'s husband Samuel gave evidence in her defence at her trial for the murder of their female infant in September 1930. Mary pleaded guilty to manslaughter but was released on entering into a recognizance. She married the deceasedinfant's father shortly before her trial. It is disingenuous to suggest that men were never required to give evidence in infanticide cases. Gardaí investigating suspected cases of infanticide did not treat the birth of an illegitimate infant in the family home as an exclusively female concern and it was not always assumed that Irish men were ignorant of the matter.

For Guilbride, the most striking aspect of the records of infanticide trials is 'the absence of the man outside his role within the criminal justice system'.[134] Ryan has also asserted that men were rarely implicated in infanticide cases.[135] While infanticide was undoubtedly a crime associated with women, and male relatives were less likely to have been suspected of assisting an unmarried sister or daughter in killing an illegitimate newborn or concealing its birth than female relatives of the birth mother, a number of Irish men were implicated in infanticide cases during the years 1900 to 1950.[136] The male relatives of three single women in the pre-independence sample were charged with concealment of birth, whereas the female relatives of fourteen women in the same sample stood trial for the murder or concealment of birth of their illegitimate infants. Eight male relatives in the Twenty-Six Counties sample were charged with murder or concealment of birth, while twenty-three female relatives of the birth mother stood trial. The absence of men in studies of infanticide in Ireland during the first half of the twentieth century has been overstated. While Irish men are absent from a number of trial records, they are present in many more. Previous studies have neglected the fact that a number of men were tried and convicted for the murder or concealment of birth of newborn infants. It was not uncommon for the male relatives of women charged with or suspected of infanticide to be questioned by the gardaí and in the courtroom. Irish men were not as far removed from crimes associated primarily with women as has hitherto been suggested.

It is clear, in most infanticide cases, that if an unmarried mother sought help from a relative or confided in a family member it was generally a sister, mother or grandmother that they turned to, but this was not always the case. Although unmarried pregnant women were far less likely to confide in a male relative, it was not unknown. One defendant in the northern sample confided in a male relative. S.M. had been living with a male relative and his wife in their Belfast home for a period of twenty-one months prior to her arrest for the murder of her female infant child. In his deposition, J.M., the male relative, told the police that S.M. had informed him about her pregnancy three months prior to the birth. He said that he did not tell his wife. It is not clear how he felt about S.M.'s pregnancy or if he offered her any advice or support. He may well have informed the police when his wife discovered the body of her infant in their house. From the available evidence it is rarely apparent, in cases where the male relatives were charged with the murder or concealment of birth of an unmarried sister or daughter's infant, whether the birth mother had confided in her male kin in advance of the birth. In some instances, such as a 1936 Co. Mayo case, the birth mother's brother, who was charged with the murder of his sister's infant, was probably not aware of his sister's pregnancy until she returned from Galway to the family home in Co. Mayo with her infant in March 1936.[137]

While S.M.'s male relative did not assist her on learning of her predicament, the fathers of three single women in the Twenty-Six Counties sample and one single woman in the northern sample were charged with the murder or concealment of birth of their daughters' illegitimate infants. Only one woman's father in the pre-independence sample was charged with concealing the birth of her illegitimate newborn. Bridget S.'s father Dan was tried for concealing the birth of Bridget's illegitimate infant at the Limerick Summer Assizes in 1901. Dan S. seems to have lied several times in order to protect both himself and his daughter. When the police first called to his house to question them he told them that Bridget was not in the house, but the police went upstairs and found her there. He also lied about where his daughter's baby was buried. 'I told Dr Lee at 7:30 o clock last night that the child was buried in Glenlara. That was not true. I showed the body to Dr Lee and the Head Constable. I did not put the child there or does [sic] not know who did it.'[138] Dan S. also told the police that he had brought a woman to attend to his daughter but the police were unable to locate the woman, and it seems likely that this was untrue.

In April 1935, a Co. Mayo father and daughter were indicted for the murder of an illegitimate male child. Delia M. pleaded guilty to manslaughter. Her father, John M., pleaded guilty to concealment of birth. Delia's father, the *Irish Times* noted, was 'anxious not to shame his daughter and did what he did'.[139] He asked the judge not to send his daughter to prison and suggested that she be sent to a home instead. The newspaper account portrayed John M. as a hard-working old man who stood by his daughter, even though 'the girl's character in general was bad'.[140] It was not the first time John M. had been involved with the gardaí because of his daughter's behaviour. In November 1931, Delia M. gave birth to a stillborn child. Her father reported the birth on that occasion and no charge was brought against her. She had also been found guilty of concealment of birth in October 1929 after the birth of her first child. Gardaí may have suspected that the infanticide case they were investigating was also a case of incest. They inquired about sleeping arrangements in the M. household.

Delia's father said that he always slept in 'the room of the house with my son in the one bed'.[141] Delia, he stated, slept alone in the kitchen. At one point she had, however, slept in the same room as her father, but John M. insisted that she had not shared a room with him 'since she was in trouble before since her mother died'.[142] It is not clear what Delia's father meant by this. There is nothing else in this particular infanticide case to suggest that Delia M. had been a victim of incest. Incest, as Davidoff et al. have noted, 'is almost impossible to uncover historically because its existence has been denied within most families and communities'.[143] However, in the only northern case where the birth mother's father was charged with the concealment of birth of an illegitimate infant, the man in question was, admittedly, both the birth mother's father and the deceased infant's father. This case is discussed at length in Chapter 3. Nora C. may have been sexually abused by her father or brothers. Nora's father, an engine driver, who was 'at times away from the house for two or three months in the course of my employment', seems to have been tolerant of his daughter's sexual activity.[144] During the course of a garda investigation into the death of Nora C.'s unnamed male infant in February 1929, it emerged that six years previously, in 1923, Nora had had an illegitimate child. Nora's father confirmed that the child in question 'is still living'.[145] Nora and her child resided with her father in his labourer's cottage in Co. Cork until she was arrested in February 1929. In his evidence Nora's father admitted being aware that his daughter had also been pregnant on two other occasions. Neither Nora nor her father referred in their evidence to the man or men responsible for her pregnancies. It is possible that Nora was the victim of incest. However, it should not always be assumed that unmarried women whose male relatives appear to have tolerated multiple pregnancies had been sexually abused. When she was charged with the murder of her illegitimate newborn in April 1931, Nora H. told investigating gardaí that her father was the father of the deceased infant. Nora was convicted of concealment of birth. The trial records do not reveal whether gardaí followed up on the allegations Nora made against her father, but it is unlikely that charges were brought against him. This is unremarkable for the period. According to Ferriter, incest cases did not often appear in the court records between 1922 and 1940.[146] It is possible, however, that other women in the cases sampled were the victims of incestuous abuse perpetrated by male relatives, and that this may have supplied some brothers and fathers with a motive for child murder and/or concealment of birth.

'I TOLD HER WE WOULD BE FOUND OUT':
THE BIRTH MOTHERS' BROTHERS

While brothers of the birth mother were less likely than sisters to have been involved in infanticide cases, the brothers of two unmarried woman in the pre-independence sample (2 per cent) were charged with concealing the birth of their sisters' illegitimate infants, and there are at least three recorded instances in the Twenty-Six Counties sample where the brothers of an unmarried woman helped her kill her newborn infant or helped her to dispose of the body. The brothers of three unmarried women in the Twenty-Six Counties sample (2 per cent) were charged with the murder or concealment of birth of their sisters' illegitimate infants. Martin D., aged 22, was one of these men. In April 1936, when approached by Detective Garda Keegan who asked him where his sister Mary Anne was, Martin D. apparently 'became excited' and confessed almost immediately.[147] Detective Keegan said that when they arrived at Dublin Castle Martin broke down completely, began to cry and said 'what will I do'[?] ... 'I told her we would be found out.'[148] Few defendants in infanticide cases seem to have planned their actions carefully in advance. Martin and Mary Anne D. were unusual in that they had made reasonably well-laid plans following the murder of Mary Anne's baby. They left Mayo for Dublin on 23 March 1936 after disposing of the infant's body. Mary Anne looked for work under a false name at a servants' registry office and she gave Martin enough money to travel to London. In fact, if Martin had not come to the attention of an off-duty detective on Aston Quay, the pair may never have been apprehended. Detective Garda Michael Keegan said that he approached a man who fitted the description of Martin D. There may well have been a warrant out for his arrest. It is not clear how exactly Martin caught Detective Keegan's attention. While unmarried mothers may have been pressured by relatives to take the life of an illegitimate newborn, in this particular case the younger brother of an unmarried mother insisted that she had pressured him into assisting her to commit murder. In his statement Martin claimed that his sister put him under considerable pressure to help her kill her baby and dispose of its body. Martin insisted that it was 'only for her' that he did it.[149] He said he 'nearly went on [his] knees to her 5 times and asked her not to do away with it. I would not go with her as I knew she was going to do it.'[150] Martin said that he 'didn't think she wanted the bag for to do away with the child, if [he] did [he] wouldn't go from here to the door with her'.[151] He said he eventually threw the baby into the river because Mary Anne started to cry: 'She said fling the bag into the river and I said no. She begged me against my will and then I threw the bag child and all into the river Moy, it was partly dark then, I told Mary she should have reared the child.'[152] Although Martin D.'s statement must be treated with caution, it is possible that he and other relatives of the other single women in the sample may have felt pressured into killing or concealing the birth of an illegitimate infant. It is also clear that many unmarried mothers were pressured by members of their families into killing their illegitimate infants.

'AFRAID OF HER BROTHERS TO GO HOME'

The majority of unmarried female defendants in all three samples seem to have been extremely anxious to conceal from their relatives the fact that they were pregnant. Some women worried that their parents would force them out of the home if they were discovered to be pregnant. (In fact, it was not uncommon for single pregnant women to be turned out of the family home in the later stages of pregnancy and this has been discussed at length in Chapter 1). In her petition, Mary M. said that she concealed the birth of her illegitimate infant because she was afraid that if her mother discovered that she had had a baby, she would throw her out of the house.[153] The body of Isabella S.'s infant son was found by gardaí in a drain approximately a quarter of a mile from the house in which she resided in Co. Cavan in August 1923. Isabella told Garda Michael Hayden that her newborn baby was alive when she put it in the drain. She said that she had been afraid to bring her home as '[her] uncle would have [her] life'.[154]

In her study of eighty-three infanticide cases tried at the Central Criminal Court between 1925 and 1957, Guilbride placed particular emphasis on the fear of male relatives' discovery of an out-of-wedlock pregnancy as a motivating factor in a single woman's decision to take her infant's life. Guilbride has asserted that 'if [male relatives] were mentioned by the woman, it was as objects of fear, and a number of infants were smothered at birth by their newly delivered mothers for fear that a father or brother would discover the existence of the said infant'.[155] This may have been a motivating factor in the Elizabeth and Rose E. case. In October 1934, Rose E. remarked to her sister Elizabeth that 'the old fellow will kill us if he hears about the baby'.[156] Fathers seem to have played a key role in ensuring that the family's reputation was upheld in many instances. Such fears were articulated by a number of women in the samples examined. According to the medical officer who examined Mary M. in Mountjoy Prison in September 1948, 'her one fear ... was that her brother, Tommy, would hear the child cry and be angry with her for the trouble she had brought on the family'.[157] Nora C. threw her newborn infant into a river in Co. Kerry in April 1927. According to her mother 'she was afraid of her brothers to go home'.[158] As previously discussed, the mothers of several women in the samples examined also remarked on their fear of their husbands' reaction to an out-of-wedlock pregnancy in their depositions.

Historians of infanticide in Ireland have been quick to find evidence of strained father–daughter relationships in the records of infanticide trials. Indeed, it is possible to cite many instances where a father's desire to keep up appearances took precedence over paternal concern for his daughter's welfare. Far less attention, however, has been paid to instances where mothers were mentioned as objects of fear by the birth mother. In her evidence, Deborah S., who gave birth on a Co. Kerry mountainside in February 1929, stated that she was terrified of her mother.[159] In September 1923 Anne F. called at the local police barracks in her locality in West Cork and, according to Sergeant Martin Nagle, Anne 'stated her mother had been hearing talk in the locality and requested me to give her a letter from her mother to the effect that she was not delivered of a child as she would be afraid her mother would kill her'.[160] Sergeant Nagle gave her a letter for her mother, 'directing that she (her mother) should not interfere with her in any way'.[161] An inquest had been conducted on Anne's illegitimate infant at that point and Anne had already admitted taking her baby's life. Anne was convicted of concealment of birth and ordered to spend eighteen months in the Henrietta Street Convent in Dublin. E.H. admitted putting her infant's body in an ash pit in September 1909. In her evidence E.H. said that her mother 'was down on [her]' and she was afraid of her brothers. She thought that she 'would get threw out' if they learned of the birth of her illegitimate infant in Belfast in September 1909.[162]

Single women who became pregnant understood the seriousness of their situation and knew that they faced rejection, not only by their parents, but also by the entire community. Although fathers were mentioned as objects of fear in the statements of a number of single women charged with infanticide, there are examples of fathers who were understanding and clearly concerned about their daughters' fate.

Mary M.'s father wrote to the chief clerk of the Central Criminal Court in November 1933 about '[his] unfortunate daughter'.[163] He said he was unable to attend his daughter's trial in Dublin because he was a poor man but appealed to the judge to have compassion on her. Julia S.'s father wrote to the Crown Solicitor for Co. Kerry in March 1916 to request his daughter's release from prison.[164] Kathleen D. was sent to a hospital in Kilkenny shortly after the birth of her daughter in September 1936.[165] Kathleen's father visited her twice when she was in hospital and she returned to live with her father when she was discharged. Kathleen did not bring her infant daughter with her when she returned to live in her father's home. She told her father that she had given her baby to the Legion of Mary at Waterford. As previously discussed, the fathers of a number of women in the cases sampled attended their trials and gave evidence in their daughters' defence.

In *The Family Story: Blood, Contract and Intimacy, 1830–1960*, Davidoff et al. argue that illegitimacy was among the silenced areas of family life during the first half of the twentieth century.[166] Most families considered illegitimacy shameful and as a result it was 'denied if present or discovered within their midst'.[167] Pregnancy that resulted from incestuous abuse was doubly silenced. Even when a victim of incestuous abuse such as Nora H. eventually broke her silence, the authorities seem to have ignored her allegations. She was imprisoned for two years with hard labour; charges were not brought against her father. In Ireland some families dealt with the shame of illegitimacy during the first half of the twentieth century by denying the illegitimate child life and by removing all evidence of its birth. Relatives who participated in the killing and/or concealment of an illegitimate newborn may have hoped that their drastic actions would prevent their family being associated with the shame and stigma of extramarital pregnancy. In some instances, relatives of the birth mother in southern Ireland seem to have treated the birth of an illegitimate infant as a private family matter which they could resolve themselves by killing the infant shortly after its birth and disposing of the body. John E. certainly seems to have regarded premarital conception as a private matter to be dealt with within the domain of the family. John E.'s neighbour spent 'a very troubled night' following his discovery of John's newborn illegitimate grandson concealed in a pyke of hay on his Co. Meath farmyard in November 1943.[168] Cornelius Fogarty told John that he felt it was his duty to report the matter to the guards. In response, John told him that the infant was all right and asked 'what did [he] want tormenting him, that he was a man that minded his own business and that it would be a good thing if every one minded their own business'.[169]

UNDER PRESSURE

A large number of the unmarried women who feature in the records of infanticide trials seem to have come under sustained pressure from their relatives to kill their illegitimate infants and to conceal all evidence of their existence from the wider community. Patrick M.'s sister Margaret was charged with murdering her illegitimate infant son in January 1905. Margaret must have felt under considerable pressure to take her infant's life. While Margaret's mother appears to have been sympathetic towards her daughter when she noticed that she was pregnant, Margaret's brothers appear to have been unhappy about the predicament in which she found herself. Margaret's mother said that in one letter Margaret sent home while she was in the South Dublin Union hospital, she had said 'that she did not like to come home to us: to bring the child home to us'.[170] In her evidence a nurse who worked in the South Dublin Union hospital stated that Margaret M. received a letter from her family two days after she had given birth. According to the nurse, who had read part of the letter, it said, 'you blackguard you have disgraced your poor mother; every person is asking where Maggie is gone: don't bring it home'.[171] As Margaret's mother was illiterate it seems likely that her brother Patrick wrote the letter. However, Margaret eventually returned home with her baby. In his deposition, her brother Patrick stated that the night that Margaret returned home there were neighbours in the house. He recalled how she said that 'she was ashamed to come in till they went away'.[172] Margaret only went indoors when the neighbours had left. Later that night Patrick saw the infant's body. Margaret's mother sent Patrick for the police. Given her brother's attitude, Margaret may have felt that she had little choice but to take her baby's life. The Margaret M. case was by no means unusual. A number of women in the samples examined were turned out of the family home and only allowed to return if they came back without the baby.

In some instances the relatives of the birth mothers may well have taken the decision to kill their infants for them. In all likelihood, the birth mothers would have acquiesced in this, perhaps relieved to have been rid of an unwanted burden. A number of birth mothers in the cases sampled seem to have stood by after delivery while their relatives destroyed the evidence of extramarital conception. Nora, the birth mother in a 1931 Waterford case, had even more reason to let her father handle the fate of her newborn infant as he was the father of the infant to whom she had given birth. Father and daughter do not seem to have discussed what to do. Nora said that her father took the infant from her shortly after delivery and went downstairs with it. Neither Nora nor her father said anything. She told gardaí she was 'quite sure none of us said anything'.[173] She did not want to speak to her father at the time because she was afraid he would hit her. He had already 'threatened that he would kill the child when he saw it'.[174] Nora's father drowned the infant on the night of 7 April 1931 and then went to bed. Once again neither of them uttered a word.

In certain cases there appears to have been a somewhat curious combination of concern for the birth mother and ruthlessness in killing a newborn infant and disposing of its body. John E. described his daughter Eileen as being 'a kind of half dazed' after giving birth unassisted in his Co. Meath home in November 1943.[175] He was clearly concerned about her and brought 'some tea and toast up to Eileen in her bedroom'.[176] He then proceeded to roll the baby up in some cloth and a black sack and he brought it 'out to the haggard and put it on top of a cock of hay [he] was using and covered it with straw'.[177] The newborn infant appears to have died from exposure and neglect. John E.'s daughter had married shortly before she gave birth and was living with her husband in her father's home, but neither Eileen nor her husband Michael Q. seem to have objected to John E.'s actions. In his deposition Michael stated that he 'did not enquire what had happened to it or what arrangements had been made. [He] did not tell any member of the family except [his] father-in-law that [his] wife had given birth to a baby.'[178] A number of couples married in the late stages of the woman's pregnancy yet still took drastic measures to conceal the infant's existence. These cases are explored in Chapter 3. In all other cases, either husband or wife were charged with the infant's murder.

'THE MOTHER ... DID NOTHING BUT SHIELD HER DAUGHTER'S SHAME': MOTIVES IN INFANTICIDE CASES INVOLVING THE BIRTH MOTHERS' RELATIVES

It is difficult to provide an adequate explanation to account for the forces that drove the relatives of single women to kill or conceal the birth of illegitimate children during the period under review. Some newborn infants were killed quite brutally. Shame was clearly one of the main motivating factors in a number of cases involving relatives of the birth mother. In a 1926 Co. Longford infanticide case, the birth mother's brother Thomas recalled how his mother remarked: 'your sister Bridget had a child on the floor. It is a nice shame in the face of the public.'[179] John E. was the only person tried for the murder of his daughter's infant in April 1944. It would appear that John E. killed his daughter's baby in an attempt to preserve her reputation and the family's honour. Eileen Q. had been married for less than two months when she gave birth in her father's home. The newly married couple were living in Eileen's parents' home in Co. Meath at the time. Extramarital conception was clearly considered shameful, even when marriage followed; John E. did not inform his younger daughters about the birth and death of the baby. Eileen's husband said that he 'did not tell any member of the family except my father-in-law that my wife had given birth to a baby'. Eileen did not receive any medical attention. Her father told the gardaí that 'I did not open my mouth to them about it. I did not want to let them know it.'[180] He claimed that the baby died a few hours after its birth and that he placed the dead body in a stack of hay, but it is clear from the evidence of his neighbour Cornelius F. that he took the baby from his daughter and left it to die in the farmyard. It would appear that the couple let Eileen's father handle the matter. He took the baby outside and left it to die in a stack of hay on his farm. Neither Eileen nor her husband Michael seem to have raised any objections to the way their infant son was disposed of. In her statement Eileen claimed that her son was already dead when her father removed it from her bedroom, although this was clearly not the case as a neighbour saw it alive on a visit to John E.'s farm on the day Eileen gave birth. In his evidence Cornelius F. said that he heard an infant's cries coming from a pyke of hay. He found the infant concealed in a sack: '[He] looked into the sack. [He] saw a child in it. It was alive. It made a noise like crying.'[181] The young couple in this case may well have been relieved that Eileen's father had taken charge of the situation.

The compulsion to protect a family's sense of honour and reputation in the community was obviously a very strong one in Ireland throughout the first half of the twentieth century and was often put forward by barristers defending the relatives of unmarried mothers charged with murder or concealment of birth in court in order to account for their clients' behaviour. Judges, barristers and doctors involved with infanticide cases often referred to the huge sense of shame and disgrace associated with unmarried motherhood. When Rose E. was questioned in court about the death of her sister's illegitimate daughter, Judge O'Byrne remarked, 'I take it that you felt her position keenly and you felt the great shame and disgrace brought upon yourself, your parents and your brother.'[182] Defending Mary M. at her trial in the Central Criminal Court, Dublin, in November 1929, Mr G.L. Howe said that 'the mother ... did nothing but shield her daughter's shame'.[183] Mary M. and her 19-year-old daughter Margaret were both charged with the murder of Margaret's illegitimate newborn. Mr Howe stated that the Mary M. 'had a very high character' and that her daughter Margaret committed the crime 'at a time when her mind was deranged and she was not responsible for her actions'.[184] However, the trial judge said that he could not allow mother and daughter to 'go free on such a serious charge' and they were both sentenced to six months' imprisonment.[185]

Financial worries rather than a desire to avoid shame and moral censure may have been the key motivating factor in some family members' decision to take illegitimate infant life. When she was arrested in July 1938, Mary S. told gardaí that she put her unmarried daughter's newborn infant 'in a well out of the house'.[186] According to the Superintendent of the Garda Síochána in Monaghan, Mary and her children were not well housed or well clothed. As noted in Chapter 1, they lived in 'a small corrugated iron-roofed house and a number of rooms were described as 'barely habitable.'[187] Mary was in receipt of financial assistance from the County Monaghan Protestant Orphan Aid Society. As a widow struggling to provide for her children, Mary S. may have been motivated to kill her daughter's infant because she would have found it difficult to support another child. A garda superintendent in Co. Monaghan doubted whether Mary S. had killed her daughter's illegitimate infant because she was anxious to protect the honour of her family. The superintendent described Mary S. as 'a rough masculine type'[188] who had 'the reputation of being of loose moral character'.[189] According to the author of the report, Mary S. 'did not appear to worry in the least as to the views, or opinions, regarding her which were held by her neighbours'.[190] The author of the report also stated that 'Having regard to the character and reputation of the family, the ruthless disposal of the infant can hardly be attributed to those motives which might in other cases be responsible, namely, the anxiety to protect the family from the shame attaching to such a misfortune.'[191]

As Arnot and Usborne have observed, 'historical studies in different contexts on topics such as childcare, infanticide and abortion have shown that there could be major disjunctures between official penal prescription and popular perceptions and practices'.[192] That there was a disjuncture between church teaching and the law on one hand, and attitudes held by many Irish families with regard to illegitimate child life on the other, is evident from an examination of Irish infanticide cases. The relatives of some single women displayed a complete lack of regard for the lives of children born outside wedlock.[193]

Ryan has examined representations of deviant Irish families in Irish newspapers between 1922 and 1937. She argues that 'while the idealised Irish family was the bedrock of the nation, particular types of families were especially liable to official scrutiny and sanction'.[194] The deviant families Ryan identified, 'who showed no respect for authority, and the poor inadequate, dirty, diseased family',[195] also feature in the records of infanticide cases. When three members of a Co. Longford family, a mother, son and daughter, were charged with murder and concealment of birth in August 1926, the judge who heard the case commented unfavourably on the 'levity of the accused in court'.[196] The judge remarked that one of the accused was apparently, from her demeanour, regarding the affair lightly. He told her that her demeanour in court was appalling and reminded her that she was in court under a most serious charge. While the state may have regarded the murder of infants as a serious charge, the attitudes displayed by the relatives of some unmarried mothers suggest that some Irish people did not regard infanticide as a serious crime. The Bishop of Ossory stated that the illegitimate child was 'less valued than the life of the ordinary child' in post-independence Ireland.[197] The records of infanticide cases reveal that this was so. The relatives of some single women displayed a complete lack of regard for the lives of children born outside wedlock. Irish society, as Smith notes, 'viewed illegitimate and legitimate children in starkly different terms'.[198] He has argued that 'tolerance for infant mortality reflects this bias'.[199] Maguire has argued that 'the Catholic doctrine of the sanctity of human, and especially child, life, and the value that early nationalist lawmakers placed on child life, bore no resemblance to the way church and state dealt with illegitimate, problematic, and vulnerable children in the twentieth century'.[200] Her research has suggested that illegitimate children were not always regarded as potentially valuable citizens but as 'dangerous and burdensome populations to be confined, regulated, and controlled'.[201] It is clear from the records of infanticide trials that illegitimate children were not valued in Irish society during the first half of the twentieth century. Thomas K. claimed that when he asked his mother why she did not remove the child from the floor 'as it would die with the cold, she said "to hell with it. What would I be bothering myself taking pain with it for" '.[202] The Catholic moral code was, according to one senior cleric, most likely to have been flouted by the poorer classes within Irish society. In his 1929 Lenten pastoral the Bishop of Ossory stated that the 'humbler classes in our country seem to have less regard for purity and morality than in the past' and appealed to employers and the clergy to help bring them back into line, 'to keep a more stringent control over these poor people' and to 'keep them from occasions of sin'.[203] Whether 'the poorer classes' were more likely to have flouted the moral code is impossible to determine, but it is apparent that poor Irish women were subject to a surveillance within their communities and by their employers that did not apply to unmarried middle-class women. Catholic priests do not play a prominent role in infanticide cases. There are references to clerics in only a very small number of files. Johanna D.'s parish priest was contacted by the county registrar at the Central Criminal Court in October 1926 and asked to 'keep a friendly eye on this poor girl, who is only 19'.[204] Johanna had attempted suicide by cutting her throat with a razor. Mary Anne M.'s parish priest made arrangements for her to be sent to the Good Shepherd convent in New Ross at the request of her father.[205] One woman's parish priest may have played a part in organising her marriage to the father of her deceased infant after her conviction for concealment of birth in 1934.[206]

INFANTICIDE AND FAMILY LIFE

Infanticide trials must have strained familial relationships and divided Irish families. It would presumably have been the source of a great deal of stress, fear and anger. It was a crime that, in many cases, may have led to the breakdown of close personal relationships and blighted the lives of all those involved. Watching an unmarried female relative give birth and subsequently committing a crime must have been a traumatic experience for the relatives of many single women in this sample. The relatives of some single women appear to have been extremely distressed because an unmarried female family member was pregnant. The pressure to assist a single woman to conceal her pregnancy and to dispose of her infant's body seems to have been a source of intense anxiety to some. When he was cross-examined, the district inspector of the RIC in Co. Louth said that when Mary C.'s mother Margaret saw the sergeant, 'she was overwhelmed – half-distracted – whether from grief or fear and was in that state when she made the statement'.[207] Margaret had attempted to refute claims that her daughter was pregnant on several occasions when her neighbours inquired, and she appears to have buried the body of her daughter's illegitimate newborn in their back garden in Drogheda, Co Louth, in August 1910. Margaret apparently 'got very nervous and excited' when the police arrived, and judging by her statement and behaviour she was extremely anxious to avoid being disgraced.[208]

Family members who assisted an unmarried relative in giving birth did not always support the mother's evidence in court. Such a secretive, shameful event clearly strained close relationships. Margaret F. and her cousin Bridget C. were charged with the murder of Margaret's infant son in June 1930. Bridget worked as a domestic servant and spent her holiday with her cousin Margaret. Margaret was in pain on 17 June and told her cousin that she was about to give birth. As Margaret's mother was out of the house at the time, they both left the house and Margaret gave birth in a field at the back of the house. Shortly after the birth, Bridget claimed that Margaret asked her to remove the lace from her boots. Bridget complied and recalled how Margaret 'took the lace and tied it round the child's neck a number of times in such a way that the child's eyes opened wide'.[209] Margaret then dragged the baby along the ground and covered the body with stones. Bridget stated that though she witnessed the infant's death she had no role in the murder. 'All there is to say is that I have nothing to do with her only that I was there standing by.'[210] Margaret F.'s statements differ from her cousin's and it is unclear, therefore, whether Bridget assisted with the death of the child or whether she simply observed what took place. Margaret insisted that Bridget urged her to choke the baby. 'The child started to cry and she told me to catch it by the neck and choke it.'[211] She also insisted that Bridget had helped her bury the body. It is difficult to ascertain whether Margaret was trying to implicate her cousin in the crime or whether she was in fact telling the truth. Bridget's detailed descriptions of how Margaret had killed her baby certainly did not help her cousin's case. It is perhaps understandable that when on trial, women who had assisted unmarried female relatives in giving birth were generally more concerned with proving their own innocence than protecting family members. Bridget C. was found 'not guilty'. She maintained that when she gave Margaret her bootlace she thought it was for the purpose of tying up her cousin's clothes. Margaret F. was found guilty and sentenced to death but the sentence was later commuted.

Little is known about the fate of single women who were convicted of the murder or concealment of birth of their illegitimate infants between 1900 and 1950 following their terms of incarceration. Some women's relationships with their close relatives may have been ruptured following their arrest, trial and imprisonment, and they may not have returned to their parents' home when they were released from prison. However, others may have not encountered as many difficulties and some women may have been welcomed back into the family fold when their term of detention had expired. Women whose parents were poor and required part of their daughters' earnings or their labour at home may have forgiven them more readily than parents who were not reliant on their daughters' assistance. Bridget R. was convicted of concealing the birth of her illegitimate infant in March 1912 and sentenced to twelve months' imprisonment with suitable labour. According to a Co. Wicklow-based RIC sergeant, Bridget's parents were 'most anxious to have their daughter Bridget home again'.[212] In her petition to the Lord Lieutenant, Bridget stated that her 'mother and father is forgiving me and taking me home under their care'.[213] Although Julia S.'s grandmother told the police to take her granddaughter away and said that she did not care what they did with her, Julia's father wrote to the Crown Solicitor for Kerry in March 1916 in order to petition him for her early release. He seems to have been dependent economically on his daughter.

FAMILY INVOLVEMENT IN NORTHERN IRELAND AND THE TWENTY-SIX COUNTIES

Infanticide cases that came to light in the southern twenty-six counties and those tried in the six northern counties varied little, but proportionately more relatives of the birth mother were charged with murder of concealment of birth in the Twenty-Six Counties both before and after independence than was the case in the six northern counties between 1920 and 1950. As the post-independence Twenty-Six Counties sample is larger than the northern sample, this may help to account for the higher level of family involvement. Further research into the history of infanticide in Northern Ireland may well bring more cases of family involvement to light. It would appear, however, that in Northern Ireland the relatives of the birth mother were less likely to have been considered suspects in the crime than their southern counterparts. In the post-independence period, policing methods may help account for the fact that charges were brought against a number of family members in infanticide cases tried in the South. There were several instances in southern Ireland where charges were brought against the relatives of the birth mother when there was little if any evidence to link them to the crime, and such cases generally collapsed when they were brought to court.[214] There appears to have been a tendency for gardaí investigating infanticide cases in the South to spread the charges against co-resident family members. Such relatives may have been arrested in the hope that when they were put under pressure they would reveal more information about the circumstances surrounding an infant's death, or contradict or add to the evidence given by the birth mother. In a 1929 Co. Monaghan case, Maggie D., the 15-year-old daughter of an unmarried woman suspected of murdering her illegitimate infant, was questioned. Maggie said that 'the inspector made [her] make a statement by telling [her] [her] mother would be hanged and that he would send [her] up to the gaol to [her] mother'.[215] She insisted that there was no truth in the statement she made. She 'answered all lies' because gardaí shook her.[216] She also said that when the gardaí arrived at their house they sent the other members of the household away and barred the door to their home. Inspector Neville's evidence contradicted Maggie's version of events. He said that he did not lock the door to the house and that the other family members left at the defendant's suggestion. He also insisted that 'it was quite proper to seek information from the daughter of the accused' and claimed that Maggie was not frightened when she was questioned; she 'smoked a cigarette placidly while being questioned'.[217] In her statement, Mary M. said:

> on the occasion when the statement was obtained from me I was sitting in the day room when the inspector questioned me about the offence. He said if I did not tell the truth my mother and step-father and my daughter would be arrested. He asked whether I wanted my daughter to go to gaol along with me. He asked whether I would let that happen or tell the truth and take the consequences.[218]

It is possible that investigating gardaí did pressure Mary and her daughter. Their interrogation of Mary's teenage daughter may well have produced results and helped incriminate her. She was found guilty of concealment of birth. In a 1940 Co. Cavan case, a recently married husband and wife were charged with the murder of their infant daughter. They had been living with James B.'s parents at the time of the birth. Even though James, Jean and their infant daughter were away from home when the infant had allegedly died – the couple said they had travelled across the border to Enniskillen and had buried the baby there – James B.'s mother Annie was also arrested and charged with murder and conspiracy to murder. When Annie B. was arrested she protested and, according to Sergeant Thomas Delaney, said 'it's a notorious mistake. He will not arrest me at all. I will resist it. I was not away from home at all. I told you all when you were here before.'[219] Annie B. seems to have been arrested simply because she was aware of the infant's existence and was acquitted when the case went to court.

While close female relatives of single women charged with infanticide in Northern Ireland were, in most instances, clearly concerned for their sisters' well being, they were not prepared to break the law in order to conceal the crime. In the south, several family members sometimes collaborated and cooperated in order to conceal the shame and disgrace of a birth outside marriage.

The relatives of sixteen unmarried mothers in the pre-independence sample were charged with murder or concealment of birth; more than half (58 per cent) were not convicted.[220] The relatives of five women in the pre-independence sample were acquitted, while the relatives of four women who were convicted of manslaughter or concealment of birth served prison sentences. The relatives of two women were found guilty of concealment of birth but were discharged on entering into a recognizance. Bridget S.'s father was probably discharged even though he was convicted of concealing the birth of her illegitimate infant at the Limerick Summer Assizes of 1901. The jury strongly recommended him for mercy because they felt that he was ignorant of the law. Men, it would appear, were not to be expected to know that the birth of an infant had to be registered and its death reported. Eight male relatives and twenty-three female relatives of the birth mother in the southern sample were charged with murder or concealment of birth in twenty-eight cases that went before the Central Criminal Court, Dublin, between 1922 and 1950. This accounts for 14 per cent of all cases in the sample for the Twenty-Six Counties. There were several more cases in the southern sample where criminal charges were not brought against relatives of the birth mother although it seemed quite clear that they had assisted her in some way.

Five out of the thirty-one relatives charged with the murder or concealment of birth of an unmarried female relative's infant were acquitted; *nolle prosequi* was entered in a further four cases. The majority of relatives in the southern sample were convicted. In the northern sample there was only one case (2.6 per cent) where a relative of the birth mother was charged with infanticide.[221] As the southern sample is larger than the northern sample, this may account for the higher level of family involvement.

CONCLUSION

Elizabeth C., who was 31 years old, stood trial for the murder of her twenty-seven-day-old infant daughter Ellen at the Central Criminal Court in June 1934. Elizabeth, an unmarried woman, gave birth in the Mullingar County Home. When she was discharged she had to seek shelter with a woman from her neighbourhood because her relatives refused to let her return home with her illegitimate infant daughter. In her deposition Bridget F. recalled making Elizabeth tea when she arrived at her doorstep. Bridget explained that she gave Elizabeth and her baby a room for the night. She also said that Elizabeth had told her that although 'the family would not let her into the house with the baby … they would let her in without the baby'.[222] Elizabeth and her brothers lived with their aunt. When her aunt was questioned by gardaí she confirmed what Elizabeth had said about her family to Bridget F. Mary K. stated that when her niece arrived at the house 'she said was she not going to be let in and I said no'.[223] Elizabeth left fifteen minutes later. Her aunt saw Elizabeth in a barn the following day and she told her that the baby had died. Elizabeth's infant daughter died of haemorrhage due to violence. In her statement Elizabeth said that 'it was through worry and annoyance I did it'.[224]

Elizabeth was faced with a stark choice. She could either return to the family fold without her infant daughter or face a very uncertain future as a single mother. Elizabeth probably had very little money of her own. She may not have had any occupational skill. It is likely that, when forced to decide on a course of action, she was emotionally drained. She had been effectively homeless since leaving the Mullingar

County Home. She was probably physically exhausted after the ordeal of giving birth. It may have seemed easier to slip back into family life after disposing of her infant daughter Ellen than embarking on a very insecure existence. But killing the infant may have proved more difficult and more traumatic for Elizabeth than some mothers in the cases sampled. The vast majority of infants in the cases sampled were killed immediately after the birth, but Elizabeth's daughter Ellen was twenty-seven days old. She had a name. Elizabeth may well have bonded with her baby; she had fed and cared for Ellen for almost a month. Many women who, like Elizabeth, faced an impossible choice in this period must have been haunted by their actions in later life. Elizabeth's aunt seems to have approved of her niece's decision. She gave her tacit support. After the baby's death, Mary K. gave Elizabeth a box for the body and asked her nephew to bury Ellen. The doors of her home were reopened to her wayward niece. In a sense, Elizabeth's aunt was almost as culpable for the baby's death.

Without the support of families or friends, adoption services or social welfare, and with little, if any financial resources of their own, unmarried women like Elizabeth C. who became pregnant in Ireland during the first half of the twentieth century were marginalised and vulnerable. Many women came under pressure from their relatives to conceal the existence of their illegitimate infants and in some cases to take their infants' lives. Others were assisted in killing their newborns or concealing the birth by secretly disposing of the body. However, the case of Elizabeth C. also reveals that despite having become pregnant outside wedlock, some women were permitted to return to the family fold once they had destroyed the evidence of extramarital sex. Many Irish families clearly prioritised their moral reputation over the welfare of an illegitimate infant during the period and were prepared to break the law rather than live with the stain of illegitimacy.

NOTES

1. *Irish Catholic*, 16 February 1929.
2. Ibid.
3. Ibid.
4. Ibid.
5. National Archives of Ireland [hereafter NAI], Court of Criminal Appeal [hereafter CCA], 36/38.
6. *Connacht Tribune*, 9 May 1936.

7. S. D'Cruze and L.A. Jackson, *Women, Crime and Justice in England since 1660* (London: Palgrave Macmillan, 2009), p.77.
8. J.R. Dickinson and J.A. Sharpe, 'Infanticide in Early Modern England: The Court of Great Sessions at Chester, 1650–1800', in Mark Jackson (ed.), *Infanticide: Historical Perspectives on Child Murder and Concealment, 1550–2000* (Aldershot: Ashgate, 2002), p.43.
9. Ibid.
10. M. Jackson, *New-Born Child Murder: Women, Illegitimacy and the Courts in Eighteenth-Century England* (Manchester: Manchester University Press, 1996), p.80, n.33.
11. L. Ryan, *Gender, Identity and the Irish Press, 1922–1937* (Lampeter: Edwin Mellen, 2002), p.282.
12. NAI, Co. Clare, Crown Files at Assizes, 1903.
13. Ibid.
14. NAI, Central Criminal Court [hereafter CCC], Co. Kilkenny, 1944.
15. Ibid.
16. NAI, Crown Files at Assizes, 1900–02.
17. 'A short stump of a girl *Dumfriesshire*', or 'a term of reprobation for a testy, or naughty girl or woman; but often used playfully.' *The Oxford English Dictionary*, 2nd ed. (Oxford: Clarendon, 1989), Vol. 4.
18. NAI, Crown Files at Assizes, 1900–02.
19. Ibid.
20. Ibid.
21. NAI, CCA, 30/1928, Co. Cork.
22. Ibid.
23. Ibid.
24. NAI, CCC, Co. Leitrim, 1944.
25. Ibid.
26. NAI, CCC, Co. Mayo, 1935.
27. Public Record Office of Northern Ireland [hereafter PRONI], BELF/1/1/2/45/7, 1914.
28. R. Schulte, *The Village in Court: Arson, Infanticide, and Poaching in the Court Records of Upper Bavaria, 1848–1910* (Cambridge: Cambridge University Press, 1994), p.98.
29. Andrew Blaikie, *Illegitimacy, Sex, and Society: Northeast Scotland, 1750–1800* (Oxford: Clarendon, 1993).
30. C. Rattigan, ' "Dark spots" in Irish society: Single Motherhood, Crime and Prosecution in Ireland, 1900–1950' (PhD thesis, Trinity College Dublin, 2008).
31. M. Hill, *Women in Ireland: A Century of Change* (Belfast: Blackstaff, 2003), pp.27–9.
32. PRONI, BELF/1/2/2/56/4, 1946.
33. Ibid.
34. PRONI, BELF/1/2/2/40/67, 1930.
35. NAI, CRF S 2/1916.
36. NAI, CCC, Co. Clare, 1927.
37. NAI, CCA, 30/1928, Co. Cork.
38. Ibid.
39. Ibid.
40. Ibid.
41. Ibid.
42. Hill, *Women in Ireland*, p.29.
43. When E.S. asked J.M. to take her in as a lodger in May 1925, E.S. 'had a black eye which she said her father had given her', according to her landlady (PRONI, BELF 1/1/2/77/5, 1925). D.G.'s father turned her out of their home one week before she gave birth in November 1927 (PRONI, BELF1/1/2/86/5, 1927).
44. NAI, Co. Dublin, Leinster Winter Assizes, 1917.
45. NAI, Co. Donegal, Crown Files at Assizes, 1900–02.
46. Ibid.
47. D'Cruze and Jackson, *Women, Crime and Justice*, p.80.
48. NAI, CCC, Co. Offaly, 1934.
49. NAI, Co. Clare, Crown Files at Assizes, 1914.

50. Ibid.
51. PRONI, BELF/1/1/2/31/5, 1910.
52. NAI, CCC, Co. Limerick, 1935.
53. Ibid.
54. Ibid.
55. NAI, CCC, Co. Longford, 1926.
56. Ibid.
57. Ibid.
58. *Cork Examiner*, 25 July 1919.
59. Ibid.
60. PRONI, BELF/1/1/2/33/6, 1909.
61. NAI, CCC, Co. Monaghan, 1924.
62. Ibid.
63. Ibid.
64. *Cork Examiner*, 30 November 1928.
65. *Cork Examiner*, 29 November 1929.
66. *Anglo-Celt*, 14 December 1940.
67. *Irish News*, 25 May 1931.
68. In total, charges were brought again thirty-one relatives of the birth mother in twenty-eight cases in the Twenty-Six Counties sample. In two cases charges were brought against a male and a female family member.
69. NAI, CCA, 36/1938, Co. Monaghan.
70. NAI, Co. Clare, Crown Files at Assizes, 1903.
71. NAI, Co. Donegal, Crown Files at Assizes, 1909–11.
72. NAI, Co. Carlow, Crown Files at Assizes, 1887–1906.
73. Ibid.
74. NAI, CCA 36/1938.
75. NAI, Co. Carlow, Crown Files at Assizes, 1887–1906.
76. NAI, Dublin, Crown Files at Quarter Sessions, 1900.
77. NAI, CCA, 24/1930.
78. PRONI, BELF/1/1/2/24/10, 1907.
79. PRONI, BELF/1/1/2/31/5, 1910.
80. PRONI, BELF/1/1/2/91/6, 1929.
81. PRONI, BELF1/1/2/76/5, 1925.
82. Ibid.
83. NAI, CCC, Co. Kilkenny, 1944.
84. NAI, CCC, Co. Meath, 1935.
85. NAI, CCC, Co. Kilkenny, 1937.
86. NAI, Co. Dublin Crown Files at Commission, Leinster Winter Assizes, 1917.
87. Ibid.
88. Ibid.
89. Ibid.
90. Ibid.
91. This figure includes one woman's mother-in-law.
92. NAI, CCC, Co. Clare, 1933.
93. NAI, CCC, Co. Waterford, 1942.
94. NAI, Department of the Taoiseach, S 7788A.
95. NAI, CCA, 13/1935.
96. *The Irish Reports*, 1935, p.500.
97. Ibid.
98. NAI, CCC, Co. Galway, 1941. Cáit and Máire ní C. were from an Irish-speaking part of Co. Galway and their statements and many of the witness statements were made in Irish.
99. Ibid.
100. NAI, CCC, Co. Kilkenny, 1944.
101. Ibid.

102. NAI, CCC, Co. Roscommon, 1948.
103. NAI, CCC, Co. Donegal, 1926.
104. NAI, CCC, Dublin, 1938.
105. Ibid.
106. NAI, CCC, Co. Tipperary, 1949.
107. NAI, CCC, Co. Kilkenny, 1944.
108. Ibid.
109. NAI, Limerick City & County, Crown Files at Assizes, 1908–10.
110. Ibid.
111. S. Lambert, 'Irish Women's Emigration to England, 1922–60: The Lengthening of Family Ties', in A. Hayes and D. Urquhart (eds), *Irish Women's History* (Dublin: Irish Academic Press, 2004), p.156.
112. L. Earner-Byrne, 'Reinforcing the Family: The Role of Gender, Morality and Sexuality in Irish Welfare Policy, 1922–1944', *History of the Family*, 13, 4 (2008), p.363.
113. NAI, CCC, Co. Cavan, 1940.
114. *Anglo-Celt*, 14 December 1940.
115. NAI, CCC, Co. Cavan, 1940.
116. NAI, CCC, Co. Mayo, 1931.
117. PRONI, BELF/1/1/2/95/6, 1931.
118. The evidence in a 1940 Belfast case suggests that one woman's mother put her under considerable pressure to consent to an abortion. Indeed, E.F.'s mother made all the arrangements for the abortion. When she discovered that her daughter was four months pregnant, E.F.'s mother first invited the man responsible for her daughter's condition to her house to discuss the matter. However, when T.B. refused to marry her, saying that 'I cannot keep a wife', M.F. approached a woman she knew and asked her 'if she would give her [daughter] a soap injection to relieve her of her pregnancy or if she knew of any other person who could do so'. Mrs F. was clearly anxious for her daughter to avoid the shame associated with single motherhood. E.M. told the police that she heard her say that she was 'not going to have [her] daughter disgraced[,] she has got to be cleared'. In his statement E.F.'s boyfriend said that she was very upset the last time he saw her and told him that 'all those people downstairs except my grandmother want me to go to a woman and have threatened to bring her here to me'. Although Mrs F. said she would never 'do anything to my wee girl', her actions led to her daughter's death (PRONI, Belf/1/1/2/123/5, 1940).
119. NAI, CCA, 24/1930.
120. Ibid.
121. Bridget and her mother Mary were also charged with murder and conspiracy to murder. NAI, CCC, Co. Longford, 1926.
122. NAI, CCC, Co. Meath, 1944.
123. NAI, CCC, Co. Mayo, 1935.
124. *Irish Independent*, 25 June 1929.
125. NAI, Co. Limerick Crown Files at Assizes, 1908–10.
126. Ibid.
127. Ibid.
128. NAI, CCC, Co. Limerick, 1935.
129. NAI, CCC, Co. Kilkenny, 1944.
130. PRONI, BELF1/1/2/76/5, 1925.
131. The fathers of three women and one woman's stepfather submitted evidence. One woman's grandfather made a deposition while the brothers of five women submitted evidence. In addition, one woman's half-brother and another woman's brother-in-law made depositions. Two of the twelve men were also defendants in the cases.
132. The fathers of four women gave depositions. One woman's brother submitted evidence and the male relative of another woman made a deposition. In that particular case it is not clear how the birth mother and the male relative were related. One of the six men was also a co-defendant in the case.
133. The fathers of eight women and the brothers of three women in the cases sampled gave

evidence in their defence. The mothers of six women and one woman's sister gave evidence in favour of unmarried female defendants in the cases sampled.

134. A. Guilbride, ' "I Went Away In Silence": A Study of Infanticide in Ireland from 1925 to 1957' (Minor MA thesis, University College, Dublin, 1994), p.28.
135. L. Ryan, 'The Press, Police and Prosecution: Perspectives on Infanticide in the 1920s' in Hayes and Urquhart (eds), *Irish Women's History*, p.144.
136. The fathers of illegitimate infants were charged with murder or concealment of birth in seven cases tried at the Central Criminal Court between 1922 and 1950 (3.5 per cent). It is also possible that John M. was the father of his girlfriend's illegitimate infant, even though he insisted that he was not the infant's father and his girlfriend thought that another man was responsible for her pregnancy (NAI, CCC, Co. Wexford, 1949). Myles D. may well have been the father of Mary C.'s illegitimate infant. Mary had intercourse with Myles, her employer, and his son (NAI, CCC, Co. Wexford, 1928). The father of one illegitimate infant in the pre-independence sample was tried for concealment of birth (1 per cent) while in the northern sample the putative fathers stood trial in three cases (8 per cent). Men, both relatives and the putative fathers, stood trial in 4 per cent of cases in the pre-independence sample and in 8 per cent of cases in the Twenty-Six Counties and northern samples.
137. NAI, CCC, Co. Mayo, 1936.
138. NAI, Co. Limerick, Crown Files at Assizes, 1901–02.
139. *Irish Times*, 2 April 1935.
140. Ibid.
141. NAI, CCC, Co. Mayo, 1935.
142. Ibid.
143. L. Davidoff et al., *The Family Story: Blood, Contract and Intimacy, 1830–1960* (London: Longman, 1998), p.246.
144. NAI, CCC, Co. Cork, 1929.
145. Ibid.
146. D. Ferriter, *Occasions of Sin: Sex and Society in Modern Ireland* (London: Profile, 2009), p183.
147. NAI, CCC, Co. Mayo, 1936.
148. Ibid.
149. Ibid.
150. Ibid.
151. Ibid.
152. Ibid.
153. NAI, CRF M 37/1916.
154. NAI, CCC, Co. Cavan, 1924.
155. Guilbride, 'I Went Away in Silence', p.29.
156. NAI, CCA, 13/1935.
157. NAI, CCC, Co. Kilkenny, 1948.
158. NAI, CCC, Co. Kerry, 1927.
159. NAI, Department of Justice, 234/2590.
160. NAI, Crown Book at Assizes, Co. Cork, 1924.
161. Ibid.
162. PRONI, BELF/1/1/2/33/6, 1909.
163. NAI, CCC, Co. Tipperary, 1933.
164. NAI, CRF S 2/1916.
165. NAI, CCC, Co. Waterford, 1936.
166. Davidoff et al., *Family Story*, p.245.
167. Ibid., p.246.
168. NAI, CCC, Co. Meath, 1944.
169. Ibid.
170. NAI, Co Carlow, Crown Files Assizes, Depositions 1887–1906.
171. Ibid.
172. Ibid.

173. NAI, CCC, Co. Waterford, 1931.
174. Ibid.
175. NAI, CCC, Co. Meath, 1944.
176. Ibid.
177. Ibid.
178. Ibid.
179. NAI, CCC, Co. Longford, 1926.
180. NAI, CCC, Co. Meath, 1944.
181. Ibid.
182. NAI, CCA, 13/1935.
183. *Cork Examiner*, 29 November 1929.
184. Ibid.
185. Ibid.
186. NAI, CCA, 36/1938, Co. Monaghan.
187. Ibid.
188. NAI, CCA, 36/38. Report by Superintendent of Garda Síochána, Monaghan, in a letter sent to the Registrar at the Court of Criminal Appeal by the Vice Commissioner of the police force.
189. Ibid.
190. Ibid.
191. Ibid.
192. M.L. Arnot and C. Usborne, 'Why Gender and Crime? Aspects of an Institutional Debate', in M.L. Arnot and C. Usborne (eds), *Gender and Crime in Modern Europe* (London: Routledge, 1999), p.20.
193. NAI, CCC, Co. Longford, 1926.
194. Ryan, *Gender, Identity and the Irish Press*, p.286.
195. Ibid.
196. *Longford Leader*, 28 August 1926.
197. *Irish Catholic*, 16 February 1929.
198. J.M. Smith, *Ireland's Magdalen Laundries and the Nation's Architecture of Containment* (Manchester: Manchester University Press, 2008), p.55.
199. Ibid.
200. M.J. Maguire, 'The Myth of Catholic Ireland: Unmarried Motherhood, Infanticide and Illegitimacy in the Twentieth Century' (PhD thesis, American University, Washington, DC, 2000), p.161.
201. Ibid. pp.161–2.
202. *Longford Leader*, 28 August 1926.
203. *Irish Catholic*, 16 February 1929.
204. NAI, CCC, Co. Limerick, 1926.
205. NAI, Trial Records Book, CCC, June 1925 to June 1927.
206. *Clare Champion*, 22 December 1934.
207. NAI, Co. Louth, Crown Files at Leinster Winter Assizes, 1906–10.
208. Ibid.
209. NAI, CCC, Co. Clare, 1930.
210. Ibid.
211. Ibid.
212. NAI, CRF R 26/1912.
213. Ibid.
214. NAI, CCC, Co. Cavan, 1940.
215. NAI, CCC, Co. Monaghan, 1929.
216. Ibid.
217. Ibid.
218. Ibid.
219. NAI, CCC, Co. Cavan, 1940.
220. Charges were brought against the relatives of sixteen unmarried women in this sample. In

one case charges were brought against the birth mother's mother and grandmother. This figure includes three cases where the verdicts are unknown and two cases that were not proceeded with.

221. Irish News, 25 May 1931.
222. NAI, CCC, Co. Westmeath, 1934.
223. Ibid.
224. Ibid.

CHAPTER THREE

'Shocking Revelations': Single Women and Sex

Edward C., a 31-year-old grocer's porter from South Lotts Road in Dublin, was charged with the murder of his nine-day-old infant son in June 1948. Edward had been involved with the infant's mother, 26-year-old Peggy S., 'on and off' over the course of several years.[1] The couple went on dates to the cinema and for walks together. While Peggy may well have expected the courtship to eventually lead to marriage, Edward does not seem to have shared his girlfriend's expectations. In the opening section of his statement, taken at the Bridewell Garda station in Dublin shortly after his arrest on 5 June, Edward explained that when he first met Peggy she was 'pregnant for a taxi-man across the road' from her mother's house in Irishtown.[2] While seemingly irrelevant to Edward's evidence, he presumably mentioned Peggy's previous pregnancy in order to cast aspersions on her reputation. Peggy, we are led to understand, was a loose woman with a history of out-of-wedlock pregnancy. Edward also spoke about his mother's disapproval of his relationship with Peggy. Edward recalled how his mother 'gave [him] a lecture over it' and 'told [her son] she didn't wish [him] to be with Peggy S.'[3] Edward did his utmost to portray Peggy in an unfavourable light.

'In or about the month of December 1947' Peggy informed Edward that she was pregnant.[4] She also told him that he would have to do something about it but Edward refused to help and 'said [he] was going to do nothing about it; that [he] wouldn't marry her'.[5] Edward stopped seeing Peggy in January 1948. He next saw her just after she had given birth in May of the same year. On that occasion Edward was summoned to the house by Peggy's sister. Peggy's mother and sister must have pressured him into taking action during the course of his visit as Edward finally agreed to face up to his responsibilities. He told Peggy he would help her 'the best [he] could' but once again he refused to marry her.[6]

While Edward said that he had been 'knocking around with her', Peggy described the relationship differently.[7] For her it seems to have been more serious. She said that they 'went out occasionally together for the first six months' but then they 'started to go out regularly'.[8] She seems to have expected that marriage would eventually follow. When Peggy realized that she was pregnant she asked Edward if they could get married. She even suggested keeping on her job as a dressmaker after the marriage, correctly anticipating his excuses about lack of money as an obstacle to marriage. That would mean that Peggy 'would then be in a position to support the child without support from him'.[9] However, Edward refused to contemplate marriage. Peggy asked him why but Edward did not respond. On another occasion he said that his job was not sufficient to keep three and that it was impossible to get married. The case is a typical example of what D'Cruze has termed 'courtship gone wrong'.[10]

Peggy found a foster mother for her infant son shortly after the birth and at her insistence Edward agreed to pay towards the cost of the service. The arrangement with the foster mother fell through soon afterwards and Peggy urged Edward to find another foster mother for their son. He agreed to do so and told Peggy that he would take the baby to a family in Tipperary. Edward assured Peggy that all the appropriate arrangements had been made. Instead, he drowned the baby in the Tolka River on Dublin's north side. When gardaí arrived at Edward's home to question him about the baby's disappearance he confessed immediately, saying 'To tell the truth, sir, I drowned it.'[11] Edward was convicted of the murder of his infant son at the Central Criminal Court, Dublin, in October 1948 and sentenced to death, but the sentence was later commuted to penal servitude for life. While some single women in the samples studied appear to have collaborated with the men charged with the murder of their infant sons or daughters, Peggy S. seems to have been unaware, when she handed her nine-day-old son over to Edward C., that he intended to drown the baby. Peggy was not entirely comfortable with handing her infant son over to Edward late at night on 1 June 1948. She worried about where Edward was taking her son and about the type of home the baby was going to. She said that she 'would have kept it if [she] could have done so, but [she] was trying to please everybody and there was nothing else [she] could do and at the same time avoid trouble with [her] family'.[12]

This chapter examines the records of infanticide cases that feature single working-class women like Peggy S. who experienced failed courtships during the first half of the twentieth century. For a pregnant woman, failed courtship meant facing the ordeal of childbirth and single motherhood alone. But this is only part of the picture. It was, as the records make clear, possible (in the Twenty-Six Counties from 1922 onwards at least) for couples to repair a failed courtship and to resume relations in the wake of trial and conviction. A small number of women who stood trial for the murder of their illegitimate infants in the Twenty-Six Counties between 1922 and 1950 were released on condition that they marry the deceased infant's father. These more fortunate women were handed a lifeline from prison that enabled them to embark on married life, but in circumstances that must surely have been fraught. Most women were far less fortunate. Failed courtship or casual sexual encounters, if followed by infanticide, meant that most faced several years in a religious-run Magdalen asylum. Not all single women who stood trial for infanticide had been in steady relationships with the men who fathered their illegitimate offspring. This chapter also looks at other types of relationship that appear in the judicial records. All too often the history of sex in Ireland is a history of transgressive activity. Legal sources reveal much about what went wrong. Yet close readings of infanticide cases can also offer new insights into 'individuals sharing pleasure', as Wills put it.[13] This chapter explores the sexual experiences of unmarried women who feature in the records of infanticide trials in Ireland, both North and South, over a fifty-year period. While judicial records spanning the fifty-year period under review on an all-island basis are used in the discussion of single women's experiences of sex in this chapter, there is an unavoidable bias towards women's experiences in the Twenty-Six Counties between 1922 and 1950.

SOURCES ON THE HISTORY OF SEXUALITY IN IRELAND

While historical sources on sexuality in Ireland are no doubt limited, sources that are available have been under-utilized. Inglis has noted that 'the history of Irish sexuality remains a relatively hidden, secretive area'[14] and has suggested that 'the reason why this subject has been ignored by historians is that there is an absence of revealing historical records and archives'.[15] In fact, the sexual activities of unmarried daughters of landless labourers, the urban and rural poor are quite well documented in the records of infanticide trials. The records of infanticide and abortion trials indicate, as McAvoy has suggested, that there was a section of society in post-independence Ireland 'identified by a number of observers as working class, whose sexual behaviour was not influenced by the dominant middle-class, Catholic sexual values'.[16] The level of detail captured in the judicial records of infanticide trials varied considerably. The judicial records examined reveal far more about patterns of sexual behaviour in the southern state after 1922, than the country as a whole from 1900 to 1921 or Northern Ireland from 1921 onwards. A more detailed and nuanced picture of sexual relationships between single mothers charged with infanticide and the fathers of their infants emerges in the trial records of cases tried at the Central Criminal Court, Dublin between 1922 and 1950. This is partly due to the disparity in the numbers of cases in the Twenty-Six Counties sample. A smaller sample of cases was examined for the period 1900–21 and for Northern Ireland. Central Criminal Court files often contain more information about the kinds of relationships single women suspected of having killed their infants had with the fathers of the murder victims. Overall, single infanticidal women in the pre-independence period and in Northern Ireland appear to have been far more reticent about sex and relationships than defendants in the Twenty-Six County state. It is not clear, however, whether this was due to the manner of the police interrogation – women's statements were clearly shaped by the way in which they were questioned – or whether other factors came into play. All suspects in the samples studied were questioned by male police officers, with the exception of K.M. whose statement was taken by a female police constable in Belfast in January 1946. Did the gardaí pressure single women suspected of murdering their newborn infants to discuss their sexual experiences more than their RIC predecessors or the police in Northern Ireland? Police in pre-independence Ireland and in Northern Ireland may not have interrogated unmarried women charged with murder or concealment of birth about the fathers of their infants, whereas it is quite apparent from the evidence in a number of Central Criminal Court files that unmarried women were consistently questioned about the infants' fathers. It is possible that in the early decades of independence the gardaí were determined to stamp out 'immoral' sexual behaviour and, in order to secure the convictions of infanticidal women, they may have been more aggressive in their method of interrogation. Few women in Northern Ireland referred to their sexual experiences in any detail. It seems unlikely that single women in the Twenty-Six Counties would have been naturally less reticent on such matters than their northern counterparts in the same period. In her analysis of defendants' statements, Maguire shows very little awareness of the processes of filtering and distortion involved, claiming that single, sexually experienced Irish women were not 'always shy and embarrassed about discussing sexual matters with gardaí and court officials'.[17] It is improbable, in a society that placed such value on female chastity, that women suspected of taking their infants' lives would have felt comfortable discussing their sexual experiences with gardaí. Maguire takes no account of the circumstances in which statements were made. The fact that female suspects may well have been pressurized or intimidated by their male interrogators to disclose information about their sexual encounters cannot be discounted. As Jackson has observed, 'depositions are complex documents with no clear authorial voice. Each witness testimony was shaped by the questions of police officers, lawyers and judges.'[18]

'Prying into the sex lives of young people in the past', as Heywood noted, 'has always proved a challenging exercise.'[19] As he observed, 'there are few sources available to throw light on the private life of the mass of children and adolescents in the past'.[20] Even if the encounter which led to pregnancy was pleasurable, the female voice captured in the judicial record is that of a woman who has been arrested and perhaps charged with a capital offence. The defendant is, at that point, unlikely to reflect positively on the encounter that led to pregnancy and eventually to infanticide. Her feelings in the circumstances she finds herself in are liable to be, like those expressed by Mary C., bitter and regretful. Mary C. told the doctor who treated her following the birth of her illegitimate infant in May 1943 that the man responsible for her pregnancy 'wasn't worth it'.[21] Mary was very ill and in a 'collapsed' condition at the time. Mollie H. told gardaí that she 'used to feel queer every night' after the man she was keeping company with had 'carnal connection' with her.[22] The manner in which Mollie described sexual intimacy with men – 'he used to interfere with me every night'[23] and 'they used to interfere with me also'[24] – suggests that sex was not necessarily an enjoyable experience. However, this may have been the only way in which Mollie could describe sex. Moreover, once Mollie had given herself up for arrest she may have deliberately sought to present herself as victim rather than agent. Although the issue of 'voice' in the judicial records 'is a vexed one', as Arnot and Usborne have noted, 'because words are mediated through (male) court officials who transcribe testimony and what people say is strongly structured by questions coming from the court', close readings of the trial records of infanticide cases can contribute to our knowledge of patterns of sexual behaviour among working-class women in Ireland between 1900 and

1950.[25] The records of infanticide trials indicate that not all pregnancies followed on from unexceptional or even injurious experiences. There are also instances of young couples in love, of tenderness, passion and recklessness.

Most single women in the case files would have been unaware of their legal rights. Most suspects would have been alone when questioned. Very few women were able to afford or access legal advice in the initial stages of the investigation. Nonetheless, a number of women refused to divulge intimate personal information that had no bearing on the case. It is clear from the manner in which their statements were worded that several women in the post-independence sample were questioned by the gardaí about their relationships with the fathers of their infants or about previous sexual partners and that they refused to respond. When asked about her infant's father, Christina M. told gardaí that in October 1940 a man had taken her up Dalkey hill, but she claimed that she could not remember what occurred there.[26] The gardaí who interrogated her may have tried to induce her to describe her encounter with this man but Christina refused to answer their questions. Mary Ellen T. told gardaí that she had a 4-year-old daughter but refused to name the girl's father: 'I do not wish to say who the father of my first child is.'[27] The gardaí must have pressed her for this information even though it had no bearing on the case. While some women clearly refused to discuss their sexual partners, others succumbed to that pressure.

'SEDUCED UNDER PROMISE OF MARRIAGE AND THEN DESERTED'?

In her study of adolescent female sexuality in the United States between 1885 and 1920, Odem argued that the sexual encounters described by young women in statutory rape cases in the Alameda and Los Angeles courts 'did not fit the image of male lust and female victimisation promoted in the seduction narratives of purity reformers. Instead of being the helpless victims of evil men, most of the young women were willing participants in a more complicated sexual drama than middle-class reformers or public officials could imagine.'[28] The discourse on single motherhood in Ireland during the period under review also often presented the unmarried mother as a passive victim who had been seduced or led astray. However, from the records of infanticide cases tried at the Central Criminal Court, Dublin, between 1922 and 1950 it would appear that single women were generally not the passive victims

of male lust and that many had willingly engaged in sexual relationships with men of the same class background. Many of the men who
fathered infants out of wedlock were labourers and, like the women
who feature in the trial records examined, they would have received
little formal education. For instance, John M. had a very poor educational standard. He told the medical officer in Mountjoy Prison that he
was unable to read or write. Apparently 'his school career was of very
short duration'.[29] A similar pattern emerges from the small number of
cases where a single woman charged with infanticide in the North
referred to the infants' father. Judicial records for cases in the pre-1922
sample contain far less information about the relationships single
women had with the fathers of their infants, but it is probable that
many unmarried women in the sample had also willingly engaged in
sexual encounters with men of the same class background. My findings
for cases tried at the Central Criminal Court are echoed by Maguire,
who has noted that 'unmarried women and men tempted fate and
engaged in unmarried sex more frequently than historians have thus
far acknowledged, and women were not always passive in these
encounters. Nor were they always the victims of male seduction or
sexual aggression portrayed in official rhetoric.'[30] Some of the judicial
records examined suggest that sexual relationships may have been
somewhat more fluid among working-class men and women. Hearn
has noted that 'in spite of dire consequences for women, seduction of
servants and premarital sexual relationships seem to have been fairly
common among servants in Ireland'.[31] This also seems to have been the
case in England. Irish working-class culture in the twentieth century
has, perhaps, not been adequately represented.

In her study of sex, violence and Victorian working women, D'Cruze
has highlighted the fact that young working women 'might also want to
indulge in courting only for leisure and pleasure purposes'.[32] The
records of Irish infanticide cases reveal that some single women became
involved with men without intending to marry them. Some of the
sexual encounters described by single women in their statements suggest
that they were of a casual nature. Some single women charged with
infanticide seem to have been uncertain about the identity of the father
of the deceased infant. Hotel maid Bridie C. was charged with the
murder of her illegitimate female infant in January 1939. She stated that
she had been keeping company with a man 'whose name [she] did not
know'.[33] She claimed that she did not know where he worked or where
he lived. Although Belfast-based housekeeper S.W. mentioned the

father of her infant in her statement, she claimed not to know his name. She told police that 'a good while ago [she] met a boy in the village' who 'took [her] down the King's road and had connection with [her] a few times'.[34] Some women may have only met the infant's father on one occasion. Jane M. was convicted of infanticide in November 1945. When Dr McDonagh asked her who the infant's father was, she claimed that she did not know, before adding that 'it was a stranger I met coming out of the bog'.[35] Christina M. was questioned about the murder of her illegitimate female infant after being admitted to Holles Street Hospital in Dublin in May 1941. She stated that she did not know who the father of her baby was. Her pregnancy seems to have been the result of a one-off encounter in October 1940.[36] Some women may have been uncertain of the man's identity, particularly if they had had sexual relations with more than one man. Gladys M. told gardaí that in June 1928 she had started 'going about' with two men.[37] She said she had permitted both men 'to have connection with [her]', but because Ned W. was 'mostly with [her]', Gladys believed that he was the father of her infant son.[38]

Maguire has asserted that 'many of the women accused of killing or concealing the birth of their infants acknowledged that they had numerous sexual partners'.[39] Maguire never states how many women in the cases examined had had several sexual partners. Nor does she indicate whether there were variations between Central Criminal Court and the Circuit Court cases she examined. My research indicates that women who acknowledged having had more than one sexual partner account for a very small proportion of the cases sampled. At least two women (2 per cent) in the pre-independence sample seem to have had more than one sexual partner. Hannah A. was convicted of conceal-ment of birth in 1903 and in 1910 she was convicted of the murder of her illegitimate infant. It is probable that the same man was not responsible for both pregnancies. In her statement, Kate H. explained that she had been 'with child' when she married in August 1907. Her husband was not the father of the child. The proportion of single women who admitted to being sexually experienced is higher in post-independence Ireland. In their statements a total of fifteen women referred to having had more than one sexual partner. None of the women charged with infanticide in Northern Ireland referred to pre-vious sexual partners in their statements. In fact, in their statements several women insisted that they had only had one sexual partner. K.M. said that the father of her infant was 'the only man who ever had intercourse with [her]'.[40] When she was questioned, E.H. said that she 'did not keep company with any other boy'.[41]

Margaret W. was charged with the murder of her infant in July 1933. Upon seeing Margaret in the barracks, a garda stationed there remarked, 'we've met before', and asked her who was responsible for her condition this time.[42] Margaret replied that it was 'the same fellow as before Mick T. – it is three times – he is the father of my third baby and the third time I have been arrested'.[43] Margaret W. was not the only single woman charged with infanticide who confessed to having given birth to an illegitimate infant previously. In Ireland, both North and South, the fact that single women charged with infanticide had given birth previously occasionally came to light during the course of an investigation into a suspected case of infanticide. At least five single women in the pre-independence sample had given birth once previously, while N.G.[44] had already had two children when she was arrested and charged with concealing the birth of her illegitimate newborn in Belfast in June 1915. M.S. had already had two children before the birth of her infant son in April 1917.[45] It would appear, from the information in her file, that M.S.'s other two children were boarded out. Nineteen women in the Twenty-Six Counties sample had given birth on at least one other occasion. Eleven women said that they had given birth once previously.[46] Five women had given birth twice previously.[47] Two women had had three infants and one woman had given birth five or six times previously. During questioning in May 1943, Kate O. told gardaí that 'nearly every year for the past five or six years I had a baby. I had all the babies in the house. They were all born alive but one, which was dead born.'[48] Women who had their first-born infants fostered or placed in an institution or whose parents permitted them to raise their children in the family home often concealed subsequent pregnancies, gave birth alone and killed their infants. Lucy B. and her 4-year-old daughter had both been living with her parents when Lucy was charged with the murder of her newborn infant in August 1929.[49] While Lucy's family were willing to accept one child born outside wedlock they may have been unwilling to accept a second transgression, and this may have motivated Lucy to kill her second illegitimate infant. Some women like Elizabeth H.,[50] Kate O.[51] and Margaret W.[52] seem to have killed all of their newborn infants. In the North at least seven single women (18.4 per cent) had given birth on another occasion. A.H. had given birth on four occasions over a twelve-year period prior to her marriage.[53] In a 1929 Belfast case the doctor who examined the defendant noted that J.M. had had a child before.[54] A.M. was charged with concealment of birth in August 1931.[55] In her deposition M.S. said that A.M. had given her a child to nurse in November 1928. L.R. was charged with infanticide in March 1929 while she was a patient in a workhouse hospital in Co. Down.[56] Dr Boyd gave evidence in the case and noted that L.R. had given birth in the institution on one other occasion in June 1929. Poor unmarried women who had already attempted to raise one infant may have been reluctant to try to maintain a second baby and this may have prompted them to take the lives of subsequent infants born out of wedlock. In her discussion of institutional provision for illegitimate children, Maguire noted that many unmarried mothers struggled to raise their children for several years before giving up 'in the face of abject poverty, the rejection of family and friends, and the censure of their neighbours'.[57] Infanticide may have been the only available means for poor sexually active women who were uninformed about contraception and unaware of effective abortion methods to control their fertility during the period. According to Maguire, infanticide enabled numerous Irish women to enjoy sex before marriage or outside marriage without having to care for the offspring that might result. Maguire implies that infanticide was widely employed as a primitive form of birth control. The trial records do not support her claim. The samples studied here suggest that infanticide may have been deliberately used as a means of regulating fertility for no more than a small minority of women.

'COURTING CUSTOMS IN IRELAND ARE NOT ALWAYS UP TO THE CATHOLIC IDEAL.'

The judicial records of infanticide cases tried in the pre-independence period reveal little about courtship practices in early-twentieth-century Ireland. Single women questioned about the deaths of their illegitimate infants rarely referred to the fathers of their infants in any detail. The putative fathers were named in a total of sixteen cases (16.8 per cent) in the cases examined for the pre-independence period. Only a small minority of female defendants in these cases discussed the dynamics of the relationship they had with their infant's father. In fact, the vast majority of unmarried women who stood trial between 1900 and 1921 did not mention the men responsible for their pregnancy. Arrested in October 1901 for the murder of her newborn infant, Minnie M. named the baby's father in her statement.[58] Bridget M., tried at the Co. Clare Assizes in December 1915 for the murder of her infant, said that she had been keeping company with a man for 'about' two years. He lodged in the house where she was employed as a domestic servant and she identified him as the father of her child. However, Bridget revealed little about their relationship in her statement. She did not say whether she had informed John L. of her pregnancy or whether they were still in touch with each other.[59] A maternity nurse recalled how Mary O. had told her the name of her infant's father. According to the nurse, Mary had wanted the baby to 'be baptised in that surname'.[60] Mary's baby died in suspicious circumstances and she was tried at the Clare Summer Assizes in 1917. When she was arrested in October 1913, Margaret C. 'mentioned to [Sergeant Gaffney] the name of the man responsible for her misfortune'.[61] She claimed that he had left the country six months previously. Several women in this sample claimed that the fathers of their deceased infants had emigrated. It is possible that the men in question were not aware that these women were pregnant, but they may have left the country in order to avoid paying maintenance costs. It is also possible, however, that some women in this sample lied about the whereabouts of the fathers of their deceased infants in order to gain sympathy on the basis that they had been seduced, betrayed and abandoned.

The women in the pre-independence sample who referred to the fathers of their deceased infants generally said very little about them. They usually only named them and mentioned their place of residence or place of employment. Unlike in the evidence gathered for infanticide cases that were tried at the Central Criminal Court between 1922 and 1950, where unmarried female suspects sometimes provided a considerable amount of information about the nature of their relationship with the father of the infant whose death was being investigated, the case files in this sample up to 1921 reveal little information about the women's feelings towards the fathers of their infants or the kinds of relationships they had had. It is only in cases where the fathers of illegitimate infants whose deaths were being investigated gave evidence that light is shed on the nature of the couple's relationship and the role the male partner played in the events leading up to the birth and after the birth.

It would appear, however, that in three of these cases the women had been involved with the fathers of their infants for a considerable length of time. Some single women who feature in the records in the pre-independence sample also seem to have maintained close contact with their infants' fathers until they were arrested and charged. Some

couples may have intended to marry. Hannah K. may well have been
keeping company with the father of her infant for a considerable length
of time.[62] When she went to Dublin in search of work to support her
family in March 1900 he followed her and apparently promised that he
would marry her later that year. When the father of Kate M.'s infant,
James H. was questioned about the death of her unnamed female infant
in June 1903 he told the police that 'she and I have been keeping company
for some time past'.[63] He also said that he intended to marry her. James
told the police that he had been in Kate M.'s company until the week before her arrest. Kate M. and James H. were clearly an established couple.
Kate's former employer 'knew that [James H.] and she kept company together'.[64] A policeman stationed in the town had often seen the pair out
walking together. They may not have planned to marry in the immediate
future; although Kate's sister knew that they were 'keeping company',
she said she did not know if the pair were to be married. It seems
unlikely that James proposed marriage when Kate informed him that
she was pregnant.

The exact length of the relationship between female defendants and
the putative fathers of their infants in the judicial records examined is
known only in a very small number of cases in the Twenty-Six Counties sample. In her statement, Margaret D. said that she and her husband (the couple married in August 1934, shortly before Margaret
gave birth) 'were keeping company for about five years before our
marriage'.[65] When she was arrested in November 1934 on suspicion of
murdering her infant daughter, Teresa C. said that she had been keeping company with the father of her infant for almost two years. She
told gardaí that 'he is the father of the child that was born for me'.[66]
A substantial number of women charged with infanticide in the
Twenty-Six Counties sample became pregnant as a result of casual sex
– in twenty-two out of fifty-six cases where information is available. A
small number of the single women in these files had had affairs with
married men. A further eleven women had had short-term relationships with the fathers of their infants. Often these women lost touch
with the infants' fathers months before they were due to give birth and
in some cases contact had ceased before the woman even realized she
was pregnant. Margaret H. was charged with murder and concealment
of birth in June 1944. She said she 'kept company' with a soldier for
two months and during that time 'he had connection with [her] nearly
every time [they] met', but she had lost touch with him eight months
before she gave birth.[67] Many unmarried women had been involved

with the father of their infant for a considerable length of time. Some women maintained close contact with the fathers of their infants until they were tried for infanticide, and a number of women seem to have expected that they would eventually marry the fathers of their infants. In twenty-three out of fifty-six cases, sex took place in the context of a relationship that seemed stable and, like many of the cases D'Cruze examined, 'probably apparently on the road to marriage'.[68] In fact, four couples had married shortly before the birth and a further eight couples married after the birth. In some cases the convicted woman's sentence was suspended once she married the putative father of her deceased infant. None of the women convicted of murder or concealment of birth in the pre-independence sample were released on marriage to the fathers of their deceased infants. Nor was it a feature of the cases examined for Northern Ireland. It seems to have been adopted as an alternative to incarceration for women convicted of the manslaughter or concealment of birth of their illegitimate infants in the Twenty-Six Counties from the early 1930s onwards. It is not known whether it was also used as an alternative to a prison sentence in the lower courts.

In the North only nine women mentioned the infant's father in their statements. Whether that information was voluntary or not is unclear. The identity of the infant's father was known in a further three cases as two men were charged with the murder of illegitimate infants during the period. Six women named the fathers of their infants, although it is worth noting that in one of these cases the defendant did not know the man's surname. K.M. told the constable who questioned her that the father of her child was an Englishman. She said that she 'only remember[ed] his name was Brian' and claimed not even to know what part of England he lived in 'as [she] kept company with him just for a week and never corresponded with him'.[69] Three women seem to have had casual relations with the fathers of their infants. S.W. met the father of her infant 'a few times'.[70] She may have made his acquaintance some time before their relationship began, however, as she said that she met him 'a good while ago.'[71] E.H. went out with the father of her infant intermittently over a ten-month period:

> About June last year I kept company with J.D. of 30 H. Street Belfast. I went with him for some time and then fell out with him. I again got great with him about September or October. About October he had connection with me and continued for about twice a week. I again fell out with him about March of this year and never went out with him since.[72]

The remaining six women seem to have had long-term relationships with the fathers of their infants. One couple had married before the woman's arrest and another woman claimed she had married shortly before giving birth. M.B. did not state how long she had been keeping company with the father of her infant but her landlady's neighbour knew that she 'used to keep company with a young man' and had often seen him 'sitting on the window stoll [sic] of Mrs G.'s house waiting for her'.[73] Again, this would suggest that theirs was a long-term relationship. According to one witness, the father of S.C.'s infant 'was in the habit of visiting the accused' at her lodgings.[74] S.C.'s landlady said that she had spoken to him about S.C.'s condition but she did not state how he had responded.

In her study of sex, violence and Victorian working women, D'Cruze noted that 'courting often took place in the shadowy evening spaces at the fringes of the neighbourhood and domestic space, placing it outside normative respectable conventions of social behaviour'.[75] In the nineteenth-century cases D'Cruze studied, fields, barns, sheds and back alleyways were often the sites of courtship. Fields, farmyard buildings and other public spaces out of doors were the key sites of courtship for poor, unmarried Irish couples in the first half of the twentieth century. In an article published in the American journal *Survey* in August 1929, entitled 'Why Girls Leave Ireland,' Signe Toksvig, a Danish-born American who lived in Ireland from 1926 to 1937, argued that because there were generally no village halls or community centres in the countryside, 'young people have no way of decently meeting'.[76] This is apparent in the cases sampled in this study. Most of the women in the samples examined worked as domestic servants. Few, if any, among them would have been permitted to entertain men in their employer's household. Fr Flanagan, parish priest of Fairview, Dublin, informed the Carrigan Committee that 'conduct that in other countries is confined to the brothels is to be seen without let or hindrance on our public roads'.[77] Ferriter has suggested that Fr Flanagan's remarks, while regarded sceptically by the Department of Justice, were probably not that wide of the mark.[78] According to Ferriter, roads were frequently mentioned in witness depositions as the scenes of sexual assault.[79]

The pattern among working-class courting couples in Ireland was similar to the pattern described by D'Cruze for Victorian England. In Irish infanticide cases where the location of intercourse was noted (7 per cent of all cases in the Twenty-Six Counties sample), most couples had sex outdoors or in farmyard buildings. In her statement Mollie H. recalled that she and her boyfriend were standing against a fence when intercourse took place. She said that he 'rose up [her] clothes and had carnal connection with [her]'.[80] Mary T. met her boyfriend outside in the evenings.[81] Mary K. also met the father of her infant in a field in the evenings.[82] As many of the women in the post-1922 sample were employed as servants in rural areas, it is hardly surprising that farm buildings are mentioned as a place where unmarried couples went to have sex. Mary C. had sex with her employer's son in the cowhouse on their farm.[83] Bridget C. had sex with the father of her infant in a 'haggard'[84] on a farm on her way home from a dance in Co. Galway, and Margaret D. 'used to meet [the father of her infant] in a shed attached to his house' in Co. Limerick.[85] Michael C. and his girlfriend Mary Anne were both employed as servants in the same Co. Longford household. When they wanted to spend time together they had to go outdoors. One witness said that he 'often saw defendants walking the road together'.[86] Michael also ran a considerable risk by inviting Mary Anne to spend the night with him in the harness room where he slept. In early June 1924 Michael's employer reprimanded him for 'keeping a girl in his bedroom' and threatened to inform his parish priest.[87] Michael told his employer 'that he was going to be married to the girl in some short time'.[88] When Mary Anne was questioned about the death of a newborn infant in June 1924, she said that the pair 'were to be married on Monday or Tuesday'.[89] It is not clear what prevented the couple from marrying sooner; they may have postponed marriage because they did not have a home or enough money. Many poor Irish couples seem to have had difficulty in securing accommodation, even after marriage. In 1926, 800,000 people were living in overcrowded conditions in the Twenty-Six Counties, while 'outside the cities, where 61 per cent of the population resided, 36,000 farm labourers were still living in their employers' housing'.[90]

The location of intercourse was not noted in any of the pre-1922 cases. However, patterns of courtship are likely to have been similar to the post-independence period, with many couples meeting outdoors or in farm buildings. The location of intercourse can be inferred in four cases in the Northern sample (11 per cent). S.W. 'had connection' with the father of her infant outdoors, somewhere on the King's Road in Belfast.[91] This also seems to have been the case for L.T.[92] The father of her infant was employed as a trapper. He had a hut of his own and she spent some time there with him. The father of L.M.'s infants was her employer. As he lived alone it seems likely that intercourse also took place indoors.[93]

Judging by the records of infanticide cases tried in Ireland between 1900 and 1950, it would appear that few young, working-class couples went on dates or participated in leisure activities together. Their lack of disposable income would have meant that they could not afford much in the way of entertainment activities. Their choice of activity would have been further curtailed by the fact that many lived in rural parts of Ireland where there were few amenities for young people. Some women attended dances, though there are no references to courting couples attending dances together; the women who mention dance halls in their statements seem to have met men at the dances and engaged in casual sex on the way home. Instead, most couples seem to have spent their time together walking through the countryside. However, there were regional variations, with city-based working-class couples more likely to have participated in leisure activities. Dubliners Edward C. and Peggy S. went to the pictures together. Belfast-based working-class couples may also have gone to the cinema or to the theatre together but the northern infanticide trials contain no references to leisure activities.

A different picture emerges from the records of abortion cases, where couples were more likely to have enjoyed recreational activities together. Bridie K. went to the races a number of times with John D.[94] Carrie D. said that she used to go to shows in the city with her boyfriend George J.,[95] and Marks R. took Bridie K. to the pictures and to the theatre 'now and again'.[96] The difference between patterns in Irish infanticide and abortion cases in this period may be explained, in part, by the fact that a number of the single women who featured in the records of abortion trials were involved with older affluent married men who could afford to cover the costs of excursions and visits to the theatre and/or cinema.

In an article, 'The Dance Halls', published in *The Bell* in February 1941, Flann O'Brien made a mockery of the moral panic that surrounded the jazz dancing 'craze' that had gripped the country in the interwar period. He queried whether 'the rural dance hall is a place to be avoided by our sisters?'[97] O'Brien viewed it as 'a harmless enough business'.[98] Influential Catholic clergymen and district court judges, he noted, were convinced that dance halls were not harmless. 'Many of our clergy do not think it is and several of the Solomons of the district court are quite certain that it isn't.'[99] Most bishops seem to have felt that the rise in the numbers of unmarried mothers could be directly attributed to the dance hall craze. Following a meeting of the Catholic hierarchy in

Maynooth in October 1925, a statement was issued condemning dance halls, the cinema, excessive drinking and the 'spiritual dangers associated with dancing'.[100] Dance halls, according to the members of the Irish hierarchy, 'had brought many a good, innocent girl into sin, shame and scandal'.[101] The Catholic Church was not alone in linking unsupervised dance halls to single motherhood. Many people were concerned about the connection between dance halls and illegitimacy in post-independence Ireland. For instance, a superintendent home assistance officer in Co. Galway commenting in 1928 believed that dance halls were 'a great source of evil to girls'.[102] At a meeting of the Galway Homes and Home Assistance Committee in December 1928, Mr Heneghan referred to one particular unmarried mother who had met a stranger at a dance. The stranger was the father of her illegitimate infant but she never saw him again.[103] Few single women charged with murder or concealment of birth between 1922 and 1950 referred to dance halls in their statements. Unsupervised dancing does not appear to have been the cause of the 'lapse' of many women in the judicial records of infanticide trials. Maguire's study of infanticide cases tried at circuit courts and in the Central Criminal Court between 1922 and 1960 also 'suggests a negligible link between dance halls, illegitimacy, and infanticide'.[104] Few women in the samples examined met men in dancehalls. When Mary Ellen T. was charged with the murder of her infant in December 1941 she named her infant's father and said that he had had 'connection' with her while they were at a dance.[105] Bridget C. attended a dance in Co. Galway in March 1932. She left the dance at 6 a.m. and was accompanied home by a man she had met there. Bridget said that she 'went into [a] haggard' with the man and 'he did it'.[106] She said that she then 'went home and he went home his own way'.[107] Bridget M. may also have met the father of her illegitimate infant at a dance. She said that she 'went with fellows now and again' and she 'often attended dances'.[108] It is, of course, possible that more women did meet the father of their infants at dances but chose not to refer to that in their statements.

Although a number of commentators expressed concern about the use of the motor car by 'male prowlers'[109] in order to bring 'ignorant girls to ruin',[110] only one woman charged with infanticide in Ireland between 1900 and 1950 referred to sex taking place in a car. Mary M. was tried for the murder and concealment of birth of her female infant at the Central Criminal Court, Dublin, in October 1939. She named Jack W., a married man, as the father of her infant. In her statement Mary said that she travelled from Bray to Greystones with Jack in his van: on one occasion 'he stopped the van on the back road between Bray and Greystones and he had connection with [her]'.[111]

Many women conceived outdoors and a substantial number also gave birth outdoors or in farmyard buildings. Deborah S. had sex with the father of her infant in a field in July 1928. She gave birth alone 'on a mountain side in Co. Kerry on a cold and snowy day' in February 1929.[112] Rebecca A. went into the yard to give birth in May 1927; her father was in the house at the time and she did not want him to discover the baby's existence.[113] Mary W. gave birth 'near a cock of hay in the haggard' on her father's land.[114] Bridget C. gave birth in June 1940 in a field 'away from the house' where she was employed as a servant.[115] Margaret S., who was 30 years old, gave birth in a field in Co. Tipperary June 1928. The infant's father, John L., a farmer from the area, was the only person present when Margaret gave birth.[116] Margaret, who was originally from neighbouring Co. Limerick, had lived in an open field for a few days prior to the birth. She slept in a ditch at night. John L. provided her with food while she lived outdoors. Margaret was employed as a servant in a nearby farmhouse. She may have lost her job in the later stages of pregnancy or she may have left her position temporarily until after the birth. Mary T., aged 19, left her position in a Co. Cork household in the later stages of pregnancy.[117] She gave birth unassisted in a disused house she came across on the back road between Carrick-on-Suir and Clonmel. Mary said that she 'stayed in the house that night with the dead child' until 8 a.m. the following morning when she buried the infant.[118] Nora C. left her parents' Co. Limerick home shortly before she was due to give birth in July 1941 and cycled in the direction of a nearby town. She slept outdoors for almost ten days before giving birth in a field.[119]

'ALTHOUGH I MISSED MY USUAL MONTHLY ILLNESS I DID NOT KNOW WHAT WAS WRONG WITH ME'

Mary T., who was 17 years old, said that she 'did not touch the cord at all' after giving birth alone in January 1930. She claimed that she 'knew nothing about it or the way children are brought into the world'.[120] Mary also stated that she 'had no knowledge of the fact that [she] was pregnant' although she had had sex with several different men.[121] When she stopped menstruating she went to see a doctor; he told Mary that there was nothing wrong with her and prescribed her some medication. Mary was not the only unmarried woman tried for infanticide in Ireland

between 1900 and 1950 who professed ignorance about the consequences of sexual intercourse and childbirth. Although no single women
in the sample for the period 1900–21 referred to their ignorance
regarding reproduction (in general they were far more reticent on the
subject of sex) it is likely that many were very poorly informed. A number of doctors were of the opinion that single women who gave birth
alone and unassisted were often ignorant about aspects of childbirth.
The doctor who examined Catherine O. in September 1902 said that
'through ignorance she may have destroyed the chord [sic]'[122] and Dr
J.P. McGinley conceded in court that as it was Mary C.'s 'first confinement she would not probably know to tie the cord'.[123] S.W.'s newborn infant died from inattention at birth in August 1930. The cord
had not been cut.

When 20-year-old Margaret H. stopped menstruating in April or
May 1947 she recalled that she 'did not take any notice of that' as she
'did not understand what that meant'.[124] Similarly, when 26-year-old
Margaret H. was questioned in September 1931 she said: 'I now want
to say that although I missed my usual monthly illness I did not know
what was wrong with me.'[125] As D'Cruze and Jackson have noted, 'poor
nutrition and health problems made menstruation a more uncertain
phenomenon'.[126] In her discussion of female sexuality during childhood
in 1930s and 1940s Dublin, Lyder has observed that 'discussion of,
or instruction in, sexual matters appears to have been virtually non-
existent'.[127] It is clear from the records of infanticide cases that were
tried at the Central Criminal Court between 1922 and 1950 that a
number of single women were very poorly informed about pregnancy
and/or childbirth. The medical officer who examined the defendant in
a 1948 Co. Kilkenny case remarked that 'from examination it appears
that this girl was completely ignorant of the dangers connected with
child birth and also with some of the essential physical facts'.[128] Some
women claimed that they did not realise that they were pregnant for a
considerable length of time. For some, it was not until they had become
particularly 'stout' that they realised they were pregnant.

Discussion of sex remained taboo throughout the period under
review: 'From the 1920s onwards, libraries were obvious targets in the
battle to prevent people from reading about sex or instructing themselves
on the facts of life.'[129] According to Ferriter, while there 'was the
occasional reference to the need for young people to be better educated
about sex and reproduction' in the 1940s 'there were significant barriers
in the way of this becoming widespread'.[130] The extent of Irish women's

lack of knowledge in sexual matters was recognised by a number of groups and individuals concerned with sexual morality in independent Ireland. Several of those who gave evidence to the Carrigan Committee commented on the high level of sexual ignorance among Irish women. Widespread ignorance about sex persisted into the 1960s. While it seems probable that many unmarried women charged with infanticide in this period would have been uninformed or poorly informed about pregnancy and childbirth, it is also possible that some may have exaggerated their ignorance when they were asked why they had failed toprepare for the birth of their infants or to seek medical assistance. Ignorance about sex and childbirth was not confined to Ireland. McCray Beier's research suggests that parental silence about sexual matters was normative in working-class communities in Lancashire during the first half of the twentieth century.[131] For the women McCray Beier interviewed, the experience of their first menstrual period was traumatic, as they had not been informed that it would occur or that it was normal and healthy.[132]

COURTSHIP GONE WRONG

As D'Cruze has noted, 'for women, courtship meant negotiating access to the next life-cycle stage of marriage'.[133] The records of infanticide cases tried in Ireland during the first half of the twentieth century contain numerous instances of what D'Cruze termed 'courtship gone wrong'. 'Courtship', D'Cruze writes, 'was seen as a transitional life-cycle state that led to marriage.'[134] It seems likely that many unmarried Irish women charged with the murder of their illegitimate infants in the first half of the twentieth century may well have viewed their period of courtship with the fathers of their infants as a step en route to marriage and, like the women in D'Cruze's study, the single women in my sample also 'had to take sexual risks in order to approach the desirable (virtually the imperative goal of marriage)'.[135] For these women courtship involved sex and unmarried women ran risks in consenting to intercourse before marriage. References to contraception in infanticide cases tried in Ireland during the first half of the twentieth century are slight. Few, if any, single women charged with the murder or concealment of birth of their illegitimate infants seem to have used any form of contraception and, as already discussed, a number of women seem to have been quite ignorant about reproduction. There

All photographs reproduced courtesy of the National Archives of Ireland.

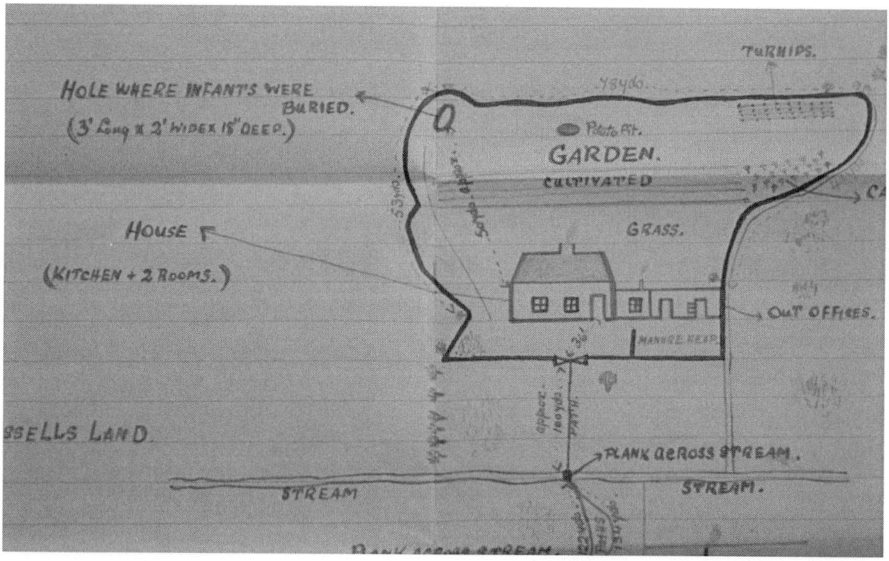
HOLE WHERE INFANTS WERE BURIED.
(3' Long x 2' WIDE x 15" DEEP.)
TURNIPS.
GARDEN.
CULTIVATED
GRASS.
HOUSE
(KITCHEN + 2 ROOMS.)
OUT OFFICES.
SSELLS LAND.
PLANK ACROSS STREAM.
STREAM
STREAM.

1. A rough plan of Kate M.'s mother's house and potato garden. The hole where Kate's twin infants were buried is marked on the top left-hand corner of the drawing. Kate had given birth in England one month previously. She returned to Ireland with her infants and came into contact with a social worker in Dublin. The gardaí went to her mother's home in Co. Westmeath as they were informed by the Catholic Young Girls Protection Society that Kate had left Dublin for Athenry with two babies. However, Kate did not arrive in Athenry as expected in January 1930. Central Criminal Court, Co. Westmeath, 1930.

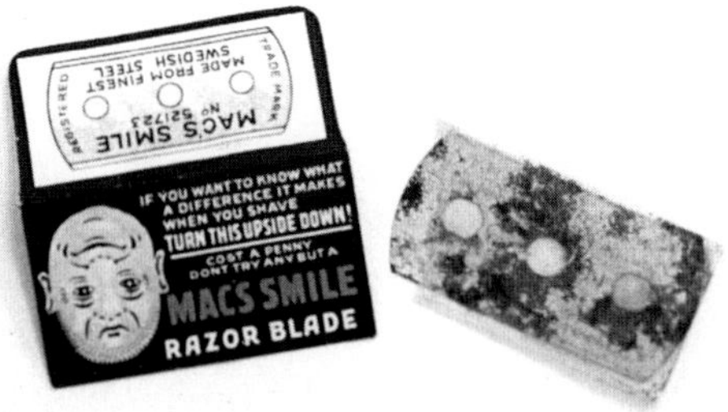
IF YOU WANT TO KNOW WHAT A DIFFERENCE IT MAKES WHEN YOU SHAVE
TURN THIS UPSIDE DOWN!
COST A PENNY DON'T TRY ANY BUT A
MAC'S SMILE
RAZOR BLADE

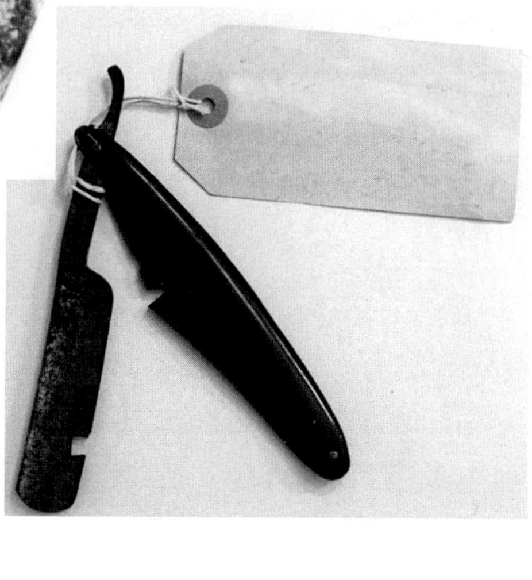

2. Razor blades found in the defendant's bedroom in a 1939 Co. Roscommon case. Most infants in the cases examined were suffocated shortly after their births but this was a particularly brutal case. One of the investigating sergeants noted that 'there were two cuts or gashes on the [infant's] throat that appeared to be fairly deep'. Central Criminal Court, Co. Roscommon, 1940.

3. The orchard near the E. sisters' Co. Roscommon
home. When the sisters returned from the County Home
where Elizabeth had given birth they said they left the
baby near a little 'groveen' of trees before going into the
house. They wanted to make sure there was nobody in
the house before bringing the baby upstairs. Central
Criminal Court, Co. Roscommon, 1935.

4. Gardaí on a ladder at the gable end of the defendants' house in a 1934 Co. Roscommon case.
Sisters Elizabeth and Rose E. were charged with the murder of Elizabeth's infant daughter in
October 1934. The gardaí conducted an extensive search of the area but the infant's body was
never discovered. Elizabeth and Rose were both sentenced to death but their sentences were
commuted to penal servitude for life. Central Criminal Court, Co. Roscommon, 1935.

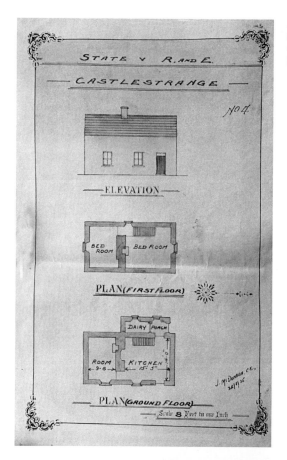

5. Plan of the family home of sisters Elizabeth and Rose E. Central Criminal Court, Co. Roscommon, 1935.

6. The hollow where Rose E. said she buried her sister's infant daughter in October 1934. The baby's body was never located. Central Criminal Court, Co. Roscommon, 1935.

7. Trials Record Book entry for Mary Anne M. who was convicted of concealment of birth at the Central Criminal Court in July 1927. Trials Record Book, Central Criminal Court, Change of Venue Dublin June 1925 – December 1926.

8. Mary C. was convicted of concealment of birth at the Central Criminal Court in November 1943. Like many single women convicted of the same offence in post-independence Ireland, Mary C. agreed to serve her sentence in a convent rather than in prison. Central Criminal Court, City of Dublin, 1943.

PREVIOUS CONVICTIONS (**One**)

Date	Court and Place	Offence	Sentence	Christian and Surname under which convicted
25 10 40	District,Dublin	Soliciting.	P.O.to 16.10.42 O.B. £5.	Mary

Governor,Mountjoy Prison.

THE CO.REGISTRAR,

COURTHOUSE,GREEN ST.

DUBLIN.

9. Mary C. was convicted of soliciting in October 1940. Central Criminal Court, City of Dublin, 1943.

10. and 11. Wards in the South Dublin Union hospital where Mary C., who was recovering from a scabies infection, was employed as an inmate worker. Mary C. gave birth in the lavatory of Ward 23 in the Female Chronic Hospital in May 1943. Central Criminal Court, City of Dublin, 1943.

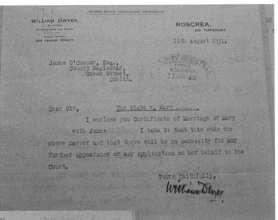

REGISTRATION OF ROMAN CATHOLIC MARRIAGES IN IRELAND.

12. Marriage certificate documenting the marriage of nineteen-year-old Mary H. to the father of her infant, James M., a labourer nineteen years her senior in August 1931. Mary was convicted of concealment of birth but was released on condition that she marry James M. Central Criminal Court, Trials Record Book (Change of Venue cases) Nov 1927 – June 1933.

13. Letter for Mary H.'s solicitor to the County Registrar in Dublin following her marriage to James M. Central Criminal Court, Trials Record Book (Change of Venue cases) Nov 1927– June 1933.

14. Nora C. was convicted of manslaughter in July 1927. The entry in the Trials Record Book notes that she enter the High Park Convent in Dublin 'until the Superioress consents to her discharge'. Central Criminal Court, Trials Record Book, (Change of venue cases), June 1925 – Dec 1926.

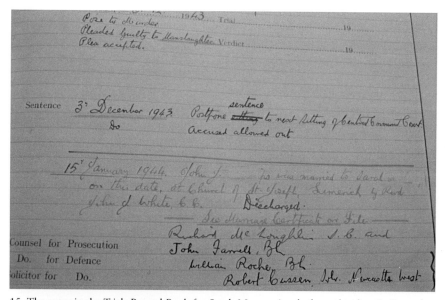

15. The entry in the Trials Record Book for Sarah M., convicted of manslaughter in December 1943, notes that she married the father of her deceased infant in January 1944. By marrying the father of her deceased infant Sarah M. avoided serving time in prison or in a religious institution. Central Criminal Court, State Book at Central Criminal Court 1941–45.

16. 23-year-old Mary B. gave birth in her bedroom in her mother's home in May 1939. Mary's mother said she 'wanted the child removed' as soon as she learned that her unmarried daughter had given birth. Shortly after the baby was born the doctor who had attended to Mary made enquiries regarding the adoption of her infant and managed to find three addresses for her. However, by the time the doctor returned to the B. household Mary's infant had died. Mary claimed that her infant daughter died soon after she was born as the baby fell off the bed and hit her head against Mary's dressing table. She was found not guilty by direction at the Central Criminal Court, Dublin. Central Criminal Court, Co. Tipperary, 1939.

17. A market bag taken possession of by gardaí at the defendant's home and handed to the State Pathologist in a 1936 Co. Tipperary case. In this particular case the woman gave birth while cycling to a nearby town. She said that she put the infant's body in her market bag and later 'dumped it in a bucket' in the fowl house on the grounds of her aunt's home. Central Criminal Court, Co. Tipperary, 1937.

18. Garda standing at the edge of the lake in Co. Cork where Eithna M. drowned her seven month-old son in September 1940. In her statement the nineteen-year-old mother told gardaí that on 17 September 1940 she 'made up her mind to drown the child in G. lake as [she] [had] been annoyed from it since it was born'. Eithna M. spent the entire day at the edge of the lake after she had killed her son. According to Eithna's second cousin, with whom she and her baby lived, two days before the incident, when asked to attend to her baby, Eithna had remarked 'Am I going to be all my life watching the baby?' The young mother may well have been suffering from depression but, as there are no medical reports in her file, this is by no means certain. She may simply have resented the responsibility of motherhood and deliberately decided to take her son's life. Central Criminal Court, Co. Cork, 1941.

19. The lake in Co. Cork where Eithna M. drowned her infant son. Central Criminal Court, Co. Cork, 1941.

are few references to fertility control. John M. was charged with the murder of his girlfriend's illegitimate infant in May 1949. In his statement he said that he had been having sex with Florence B. several times a week for a number of years but that he 'always withdrew before [he] discharged'.[136] When she was arrested in January 1935, Margaret D., who married shortly before giving birth, told gardaí that she had sexual intercourse with her husband in a shed attached to his house every night. Margaret explained that while she was anxious to have children, her husband was not. She said that she was able to avoid becoming pregnant although she did not specify how she was able to prevent conception.

Contraception was prohibited in southern Ireland in 1935. Although contraception was legal in Northern Ireland it was not widely available there between 1920 and 1950, and as Hill has observed, there was no 'widespread public demand for easier access' at the time.[137] Similarly, Howes has drawn attention to the fact that while 'at least theoretically, women in the North of Ireland enjoyed opportunities and freedoms not available to women in the Free State',[138] in general women in Northern Ireland do no appear to have taken advantage of those opportunities and freedoms. She has argued that 'the sexual culture of the North had a great deal in common with that of the new Irish state'.[139]

In contrast to this, several single Irish women who terminated their pregnancies between 1900 and 1950 had used contraception on a regular basis. Judith M.'s fiancé said that he 'always used contraceptives except in the safe periods, immediately before and immediately after menstruations'.[140] Alphonsus M. usually purchased the contraceptives in Northern Ireland but he bought them from northern students in Trinity College 'a couple of times'.[141] 'A whirling spray' was, according to Dr O'Donnel Browne, who gave evidence in a 1937 Dublin abortion case, a vaginal douche usually used for 'contraceptive cases'. It was found in Margaret B.'s bedroom.[142] When he was questioned in court, Dennis B., referred to the fact that coitus interruptus was 'the usual practice' with Karmel M.[143]

Schulte's research on the court records of infanticide trials in Upper Bavaria has shown that in some instances infanticide had been preceded by attempts to abort.[144] There are few references to attempts to abort in the Irish cases sampled. Only one unmarried woman in the Central Criminal Court sample referred to the fact that she attempted to terminate her pregnancy by consuming abortifacient drugs: Mary C. was tried for infanticide and concealment of birth at the Central Criminal Court in Dublin in October 1941. In her statement she said that her boyfriend 'suggested getting [her] a bottle to get rid of [her] trouble'.[145] They shared the cost of the medication but it did not have the intended effect. There were attempts to cause a pregnant woman to miscarry in other samples as well, but this appears to have been relatively rare. Of course, such attempts are unlikely to have come to the attention of the police unless serious harm was done to the woman involved. Bridget M. may have attempted to induce a miscarriage by taking salts and other medication during her pregnancy. In her deposition, Bridget M.'s mother told the police that Bridget 'had her stomach sick from the pills and the salts' she had been taking. When questioned about it, Bridget insisted that 'before the birth [she] never took any medicine but salts'.[146] When L.T. informed her boyfriend that she was pregnant in February 1933 'he procured a box of pills and gave them to her to take telling her that she would be all right and that there would be no baby'.[147] L.T. took the medication as directed but it had no impact on her pregnancy.

As already detailed, many single women charged with infanticide in the Twenty-Six Counties between 1922 and 1950 had been involved with the father of their infant for a considerable length of time. Some women maintained close contact with the fathers of their infants until they were tried for infanticide. A number of women seem to have expected that they would eventually marry the fathers of their infants. Annie R. had made long-term plans with the father of her infant. She told gardaí that she was keeping company with a man named Patrick R. and that she intended to marry him. She said that she was 'fairly intimate with him' and he came to see her twice a week.[148] Similarly, Nora C. told gardaí that she had been keeping company with a boy for the past year. They met once a week and she said that they 'had an understanding that we would be married'.[149] Elizabeth E., aged 23, gave birth in October 1934. According to her sister, the father of her infant, Tom M., 'used to come up' to see Elizabeth 'every Sunday night until about a week before the child was born'.[150] His last visit occurred less than a week before Elizabeth went to the Roscommon County Home to give birth. Theirs seems to have been a well-established courtship and Elizabeth may have hoped that she and Tom would eventually marry. She said that if her infant daughter had lived she could have made Tom marry her. She also spoke about Tom M. making 'provision' for her and the baby in the future, although Elizabeth may have mentioned that when she was being questioned by gardaí, to make her infant daughter's death appear accidental rather than deliberate and premeditated. Tom must have known about Elizabeth's pregnancy and it is questionable whether he genuinely intended to marry her. He provided little, if any, support and Elizabeth had to rely on her younger sister Rose to make all the necessary arrangements for her confinement in the Roscommon County Home. Both sisters were sentenced to death in March 1935 for the murder of Elizabeth's illegitimate newborn. Elizabeth had taken a considerable risk in her courtship. Her risky behaviour eventually led to the arrest, trial and imprisonment both of her and her younger sister. Although the sentence was commuted, Elizabeth and her sister faced penal servitude for life.

Men's reluctance to marry their long-term girlfriends, even when they became pregnant, is also evident in Northern Ireland. It is not clear whether M.M. was sincere in his intentions to marry L.T. The latter told the court that after the birth of her daughter M.M. had said that 'as soon as they were able they would get married'.[151] The pair had been keeping company for approximately three years before L.T. gave birth in September 1933. According to a police report there was 'intimacy' between them 'soon after they began keeping company'.[152] In November 1931 the couple made arrangements to get married, but M.M. left the area a few days before the wedding day and 'there was a coolness betwen Miss T. and he then until December of the same year when the intimacy began again'.'[153] As M.M. provided his pregnant girlfriend with abortifacient pills rather than offering to marry her again, this may indicate that he was insincere about marriage.

While many men may have shirked their responsibilities during the period under review and abandoned their girlfriends when they became pregnant, some men were prepared to stand by the women with whom they were involved. A 1945 Co. Cork case highlights the obstacles that young couples could come up against when attempting to get married. Kathleen L. told gardaí that when she told Patrick M. that she was pregnant he agreed to marry her. As Patrick was under the age of 21 he needed his mother's consent to marry, but she refused to give her consent. Kathleen L. told the gardaí who questioned her that her sister and the parish priest had gone to speak to Patrick's mother about their marriage but that she withheld her consent. The young couple even appealed to the Bishop of Kerry, but he refused to intervene and said 'he had nothing to do with marriages'.[154] In July 1945 Kathleen and Patrick left Kerry 'with the intention of getting married in Cork', but the priest they went to see in Cork refused to marry them unless they could provide a letter from their priest in Kerry.[155] Kathleen gave birth in a boarding house in Cork and Patrick was later charged with the infant's murder.

A history of long-term involvement with the father of their baby often worked in favour of women who were charged with infanticide in the Twenty-Six Counties between 1922 and 1950. If the father of the infant agreed to marry a woman charged with infanticide, she could often avoid serving a prison sentence or spending time in a religious-run institution. There is no evidence to suggest that this practice existed in Ireland prior to 1922 or in Northern Ireland. Yet in the Twenty-Six County state, eight women were released from custody following their marriage to the putative fathers of their illegitimate infants.

Domestic servant Mary H., aged 19, was found guilty at the Central Criminal Court, Dublin, in June 1931 of concealing the birth of her illegitimate male infant. However, it was noted that 'on the undertaking of the accused to marry James M. the court ordered that she be released from custody'.[156] Mary and James M., a labourer nineteen years her senior, married on 5 August of the same year. Writing to the county registrar on 11 August, Mary's solicitor enclosed the marriage certificate, noting: 'I take it that this ends the above matter and that there will be no necessity for any further appearance or any application on her behalf to the Court.'[157] Seven more couples married after the woman had been charged with the murder and/or concealment of birth of her infant in the Twenty-Six Counties. Kate H. married in July 1932 while she was still a prisoner in Sligo Jail.[158]

From the available evidence it is not clear what prompted the fathers of some women's murdered infants to offer to marry them, thereby securing their release. These men may have acted of their own free will or they may have been subject to pressure by the woman's family, by members of their own family or by the wider community. Local priests may also have played a role in engineering these marriages. In a 1934 Co. Clare case, the father of the deceased infant wrote to Teresa C. who was being held in Mountjoy and expressed his willingness 'to make atonement and to marry her'.[159] The *Clare Champion* noted that the parish priest 'entirely approved of the attitude of the parties'.[160]

In January 1946 the gardaí in Fermoy, County Cork wrote to the county registrar, informing him that Nora S. and the putative father of her infant, Edmund W., married 'according to the Rites of the Catholic Church' on 19 January. It was noted that 'husband and wife are residing at S., Glanworth in the home of Norah S.'s surviving parent'.[161] Couples who married shortly before the birth or following the woman's trial may not always have lived together immediately after the marriage. Relations between couples who married in such circumstances and their families may often have been strained. The garda who wrote the letter in the Nora S. case remarked that 'the relations existing between the two people concerned and their parents, brothers and sisters are satisfactory'.[162] These women were certainly fortunate in that they managed to avoid serving a prison sentence or spending time in a Magdalen asylum. However, one wonders to what extent they would have been emotionally scarred by their experience of giving birth alone, being apprehended by the police, imprisoned and tried, and how these experiences would have impacted on their married life.

While a small number of women married the fathers of their infants after they had been charged (and in some cases convicted), other women had married shortly before they gave birth. It is clear from the records of infanticide trials that premarital conception was clearly considered shameful, even in cases where couples married shortly before the birth of their child. The *Anglo-Celt* newspaper, which covered the trial of James B., his wife Jean and his mother Annie for the murder of a newborn infant in December 1940, referred to James and Jean's recent marriage as a 'hasty marriage by force of circumstances'.[163] The report suggested that the three defendants had 'early on at all events, the intention of hiding the fact of this hasty marriage'.[164] Although Jean B. said that she had not been 'anxious to conceal the child's early arrival ... her husband, mother-in-law and sister-in-law were anxious to conceal it'.[165]

Margaret D., aged 22, stood trial for the murder of her unnamed female infant at the Central Criminal Court, Dublin in March 1935. Margaret had married the infant's father, Patrick D., about a month before she gave birth. Margaret said that they had been 'keeping company for about five years before our marriage' and explained that they 'would have been married long before only that we could get no house'.[166] The couple were unable to live together after the marriage, as they had still not secured appropriate accommodation; they were waiting to get a cottage. Margaret was clearly not welcome in her husband's family home. Her husband's sister was not on speaking terms with her and rarely spoke to her brother either, presumably because she suspected that Margaret had become pregnant before the marriage. Margaret's sister-in-law informed her 'that she heard when [Margaret]

was coming [to her husband's family home] [she] wouldn't be here in
Kilross a fortnight when [she] would have to go to hospital' to give
birth.[167] Margaret strenuously denied that she was pregnant. She clearly
felt under pressure to conceal the fact that she and her husband had
had sexual intercourse before marriage. Margaret lived with her
parents, paying regular visits to her husband. She said she 'used to come
to [her] husband's place at Kilross nearly every night but during that
period [she] never came into the house. [She] used to meet him in a
shed attached to his house.'[168] Margaret gave birth unassisted in her
parents' home: 'No body attended me or anything and nobody knew
anything about it except myself.'[169] Shortly after the birth Margaret said
she 'tied a string around [her baby's] neck and it died'.[170] She then hid
the body and the following day she said that she carried the body 'up
on the hill'.[171] A few months later the body was found in a freshly dug
hole in a disused quarry. The man who found the body reported his
discovery to the gardaí. This Co. Limerick case highlights the fact that
in the Ireland of the 1930s, economic circumstances often prevented
well-established couples from poor rural backgrounds from getting
married. There was such a stigma associated with premarital sexual
activity that women like Margaret D. who married in the later stages of
pregnancy chose to kill a newborn infant rather than face the disapproval and hostility of family and neighbours. This was not an isolated
instance. Four couples married shortly before the birth in the Twenty-
Six Counties sample. None of the couples in the pre-1921 sample
married either just before or shortly after the birth and only one woman
in the northern sample appears to have married the father of her infant.
Another married after the birth of her infant. The fact that newly-wed
women who gave birth shortly after marriage felt compelled to
conceal all evidence of premarital sex by taking the infant's life shortly
after delivery indicates that sexual relations (or 'illegitimate intercourse
between the sexes' as an editorial in the *Irish Independent* in 1931 put
it), even among couples who went on to marry, was severely frowned
upon in Ireland during this period.[172]

  Catherine N. and Lawrence A. married a month before Catherine
was due to give birth. 'I was pregnant when married', she stated, 'and
Lawrence A. was responsible.'[173] While Margaret D. seems to have had
a strong, long-standing relationship with her husband, relations
between Co. Wexford newly-weds Catherine and Lawrence A. appear
to have been more strained. Although the couple spent their wedding
night in her parents' home, Catherine stated that her husband had only

'stayed an occasional night since'.[174] The couple did not live together after the marriage; Catherine continued to reside with her parents and she gave birth in their home. The sources reveal very little about their relationship but it seems likely that Lawrence may have been under pressure to marry Catherine in the later stages of her pregnancy. Lawrence was informed of the birth the following day. Catherine told him that the baby 'was dead born'.[175] Initially Catherine told the police that her husband had buried the infant but she later admitted that she buried the baby herself. In his statement Lawrence expressed little concern for his wife although this may, of course, have been due to the manner in which he was questioned.

Not all single women who became pregnant necessarily wished to marry the men who were responsible for their condition. James N. told gardaí that when he noticed that his girlfriend was 'remarkably stout'[176] in the summer of 1936 he asked her 'was there anything wrong or who was the father of it',[177] but Margaret denied she was pregnant. Although James had known Margaret 'all her life' and was keeping company with her, Margaret does not seem to have confided in him.[178] There is evidence to suggest that a number of women like Margaret S. seem to have been reluctant or unwilling to confide in the men with whom they had had sexual relations. Margaret may not have wanted to marry James N. or she may have considered that giving birth secretly and killing the infant was preferable to living with the stigma of single motherhood. When Mary C. found that she was pregnant a few months later she told Jim M. and he offered to marry her. However, she said that she did not want to marry him. According to Mary, Jim said 'there is no need to worry I will stand by you and he said that he would marry me. I said that I would not marry him.' [179]

'IRREGULAR' SEXUAL PRACTICES

Most single Irish women charged with infanticide appear to have willingly engaged in sexual encounters with men of the same class background. However, a small number of women told the gardaí who questioned them about the death of their infants that they had not consented to sex. Some women may well have been forced into sex. When Hannah B. was arrested and charged with the murder of her infant she told gardaí that she had been raped by a middle-aged man when she was leaving her sister's house late one night in October 1931. She said that she 'did not tell any person that this happened to [her]'.[180] While Hannah

B. claimed to have been raped by a stranger, a small number of women alleged to have been raped by the men who were courting them. Although Mary T. was not raped, when she described her experience with the father of her infant she suggested that he used some degree of force. Mary said that she tried to stop John C. 'when he lifted [her] clothes up' but when he used force she said she then decided to 'let him do whatever he wanted'.[181] Similarly, Elizabeth K. said that the father of her infant 'more or less did it against [her] will'.[182] Ferriter's research demonstrates that sexual crime was quite prevalent in Ireland both before and after independence. However, it remained difficult for victims to get justice. The circuit court records that Ferriter examined show a high number of acquittals for rape and carnal knowledge cases in the 1920s and 1930s. Ferriter argues that 'the preponderance of men and the prevailing view of the status of women, as well as comments from judges about "the natural, irresistible impulse animating the man", ensured that the women who appeared in court as witnesses or victims were at a distinct disadvantage'.[183] This helps explain women's reluctance to press charges.

While some women charged with the murder of their illegitimate infants may have been raped, it is also possible that women may have claimed that they had not consented to sex because they were concerned about their reputation. Kate Anne F.'s statement appears in question and answer format. Questioned on 9 April 1936 on suspicion of murdering her illegitimate newborn, Kate Anne identified her deceased infant's father and implied that intercourse had not been consensual. The male in question was not unknown to Kate Anne; she had often seen him in the area prior to the incident and she knew his name but she was not in a relationship with him. When asked if she struggled with him, Kate Anne replied in the affirmative but she was unable (or unwilling perhaps) to say how long she had spent with him and did not supply gardaí with any more information.

Odem's study of adolescent female sexuality in the United States between 1885 and 1920 has shown that some 'girls were sexually abused by stepfathers, uncles, brothers or other male relatives in a position of authority over the girls'.[184] Instances of incest and abuse occasionally came to light during the course of investigations into suspected cases of infanticide. In a small number of cases, women charged with infanticide had been sexually abused by male relatives or by male employers who were in a position of authority over them. Nora H. was charged with the murder of her infant in April 1931. She lived alone with her father in their home in Waterford city. Nora seems to have feared her violent father. In her evidence she said she was afraid he would hit her. She explained to gardaí that she did not go to hospital to have the baby; '[she] said [she] would have it at home and leave it to [her father] because he owns it'.[185] A week before the birth, Nora's father had said that if he saw a child in the house he would kill it. When Nora reminded him that he 'owned' the child she said 'he got into a temper then and was fighting all the night'.[186] Nora was convicted of concealment of birth at the Central Criminal Court, Dublin. According to the Trials Record Book Nora undertook to spend two years in the Magdalen Asylum in Donnybrook. However, the Reverend Mother of the convent wrote to the registrar at Green Street courthouse seven months after Nora's admission to request that she be 'removed without delay'.[187] Nora had endangered the lives of some of the other inmates and had 'to be kept apart from the other inmates of the institution'.[188] She was then sentenced to two years' imprisonment with hard labour. It is unlikely that charges were brought against Nora's father despite his daughter's allegations. He denied all knowledge of the infant's existence. Nora's behaviour in the convent may well have been due to the abuse she experienced but she was evidently treated as a criminal rather than a victim.

While there may have been a general cultural silence about sexual abuse within the family in Ireland, as elsewhere during this period, and cases may have been only rarely pursued through the courts, the questions put to unmarried women living in households with male relatives only by the gardaí in the samples studied suggest that they were not unaware of incidences of incestuous abuse. Margaret W. was questioned about the death of a newborn infant by gardaí in Co. Kildare on 12 July 1933. Margaret began her statement by stating her age, her marital status and her place of residence. Margaret then asserted that she slept by herself in one room. Her father and three brothers, the gardaí were informed, slept in the kitchen. It is probable that Margaret's description of her family's sleeping arrangements was prompted by questions from the gardaí responsible for taking her statement. It is surely significant that questions were asked about sleeping arrangements so early on in the investigation of the death of an illegitimate infant born to an unmarried young woman in a working-class household without a mother figure. The gardaí who handled the initial stages of the investigation may have regarded Margaret's father and brothers as potential suspects. It seems to have been an obvious line of inquiry at the time, particularly in working-class households without a mother figure, and is discussed at length in Chapter 5. This line of inquiry was soon derailed in this particular case, for Margaret named the father of her deceased infant. He had been responsible for Margaret's three pregnancies. Margaret had been arrested three times on suspicion of killing a newborn infant or concealing its birth, and had been convicted for concealing the birth of an illegitimate infant prior to her arrest in July 1933.

There was one case of incest in the northern sample. As noted in Chapter 5, J.R., 'a grey-haired farmer about 66 years of age'[189] was charged with the murder of his daughter's female infant and with having had 'carnal knowledge' of his daughter in May 1931. One of the investigating officers in the case said that J.R. admitted that he had carnal knowledge of his daughter A.R. at least five or six times and said that they had both slept in the same bed for the past nine months.[190] J.R.'s wife, who had been 'residing apart from [her] husband four and a half years', said that her husband had nodded his head 'as if to say he could not help it' when he admitted that he was the father of their daughter's infant.[191] A.R.'s mother and uncle appear to have been profoundly shocked when they learned of the incestuous relationship she had had with her father. According to a report in the *Belfast Telegraph*, J.R.'s brother-in-law 'was overcome and collapsed in the hall leading to the office and did not revive for a considerable time'.[192] J.R.'s wife said that when her daughter told her what had happened she believed that 'if [she] had got a knife [she] would have struck the two of them'.[193] As A.R. did not make a statement there is little to indicate how she felt towards her father; according to the *Belfast Telegraph*, both the accused cried in court.[194]

Odem's discussion of a case of sexual abuse where a young girl's uncle 'used his position of authority within the home to compel the girl to submit to his sexual demands'[195] is reminiscent of a 1938 Co. Dublin infanticide case involving a 20-year-old woman and her maternal uncle. At first glance the case appears to be yet another incidence of sexual abuse of a young, economically dependent woman by an older male relative. Following the death of Margaret's newborn infant in September 1938 it emerged that, as Justice Maguire put it, Margaret's uncle had seduced his niece. Margaret M. was charged with the murder of her illegitimate infant in September 1938. Her uncle Laurence B. was charged with concealment of birth. Laurence told gardaí that he had been keeping company with his niece for two years. In her statement Margaret said that she went to live with her uncle 'the day before Christmas Eve last and since then [they] [had] lived together as man and wife'.[196] She said that they slept in the same bed and that she had 'connection' with her uncle on and off since she went to live with him.[197] Margaret was 20 at the time of her arrest and her uncle was 48. According to newspaper reports on the case, Margaret's father was an alcoholic. The *Irish Times* claimed that Margaret M. had 'been brought up in circumstances of extreme unhappiness' and alleged that Margaret and her mother 'sometimes had to leave the house and seek refuge with an uncle' as her father often turned his family onto the road.[198] It is possible that Margaret went to live with her uncle because she had very few options. While Margaret may have had genuine feelings for her uncle, the fact that she attempted to commit suicide shortly after she had killed her newborn infant suggests that she may have been less than happy with the situation in which she found herself. Yet it is possible that Margaret's feelings for her uncle were genuine. Sexual relations had begun even before Margaret went to live with her uncle. Probation officer Elizabeth Carroll said that she was convinced 'from conversations with her and other evidence that her whole desire is to get out as soon as possible and go back to her uncle'.[199] The couple may have married following Margaret's release. Laurence was apparently 'most ready and willing to marry' his niece and intended to get the dispensation required at the earliest opportunity.

According to D'Cruze, in nineteenth-century England many servants were raped by their employers.[200] In her study of domestic service in Dublin between 1880 and 1922, Hearn argued that servants were particularly vulnerable to sexual exploitation by the master, sons and male visitors to the house in which they worked.[201] She has also suggested that unmarried domestic servants 'were often lonely, deprived of the companionship of members of the opposite sex and so were particularly vulnerable: employers and their friends frequently took advantage of this situation'.[202] More recently, Ferriter has highlighted the fact that large numbers of cases involving the sexual exploitation and abuse of servants came before the courts in late-nineteenth- and early-twentieth-century Ireland. It was, he argues, a recurring problem.[203] Contemporaries regarded it as a persistent problem. A number of witnesses who gave evidence before the Carrigan Committee were of the opinion that employers often seduced young women who worked for them by intimidating them. For instance, at the eleventh meeting of the Carrigan Committee, representatives from the Committee of Medical Women stated that 'it is believed that in many cases an evilly-disposed employer intimidates girls in his employment e.g. domestic servants,

Clerks, Shop Assistants etc into yielding to his wishes by threats of dismissal'.[204] There may well have been many such instances in Ireland during the first half of the twentieth century, but single women charged with infanticide between 1900 and 1950 rarely referred to being seduced by their employers in their statements. In fact, only three women in the samples studied claimed that their employers were the fathers of their infants. Mary G. and her employer Robert M. were both charged with concealing the birth of their infant daughter in December 1902. Mary had worked as a servant in Robert's household for three years prior to the birth of her infant. She told police that he was the father of herinfant. Mary said that she gave birth in the loft of Robert M.'s house. She claimed that the baby was stillborn and said that 'when it was born [she] called down to [Robert] that it was born and was dead'.[205] In his statement Robert claimed that he knew 'nothing about Mary G. having a child'.[206] He did admit that he knew that she was pregnant but claimed he told her she should not stay in his house any longer. It is possible that Mary G. lied and that Robert M. was not the infant's father, but given that Mary and Robert lived together in close proximity for three years it is not improbable that a sexual relationship developed between them. This relationship may not have been exploitative. Hearn acknowledged the fact that 'not all servants were innocent victims of sexual liaisons'.[207] However, given the lack of available evidence it is not possible to do more than speculate on the dynamics of Robert and Mary's relationship. As D'Cruze has observed, 'where sex-in-the-workplace was not directly coerced, elements of power inequalities imported from the structure of workplace hierarchies may well have overlaid the relationship'.[208]

In a 1928 Co. Wexford case it emerged that Mary C., who had been employed by Myles D. as a domestic servant, had had sexual intercourse with both her employer and her employer's son.[209] They had all shared the same bed for a number of months. In his statement, Myles D. said that Mary had slept between him and his son. Although Mary C. seems to have consented to sex with her employer's son, it is not possible to determine whether she also consented to sex with her employer on two occasions. Mary C. gave no indication of her feelings towards either man in her evidence although she mentioned that at one point there 'was a conversation about John marrying [her]'.[210] The case differs from the bulk of the cases studied in that the unmarried servant in question had had sexual relations with both her employer and her employer's son, and also in terms of the way her father was compensated for his daughter's loss of reputation. Mary's employer Myles told gardaí that once the infant's body was disposed of he went to the National Bank in Wexford, where he withdrew sixty pounds. He gave Mary's father fifty pounds in a public house close by. In his statement Myles explained that 'the fifty pounds was paid for the wrong done to his daughter. Mary's father Patrick had allegedly said that they 'would be no worse friends if I paid him fifty pounds'. Mary also referred to the money payment in her statement. She said it was 'to hide the shame'. Patrick may well have threatened Myles and his son with legal proceedings. A newspaper report on the case recorded Myles claiming to have paid Patrick C. fifty pounds because he had informed him that he was going 'to take an action against [Myles]'.[211] In her study of child sexual abuse in Victorian England, Jackson referred to the offering of payments in sexual assault cases, a practice she identifies with the 'long-established conception of working-class women's bodies as property or commodity which could be bought or bartered for'.[212] In some parts of England 'the practice of settling sexual assault cases through financial payment was still accepted by the courts at mid-century'.[213] This 1928 Co. Wexford case indicates that informal, out-of-court payments were accepted as a settlement in such cases in some parts of Ireland well into the twentieth century. It is not clear from the case files whether Mary would have received a share of the compensation paid to her father.

There was only one northern case where the father of an illegitimate infant whose death was being investigated was also the woman's employer. J.M. was tried for the murder and concealment of birth of two illegitimate infants in October 1924. The mother of the infants, L.M., had already been convicted of concealing the birth of one of the infants. When she was imprisoned in Armagh Jail, she made a statement implicating J.M., the father of the deceased infants. L.M. was a married woman and she was employed by J.M. as his housekeeper. From the information available in this case it does not appear that L.M. was exploited by her employer. She seems to have left his employment after her marriage but when she argued with her husband she returned to J.M.'s house and resumed her work as his housekeeper. L.M. told the police that J.M. attended her during her confinement in his home. J.M. seems to have assumed responsibility for removing the body and disposing of it after the birth. L.M. said that 'after the child was born [the] prisoner took it away and [she] never saw it again. [She] never asked him what he did with it.'[214] This happened on three separate occasions. J.M. and L.M. had an ongoing sexual relationship and they seem to have used infanticide as a means of fertility control. L.M.'s husband gave evidence in the case. He said that he was not aware when he married L.M. that she had already had a child. He also said that he 'tried to get her to come back to [him]' when she was in her employer's house but L.M. clearly preferred to stay with J.M.[215]

THE INFANTS' FATHERS AND INFANTICIDE

While many men were unsupportive of unplanned pregnancies, the records of infanticide trials in Ireland indicate that in some cases the fathers of illegitimate infants were supportive of their unmarried girl-friends, in that they assisted them in making plans to give birth secretly. John M. and Mary Kate M. were charged with murder and conspiracy to murder in April 1943. A report in the *Irish Times* noted that Mary Kate M. 'was unmarried, while Mr M., who was married, lived about four miles from M.'s house. He worked for the M.'s and occasionally slept at their home.'[216] John M. told gardaí that 'it was my wish and hers to hide the birth of the child'.[217] In his statement John M. referred to the plans they made together before the baby was born:

> Before she left home it was our intention that she should give birth to the child at some place where it would not become known that the child had been born. My object in going to Galway was to get the quietest nursing home I could for her to enter and my reason was to hide the birth of the child.[218]

John M. called to the nursing home and said he was Mary Kate's husband. He arranged to have the baby baptized and ordered a car to take Mary Kate and the baby home. John M. may have been suspected of putting pressure on Mary Kate to kill the infant. He told gardaí that '[he] didn't murder it and [he] didn't say it to her to murder it'.[219]

The fathers of illegitimate infants were rarely questioned during the course of investigations into suspected cases of infanticide. In the vast majority of cases the putative fathers were not suspected of having played any part in the infant's death. Ryan has noted how 'unmarried young women were held entirely responsible for their predicaments'.[220] This is true to a point. When the father of an illegitimate infant whose death was being investigated or relatives of the birth mother were suspected of having played a part in the infant's death, then they were questioned and charged where appropriate. In most cases examined the unmarried mother acted alone and she alone was held responsible for the infant's death. The fathers of only fourteen infants (7 per cent) in the post-independence southern sample were questioned by the gardaí and submitted depositions. Ryan has asserted that 'men were very rarely charged with complicity in infanticide'.[221] In *Occasions of Sin*, Ferriter refers to male involvement in concealing the birth of illegitimate new-borns as unusual.[222] Despite having identified almost 600 cases of infanticide tried at Irish circuit courts and the Central Criminal Court, Maguire has referred only briefly to men implicated in infanticide cases, noting that male defendants appeared before the courts on rare occasions. Maguire does not offer a sustained discussion of men's role in the murder or concealment of birth of illegitimate newborns and does not indicate how many men stood trial in the circuit courts. The fathers of nine illegitimate infants whose deaths were investigated in the Twenty-Six Counties sample were charged with murder or concealment of birth (4.6 per cent).[223] Seven of the nine men were convicted. One man was convicted of murder, two were convicted of manslaughter and a further four men were convicted of concealment of birth. Two cases were not proceeded with. In three cases these men were the sole defendants, while in a further six cases the fathers of the infants stood trial along with the infants' mother and or others. In total, sixteen men (8 per cent) were charged with the murder or concealment of birth of an illegitimate infant in the Twenty-Six Counties sample. Charges were less likely to have been brought against male relatives of the birth mothers than the fathers of their infants. In the pre-independence sample, charges were more likely to have been brought against male relatives of the birth mothers than the fathers of their infants, whereas in the northern sample, charges were more likely to have been brought against the fathers of illegitimate infants.[224] The role played by male relatives of the birth mother has been discussed in Chapter 2. The sentences handed down to men convicted of murder, manslaughter or concealment of birth is examined in Chapter 5. While male involvement in the murder or concealment of birth was certainly not customary it was perhaps less unusual than historians have hitherto realised.

Three putative fathers in the pre-independence sample gave depositions. Charges were brought against the alleged father of only one infant (1 per cent). Mary G., a domestic servant and her employer Robert M. were both due to be tried for concealment of birth at the Donegal Spring Assizes in 1903. The case against Robert M., detailed earlier in the chapter, was not proceeded with. The fathers of four infants (11 per cent) in the northern sample were questioned by the police in relation to the deaths of their illegitimate infants. Three of the four men were charged with murder or concealment of birth (7.8 per cent). One man was also the birth mother's father and he was charged with concealment of birth and carnal knowledge. If he is excluded from the infants' fathers category and included in the category of male relatives charged, then the percentage of infants' fathers charged is reduced to 2 (5 per cent). In December 1933, M.M., who was employed as a trapper by the Northern Ministry of Agriculture and lived in a hut in Co. Down, was sentenced to death for the murder of his nine-day-old infant daughter. J.R. was charged with the murder of his daughter's female infant and with having had carnal know-ledge of his daughter in May 1931. J.M. was tried for the murder and concealment of birth of two illegitimate infants in October 1924.

Police investigating infanticide cases throughout the period under review, both North and South, seem to have had little interest in the infants' fathers. Presumably they were not questioned because they were not suspected of having played a part in the infant's death or because they were no longer in the area and the woman had lost touch with them. It would appear that men who fathered children outside wedlock were not regarded as 'real' fathers by the Irish authorities unless they married the child's mother.

There is evidence to suggest that other men in pre-independence Ireland may have conspired with the birth mothers but there may not have been enough evidence to bring charges against them. When James R. was questioned by the police he admitted knowing about Ellen C.'s pregnancy.[225] He said that he realised from her appearance that she was pregnant but said that they had never discussed it. He swore that he was not in her room the night she gave birth. In her statement Ellen said that Jim R. came into her room the evening after she had given birth. She also stated that she had told him that their twin infants were dead and that she had wrapped them up in her bed. Ellen alleged that Jim had asked her 'was there anything he could do for [her]'.[226] 'He had a half pint of whiskey in his pocket and wanted [her] to drink some of it … He then asked me did I want anything else and I said no except he brought in some milk from the barn and boiled it'.[227] Ellen also claimed that Jim said that he would bury the infants. From the evidence available in this case it seems that Ellen and Jim may have conspired together. Jim may have assisted her in concealing the births of her infant twins. However, charges were not brought against him.

As we have seen, there were a number of instances where couples, both unmarried and newly wed, conspired to kill and bury a newborn infant in the South between 1922 and 1950, but there is less evidence of similar conspiracies in the judicial records of cases tried in Northern Ireland. J.M. and the mother of his deceased infants, L.M., seem to have conspired together to conceal the birth of three infants to whom the latter gave birth in secret over the course of several years. When she was questioned, L.M. said that each time she gave birth J.M. took the bodies away. She said that she never questioned him about what he did with the bodies and that on the second occasion 'he told [her] not to tell no one'.[228] Although the evidence in this file is not very detailed, the fact that L.M. returned to live with and work for J.M. after her marriage to a third party, and following the birth and death of her first infant with J.M., suggests that she played an active part in the conspiracy to dispose of the babies' bodies. J.R. was charged with the murder of his daughter's female infant and with having had carnal knowledge of his daughter in May 1931. J.M. was tried for the murder and concealment of birth of two illegitimate infants in October 1924. The mother of the infants was his housekeeper and she was convicted of concealment of birth but the couple were tried separately.

Like Peggy S. in a 1948 Dublin case discussed earlier in this chapter, it would appear that L.T. was not aware that her infant's father intended to kill their newborn daughter. The barristers who defended M.M. in court in December 1933 suggested that L.T., the mother, had been aware of M.M.'s intentions, but the presiding judge objected to the allegations. When L.T. left the baby at M.M.'s hut she had prepared two bottles of milk, and when M.M. told her that he had given the baby to his sister in Glasgow she claimed she had offered to send her money to pay for the baby's upkeep. The *Northern Whig* reported that during the course of the trial L.T. 'broke down momentarily when a shawl was produced, which she identified as that which was around the child when it was taken to the hut'.[229] It seems unlikely that L.T. had been involved in her daughter's death. While some single women appear to have collaborated with the men charged with the murder of their infant sons or daughters, neither Peggy S. nor L.T. seem to have been aware that their partners intended to take the lives of their infants. From the evidence available in the case files, both women seem to have been loving mothers.

CONCLUSION

While the discourse on single motherhood in Ireland during the first half of the twentieth century often presented the unmarried mother as a passive victim who had been seduced or led astray, the statements of single women charged with the murder or concealment of birth of their illegitimate infants between 1900 and 1950 suggest that the reality was far more complex. Some women may have been unsophisticated and uninformed about sex and pregnancy and a smaller number had 'fallen' more than once, but the records suggest that the experiences of single working-class women during the period varied considerably and in many cases did not conform to the stereotypes in discourses on unmarried motherhood prevalent in post-independence Ireland. Contemporary observers tended to group unmarried mothers into overly neat categories. Dr Fogarty, Bishop of Killaloe, writing to the Co. Clare Board of Health in November 1933, divided unmarried mothers into three 'classes': 'the feeble or weak minded sort (and a great many of them are such) who will never be able to take care of themselves and are easy victims to the wrecker', 'girls who are naturally decent, but have fallen through accident or environment' and 'women of a wild or vicious nature who are a harmful influence wherever they prevail'.[230] However, the range of sexual experiences and of contrasting attitudes towards sexuality evident in the statements of single women charged with the murder or concealment of birth of their illegitimate infants between 1900 and 1950 defy such clear-cut categorisation. Some women had been involved with the fathers of their infants over a considerable period of time, others had had brief encounters with the men they named as the infant's father and a very small number of women had been raped or abused.

Given that these statements were made at a time when sexual activity among unmarried couples was seriously frowned upon officially and the discussion of sexual matters was considered taboo, the level of detail in many of the statements of single women charged with infanticide is quite striking. The records of infanticide trials certainly raise questions about the manner in which gardaí conducted investigations into suspected cases of infanticide. While some women may not have been interrogated about their sexual experiences, others were questioned about the most intimate aspects of their relationships with the fathers of the deceased infants.

Although the records of infanticide trials bring to light the sexual experiences of single working-class women in Ireland, both North and

South, during the first half of the twentieth century, given the dearth of information available for the pre-independence period, they do not indicate whether patterns of sexual behaviour changed over time. It may well be that little changed between 1900 and 1950. Levels of ignorance about human sexuality remained high. Throughout the period, unmarried Irish women defied church teaching on celibacy and engaged in premarital sex. The working-class Irish women who feature in the trial records examined engaged in risky behaviour which ended, in many cases, in self-delivery followed by arrest, trial and conviction for the murder or concealment of birth of an illegitimate infant. Small wonder, then, that Mary C., reflecting on the man responsible for her pregnancy in May 1943 would remark that 'he wasn't worth it'.[231]

As Ferriter has noted, for much of the twentieth century 'it was assumed that in terms of sexual morality Ireland was different to other countries. There was a delusion Ireland was immune from certain sexual problems; they were deemed to be "foreign vices", usually associated with England.'[232] There was, he reminds us, a significant gulf between the rhetoric of Irish chastity and the reality.[233] Both Luddy and Ferriter have argued that Inglis has failed to take adequate account of the extent to which Irish people defied church teachings on sexuality. Luddy's *Prostitution and Irish Society* complicates the image of Ireland as a sexually pure nation and demonstrates that prostitution survived in Ireland with little interference from the church: 'Between 1800 and 1940 thousands of women worked as prostitutes in Ireland.'[234] In *Occasions of Sin*, Ferriter highlights discourses that were independent of or opposed to the Catholic Church. According to Ferriter, there was no shortage of sexual transgressions in modern Ireland. Close readings of the judicial records of infanticide trials confirm this; they remain one of the most revealing documentary records of sexual behaviour among poor, unmarried Irish women during the first half of the twentieth century.

NOTES

1. National Archives of Ireland [hereafter NAI], Central Criminal Court [hereafter CCC], Dublin, 1948.
2. Ibid.
3. Ibid.
4. Ibid.
5. Ibid.
6. Ibid.
7. Ibid.
8. Ibid.

9. Ibid.
10. S. D'Cruze, *Crimes of Outrage: Sex, Violence and Victorian Working Women* (London: University College London Press, 1998), p.130.
11. NAI, Central Criminal Court [hereafter CCC], Dublin, 1948.
12. Ibid.
13. C. Wills, 'All Pleasure Now', *Times Literary Supplement*, December 18 and 25 2009 (*Review of Occasions of Sin*).
14. T. Inglis, 'Origins and Legacies of Irish Prudery: Sexuality and Social Control in Modern Ireland', *Éire Ireland*, 40, 3 & 4 (2005), p.9.
15. Ibid., p.10.
16. S. McAvoy, 'The Regulation of Sexuality in the Irish Free State, 1929–1935', in E. Malcolm and G. Jones (eds), *Medicine, Disease and the State in Ireland, 1650–1940* (Cork: Cork University Press, 1999), p.264.
17. M.J. Maguire, *Precarious Childhood in Post-Independence Ireland* (Manchester: Manchester University Press, 2009), p.206.
18. L.A. Jackson, *Child Sexual Abuse in Victorian England* (London: Routledge, 1999), p.29.
19. C. Heywood, 'Innocence and Experience: Sexuality Among Young People in Modern France, c. 1750–1950', *French History*, 21, 1 (2007), p.44.
20. Ibid., p.45.
21. NAI, CCC, Dublin, 1943.
22. NAI, CCC, Co. Dublin, 1926.
23. Ibid.
24. Ibid.
25. M.L. Arnot and C. Usborne, 'Why Gender and Crime? Aspects of an Institutional Debate', in M.L. Arnot and C. Usborne (eds), *Gender and Crime in Modern Europe* (London: Routledge, 1999), p.22.
26. NAI, CCC, Co. Dublin, 1941.
27. NAI, CCC, Dublin, 1942.
28. M.E. Odem, *Delinquent Daughters: Protecting and Policing Adolescent Female Sexuality in the United States, 1885–1920* (Chapel Hill, NC: University of North Carolina Press, 1995), p.53.
29. NAI, CCC, Co. Wexford, 1949.
30. Maguire, *Precarious Childhood*, p.203.
31. M. Hearn, *Below Stairs: Domestic Service Remembered in Dublin and Beyond 1880–1922* (Dublin: Lilliput Press, 1993), p.97.
32. D'Cruze, *Crimes of Outrage*, p.135.
33. NAI, CCC, Co. Longford, 1939.
34. Public Record Office of Northern Ireland [hereafter PRONI], BELF/1/1/2/94/6, 1930.
35. NAI, CCC, Co. Sligo, 1945. Dr McDonagh concluded that Jane M. was subnormal in intelligence.
36. NAI, CCC, Co. Dublin, 1941.
37. NAI, CCC, Co. Wicklow, 1929.
38. Ibid.
39. Maguire, *Precarious Childhood*, p.220, fn.2.
40. PRONI, BELF/1/2/2/56/4, 1946.
41. PRONI, BELF/1/2/2/40/67, 1930.
42. NAI, CCC, Co. Kildare, 1933.
43. Ibid.
44. PRONI, BELF/1/1/2/47/7, 1915.
45. PRONI, BELF/1/1/2/53/7, 1917.
46. Seven of these infants were alive when the mother was arrested, two resided with foster mothers, two children lived with their mothers and her parents, and one woman's child lived in a Catholic home. One woman's baby had died, and this information was not recorded in two cases.
47. Seven of these infants had died.
48. NAI, CCC, Co. Westmeath, 1943.
49. NAI, CCC, Co. Carlow, 1929.
50. NAI, CCC, Co. Westmeath, 1927.

51. NAI, CCC, Co. Westmeath, 1943.
52. NAI, CCC, Co. Kildare, 1933.
53. PRONI, BELF/1/1/2/98/6, 1932.
54. PRONI, BELF/1/1/2/91/6, 1929.
55. PRONI, BELF/1/1/2/97/5, 1931.
56. PRONI, DOW/1/2B/36/6, 1929.
57. Maguire, *Precarious Childhood*, p.108.
58. NAI, Co. Limerick, Crown Files at Assizes, 1901–02.
59. NAI, Co. Clare, Crown Files at Assizes, 1915.
60. NAI, Co. Clare, Crown Files at Assizes, 1917.
61. NAI, Co. Clare, Crown Files at Assizes, 1914.
62. See NAI, CRF/1911/A 11 for Hannah K. file (1900).
63. NAI, Co. Clare, Crown Files at Assizes, 1903.
64. Ibid.
65. NAI, CCC, Co. Limerick, 1935.
66. NAI, CCC, Co. Clare, 1934.
67. NAI, CCC, Co. Cork, 1944.
68. D'Cruze, *Crimes of Outrage*, p.4.
69. PRONI, BELF/1/2/2/56/4, 1946.
70. PRONI, BELF/1/1/2/94/6, 1930.
71. Ibid.
72. PRONI, BELF/1/2/2/40/67, 1930.
73. PRONI, BELF 1/1/2/73/7, 1923.
74. PRONI, BELF/1/1/2/62/5, 1920.
75. D'Cruze, *Crimes of Outrage*, p.4.
76. S. Toksvig, 'Why Girls Leave Ireland', *Survey* (August 1929), pp.484–5.
77. NAI, Department of Justice, 90/4, Minutes of Evidence, Carrigan Committee.
78. D. Ferriter, *Occasions of Sin: Sex and Society in Modern Ireland* (London: Profile, 2009), p.179.
79. Ibid.
80. NAI, CCC, Co. Dublin, 1926.
81. NAI, CCC, Co. Leix, 1930.
82. NAI, CCC, Co. Limerick, 1931.
83. NAI, CCC, Co. Wexford, 1928.
84. NAI, CCC, Co. Galway, 1933. A haggard is a traditional storage area for crops.
85. NAI, CCC, Co. Limerick, 1935.
86. NAI, CCC, Co. Longford, 1925.
87. Ibid.
88. Ibid.
89. Ibid.
90. D. Ferriter, *The Transformation of Ireland 1900–2000* (London: Profile, 2005), p.319.
91. PRONI, BELF/1/1/2/94/6, 1930.
92. PRONI, HA 9/2/4, 1933.
93. PRONI, TYR1/2B/34, 1924.
94. NAI, CCC, Cork, Attorney Generals Office [hereafter AG] 2002/16/480.
95. NAI, CCA, 60/1945.
96. NAI, CCA, 23/1931.
97. F. O'Brien, 'The Dance Halls', *The Bell* (February 1941), p.44. 8
98. Ibid.
99. Ibid.
100. *Irish Independent*, 7 October 1925.
101. Ibid.
102. *Connacht Tribune*, 8 December 1928.
103. Ibid.
104. Maguire, *Precarious Childhood*, p.191.
105. NAI, CCC, Dublin, 1942.
106. NAI, CCC, Co. Galway, 1933.
107. Ibid.

108. NAI, CCC, Co. Mayo, 1931.
109. NAI, Department of the Taoiseach, S5998, Report of the Committee on the Criminal Law Amendment Acts (1880–1885), and Juvenile Prostitution, p.20.
110. Ibid.
111. NAI, CCC, Co. Wicklow, 1939.
112. NAI, Department of the Taoiseach, S5886.
113. NAI, CCC, Co. Donegal, 1927.
114. NAI, CCC, Co. Kilkenny, 1944.
115. NAI, CCC, Co. Longford, 1939.
116. NAI, CCC, Co. Tipperary, 1928.
117. NAI, CCC, Co. Waterford, 1935.
118. Ibid.
119. NAI, CCC, Co. Limerick, 1941.
120. NAI, CCC, Co. Leix, 1930.
121. Ibid.
122. NAI, Louth Crown and Peace Office, Crown Books at Assizes, Leinster, Winter 1900–05.
123. NAI, Co. Donegal 1919–21, Crown Files at Assizes.
124. NAI, CCC, Co. Cork, 1947.
125. NAI, CCC, Co. Meath, 1931.
126. S. D'Cruze and L.A. Jackson, *Women, Crime and Justice in England since 1660* (London: Palgrave Macmillan, 2009), p.76.
127. H. Lyder, ' "Silence and Secrecy": Exploring Female Sexuality during Childhood in 1930s and 1940s Dublin', *Irish Journal of Feminist Studies*, 5, 1 & 2 (2003), p.80.
128. NAI, CCC, Co. Kilkenny, 1948.
129. Ferriter, *Occasions of Sin*, p.205.
130. Ibid., p.293.
131. L. McCray Beier, 'We were green as grass': Learning about Sex and Reproduction in Three Working-Class Lancashire Communities 1900–1970', *Social History of Medicine*, 16, 3 (2003).
132. Ibid., p.467.
133. D'Cruze, *Crimes of Outrage*, p.3.
134. Ibid., p.130.
135. Ibid., p.135.
136. NAI, CCC, Co. Wexford, 1949.
137. M. Hill, *Women in Ireland: A Century of Change* (Belfast: Blackstaff, 2003), p.106.
138. M. Howes (ed.), 'Public Discourse, Private Reflection, 1916–70', in A. Bourke, S. Kilfeather. M. Luddy, M. McCurtain, G. Meaney, M. Ní Dhonnchadha, M. O'Dowd, C. Wills (eds), *The Field Day Anthology of Irish Writing: Irish Women's Writing and Traditions, Vol. 4* (Cork: Cork University Press, 2002), p.924.
139. Ibid.
140. NAI, CCA, 83/1944.
141. Ibid.
142. NAI, CCA, 8/1937.
143. NAI, CCA, 72/1944. See C. Rattigan, ' "Dark spots in Irish society": Single Motherhood, Crime and Prosecution in Ireland, 1900–1950' (PhD thesis, Trinity College Dublin, 1998), for a discussion of single women and abortion.
144. R. Schulte, *The Village in Court: Arson, Infanticide, and Poaching in the Court Records of Upper Bavaria, 1848–1910* (Cambridge: Cambridge University Press, 1994), p.110.
145. NAI, CCC, Co. Meath, 1941.
146. NAI, Co. Clare, Crown Files at Assizes, 1915.
147. PRONI, HA 9/2/4, 1933.
148. NAI, CCC, Co. Cavan, 1946.
149. NAI, CCC, Co. Roscommon, 1943.
150. NAI, CCA 13/1935.
151. *Northern Whig and Belfast Post*, 14 December 1933.
152. PRONI, HA 9/2/4.
153. Ibid.
154. NAI, CCC, Co. Cork, 1945.

155. Ibid.
156. NAI, CCC, Co. Leix, 1931.
157. Trials Record Book, CCC, Change of Venue Cases, November 1927 Sittings – June 1933 Sittings. Letter from William O'Dwyer, Solicitors, Roscrea, Co. Tipperary, to James O'Connor, County Registrar, Green Street, Dublin, 11 August 1931.
158. NAI, CCC, Co. Mayo, 1932.
159. *Clare Champion*, 22 December 1934.
160. Ibid.
161. NAI, CCC, Co. Cork, 1945.
162. Ibid.
163. *Anglo Celt*, 14 December 1940.
164. Ibid.
165. Ibid.
166. NAI, CCC, Co. Limerick, 1935.
167. Ibid.
168. Ibid.
169. Ibid.
170. Ibid.
171. Ibid.
172. *Irish Independent*, 16 February 1931.
173. NAI, CCC, Co. Wexford, 1929.
174. Ibid.
175. Ibid.
176. NAI, CCC, Co. Tipperary, 1937.
177. Ibid.
178. Ibid.
179. NAI, CCC, Co. Meath, 1941.
180. NAI, CCC, Cork, 1931.
181. NAI, CCC, Co. Leix, 1930.
182. NAI, CCC, Dublin, 1935.
183. Ferriter, *Occasions of Sin*, p.41.
184. Odem, *Delinquent Daughters*, p.59.
185. NAI, CCC, Co. Waterford, 1931.
186. Ibid.
187. NAI, Trials Record Book, CCC, Change of Venue Cases, November 1927 Sittings – June 1933 Sittings.
188. Ibid.
189. *Irish News*, 25 May 1931.
190. PRONI, DOW1/2B/38/7, 1931.
191. Ibid.
192. *Belfast Telegraph*, 23 May 1931.
193. Ibid.
194. Ibid.
195. Odem, *Delinquent Daughters*, p.61.
196. NAI, CCC, Co. Dublin, 1938.
197. Ibid.
198. *Irish Times*, 3 May 1938.
199. NAI, CCC, Co. Dublin, 1938, Letter dated 30 September 1938 from Elizabeth Carroll, Probation Officer, to J.J. O'Connor, Circuit Court Office.
200. D'Cruze, *Crimes of Outrage*, p.45.
201. Hearn, *Below Stairs*, p.96.
202. Ibid.
203. Ferriter, *Occasions of Sin*, p.81.
204. NAI, Department of Justice, H247/41D, Criminal law Amendment Committee (1930) Minute Book, 90/40/1.
205. NAI, Co. Donegal, Crown Files at Assizes, 1903–05.
206. Ibid.

207. Hearn, *Below Stairs*, p.97.

208. D'Cruze, *Crimes of Outrage*, p.109.

209. NAI, CCC, Co. Wexford, 1928.

210. Ibid.

211. *Wexford People*, 2 June 1928.

212. Jackson, *Child Sexual Abuse*, p.39.

213. Ibid.

214. PRONI, HA 9/2/4.

215. PRONI, TYR1/2B/34, 1924.

216. *Irish Times*, 25 November 1943.

217. NAI, CCC, Co. Galway, 1943.

218. Ibid.

219. Ibid.

220. L. Ryan, *Gender, Identity and the Irish Press 1922–1937: Embodying the Nation* (Lampeter: Edwin Mellen, 2002), p.274.

221. Ibid., p.253.

222. Ferriter, *Occasions of Sin*, p.247.

223. Myles D. and John M. are treated as infants' fathers here although it is possible that they may not have been the fathers of the deceased infants. John M. insisted that he was not the father of his girlfriend's illegitimate infant. He thought that another man was responsible for her pregnancy. In her evidence his girlfriend admitted that she had had intercourse with other men (NAI, CCC, Co. Wexford, 1949). Both Myles D. and his son had had sexual relations with their live-in servant Mary C. It was not clear which man was the father of the deceased infant. Laurence B., who was both the father of an infant and a male relative (uncle) of the birth mother, is included here (NAI, CCC, Co. Dublin, 1938).

224. In the northern sample, one male relative of the birth mother (3 per cent) stood trial for the concealment of birth of an illegitimate infant. In fact, he was also the birth mother's father and was charged with carnal knowledge of his daughter. If he is included in the category of infants' fathers charged then it brings the number of infants' fathers charged in the northern sample to three (8 per cent). If he is included in the male relatives charged category then the figure for male relatives charged in the northern sample is one (3 per cent) and the figure for infants' fathers charged is reduced to two (5 per cent).

225. NAI, Limerick City & County, Crown Files at Assizes, 1903.

226. Ibid.

227. Ibid.

228. PRONI, TYR1/2B/34, 1924.

229. *Northern Whig and Belfast Post*, 14 December 1933.

230. *Clare Champion*, 25 November 1933.

231. NAI, CCC, Dublin, 1943.

232. Ferriter, *Occasions of Sin*, p.4.

233. Ibid., p.6.

234. M. Luddy, *Prostitution and Irish Society 1800–1940* (Cambridge: Cambridge University Press, 2007), p.239.

CHAPTER FOUR

'I thought from her appearance that she was in the family way': Detecting Infanticide Cases in Ireland, 1900–50

In July 1923, Maggie R. was arrested on suspicion of murdering her un-named male infant. Maggie had given birth in Holles Street maternity hospital in Dublin. She had done her utmost to conceal the pregnancy from her family, telling them she needed hospital treatment for a tumour in her side. While in police custody, Maggie asked Sergeant Thomas Hughes if he thought she would 'have to go to gaol, or will I get out of it?' She was also concerned about the crime being reported in the press. 'Will this go in the papers[?]' she inquired, adding that she did not 'want to let [her] people at home know about it'.[1] Maggie R. was not the only defendant anxious about the consequences of her actions and the publicity that might ensue. When Superintendent James Kelly confronted Margaret R. about the discovery of the body of a newborn female infant in a rabbit burrow near her Co. Galway home in February 1942, she confessed immediately and asked him not to bring the case to court and to keep it out of the papers. Superintendent Kelly said that 'just then Margaret R., the accused, became weak and hysterical' and fainted.[2] Most women grew distressed when they were charged and taken into custody. When Margaret M. was charged with murdering her illegitimate infant in September 1910, she 'burst out crying' and said she was a disgrace to her brothers and sisters.[3] When K.F. was arrested and charged with concealing the birth of her illegitimate infant in Belfast in November 1914 she begged the police not to inform her parents of her arrest. She said that it would 'break their hearts and disgrace them for life'.[4] Similarly, when Sergeant Patrick O'Connor arrested Bridget C. in June 1940 in her employer's Co. Limerick home, she asked him where he was going to take her, adding that she hoped it will not be Tournafulla. Bridget was anxious to avoid seeing her family and members of the community she grew up in while she was in police custody. She told Sergeant O'Connor that she 'would go down through the ground with shame after this if [she] saw any of them again'. He noted that 'at this time she was crying and sobbing'.[5]

Many women were visibly upset when arrested; others attempted to bargain with the police or talk their way out of arrest. When Catherine C. was arrested in February 1924 on suspicion of murdering her infant daughter she attempted to bargain with Sergeant Thomas Connaill en route to the Garda Barracks at Raphoe, Co. Donegal. Sergeant Connaill reported that Catherine had said 'you can get me out of this if you want to. Do not be too hard on me.' She also tried to bribe Sergeant Connaill. Catherine allegedly said: 'I will give you a handful of money and so shall my people.' When her attempts at bargaining failed, Catherine reflected on her predicament out loud, saying, 'I suppose I will not be coming home again.'[6] M.C. was arrested in Belfast on 22 May 1924. She told the policeman who arrested her that she was feeling nervous. She asked him if she would get time and remarked that going in is the worst.[7] Many of the unwed women who feature in the trial records examined had done their utmost to conceal an unplanned pregnancy from friends, family and employers for months. Small wonder, then, that most were distraught on arrest. Not only had they endeavoured to conceal a crime, the murder of an infant, but they had also laboured to safeguard their own reputations and the reputations of their families, which would be tainted, both because of the woman's criminal actions and the 'illegitimate intercourse' in which she had partaken.[8]

DETECTING CASES OF INFANTICIDE INVOLVING UNMARRIED WOMEN

Nine hundred cases of murder, where the victims were aged one year or under, and concealment of birth were recorded as being known to the police in Ireland between 1900 and 1919. Such cases slightly increased in number after independence with 141 murder of infant cases and over 850 cases of concealment of birth being known to the gardaí between 1927 and 1950.[9] Many of these infants were born outside wedlock and were killed shortly after birth. In a large number of cases a suspect was never identified and the crime was not prosecuted. There was often no suspect in these cases and many more infanticides must have gone undetected during the first two decades of the twentieth century. We simply do not know what proportion of infanticide cases were brought to justice. At least two single women tried at the Central Criminal Court, Dublin, between 1922 and 1950 appear to have given birth secretly without assistance on several occasions and committed infanticide shortly after delivery each time without being detected. Two other women managed to escape the notice of the authorities several times. In May 1943 Kate O. admitted killing five illegitimate infants over the course of five or six years. She gave birth in her mother's house on each occasion and admitted killing each newborn baby apart from one infant, which, according to Kate, was stillborn.[10] Kate's crimes only came to light the fifth or sixth time she committed infanticide. In a 1928 Co. Sligo case, Garda John Leary said, in evidence, that 'in consequence of certain rumours [he] heard [he] went to see Anne B. in July' 1928. Anne B. was a neighbour who lived next to Anne H., an unmarried woman suspected of having killed and/or concealed the birth of an illegitimate infant. Following a conversation with Anne H.'s neighbour, Garda Leary questioned her and she admitted that she had killed two infants and concealed their births. While Anne's second pregnancy had clearly been talked about in the neighbourhood, her previous pregnancy may have gone unnoticed or her neighbours may not have brought it to police attention.[11] Gossip played an important role in the detection of infanticide in Ireland during the period under review. Often rumour and hearsay seems to have alerted the authorities to cases that might otherwise have gone undetected.

Yet many more cases were brought to trial. How did these cases come to light? What led to the arrest and trial of so many single women for the murder and concealment of birth of their illegitimate infants in Ireland during the first half of the twentieth century? This chapter examines the ways in which infanticide cases involving unmarried women came to police attention in Ireland during the first half of the twentieth century. Many suspected cases of infanticide at the time were investigated by the police because of 'information' they received from members of the public. A considerable number of investigations began even before a body was discovered. It is clear from an examination of these cases that the sexual behaviour of single women, particularly those living in tight-knit rural communities, was closely monitored. Members of the neighbourhoods and communities in which unmarried pregnant women lived frequently played a key role in alerting the police about suspected cases of infanticide. Within communities, employers, doctors and the relatives of unmarried women responded to suspected cases of infanticide and this chapter will explore the implications of infanticide for those outside the immediate family circle.

A Co. Tipperary case tried at the Central Criminal Court in February 1937 is, in many ways, a typical Irish infanticide case. It began, like so many other successful prosecutions, with rumours centring on an unmarried working-class woman in a small rural community. Margaret S. lived with her aunt in rural south Co. Tipperary. She was well known locally and seems to have been on familiar terms with the gardaí stationed in the area. On 11 October 1936 Garda Thomas Looney had a conversation with Margaret at her home. Margaret's appearance struck him at the time. She was, he noted, 'haggard looking and slim in appearance'.[12] Garda Looney met Margaret again three days later. She continued to deny that there was anything wrong with her. Garda Looney clearly suspected that Margaret had given birth and disposed of the infant's body even though he had no evidence to link Margaret to any such crime. In fact, the body of a deceased infant had yet to be discovered. Members of the tight-knit Co. Tipperary community, including the gardaí, must have noticed Margaret's changing physical appearance over the course of the previous few months. It may well have been remarked on by people in the area. Although Margaret had tried to conceal all signs of pregnancy, her weight gain had not gone unnoticed. Her next-door neighbour, Charles M., stated that Margaret had been 'bulky looking' in early October. When he next encountered her in mid-October she 'didn't look as bulky that day'.[13] In the summer of 1936, James N., the father of the deceased infant, noticed that Margaret was 'remarkably stout'.[14] Then, in mid-October, James noticed that Margaret 'had got slim' again.[15] The local gardaí, in the absence of a body, were surprisingly persistent in their inquiries. This persistence may reflect a determination on their part to tackle the problem of infanticide in 1930's Ireland. On 30 October Sergeant Malley approached Margaret and informed her that 'there were rumours that she had given birth to a child'.[16] Local gardaí may well have pressured Margaret into procuring a doctor's certificate to show that she had not been pregnant. In the evidence Margaret repeatedly stated that she 'intended getting a doctor's certificate to show the rumours were untrue'.[17] A considerable amount of pressure was brought to bear on Margaret. Having been approached by local gardaí on six occasions between 11 October and 31 October 1936, Margaret eventually admitted to burning her infant's body and concealing it in the fowl house.

The manner in which the Margaret S. case unfolded in Co. Tipperary in October 1936 was certainly not atypical. Many investigations into suspected cases of infanticide began before a body was found.

Margaret M. was arrested when she was participating in choir practice in her Co. Laois community in October 1928. A garda sergeant called Margaret out. He cautioned the anxious 19-year-old, having explained who he was and 'the nature of our business'. Margaret became very agitated. She protested, saying 'I did nothing, I did nothing', and then asked 'am I going to be took?' A body had not been located at the time of Margaret's arrest. Margaret was informed that 'certain rumours' had been circulating about her. The gardaí suggested that she visit the local doctor.[18] Margaret and her mother Mary were later charged with the murder of Margaret's unnamed newborn. Both mother and daughter pleaded guilty to concealment of birth and were sentenced to six months' imprisonment each.

RUMOURS AND WOMEN UNDER SURVEILLANCE

Ryan's study of newspaper coverage of infanticide cases in the Irish Free State for the years 1925 and 1926 has shown that 'based on their local knowledge, the Civic Guards seem to have played an active role in initiating investigations even before infant bodies were discovered'.[19] Cases in rural areas were, according to Ryan, often 'initiated by the suspicions of the local civic guards ... In each case, the Guards, aware that a local woman was pregnant, began investigating when it was apparent that no baby had arrived.'[20] Ryan's findings are affirmed here by close readings of over 300 infanticide trials over a fifty-year period. For instance, on 28 July 1943 in Co. Meath, Sergeant John Mahony interviewed 22-year-old Mary G. 'in connection with certain rumours' almost three weeks after she had given birth. Once again, an investigation into a suspected case of infanticide had not been prompted by the discovery of a body. Mary later showed Sergeant Mahony where she had hidden the infant's body. Mary had given birth unassisted in her uncle's backyard. She said she 'choked the child immediately after birth and put it into a ditch near where it was born'.[21] Once again we see that rumours circulating in rural Irish communities could instigate investigations which led to the arrest of women suspected of having given birth outside wedlock. In most cases, female suspects responded well to interrogation; once confronted by the authorities they were often quick to admit to the crime.

Sergeant Edmond O'Brien told the Limerick County Court that due to 'information received' he, along with another member of the RIC, went to Denis M.'s house in October 1901 and made a search of a manure heap.[22] They discovered the body of a newborn infant there and charged Denis's daughter Minnie M. with concealment of birth. Minnie admitted throwing the infant's body on the dung heap but insisted that she did not kill her baby. In this case the body of the deceased infant had been concealed for three weeks before the police began to make inquiries. Minnie's neighbours or co-workers may have alerted the police, or the RIC may have heard rumours that Minnie had been pregnant and decided to investigate the matter when it became clear that she did not have a baby, even though she was no longer visibly pregnant.

As D'Cruze has noted in relation to Victorian working women, 'patterns of work, consumption and social and cultural reproduction meant that one crossed and re-crossed one's neighbours' paths in the course of the working day or month'.[23] Like their nineteenth-century English counterparts, many of the defendants in the cases examined lived in rural areas where most people led a largely pedestrian existence. D'Cruze has argued that because people were routinely visible (and often audible) to each other both in small rural settlements and over-crowded urban areas, they moved across the grid of neighbourhood space under the regular observation of others.[24] This is also apparent in the trial records of Irish infanticide cases. Neighbours, co-workers, friends and kin clearly watched each other in rural Ireland. Gossip in Irish communities, as in the neighbourhoods D'Cruze studied, 'served to regulate behaviour and monitor the observance of norms of socia-bility and conduct'.[25] The police in many rural Irish communities seem to have been on the lookout for cases of infanticide. They, along with members of the communities they policed, appear to have kept unmarried working-class women, whose sexuality was seen to be lax, under close observation. The police pursued rumours about single preg-nant women and monitored their movements. While advice on coping with an unplanned pregnancy would not have been offered to single expectant mothers, the law enforcement authorities repeatedly showed that they were determined to hold women accountable for the crime of infanticide, particularly in rural Ireland. Unmarried working-class women were subject to forms of neighbourhood surveillance and gossip that did not apply to men.

On 6 June 1905 Sergeant William Atteridge 'made an information' before a Justice of the Peace in Co. Galway and obtained a warrant to enter and search the house where Maria O. lived with her brother John. Sergeant Atteridge said that at the time he had 'good reason to believe that [Maria] is about being or has been delivered of an illegitimate child'. He also said that he had reason to believe that her infant, 'if born may be unlawfully done away with'. He requested a warrant 'to enter the house of said Maria O. of K. and take therein such action as [he] may legally do in [his] capacity of constable to prevent or detect the commission of a crime'.[26] There is nothing in the depositions to indicate how Sergeant Atteridge knew that Maria was pregnant or why he suspected that she might kill her illegitimate infant. Rumours may have been circulating in the local area about Maria's pregnancy, or the sergeant may himself have noticed that she was heavily pregnant and suspected that she might take her baby's life. The manner in which this case was dealt with by the RIC indicates that infanticide was not uncommon in Ireland at the time and that the police may have, in some instances, tried to intervene to prevent the death of illegitimate newborns. The police seem to have thought that there was a strong possibility that unmarried, working-class women would commit infanticide as soon as they had given birth.

It is possible that the police, particularly in rural areas, would have had unmarried pregnant women under observation. They certainly seem to have been monitoring Margaret S. in south Co. Tipperary in the autumn of 1936. In the early 1930s, when the numbers of murder of infants and concealment of birth cases peaked in the Twenty-Six County state, a Co. Offaly garda was paying close attention to an unmarried 18-year-old woman. In his evidence, Garda John Lally said that he knew Bridget M., who was charged with the murder of her infant daughter in July 1933. He observed that 'for some time' prior to the date of her arrest she appeared 'as if she were pregnant'.[27] When he saw Bridget standing outside her house on 15 July 1933, he noticed that 'she looked pale and thin' and he began to ask her 'some questions relating to [her] condition'.[28] Bridget confessed quickly and showed him where she had buried her baby. In a report to the Carrigan Committee, NSPCC (National Society for the Prevention of Cruelty to Children) inspector Hannah Clarke claimed that the gardaí were 'now keeping an eye on girls in trouble to prevent infanticide'.[29] She stated that a sergeant in Maynooth 'had ten cases under observation recently'.[30] The Department of Justice may have asked the gardaí to monitor single pregnant women or it may have been an initiative in a particular area, especially if other cases in Co. Kildare or the surrounding counties had come to light at that time. Not only were guards monitoring the sexual behaviour of many young unmarried women, but the neighbours and other people with whom women charged with infanticide came into contact on a regular basis also observed their behaviour. It is apparent that while neighbours or acquaintances, on noticing that a single woman was pregnant, did not, in most instances, offer any advice or support, they were quite prepared to alert the police as soon as they suspected that the woman had given birth. In her deposition Catherine Kelly stated that her husband was 'cottier to James Watson' and she confirmed that she knew Bridget M., who stood trial for the murder of her infant child at the Donegal Winter Assizes in 1900.[31] Bridget was employed as a servant by Mr Watson and Catherine often came into contact with her. 'Sometime before May last [Catherine] noticed [Bridget] was apparently in the family way and [she] mentioned it to her.'[32] However, Bridget denied that she was pregnant. She left Mr Watson's on 12 May but told Catherine that she intended to return. According to Catherine, Bridget 'did not say why she was going further than that she was not well and was going home for some time to her people'.[33] When she returned on 22 July 1900 Catherine immediately noticed that 'there was a great change on her' and she questioned Bridget about the apparent change in her physical appearance.[34] Bridget 'said there was no change on her that she was as large as before she went away'.[35] She also told Catherine that she had had 'a power of trouble as her father had died since she went away'.[36] Bridget may have mentioned her father's death as a means of diverting Catherine's attention from her physical appearance or she may have hoped that Catherine might think that the grief she experienced following her father's death resulted in rapid weight loss. The body of Bridget's infant was eventually found in a stream near Letterkenny and the police seem to have had little difficulty in identifying their suspect, presumably because rumours had been circulating about her pregnancy in the townland of Swilly.

While women may have been particularly active as arbiters of other women's reputations, it is clear from the trial records that men were also involved in the surveillance of unmarried women in their neighbourhoods. Both men and women informed on unmarried pregnant women suspected of having harmed their infants. In a 1929 Co. Tipperary case, the infant's father informed the gardaí that the woman he had been keeping company with for a year and a half had given birth in a field on the way home from a dance and that the baby had been found dead.[37] It is not clear from the case files what motivated people to inform on single women suspected of having committed infanticide. In the Co. Tipperary case quoted here the infant's father may have been acting in his own self-interest, informing on his girlfriend to avoid being regarded as a suspect. While Catholic priests do not feature as informants in the cases examined, it is possible that some did notify the authorities about single women they suspected of being pregnant. However, priests would certainly have helped shape people's attitudes towards single mothers in this period, particularly from the 1920s onwards, when there was a renewed emphasis in sermons and pastorals on the sinfulness of sex outside marriage. Concern for infant life does not feature strongly in most cases where informants can be identified; instead, some seem to have been motivated to inform on a particular woman because of ongoing petty disputes with the woman's family; others sought to distance themselves from the defendant by reporting the case.

Many cases of infanticide were investigated by the police because of 'information' they received from members of the public. The quality of the 'information received' varied. Sometimes specific information about the location of an infant's body was provided. In other cases they seem to have been aware of rumours that had been in circulation about an unmarried woman in a particular locality.

In October 1917, Sergeant Coleman Folan, stationed at Balbriggan, Co. Dublin, received an anonymous letter. In his deposition he stated that 'in consequence [he] made certain inquiries'.[38] He questioned 24-year-old Annie T., her mother and her stepfather. Following his inquiries, Sergeant Folan obtained a written order from a magistrate to have Annie T. examined by a doctor. He also searched for the body of Annie's deceased infant. A constable found the body of Annie's infant son in the garden, fully immersed in water and mud. Annie and her mother were later charged with the murder of Annie's infant son. Rumours about Annie's pregnancy had clearly been circulating in Balbriggan. Annie had been working in the local mill prior to the birth of her son. Soon after the birth Annie and her mother visited a doctor. Annie's mother explained that her daughter had been prevented from returning to work 'on account of reports that she was pregnant or had a baby'.[39] They wanted Dr Fulham to give them a certificate stating that Annie had not been pregnant. Dr Fulham refused to provide a certificate without having examined Annie.

A Protestant clergyman seems to have alerted the police in a 1915 Co. Carlow case. Minnie E., an unmarried woman, and her grandmother Susan E. were both charged with having concealed the birth of Minnie's infant in June 1915. According to the Reverend Bradish, during the course of a conversation with 'the elder prisoner before the child was born', Susan E. threatened to kill her granddaughter's illegitimate infant.[40] The Reverend Bradish's suspicions were aroused when he saw Minnie and her grandmother at divine service in August 1915, more than a month after the baby was due. When he questioned them about the infant, 'Mrs E. said at first there was no child, but afterwards said that the child was dead-born.'[41] Minnie's grandmother had buried the infant's body in a plot in front of her house. According to the newspaper report, 'the remains were eventually exhumed when news of the birth reached the police'.[42] Sergeant R. Walker went to Susan E.'s house on 17 August 'acting on information received.'[43] The Reverend Bradish was the only other person mentioned in connection with the case and he may well have informed the police about his suspicions regarding two of his parishioners. Susan E. was rather careless in the way she handled the birth of her granddaughter's illegitimate infant. She expressed a strong sense of anger about Minnie's pregnancy during the course of a conversation with Bradish prior to the birth and even went as far as to threaten to take the baby's life. Even though the Reverend Bradish was clearly aware that Minnie was pregnant, it may not have occurred to her grandmother Susan that he would inquire about the infant after the birth. She may not have realised that the authorities would take such a strong interest in the fate of her granddaughter's illegitimate infant. However, the police in Co. Carlow followed up on the information they received about Minnie's illegitimate infant and both women were convicted of concealment of birth in December 1915.

Writing about the trial and execution of Sarah Dean in Chester in 1755, Dickinson and Sharpe noted how that case, among others, 'reveal[s] a world of gossip and rumour, in which the moral conduct and physical appearance of women were made a matter of comment among other women in the community'.[44] The records of infanticide cases in twentieth-century Ireland also suggest a world of gossip and rumour, with eyes watching the moral conduct and physical appearance of unmarried women. As McKenna has noted in her study of Irish nuns and Irish womanhood in the mid-twentieth century, women who became pregnant outside marriage 'were often excluded by a judgemental society'.[45] She has also drawn attention to the fact that local communities in Ireland could prove 'more effective than legislation at ostracizing individuals for behaviour deemed inappropriate'.[46] This is doubly apparent, to judge by the records of infanticide trials, in the first half of the twentieth century. McCarthy has referred to the ways in which gender ideology was imposed on Irish women in the 1920s. She has argued that this ideology was mediated through social structures such as the Catholic Church and has asserted that at a local level, neighbourhood gossip was often an effective way of monitoring women's behaviour.[47] McAvoy has argued that Irish women, and working-class women in particular, were exposed to scrutiny within small communities and that an informal system of neighbourhood surveillance policed women's behaviour, and in particular the sexual behaviour of young women.[48] That local communities monitored the behaviour of young women is clear in many of the cases quoted here. Many unmarried Irish women who became pregnant during the period would have been keenly aware that the people they worked for and their co-workers, neighbours and friends may have suspected that they were going to give birth, particularly during the later stages of pregnancy. Some women went to considerable lengths to avoid detection. Bridget B. may have left her local area in order to escape that kind of scrutiny. She was originally from Co. Galway but went to live in Limerick a few months before she gave birth in June 1935.[49] Mary G. tried to avoid detection by leaving the area where she resided with her family just before she was due to give birth in August 1907, returning to her parents' house after the birth.[50] She travelled to another part of Co. Donegal shortly before she was due to give birth and rented a room. She gave a false name in the house where she lodged and told the nurse who attended her that she was a married woman whose husband had deserted her. Several women in this sample gave birth in workhouse maternity wards. They often lied about their marital status when they were admitted to the institutions and gave false names. Perhaps by giving a false name they may have hoped that they would escape detection after being discharged, but this was not always possible and unmarried women who gave birth in workhouses in areas where they were not known seem to have been quite easily traced by police.

When gardaí questioned Margaret F. about the body of a newborn infant, she denied that she had given birth and insisted that the rumours circulating in the neighbourhood about her were untrue. She claimed that someone was telling lies about her. 'The talk of the people is something awful. I never had a child in my life.'[51] When Sergeant McAllister called to Bridget M.'s home to question her in August 1926 she denied having recently given birth and said that 'there were some people in Granard who would like to be talking about people who were not as bad as themselves'.[52] Bridget was eventually charged with murder,

conspiracy to murder and concealment of birth. In her study of infanticide cases in Upper Bavaria between 1848 and 1910, Schulte argued
that 'in many cases the thing that leads to the discovery of infanticide or
the exposure of the culprit is "talk" that has built up, a "rumour" that
has gotten around, or the "voice of public opinion" '.[53] This also seems
to have been the case in early-twentieth-century Ireland, particularly in
rural areas. Neighbours noted the moral conduct and the physical
appearance of unmarried women, and in many of the cases examined it
is clear that neighbours and employers often reported their suspicions
about young, unmarried pregnant women to the gardaí. McAvoy has
suggested that single women who were pregnant may have been
reported to the police, not because members of their community were
concerned about the fate of their vanished infants but because they may
have wanted to shame single pregnant women or to make examples of
them.[54] The treatment accorded to children born outside wedlock in
Ireland during the first half of the twentieth century would suggest that,
for the most part, people were less concerned with the fate of these
infants and more concerned with condemning unwed mothers.

Even when investigations began with the discovery of a body, gardaí seem to have been reliant on gossip and hearsay, about single
women who attempted to conceal their pregnancies, in their search for
suspects. Gossip was central to the investigation of infanticide. In April
1936 gardaí in Co. Sligo began investigating 'the discovery of the head
and neck of a child in the locality'.[55] It was not long before the gardaí
linked the infant's death with unmarried domestic servant Kate Anne
F. Once again rumours and gossip in small rural communities seem to
have given gardaí their lead and connected a single, working-class
woman with an illegitimate infant's death. Superintendent Devine told
Kate Anne that he 'had received certain information that she was the
mother of a child recently'.[56] Gardaí went to see Annie H. in her Co.
Sligo home in July 1928, three months after she had given birth
secretly and unassisted, 'in consequence of certain rumours'.[57] Annie
was later charged with the murder of her unnamed male infant. This
investigation also preceded the discovery of a body and was most likely
prompted by rumours circulating in the community.

VARIABLE RATES OF DETECTION

Ryan has suggested that there was a higher rate of detection of infanticide in rural areas than in large towns or cities. 'Based on their local

knowledge, the civic guards seem to have played an active role in initiating investigations even before infant bodies were discovered.'[58] Ryan's study of infanticide reports in the *Cork Examiner* in 1926 has shown that in three separate cases, investigations into the death of an infant began because the gardaí were aware that the woman in each case was pregnant, but realised that the expected infants had not appeared. Examination of the judicial records of infanticide cases involving single women tried at the Central Criminal Court between 1922 and 1950 shows that cities such as Dublin, Cork, Galway and Limerick account for only eighteen out of a total of 195 cases, indicating that reported infanticide was largely a rural phenomenon.[59] It may have been the case that rates of detection of infanticide were higher in rural areas because tight-knit communities observed the sexual behaviour of young women more closely than in the cities.

Unlike cases tried in southern Ireland, where investigations into suspected cases of infanticide were often initiated even before a body had been found, in Northern Ireland investigation of the crime of infanticide usually began when a body had been discovered, and when the relatives, employers or landladies of suspect single women reported the fact to the authorities. The phenomenon of local communities monitoring the behaviour of young women is less evident in the sample for Northern Ireland (perhaps because it was a more urbanised society).[60] In the vast majority of cases in Northern Ireland the discovery of a body of a newborn infant was reported to the police and only then an inquiry began. A 1933 Co. Down case is an exception in this regard. It highlights the fact that the sexual behaviour of young unmarried couples may have occasionally attracted the attention of the RUC (Royal Ulster Constabulary), particularly in rural Northern Ireland. The local police were aware that L.T. was pregnant and had given birth in September 1933. Soon after she returned to work, following the birth of her daughter, they began 'to make inquiries as to the whereabouts of the child and who was looking after it'.[61] This led to the arrest of the infant's father, M.M. The sergeant overseeing the case commented at length on M.M.'s relationship with L.T. in a report on the defendant's character which was compiled in January 1934. While it seems likely that most of the information contained in the report was based on interviews with L.T. following M.M.'s arrest, it is also evident that relationships between unmarried couples did not go unnoticed by the authorities in some areas.

More than half of the single women in the northern cases gave birth alone in their bedrooms in their employers' or parents' houses.[62] For the most part, the bodies of illegitimate infants were found in the bedrooms or grounds of the houses of the defendants' employer or parents. Many women were unable to leave their bedrooms after giving birth alone and a number of women concealed the bodies in suitcases or boxes in their rooms. The authorities were generally notified by the defendant's relatives, employer or landlady.

Although Ryan's research on infanticide cases in the Irish Free State has shown that there was a higher rate of detection of infanticide in rural areas in the Irish Free State than in large towns or cities, it is not clear if there was a marked disparity between the numbers of discovered infanticide cases in cities and in rural areas in Northern Ireland.[63] Overall figures for the numbers of infanticide cases that were known to the police are currently unavailable. However, nineteen out of the thirty-eight infanticide cases in the northern sample occurred in Belfast and nineteen cases occurred in small towns or rural areas.

DOCTORS AND THE DETECTION OF INFANTICIDE CASES

Mary Bridget B., a 22-year-old unmarried woman, was tried for the murder of an unnamed male infant at the Central Criminal Court in October 1944. She gave birth alone in her bedroom in June 1944. Mary Bridget's sister and mother only discovered that she had given birth the following day, when Mary Bridget asked her sister to send for a doctor 'because she was feeling weak and wanted a doctor as she had a baby'.[64] When Dr Anne Fitzgerald arrived at the family home on 18 June 1944, Mary Bridget's mother 'shut the door and said "this is an awful case Doctor. We have a very bad case here." [Dr Fitzgerald] asked what was wrong with the girl. The mother said "Oh now it's a bad case for you." [She] asked "is it a confinement case by any chance?" The mother replied "it's a confinement case and an awful one".'[65]

Cases of infanticide often came to light when a woman who chose to give birth alone subsequently required medical attention and had to send for a doctor. This is evident in the Mary Bridget B. case. Doctors were often the first people to come into contact with unmarried mothers who had committed infanticide. When they treated these women in their bedrooms they were often the first to enter what had, in effect, become a crime scene. Doctors were also often the first to attempt to find the baby's body. As soon as she reached Mary Bridget's bedroom Dr Fitzgerald 'took down the bedclothes that were over the accused in bed and [she] said [she] wanted to find the baby'.[66] Mary Bridget's mother then pointed to a suitcase on the bedroom floor. When Dr Fitzgerald opened the suitcase she 'found a bloodstained piece of brown paper covering a male child's body'.[67] Forty-two years previously, in September 1902, Dr Thomas Parr found the body of Catherine O.'s newborn infant 'wrapped in a window blind, under the hair-mattress of the bed'.[68] Doctors were also often the first to report a suspected case of infanticide to the police. Nurses also feature in the records of Irish infanticide trials. Like doctors, they too were involved at various stages of investigations into suspected cases of infanticide. In a number of infanticide cases a nurse, rather than a doctor, was the first person to treat an unmarried mother suspected of infanticide. In a 1938 Dublin case an identification parade was held at the Bridewell Garda station. Two nurses were asked to identify a woman they had treated some weeks previously. Both nurses identified Mary M., who had been a patient in St Kevin's hospital and in St Patrick's hospital. According to the nurses, Mary M. had had a baby boy with her at the time.

Doctors clearly played an important role in infanticide cases tried in Ireland during the first half of the twentieth century and were regularly called upon during the initial stages of investigations into suspected cases of infanticide, as they could easily establish whether a woman had recently given birth. In some cases doctors accompanied policemen to households where unmarried women were suspected of having recently given birth and subsequently killed their newborn infants or concealed the birth. Once a doctor had confirmed that the suspect had recently given birth, the police investigation could follow. Sergeant Atteridge obtained a warrant to search the house where Maria O. lived with her brother John in June 1905.[69] He was accompanied by a doctor when he went to investigate whether a crime had been committed. Dr O'Callaghan examined Maria O. with her consent and quickly concluded that she had recently given birth. Sergeant Atteridge then proceeded to search the house. In a 1933 Co. Limerick case an infant's body was found in the grounds of a mental hospital. Bridget M. was questioned two days later. When Sergeant Peter Higgins asked her if 'she had any objection to be examined by a medical doctor' she said 'no'.[70] In fact, Bridget's mother advised the gardaí to 'take her to a doctor and have finished with it'.[71] Following the medical examination Sergeant Higgins charged Bridget with murder and concealment of birth. As noted in Chapter 1, servants accounted for a large proportion of single women charged with infanticide in Ireland during the period under review. Servants' employers often notified the authorities if they suspected an unmarried employee was pregnant or if they discovered an infant's body on their premises.

THE EVIDENCE OF WOMEN CHARGED WITH INFANTICIDE

Unmarried women who committed infanticide during the first half of the twentieth century were not usually perceived as dangerous criminals. They were not regarded as posing a threat to society. Often physically and emotionally exhausted when they were apprehended, the women in the samples studied frequently said that they regretted their actions. A number of women expressed a sense of remorse and sorrow over the death of their infants in their statements. Following her arrest in Co. Armagh in April 1928, M.M. stated that she was not a bit worried about herself. She apologised immediately and said 'I deserve it all. It was living when it was born.'[72] When Mary Anne M. was cautioned by gardaí shortly after giving birth unassisted on 19 June 1927 she simply said 'I haven't a ha'sporth to say' and did not make a statement.[73] It is hardly surprising that Mary Anne, who had lost a lot of blood during labour (blood had dripped from the floor of the bedroom she occupied to the kitchen on the level beneath), had neither the energy or presence of mind to make a statement. In her evidence, Dr Annie Keogh said 'it is likely that defendant was in great physical and mental agony'.[74] When A.M. was cautioned by Sergeant John Park in the Belfast Union on 15 September 1931 she simply said 'I am sorry. I'm guilty.'[75] When Robert G. Shaw arrived at the house in Belfast where A.M. was employed as a nursemaid in July 1930 he explained who he was and he cautioned her. He informed her that 'she was likely to be charged with concealing the birth of her newly born male child'. A.M. responded by confessing to the crime immediately. She was recorded as saying 'I admit that sir. It is unfortunate. I am sorry for the trouble I have given. It was born at half past nine o'clock this morning.'[76] At the time A.M. was, according to Robert G. Shaw, very weak and very pale. He sent her to the Belfast Union Infirmary. She made no further statement. A.M.'s reaction is not atypical. Most women, when confronted by figures of authority, readily admitted to the crime; many expressed feelings of regret.

Nora C. said very little when she was arrested in March 1929 for the murder of her infant son. Nora responded to only one question put to her by Inspector J. O'Sullivan. When he asked her who killed 'the child found in the stable' Nora admitted that she was responsible for its death. She replied by saying 'myself. There was no earthly Christian there but myself. That's the truth. I can't do any more for ye.'[77]

The records of a small number of cases that went before the Court of Criminal Appeal in the South between 1922 and 1950 include the questions put to unmarried female defendants charged with the murder of their illegitimate infants, and the statements of a very small number of women tried at the Central Criminal Court, Dublin, in the same period were recorded in question-and-answer format, but there is no indication in most judicial files as to the manner in which female suspects were interrogated. In most cases, it is not possible to know to what extent women were responding to questions in their statements and to what extent they were telling their own narrative on their own terms. It is only possible to speculate as to what extent female suspects in the samples may have been telling the authorities what they thought they wanted to hear and whether they were conscious of the need to place their actions in a certain light as they made their statements. Some women may well have been aware of how their version of events would be received in the courtroom; others seem to have been almost completely unaware about the implications of what they stated in their evidence. A small number seem to have naïvely hoped that if they confessed to the police, the charges against them would be dropped. When a police sergeant went to S.W.'s Belfast home in September 1930 and questioned her about the body of a newborn infant that had been found nearby, she told him that she knew about and said 'Sure. There will be nothing about it if I tell you.'[78] There are a number of similar examples of such naïvety.

Single women charged with infanticide often broke down as soon as they were arrested and charged. When A.H. was cautioned in January 1932, the district inspector said that 'she merely turned pale and sat down and cried'.[79] Under cross-examination, Sergeant Hugh McKeon said that M.H. was 'excited' when he arrested her in a lodging house in Lurgan in March 1920 and that she sat on the bed crying.[80] Few women in this sample seem to have made sustained attempts to deny that they had given birth or to lie about their crime once they were apprehended. Even when they did lie about the circumstances surrounding the birth and death of their infants, most single women charged with infanticide seem to have broken down soon after being interrogated. Few seem to have thought of convincing lies to tell the authorities in advance of their arrest. This suggests that even if the women who feature in the trial records had planned to kill the infant from the outset, they had not considered the consequences of such actions; some simply may have wanted to dispose of the problem, the shame of having a baby outside wedlock, as quickly as possible. For instance, when Constable Henry asked L.M. if she was 'a Miss M.' she hesitated at first but then replied in the affirmative. When he inquired whether she had left the workhouse hospital that morning (28 May 1937) she said 'no' but following a short pause she said 'yes'.[81] When he asked L.M. where the baby was she told him a woman in Belfast was going to look after it and said that the woman had left the town by bus. L.M. claimed that she did not know the woman's address. The constable then recovered the keys to L.M.'s case and found her infant's body.

CONCLUSION

Close readings of over 300 individual case files have clearly demonstrated that in Ireland, and in rural Ireland in particular, the police pursued and investigated rumours about unmarried pregnant women. Infanticide was not uncommon during the first half of the twentieth century. The willingness of the police to initiate investigations before an infant's body had been found suggests that they were aware that there was a strong possibility that poor single women would commit infanticide soon after delivery.

The case studies explored in this chapter suggest that communities across Ireland felt they had the right to intervene and inform the authorities about unmarried women suspected of having killed an infant or concealed its birth. Sexual transgression was seriously frowned upon by most Irish people at this time. There seems to have been little sympathy for single women who became pregnant outside wedlock. Rural communities did not support such women; instead, they informed on them. In so doing they made clear their intolerance of such behaviour. In some cases there is evidence to suggest that inform- ants were motivated to report their suspicions about a single woman's pregnancy to the police because of long-standing grievances, disputes or petty rivalries with the woman herself or her extended family.

In many instances the police seem to have had detailed knowledge of the people living in the towns and villages they patrolled. Their level of knowledge of unmarried women's physical appearance points to a parochial, inward-looking society and suggests that in many rural communities the police had few serious crimes to pursue. The behaviour of poor unmarried women was closely monitored in many Irish communities. Poor unmarried men were not subject to same degree of scrutiny.

Gossip was an effective way of regulating the behaviour of unmarried women in this period. It is likely that many more infanticide cases would have gone undetected in the absence of gossip and rumour about unmarried expectant women in small towns and rural areas.

NOTES

1. National Archives of Ireland [hereafter NAI], Central Criminal Court [hereafter CCC], Co. Kildare, 1923.
2. NAI, CCC, Co. Galway, 1942.
3. NAI, Co. Limerick, Crown Files at Assizes, 1910.
4. Public Record Office of Northern Ireland [hereafter PRONI], BELF/1/1/2/45/7, 1914.
5. NAI, CCC, Co. Limerick, 1940.
6. NAI, CCC, Co. Donegal, 1924.
7. PRONI, BELF1/1/2/74/5, 1924.
8. *Irish Independent*, 16 February 1931.
9. I. O'Donnell, E. O'Sullivan and D. Healy (eds), *Crime and Punishment in Ireland 1922–2003: A Statistical Sourcebook* (Dublin: Institute of Public Administration, 2005), pp.2–11. Statistics are not currently available for Northern Ireland.
10. NAI, CCC, Co. Westmeath, 1943.
11. NAI, CCC, Co. Sligo, 1928.
12. NAI, CCC, Co. Tipperary, 1937.
13. Ibid.
14. Ibid.
15. Ibid.
16. Ibid.
17. Ibid.
18. NAI, CCC, Co. Leix, 1928.
19. L. Ryan, 'The Press, Police and Prosecution: Perspectives on Infanticide in the 1920s', in A. Hayes and D. Urquhart (eds), *Irish Women's History* (Dublin: Irish Academic Press, 2004), p.145.
20. Ibid.
21. NAI, CCC, Co. Meath, 1943.
22. NAI, Co. Limerick, Crown Files at Assizes, 1901–02.
23. S. D'Cruze, *Crimes of Outrage: Sex, Violence and Victorian Working Women* (London: Routledge, 1998), p.50.
24. Ibid., p.50.
25. Ibid., p.62.
26. NAI, Co. Galway, Crown Files at Assizes, 1905–06.
27. NAI, CCC, Co. Offaly, 1933.
28. Ibid.
29. NAI, Department of Justice, H247/41D, 90/4/8.
30. Ibid.
31. NAI, Co. Donegal, Crown Files at Assizes, 1900–02.
32. Ibid.
33. Ibid.
34. Ibid.
35. Ibid.
36. Ibid.
37. NAI, CCC, Co. Tipperary, 1929.
38. NAI, Crown Files at Commission, Leinster Winter Assizes, 1917.
39. Ibid.
40. *Nationalist and Leinster Times*, 11 September 1915.
41. Ibid.

42. *Nationalist and Leinster Times*, 21 August 1915.
43. Ibid.
44. J.R. Dickinson and J.A. Sharpe, 'Infanticide in Early Modern England: The Court of Great Sessions at Chester, 1650–1800', in M. Jackson (ed.), *Infanticide: Historical Perspectives on Child Murder and Concealment, 1550–2000* (Aldershot: Ashgate, 2002), p.46.
45. Y. McKenna, 'Embodied Ideals and Realities: Irish Nuns and Irish Womanhood, 1930s–1960s', *Éire Ireland*, 41, 1 (2006), p.43.
46. Ibid.
47. Á. McCarthy, 'Hearths, Bodies and Minds: Gender Ideology and Women's Committal to Enniscorthy Lunatic Asylum, 1916–25', in Hayes and Urquhart (eds), *Irish Women's History*, p.123.
48. S. McAvoy (Larmour), 'Aspects of the State and Female Sexuality in the Irish Free State, 1922–1949' (PhD thesis, University College, Cork, 1998), p.308.
49. NAI, CCC, Co. Limerick, 1935.
50. NAI, Co. Donegal, Crown Files at Assizes, 1906–08.
51. NAI, CCC, Co. Clare, 1930.
52. NAI, CCC, Co. Longford, 1926.
53. R. Schulte, *The Village in Court: Arson, Infanticide, and Poaching in the Court Records of Upper Bavaria, 1848–1910* (Cambridge: Cambridge University Press, 1994), p.111.
54. McAvoy (Larmour), 'Aspects of the State', p.308.
55. NAI, CCC, Co. Sligo, 1936.
56. Ibid.
57. NAI, CCC, Co. Sligo, 1928.
58. Ryan, 'Press, Police and Prosecution', p.145.
59. A total of fourteen cases in the Twenty-Six Counties sample occurred in Dublin city between 1922 and 1950. There were two cases in Cork city and two in Limerick city. No infanticide cases in this sample were discovered for Galway city.
60. Belfast cases account for 50 per cent of cases in this sample.
61. PRONI, HA 9/2/4, 1933.
62. Six women (15.7 per cent) in the northern sample gave birth in their parents' house and thirteen women (34.2 per cent) gave birth in their place of employment. Three women (7.8 per cent) gave birth in the house of a relative. Six women (15.7 per cent) gave birth in a house where they had a rented room. Four women (10.5 per cent) gave birth in a workhouse hospital. One woman (2.6 per cent) gave birth in the house where her fiancé's sister lived. This information was not recorded in five cases (13.1 per cent) in the northern sample.
63. Ryan, 'Press, Police and Prosecution', p.145.
64. NAI, CCC, Co. Leitrim, 1944.
65. Ibid.
66. Ibid.
67. Ibid.
68. NAI, Co. Louth, Leinster Winter Assizes, 1900–05.
69. NAI, Co. Galway, Crown Files at Assizes, 1905–06.
70. NAI, CCC Co. Limerick, 1933.
71. Ibid.
72. PRONI, ARM1/2D/16/6, 1928.
73. NAI, CCC, Co. Wexford, 1927.
74. Ibid.
75. PRONI, BELF/1/1/2/97/5, 1931.
76. PRONI, BELF/1/2/2/40/68, 1930.
77. NAI, CCC, Co. Cork, 1929.
78. PRONI, BELF/1/1/2/94/6, 1930.
79. PRONI, BELF/1/1/2/98/6, 1932.
80. PRONI, ARM1/2D/14/5, 1920.
81. PRONI, DOW/2B/44/5, 1937.

CHAPTER FIVE

'All girls in this country ... are amenable to the law, and must suffer for this crime': Sentencing in Irish Infanticide Cases

Once a suspect (or suspects) had been identified, charges were brought against those responsible for the infant's death. How did unmarried woman and, in some instances, their relatives, fare in the courtroom? What fate were defendants likely to meet? What kinds of sentences were handed down to women convicted of murder, manslaughter, infanticide or concealment of birth? Did their treatment change over time? A discussion of the ways in which infanticide cases involving unmarried women were dealt with in the Irish courts between 1900 and 1950 is central to this chapter. This chapter examines changes in sentencing patterns in infanticide cases involving single women over a fifty-year period. Sentencing patterns in southern Ireland after independence will be contrasted with sentences handed down to defendants in northern infanticide cases.

Unmarried defendants in infanticide cases were clearly anxious to avoid the shame and publicity associated with unmarried motherhood. Many women were aware that their arrest and trial would be reported in the local press and perhaps also in the national press. In a 1942 Co. Galway infanticide case, Margaret R. was charged with the murder of her infant. Gardaí found the baby's body in a rabbit burrow and soon afterwards Margaret confessed to the crime. She begged the superintendent who took her statement 'not [to] bring the case to court and [to] keep it out of the paper'.[1] According to the superintendent she then became 'weak and hysterical' and fainted.[2] Reports on the case were published in the *Connacht Tribune* but when Margaret was tried at Athenry district court the evidence was taken 'in camera' and the newspaper report featured little detail. In a 1934 Co. Clare case, Teresa C., a 17-year-old domestic servant, was charged with the murder of her unnamed female infant. When Teresa C. was questioned by gardaí in

November 1934 the first thing she said was 'will it be in the papers?'[3] She then proceeded to make a statement. The case was reported in great detail in the *Clare Champion*. When she was convicted of concealment of birth at the Central Criminal Court in December 1934 the heading in the *Clare Champion* read 'Clare girl before Central Criminal Court.'[4] Newspaper reports will be used to shed light on this aspect of the judicial process. This chapter will analyse the outcomes in infanticide cases and investigate whether single women charged with murder or concealment of birth were more likely to have been convicted or acquitted. Contrasting acquittal and conviction rates during the period and comparing the kinds of sentences handed down to single women convicted of the murder or concealment of birth of their illegitimate infants both before and after independence reveals legislative differences, North and South, from 1920 onwards, and divergences in terms of sentencing patterns.

In the Twenty-Six County state, women were generally charged with concealment of birth rather than murder if 'there was insufficient evidence to prove either murder or manslaughter' or in cases 'where post-mortem evidence was insufficient to sustain a murder or manslaughter charge, but where a clear attempt was made to secretly dispose of the body of an infant in order to hide the fact that its mother had given birth'.[5] This also seems to have been the practice prior to independence. If the birth mother and/or others were charged with concealment of birth only, the case was tried in the circuit court rather than in the Central Criminal Court. Women who stood trial at the Central Criminal Court between 1922 and 1950 were usually charged with both murder and concealment of birth. This meant that women could be convicted on a lesser charge of concealment of birth. Juries could also return a manslaughter verdict in cases where individuals stood trial for the murder of infants. From 1922 onwards women in the northern sample were convicted of infanticide. Women in the Twenty-Six Counties sample could be charged with and convicted of infanticide from 1949 onwards, although the first recorded instance in the southern sample of a woman convicted of infanticide was in February 1950 when Margaret R., charged with the murder of her unnamed female infant, pleaded guilty to infanticide. Her plea was accepted. Until 1949 the deliberate killing of a fully delivered infant was murder and carried a mandatory death penalty under Section 1 of the 1861 Offences Against the Person Act. However, only a small number of cases prosecuted in the Central Criminal Court during the period under review actually resulted in murder convictions. The death sentence passed on women convicted of the murder of their infants between 1922 and 1949 was always commuted, and few women convicted of the murder of their illegitimate infants served more than three years in prison. In the South, the passing of the Infanticide Bill in 1949 did not mark a significant change in the way that women convicted of the murder of their infants were dealt with. Rather, it spared the indicted woman, the judge, the jury and the government 'all the distress and worry of an unreal trial for murder followed by reprieve' and sanctioned existing practice.[6] As McAvoy has observed, 'it is clear that the introduction of infanticide legislation was not perceived as a priority issue by any Irish government prior to 1949.'[7] She has suggested that this low priority was due to the fact that contemporary legal practice had ensured that most infant murder prosecutions ended in lesser verdicts.

A change in legislation had been under discussion in the Department of Justice and in the Attorney General's office for some time before the law was changed in 1949. With the passing of the Infanticide Bill in 1949, a woman charged with infanticide was no longer considered fully responsible for her actions. It was assumed that she had been suffering from a disturbed or unbalanced state of mind at the time. Infanticide became a non-capital offence. In 1951 the Attorney General, C.F. Casey, could express his sympathy in the national press with the physical and mental trauma unmarried mothers experienced: 'those who have prosecuted or defended know that death has often been inflicted on the child by the anguished mother. No one knows the mental anguish of the unmarried mother in her terrible suffering. Her mind and judgement are unbalanced. Her world is indeed black.'[8] The English Infanticide Acts of 1922 and 1938 were also introduced in Northern Ireland, reducing infanticide to a non-capital offence.

THE PRE-TRIAL PROCESS

While some juries and members of the medical profession may have sympathized with unmarried mothers accused of infanticide, the police treated it as a very serious crime.[9] It is clear that the police often went to great lengths to prosecute women suspected of giving birth outside wedlock and of murdering their infants. Nonetheless, single women suspected of murdering their infants were dealt with differently to women or men charged with the murder of an adult. Unmarried women who committed infanticide during the first half of the twentieth century were not usually perceived as dangerous criminals; they were not seen as a threat to society. Unlike adult murder trials, cases involving young, unmarried women were often described in the press as 'painful',[10] 'pitiable'[11] or 'poignant.'[12] Some, in poor health after the ordeal of giving birth alone and unassisted, were viewed as vulnerable women. A number of defendants needed medical attention at the time of arrest. When gardaí involved in a 1926 Co. Limerick infanticide case first encountered the suspect she was at her employers' house and was 'not in a fit condition to be arrested or charged'.[13] Johanna had attempted suicide by cutting her throat with a razor. At the time she had an open wound on her neck. A guard was placed over Johanna prior to her transfer to hospital. She was later sent for trial at the Central Criminal Court. Limerick doctor Cecil Molony examined Bridget B. in the Legion of Mary hostel in the city between twenty-four and thirty-six hours after she had given birth unattended in a field some five miles outside Limerick city in June 1935. He was of the opinion that Bridget, who had been homeless for some time during the later stages of pregnancy, had 'suffered greatly both physically and mentally'.[14]

Those who stood trial at the Central Criminal Court in Dublin between 1922 and 1950 were first charged at district court level. For instance, Margaret R. was remanded in custody by the district justice to the Central Criminal Court in March 1942. The evidence was taken in camera at the Athenry District Court. While some defendants may have been released on bail before standing trial, others were refused bail. At the Wexford district court in April 1929, Mr O'Connor, solicitor for Catherine A., asked that the accused be allowed out on bail. He asserted that 'it was quite usual to have bail granted in a charge of infanticide or concealment of birth'.[15] Catherine A. was apparently in a 'very delicate state of health' at the time.[16] Mr O'Connor said that another week in prison in Waterford 'would be very injurious to her health'.[17] However, the district court judge refused to grant the application for bail and remarked that there 'was an increase in these awful cases'.[18]As previously noted, in the weeks, or even months leading up to trial, many defendants were assigned defence.

Defendants often underwent a medical examination in prison before standing trial. This was particularly important in cases where women had attempted suicide or threatened to take their lives, and in cases where defendants claimed to have become temporarily insane during and just after labour. The defendant's level of intelligence was often assessed and commented on. Some women were deemed to have been 'mental defectives'. 'Repeated pregnancy outside marriage', as Luddy has observed, 'was to become closely identified with mental deficiency.'[19] Only a small number of Central Criminal Court case files contain medical reports, mainly from the 1940s onwards. Medical officers usually commented on the prisoner's physical health, level of education and intelligence. Reports were usually more detailed if the prisoner was thought to have been mentally defective or if the woman had been suicidal. 21-year-old Mary C. stood trial for the murder of her unnamed male infant at the Central Criminal Court in June 1947. She had given birth in her mother's home in April 1947. Extracts from the medical officer's journal in Sligo Prison, where Mary was held before her trial, were forwarded to the presiding judge at the Central Criminal Court shortly before her trial. Mary had expressed the desire to take her own life and she was kept under close observation in prison. It is not known whether the medical officer's reports affected the outcome in the case.[20] Although Mary was convicted of the manslaughter of her infant she was released on entering into a recognizance of twenty pounds and agreeing to keep the peace. It is possible that Mary was dealt with leniently by the courts as a result of the mental distress she had experienced.

It is not clear to what extent infanticide trials attracted public interest in Ireland during the first half of the twentieth century. Attendance levels were not always commented upon in newspaper reports. The *Connacht Tribune* reported that when sisters Elizabeth and Rose E. were tried for the murder of Elizabeth's baby in January 1935 the district courthouse was crowded.[21] It is clear, however, that some trials attracted considerably more attention than others. In Northern Ireland particularly gruesome cases (such as the trial of A.H. in Belfast in January 1932 for concealing the births of four infants[22]), cases involving men (such as the M.M. trial in December 1933[23]) and a trial held in July 1928 where a young woman was sentenced to death[24] seem to have been well attended. Trials involving the suspicious deaths of infants born outside wedlock seem to have held a certain appeal; presumably some appeared out of the ordinary and involved unmarried women and men whose behaviour did not conform to the ideal. Many of those who attended may have known the defendants. In January 1932 a 31-year-old married woman was charged with the concealment of birth of four infants. The heading in the *Irish News* when the story broke read: 'Gruesome Discovery in Belfast. Infants' Bodies in Suitcase'.[25] When A.H. was brought to trial the *Belfast Telegraph* noted that 'there was keen interest at the Belfast Custody Court to-day' and that 'the court was crowded'.[26] Indeed, since 4 January when police first began to investigate the case there had been a high level of interest in the proceedings. According to the *Irish News*, 'the dramatic swoop by the police, and the shocking discovery which followed, caused a profound sensation in the district, and the house in which the suitcase was found was the object of many curious sightseers on Monday night'.[27] On 29 January 1932 the *Belfast Telegraph* published an article on the trial of A.H. with the heading 'Babes and Books. Strange Belfast Case'.[28] The heading referred to a hymnbook, the Bible and a copy of 'The Life of Christ' that were found in the suitcase along with the remains of four infants. The A.H. case was given much more coverage than most Irish infanticide cases and the *Belfast Telegraph* even published a photograph of the house where the bodies were discovered. This particular case may have received more coverage in the press than most trials because it involved the death of several infants over the course of several years. The defendant appeared outwardly religious yet her behaviour was disturbing and seemed to fly in the face of religious teachings. Similarly, in May 1931, when a father and daughter were charged with incest and infanticide, the *Belfast Telegraph* noted that 'the arrival of the accused at the petty sessions office, where the Court was held, attracted considerable attention owing to the rather unusual features of the case'.[29]

In July 1928 the Belfast *Irish News* provided extensive coverage of J.M.'s trial for the murder of her fifteen-month-old daughter. One report detailed the atmosphere in the courtroom, noting that 'there was suppressed excitement in Court when J.M., aged 24 years, a domestic servant and native of Larne, but who had been employed in Belfast for the last seven years, was put forward charged with the murder of her illegitimate child E.M.M'.[30] News of the verdict was published under the heading: 'Girl Murderer. Swoons on Being Sentenced to Death'.[31] When the death sentence was passed on the young woman, a 'distressing scene' unfolded in the courtroom in Belfast.[32] According to the *Irish News* reporter, 'there were deep sighs in all parts of the court' as Lord Justice Best adjusted the black cap 'and the loud moans and sobs of a woman were heard coming from the public gallery'.[33] Addressing J.M., Lord Justice Best assured her that the jury's recommendation for mercy would be sent forward 'at once and if possible acted upon immediately'.[34] However, he told her that he had a duty to perform and said he had no alternative but to perform it. 'I have now to pass upon you the dread sentence of the law', he explained.[35] She collapsed in the dock when Lord Justice Best assumed the black cap.[36] She was raised up by the warders and it was reported that 'while the closing words of the dread sentence were uttered [the] prisoner lay inertly in the arms of the prison officials with her head thrown backwards'.[37] She was due to be executed on 14 August 1928, but her sentence was commuted to ten years' penal servitude by the Governor of Northern Ireland. A letter written to a Member of Parliament by the secretary of the Belfast Women's Advisory Council in August 1928 drew attention to the sense of public outcry following the outcome of the J.M. case. Miss Montgomery stated that 'in common with the rest of the public my Council has been gravely disturbed by the fact that the Jury was forced to return a verdict of "wilful murder" and the Judge was forced to pronounce the death sentence on [J.M.]'.[38] If Miss Montgomery's letter is accurate, it seems that a certain proportion of Belfast's citizens were appalled by the verdict. No other woman in the northern sample had to undergo such a traumatic experience. As J.M.'s infant was fifteen months old at the time of death, her defence counsel was not able to plead that she was suffering from the effects of childbirth or was temporarily insane after self-delivery. Such arguments were more likely to have been accepted by juries in cases where the mother took her infant's life shortly after birth. While there may have been public interest in high-profile infanticide cases, such interest did not lead to debate on the economic circumstances or lack of provision for single mothers in Ireland, North or South. Indeed, the Belfast Women's Advisory Council does not seem to have realized that the Infanticide Act (1922) had been passed in Northern Ireland.[39]

'ONE EXAMPLE OF STERNNESS WOULD HAVE MORE EFFECT IN SUPPRESSING THE CRIME IN THIS COUNTRY, THAN ANY AMOUNT OF PIOUS EXHORTATION'

Juries in pre-independence Ireland appear to have been unwilling to convict young, single women charged with the murder of their illegitimate newborns. Writing to the Chief Secretary's office about Mary M. in October 1916, Lord Justice Ronan noted that 'this was one of these cases in which the Crown accepts a plea of guilty to concealment of birth although the facts disclose strong evidence of infanticide'.[40] 'It is difficult', he added, 'to conceive a more serious case of concealment of birth.'[41] Mary's infant's died as the result of a fracture to its skull. It appeared more than likely that Mary had inflicted force on her new-born infant's head. The judge's comments suggest that there were many similar cases and that during the first two decades of the twentieth century there was a reluctance to proceed with murder charges against a single woman suspected of having killed her infant, and a readiness instead to accept pleas of guilty to concealment of birth. Judges were extremely reluctant to sentence to death single women convicted of the murder of their infants. As Arnot has observed, in some instances, the criminal justice system operated to women's advantage.[42] For instance, Mr Justice Boyd said that passing the death sentence on Hannah A., who was convicted of the murder of her infant daughter in July 1910, was 'a most disagreeable thing for [him] to do'.[43] He told Hannah that he would forward 'a strong expression on [his] own part' along with the jury's recommendation for mercy and explained that it was necessary for him to pronounce the death sentence, even though he clearly did not wish to do so.[44] Hannah A.'s case had clearly generated a great deal of sympathy and concern. There seems to have been a strong sense of compassion towards Hannah, who was perceived as a vulnerable young woman – despite the fact that she was 36 years old and had been previously convicted of concealment of birth. Solicitor Edward Coffey sent a memorial to the Under-Secretary of Dublin Castle in July 1910 appealing for mercy for Hannah A. It was signed by the Mayor and High Sheriff of Limerick city as well as 'other prominent gentlemen of the City of Limerick, and district, praying mercy for the defendant'.[45] Later in the month the death sentence passed on Hannah was commuted to penal servitude for life. This was common practice at the time.

Juries often sympathized with the plight of unmarried women in infanticide cases. According to Edward Jacob of the Waterford Discharged Prisoner's Society, the jury in the Mary B. case 'were only too glad thus to find a door of escape for the poor young thing'.[46] They found her guilty of murder but noted that at the time Mary killed her infant son she was not responsible for her actions. One of the members of the grand jury who brought in true bills against Hannah K., a 20-year-old unmarried domestic servant who was charged with murdering her infant son in September 1900, was moved to write to the Lord Lieutenant about the case. He recalled how the feeling among the other members of the panel 'was so strong that it was a case for pity; that it was arranged to ask the judge if in believing the woman to be guilty we were justified in throwing out the bills, because of the sad circumstances'.[47] Colonel Robertson of Bray wrote to the Lord Lieutenant to express his views regarding the Hannah K. case. He felt that because infanticide was not prevalent in Ireland, Hannah should 'be tenderly dealt with'.[48] Infanticide was more prevalent than Colonel Robertson realized or cared to admit. In 1900 the police recorded that twenty infants aged one year had been murdered and in the same year thirty-eight concealment of birth cases were recorded by the police in Ireland. Those figures remained stable until 1919 (from 1920 onwards crime statistics were no longer compiled on an all-Ireland basis). While the number of murder of infant cases known to the gardaí decreased in the 1930s and 1940s, concealment of birth offences recorded as being known to the gardaí were higher for the Twenty-Six Counties from 1927 to 1950 than was the case from 1900 to 1919.

The sense of sympathy with Hannah K. even extended to the judge who tried the case. He told the jury that if they recommended Hannah to mercy they would have his support. Several commentators, as Ward has noted, 'attributed acquittals to the sympathy of judges and juries for fallen women and their sense (perhaps prompted by their own sexual guilt) of the injustice of sentencing the woman to death while her seducer went free'.[49] Mr Justice Gibson was reluctant to pass the death sentence on Hannah K. This may have been partly due to the fact that she had apparently been seduced and betrayed. He chose not to address her 'in the ordinary language a judge does to a criminal'.[50] He did not exhort her to repent for her crime because he said that he had 'no reason to doubt that you are, apart from this lamentable transaction, a good girl'.[51] When Kate B. was tried for the murder of her illegitimate infant in December 1900 the trial judge stated that 'on a case of this kind the feeling was always that they had not the real criminal before them, because the woman was less guilty than the father of the child'.[52] Kate was found not guilty and she was discharged. Mary D. stood trial for concealment of birth in July 1916. The trial judge stated that he 'sympathised with prisoner in her social distress and anguish and if he had before him the man who made her his victim, he would deal very strictly with him'.[53] Indeed, there are many other cases throughout the period where the sympathy of the judge and jury with women charged with the murder or concealment of birth of their newborn infants is strongly in evidence. This sense of sympathy is in evidence throughout the fifty year period under review. As Ferriter has observed in relation to infanticide cases in the 1920s and 1930s, 'there was a recognition of the human dilemma and stark loneliness of the single mother, and a frequent refusal by juries to convict women of infanticide or impose the death penalty or unduly harsh sentences'.[54]

Did attitudes towards the murder of newborn infants harden in post-independence Ireland? There seems to have been increased concern with sexual immorality in the immediate post-independence period, and in particular with rising illegitimacy rates and single mothers. Whyte has noted that in the years following the civil war, by far the most prominent topic in the published statements of Irish bishops was the apparent decline in sexual morality in the country.[55] It also featured regularly in the Irish press. Young women were regularly singled out for censure. Bishops and journalists attributed the apparent rise in the number of unmarried mothers to modernity, which had introduced the cinema, foreign films, dance halls and 'immoral' music to Ireland. Some judges certainly issued stern statements at infanticide trials in post-independence Ireland, perhaps warning unmarried Irish women that infanticide was a crime which was taken seriously by the authorities. Sentencing one woman for the concealment of birth of her illegitimate infant at the Cork Circuit Court in October 1928, Judge Kenny stated that 'it must be brought home to all girls in this country that they are amenable to the law, and must suffer for this crime'.[56] At a Central Criminal Court trial the previous year, senior state counsel said that the death penalty would have to be imposed in some cases because such cases were 'lamentably too frequent' in post-independence Ireland.[57] Mr Carrigan, KC, argued that 'until that was done in this country the massacre of the innocents would continue'.[58] He felt that 'one example of sternness would have more effect in suppressing the crime in this country, than any amount of pious exhortation'.[59] However, in his address to the jury, the trial judge described the case as a sad one. 'He expressed a view that a change in the law might be made in the Free State, so as to obviate a charge of wilful murder in a case such as the present.'[60] Juries in post-independence Ireland also appear to have been reluctant to convict young women of murder and they were often convicted on lesser charges of concealment of birth or manslaughter.[61] Writing to the Secretary of the Department of Justice in March 1941, a civil servant in the Attorney General's Office noted that juries 'will on the slightest excuse bring in a verdict of manslaughter or acquit'.[62] Mr Carrigan, KC, seems to have felt that juries generally sympathized with defendants in infanticide cases and often opted to convict women of concealment of birth rather than find them guilty of murder. When Mary L. was tried for the murder of her granddaughter's infant at the Central Criminal Court in December 1928 the prosecution insisted that there could be 'no half-way verdict of concealment of birth in this case. It must be one of wilful murder or not.'[63] But between 1922 and 1950 many Central Criminal Court juries returned a 'half-way verdict of concealment of birth'.[64] In Northern Ireland, from 1922 onwards most single women suspected of causing the deaths of their newborn infants were charged with infanticide, a non-capital offence. Despite differences in legislation, the experiences of unmarried pregnant women living on either side of the border were remarkably similar during the period under review.

'I STRONGLY RECOMMEND THE ACCUSED TO MERCY'

James M. Donovan's study of infanticide and juries in France between 1825 and 1913 has shown that juries were quite lenient towards those tried for the crime of infanticide. While the acquittal rate for infanticide in France was 'slightly higher than the average acquittal rate for all felonies', it rose sharply after 1891.[65] In the Irish context, as Maguire has put it, 'the leniency evident in the Irish adjudication of infanticide was manifest not in a high acquittal rate but in a high rate of convictions on lesser charges'.[66]

Information on the verdicts in cases of infanticide is available in seventy-one cases (74.7 per cent) in the pre-independence sample. Information relating to the verdict is available for 193 cases in the Central Criminal Court sample. As twelve of these cases involve individuals other than the birth mother, information on the verdict in cases where an unmarried mother was tried for the murder, manslaughter or concealment of birth of her illegitimate infant is available in 181 cases. Information on the outcome in cases where single women or their male partners were charged with murder, infanticide or the concealment of birth of an illegitimate infant is available in twenty-six cases in the northern sample (68.4 per cent).[67]

Ten women (14 per cent) in the pre-independence sample were acquitted. In addition, seven more cases were not proceeded with. Just under a quarter of defendants in the pre-independence cases examined were not convicted. Three defendants (12 per cent) out of a total of twenty-six where information on the verdict was sourced in the northern sample were acquitted. Of the birth mothers who stood trial in the Twenty-Six Counties sample, 15 per cent were acquitted, and the state entered *nolle prosequi* in 1.5 per cent of cases.[68]

Arnot and Usborne have noted that although European criminal justice systems have until more recently been controlled 'either entirely or almost entirely by men', it is not clear whether such male power has disadvantaged women.[69] 'Some recent work', according to Arnot and Usborne, 'suggests its effects could sometimes be contradictory.'[70] Male power within the criminal justice system in Ireland may not have disadvantaged women. Members of the legal profession were not entirely unsympathetic to single mothers in post-independence Ireland. In their closing speeches, judges usually acknowledged the fact that unmarried motherhood was a traumatic experience for the women involved. In some instances judges and members of the juries in infanticide cases openly sympathised with the plight of unmarried mothers. Defence lawyers often attempted to use the overwhelming sense of shame and disgrace experienced by unmarried mothers and their families to account for the actions of the women they defended and to arouse pity in the members of the jury. Defending Mary S., who was tried for the murder of her daughter's illegitimate infant in November 1938, Mr Hooper argued that there was 'no calm intention of taking away the life of the child' and that the 'the shame which was brought upon house-holders by the birth of an illegitimate child' was 'a natural thing to try to avoid'.[71] The jury in the Deborah S. case found it difficult to deliver a verdict. They informed the judge 'that their difficulty was as to the state of mind of the woman at the time of the act'.[72] Deborah S. gave birth on a mountainside in Co. Kerry in February 1929 without any assistance. The infant's body was found in a stream where it had been drowned. The doctor who carried out the post-mortem in the case stated that 'in the absence of any assistance it is possible but highly improbable for a mother to help herself by putting a hand on the child's throat. In moments of great pain it is possible the mother might do the improbable thing.'[73] Deborah S.'s defence argued that she felt so weak and frightened after giving birth alone that she put the child's body in a bush but could not explain how it had drowned. The jury in the Deborah S. case found the prisoner guilty but recommended her to mercy: 'In all the circumstances of the case, I strongly recommend the accused to mercy – the act was committed immediately after birth when the accused must have still been suffering from the pangs and subse-quent prostration of child-birth.'[74] Similarly, Catherine A.'s defence ar-gued that she was so traumatised by giving birth without any medical assistance that she could not be reasonably held responsible for her actions. The jury recommended Catherine A. to mercy 'having regard to the circumstances attending the birth of the child. The accused had no attention or assistance at the birth and the child appears to have been strangled by her a short time after the birth.'[75] Doctors often played a key role in infanticide cases. Their evidence in relation to the mental health of unmarried women who had given birth unassisted may have affected the verdict and sentencing in a number of cases. In his deposition Dr Sean Travers, who treated Catherine A., explained that while he had never seen an infant injured during birth in the way that Catherine's infant had been injured, he had 'heard and read of such cases'. He believed it was possible that the injuries to her infant were 'caused by the mother without knowing what she was doing'.[76] The professional opinion of men like Dr Travers was extremely important in infanticide cases. Doctors formulated arguments that linked child-birth to mental disturbance and, in doing so, they provided a loophole that made it easier for the government and the Governor General to commute the death sentence passed on women who were convicted of the murder of their newborn infants.

VERDICTS IN INFANTICIDE CASES

TABLE 1. VERDICTS IN INFANTICIDE CASES, 1900–21

Outcome	Number	Percentage
Guilty of murder	3	4.2
Guilty of manslaughter	8	11.2
Guilty of concealment of birth	38	53.5
Guilty but insane	2	2.8
No true bill	3	4.2
Nolle prosequi	3	4.2
Not guilty	10	14.0
Not proceeded with	1	1.4
Relative	3	4.2
Total	71	100

Single women charged with the murder of their infants in pre-independence Ireland were unlikely to have been convicted of murder. Only three single women were found guilty of the murder of their illegitimate infants (4.2 per cent) in Ireland between 1900 and 1921.[77] Eight women were found guilty of manslaughter (11.2 per cent). Most women were likely to have been convicted on the lesser charge of concealing the births of their infants. Thirty-eight women were found guilty of concealment of birth (53.5 per cent). Indeed, many of these women were also charged with the murder of their illegitimate newborns but in most cases they pleaded not guilty to murder but guilty to concealment of birth. Their pleas were almost always accepted. As Ward has

TABLE 2. VERDICTS IN INFANTICIDE CASES: TWENTY-SIX COUNTIES, 1922–50

Outcome	Number	Percentage
Guilty of murder	9	4.6
Guilty of murder but insane	3	1.5
Guilty of manslaughter	67	34.3
Guilty of concealment of birth	64	32.8
Guilty of infanticide	1	0.5
Guilty of abandonment	4	2.0
Guilty of neglect	1	0.5
Guilty of cruelty to a child	1	0.5
Guilty of attempted suicide	1	0.5
Nolle prosequi	3	1.5
Not applicable*	12	6.1
Unknown	2	1.0
Not guilty	27	13.8
Total	**195**	**100**

*Cases where the birth mother was not a defendant

noted in relation to nineteenth-century England, women who faced trial for killing newborn infants were usually only convicted of concealment of birth.[78] This pattern is also evident in post-independence Ireland where almost one third of unmarried birth mothers tried at the Central Criminal Court were convicted of concealment of birth.

Between 1922 and 1950 twelve women and one man were convicted of the murder of an illegitimate infant in the Twenty-Six County state. Of the twelve women convicted of murder, nine were the birth mothers (4.9 per cent).[79] Even when single women, their relatives or male partners were convicted of murder, juries invariably strongly recommended them to mercy. Judges always strongly supported such recommendations. In all cases the death sentence was commuted to penal servitude for life and one woman was transferred to the Dundrum Central Lunatic Asylum. Information on the length of time that women convicted of the murder of their infants served in prison is available for seven individuals, and the average length of time that these women served in prison was two years. Deborah S. spent six months in prison while Catherine A. served four years in prison. Guilty of murder convictions were returned in two northern cases between 1920 and 1950, one involving the infant's mother and the other involving the infant's father. There was no separate category of infanticide in southern Ireland until the passing of the Infanticide Bill in

1949, and thus the murder of infants under the age of one year was until then a capital offence. However, in many cases, single women charged with the murder of their illegitimate infants pleaded guilty to manslaughter or concealment of birth and these pleas were generally accepted.[80] Thus we find that the vast majority of single women charged with the murder of their illegitimate infants between 1922 and 1950 were convicted of manslaughter (34.3 per cent) or concealment of birth (32.8 per cent) rather than murder. Only one woman was convicted of infanticide. Margaret R. pleaded guilty to infanticide at her trial in February 1950. She was one of the few women in the post-independence sample who stood trial after the passing of the Infanticide Act in 1949. Of single women for whom information is available, 1.5 per cent were found 'guilty but insane'. Six women were convicted of lesser charges such as abandonment, cruelty and neglect; one woman was found not guilty of concealment of birth but guilty of attempted suicide following the birth of her illegitimate infant.[81] Eight women (30.7 per cent) in the northern sample were convicted of concealment of birth, and thirteen women (50 per cent) were found guilty of infanticide.

TABLE 3. VERDICTS IN INFANTICIDE CASES: NORTHERN IRELAND, 1920–50

Outcome	Number	Percentage
Guilty of murder	1	3.8
Guilty of infanticide	13	50
Guilty of concealment of birth	8	30.7
Acquitted	2	7.6
Not applicable*	2	7.6
Total	26	100

*Cases where the birth mother was not a defendant

Ward's research on infanticide in England between 1860 and 1938 has shown that unmarried women who killed their infants were 'only rarely found insane at trial'.[82] Kramar has stressed the fact that in twentieth-century Canada, few women convicted of concealment of birth were actually detained for lunacy. According to Kramar, 'the question of mental illness in these cases was, however, never really very strong since infanticide was understood as resulting from a fleeting mental condition precipitated by childbirth and/or lactation, somewhat akin to a state of inebriety'.[83] The situation was similar in Ireland during the first half of the twentieth century. A mere two women in the pre-independence sample, Mary B. and Susan M., were found guilty but insane at the time they committed the act of murder. Mary B. was sent to the Dundrum Criminal Lunatic Asylum. However, as she had suffered from temporary insanity, Dundrum may not have been a suitable place of detention for Mary B. The legal system was perhaps not accustomed to dealing with prisoners who had been affected by a fleeting form of insanity associated with childbirth. Edward Jacob of the Waterford Discharged Prisoners Society felt that 'from the time the girl [Mary B.] was admitted into Waterford Prison until the day she left, there was no sign of her mind being in anyway affected'.[84] Mary B. had spent over one year in Dundrum Criminal Lunatic Asylum when the Catholic Discharged Prisoners' Aid Society wrote to the Lord Lieutenant noting that she was 'of quite sound mind'.[85] Ten years later, in 1915, Susan M. was also found guilty but insane at the time she committed the deed, but she was not removed to the Dundrum Criminal Lunatic Asylum. Susan was clearly not considered to be in need of psychiatric treatment as she spent just over three months in Limerick Prison before being transferred to a convent in Dublin. Susan herself was apparently 'willing and anxious to go to the Home'; the nuns at Our Lady's Home, Henrietta Street, regarded her as 'a case to be reclaimed' and accepted her. The notes in Susan M.'s case file are not very detailed and it is unclear why she was deemed insane in the first place. The jury may have felt that she suffered from temporary insanity during childbirth. Susan stated that she did not remember what happened 'when [she] was confined of the baby'. She said that she was suffering from 'terrible pains' on 31 March 1915.

Although a number of women tried at the Central Criminal Court between 1922 and 1950 referred to the fact that they had experienced mental distress, and one woman claimed she was half mad following the birth of her infant, very few single women convicted of the murder, manslaughter or concealment of birth of their illegitimate infants were actually found insane. Between 1922 and 1950 a total of three single women for whom information is available (1.9 per cent) were deemed insane and considered unfit to plead. Annie C. was found insane and considered incapable of pleading in June 1930. She was sentenced to be detained in strict custody and taken care of 'until the pleasure of His Excellency the Governor General be made known concerning her'.[86] At her trial for the murder of her twin female infants in February 1930 Kate M. was found guilty but insane at the time. Margaret F. was charged with the murder of her illegitimate male infant in June 1943. The doctor who was called to Margaret's house after she had given birth said that she was 'slow witted', and the medical officer who examined Margaret in Sligo Prison was of the opinion that she was mentally defective.[87] Margaret was found insane and ordered to be detained in strict custody until the pleasure of the government be made known concerning her. Elizabeth D. was sentenced to death, but the sentence was later commuted to penal servitude for life. She may later have been deemed insane and in need of psychiatric care as she was transferred to Dundrum Asylum in July 1926. As detailed medical reports do not exist for these individuals, it is not known how their insanity manifested itself. None of the single women convicted in the northern sample were deemed insane.

SENTENCING IN INFANTICIDE CASES

Information on the sentence in cases of the murder, manslaughter or concealment of birth of infants is available for a total of sixty-one cases in the pre-independence sample (64 per cent of the sample). Of the women convicted of murder, manslaughter or concealment of birth in this sample, 25 per cent were incarcerated in prisons.[88] The length of time women were sentenced to serve in prison ranged from one month to eighteen months. Two women convicted of the murder of their illegitimate infants were sentenced to death. In both cases their sentences were reduced to penal servitude for life; in reality few women served more than three years in prison. Two more women in the pre-independence sample were convicted of murder but both were deemed insane and were sent to institutions. However, almost 50 per cent of women convicted of the manslaughter or concealment of birth of their illegitimate infants in the pre-independence sample received non-custodial sentences.[89] They paid a recognizance and agreed to come up for sentencing if called upon, and to keep the peace and be of good behaviour for a certain length of time. The evidence suggests that unmarried women were dealt with more leniently by the courts in pre-independence Ireland. In the post-independence period, single women convicted of the manslaughter or concealment of birth of an infant were more likely to have been incarcerated in convents.

A small proportion of defendants such as Mary G., who was merely detained for a day, having been convicted of concealing the birth of her illegitimate infant, appear to have received particularly lenient sentences. However, Mary was discharged following her trial at the Donegal Spring Assizes of 1903, presumably because she had already spent a number of weeks, or perhaps even months, in custody awaiting

TABLE 4. SENTENCING IN INFANTICIDE CASES, 1900–21

Outcome	Number	Percentage
Sentenced to death	2	3.9
Prison	15	29.4
Recognizance	24	47
Dundrum Asylum	1	1.9
Discharged	7	13.7
Salvation Army Home	1	1.9
Convent	1	1.9
Total	51	100

trial. In fact, a number of women convicted of concealing the births of their illegitimate infants between 1900 and 1921 were discharged following their trials, particularly if they had been held in prison awaiting trial. Mary D. had spent over three months in prison before she was tried for concealing the birth of her illegitimate infant in July 1916, and although she was convicted she was released after her trial. The judge said that as she had been held in prison since April 1916 he felt that she had 'suffered punishment quite adequate and sufficient for her case and he ordered her to be released'.[90]

Single women convicted of infanticide or concealment of birth in Northern Ireland between 1920 and 1950 were dealt with quite leniently by the courts. Five women in the northern sample were sentenced to terms of imprisonment ranging from six weeks to nine months. The average length of time women in this sample were sentenced to serve in prison was four-and-a-half months. Eleven women convicted of infanticide or concealment of birth in this sample were released on payment of a recognizance and agreeing to keep the peace and be of good behaviour for a specified period of time. In the North this often meant entering into a recognizance of ten pounds and agreeing 'to keep the peace' for twelve months from the sentencing date.

'HER MOTHER'S HOME IS THE BEST HOME FOR HER': CONVENTS AS PLACE OF DETENTION

When Kate C. was convicted of concealment of birth in December 1915 the trial judge told her mother, who was in attendance in court, to 'take her away and look after her; no good would come of my sending her to gaol'.[91] Ellen O. pleaded guilty to concealment of birth in December 1914.

The judge said that he 'would not impose any punishment on [her] as he thought she had suffered enough'.[92] However, according to the barrister who prosecuted, the prison chaplain was anxious to have Ellen sent to a home. The chaplain presumably felt that Ellen was in need of spiritual guidance which would be provided by nuns in a convent. The judge seems to have been opposed to sending Ellen to a convent and stated that while she could 'go to one if she likes', 'her mother's home is the best home for her'.[93] Judges who tried infanticide cases in the Twenty-Six Counties from 1922 to 1950 appear to have felt that convents, or the Bethany Home in the case of Protestant women, were the most appropriate places for unmarried women convicted of concealment of birth. Dublin's Bethany Home operated from 1922 until 1972. Members of the home's nursing staff were expected to be evangelical missionaries.[94] The Bethany Home frequently served as a place of detention for non-Catholic women who had been convicted of various crimes, including infanticide. By the twentieth century a considerable number of convents run by various Catholic religious orders admitted prostitutes and unmarried mothers, along with women who had been convicted of the manslaughter or concealment of birth of their illegitimate infants. As Luddy has observed, 'while prostitutes still entered these institutions, it is likely that unmarried mothers now joined them in greater numbers'.[95] Only one woman convicted of the murder of her illegitimate infant in the pre-independence sample 'agreed' to enter a convent as part of her recognizance agreement. Susan M. was convicted of murder at the Limerick Assizes in 1915 but the jury felt that she was insane at the time she committed the deed. It would appear from the documents in her file that she was discharged upon payment of a recognizance and once she had agreed to enter a convent. In July 1915 the superioress of Our Lady's Home, Henrietta Street, Dublin, wrote to the court authorities about Susan M. She stated that Susan was 'a case to be reclaimed' and said that they were willing to admit her to the convent.[96] One woman was sent to the Salvation Army Home in Belfast in 1915. Judging by this sample, it would appear that, overall, sentences for unmarried women convicted of concealment of birth in Ireland between 1900 and 1921 were somewhat less harsh than they were to be in the southern state in the decades after independence. Sentences for concealment of birth in Ireland in the years 1900 and 1921 were similar to sentencing patterns for the same offence in Britain during the first half of the twentieth century and to those in Northern Ireland between 1921 and 1950. They differed somewhat, as we shall see, from sentencing patterns in the Twenty-Six County state after 1922.

A much larger proportion of unmarried women convicted of the manslaughter or concealment of birth of their illegitimate infants 'agreed' to serve their sentences in convents in post-independence Ireland. There was, as Luddy has noted, 'absolutely no legal basis for allowing these women to spend their sentences in convents'.[97] However, few women seem to have been aware of their rights. Single women who were thus incarcerated in convents had no right of petition to the Minster for Justice. By contrast, this was a right that women who served their sentences in prison up to 1921 had enjoyed and, judging by the convict reference files that have survived, many women made use of this right and attempted to have their sentences reduced by petitioning the Lord Lieutenant.

Prior to independence, convents were not generally used as substitutes for prison for unmarried women convicted of manslaughter or concealment of birth. Convents do not seem to have been widely used in Northern Ireland either. Convents were, however, occasionally used as rehabilitation centres for women convicted of murder, manslaughter or concealment of birth between 1900 and 1921, following their release from prison. At least one woman in the pre-independence sample spent some time in a convent following her release from prison in October 1906. Edward Jacob of the Waterford Prisoners' Aid Society felt that Mary B. should go to the Good Shepherd Convent in Waterford for several months if she was released from the Dundrum Asylum. Jacob had clearly helped to place a number of women who had served time in prison under the care of the Good Shepherd sisters. Jacob was keen to see Mary 'restored to the path of virtue', and he, like many others, may have felt that an institution run by nuns would have been the most appropriate place for a 'fallen' woman.[98]

A minority of single women (15.8 per cent) convicted of manslaughter or concealment of birth in the Central Criminal Court, Dublin, served their sentences in prison.[99] Of all single women convicted of concealment of birth or manslaughter in the Twenty-Six County state between 1922 and 1950, 49 per cent were detained in convents rather than in prisons. McAvoy has commented on the development of the practice of suspending prison sentences following manslaughter convictions, once the women in question agreed to enter a Magdalen asylum for 'a period equivalent to the length of the proposed sentence'.[100] However, it would appear that the length of time women 'agreed' to serve in a Magdalen asylum sometimes exceeded the length of time they would have spent in prison. For instance, Mary C., tried at the Central Criminal Court

in November 1943, pleaded not guilty to murder but guilty to concealment of birth and was sentenced to two years' imprisonment with
hard labour. This sentence was suspended when Mary C. agreed to
enter High Park Convent, Whitehall, Dublin, for a period of three
years. In a 1927 Co. Kerry case, Nora O'C. was charged with the
murder of her infant, Lizzie O'C., on 7 April 1927. She too pleaded not
guilty to murder but guilty to the charge of manslaughter. Her
six-month prison sentence was suspended on condition that she paid
ten pounds as a guarantee that she would keep the peace for two years
and that she go to High Park Convent and 'remain there until the
Superior consents to her discharge'.[101]

TABLE 5. SENTENCING IN INFANTICIDE CASES: TWENTY-SIX COUNTIES, 1922–50

Sentence	Number	Percentage
Sentenced to death	9	5.9
Prison	24	15.8
Convent	74	49.0
Insane*	3	1.9
Recognizance	27	17.8
Recognizance and marriage	6	3.9
Discharged	4	2.6
Bethany Home	4	2.6
Total	151	100

*All three women were ordered to be detained in strict custody and taken care of until the
pleasure of His Excellency the Governor General be made known concerning them.

In post-independence Ireland, court decisions in terms of sentencing
appear to have been affected by the gender, age and marital status of
defendants. Single women who had given birth and were suspected of
having killed their illegitimate newborns seem to have been regarded as
sexually transgressive and were, therefore, punished in a particular way.
McAvoy has suggested that convents may have been the 'only available
alternative to prison in cases in which the convicted girls were destitute
and could not be bound over to keep the peace and return to the care of
their families'.[102] However, she has also argued that the practice of con-
fining women convicted of the manslaughter or concealment of birth of
their infants in convents may have been 'motivated by contemporary
thinking on the possibility of penance, reform and redemption of women
whose sexual behaviour was considered unacceptable, more than

concern about punishment for killing or the treatment of "illness" '.[103] Maguire has also noted that 'court justices shared the hierarchy's concern for the rehabilitation of convicted women, and many of the sentences handed down to female defendants aimed less at punishing crimes than at rehabilitating moral lapses'.[104] Such explanations are plausible, given the socio-moral climate of post-independence Ireland. The fact that some women convicted of the manslaughter or concealment of birth of their illegitimate infants were released upon their marriage to the father of the deceased infant suggested that there was perhaps more concern with containing women's sexuality within marriage than with the deaths of illegitimate infants.

Gender-based assumptions about appropriate sexual behaviour, morality and respectability did not apply to Irish men in the same way that they applied to Irish women. For instance, brother and sister Martin and Mary Anne D. were both found guilty of concealing the birth of Mary Anne's illegitimate female infant in March 1936. Martin D. was discharged on entering into a recognizance of twenty-five pounds, whereas his sister Mary Anne was sentenced to spend two years at Henrietta Street Convent in Dublin. However, not all male defendants were treated so leniently. John L. and Margaret S. were charged with the murder of their illegitimate infant in June 1928.[105] John L. was sentenced to three years' imprisonment for the manslaughter of his illegitimate infant while *nolle prosequi* was entered in the case against the infant's mother, Margaret S. Mr Carrigan, who prosecuted, said that 'she was not in a condition to realise what was happening at the time'. This may have been due to the fact that, as Maguire has noted, John L. failed to provide adequately for his girlfriend's confinement; she was homeless and gave birth in a field in Co. Tipperary in June 1928.[106] Mr Carrigan seems to have sympathised to some extent with domestic servant Margaret S.'s situation. He said that 'if legislators acted rightly they would pass a law for making amenable men responsible in cases where the unfortunate children were born in such circumstances'.[107] John L. had provided Margaret with very little support. She had been reduced to living in an open field and sleeping in a ditch for some time prior to the birth. John L. brought her some food each day. In his statement he admitted that he had left the infant to die outdoors and buried the body afterwards.[108]

Detention in a religious-run institution may have been regarded by members of the judiciary and others who came into contact with unmarried women convicted of manslaughter or concealment of birth as less harsh than a term of imprisonment. At a Central Criminal Court trial in 1930, Hettie Walker, secretary of the Bethany Home, referred to a term in the home as a lenient course of action. She stated that 'in the event of His Lordship taking a lenient course the accused would be admitted to the home and kept there for twelve months'.[109] The judge agreed to send Ethel D. to the Bethany Home for at least twelve months.

In post-independence Ireland women were occasionally held in Magdalen convents even before they were tried for the murder of their infants. In July 1938 Sr Frances Eucharia Greer agreed to admit Bridget D. into the institution run by her order in Cork prior to her trial at the Central Criminal Court: 'Though we do not as a rule like to take these girls before the case is tried we will make an exception of her on the condition we will not be held responsible if she escapes. I believe there is little to fear on that score. I only mention it.'[110] On 1 December 1938 Bridget D. was found guilty of manslaughter and was ordered to serve her sentence in the convent in which she had been held before her trial. After independence, single women who had been pregnant more than once were more likely to receive prison sentences than be sent to convents. Seven women who had given birth more than once and were convicted of the murder, manslaughter or concealment of birth of their illegitimate infants were given prison sentences. Two of these women were sentenced to death but the sentences were commuted to penal servitude for life. Between 1922 and 1950 just four of nineteen women who had given birth more than once were sentenced to spend time in convents rather than in prisons. As Luddy has noted, in Ireland 'the state and the Church identified unmarried mothers as belonging to one of the following categories: those who were redeemable and those who were not'.[111] Unmarried mothers who had been pregnant more than once may have been regarded as 'less hopeful cases' and less amenable to reform and religious influence than younger, less sexually experienced single women. Widows were also less likely to serve their sentences in a convent rather than in prison. As the widows in this sample were older than most of the unmarried women who stood trial during the period under review, and as women who had been married, they may have been regarded as less amenable to reform and religious instruction in a convent. One woman was temporarily detained in a convent after her trial. Teresa C. pleaded guilty to concealment of birth at the Central Criminal Court and was allowed out on bail in December 1934 on condition that she reside in a convent pending her marriage to the father of her deceased infant.[112]

Similarly, some women charged with infanticide or concealment of birth in Northern Ireland were held in religious homes or institutions both before and during their trials. A.H. was sent from the Belfast Police Court to the Salvation Army Home in the city in February 1932. She spent a week there while on remand. According to the records of the home, 'immorality' was the cause of her fall. Her conduct was good while she was in the home but she did not profess 'to be saved'. It was noted that she did not have a drink habit and had not been in prison before.[113]

Although 49 per cent of women convicted of manslaughter or concealment of birth in the southern sample served their sentences in convents, little is known about their fate post-trial. However, a 1938 Cork case and a 1925 Co. Tyrone case shed some light on the manner in which unmarried women convicted of manslaughter or concealment of birth were treated. On 1 December 1938 Bridget D. was found guilty of manslaughter and was ordered to serve her sentence in St Vincent's Convent in Cork. In a letter to the county registrar at the Central Criminal Court, Sr Frances Greer stated that the nuns would 'do [their] best to keep her in safety even after her time has expired'.[114] It is evident from Sr Greer's letters to the county registrar that religious-run institutions were willing, even anxious, to keep a convicted woman in their care even after her sentence had expired, and that the state was aware of this practice. In such instances, nuns may have been motivated to prolong their detention in order to prevent single women who had been sexually active from 'sinning' again in the outside world. The county registrar expressed his gratitude to Sr Greer for agreeing to take Bridget D. 'for a year or more, if necessary',[115] even though she had only been sentenced to one year in the home. R.G., aged 20, was charged with killing her female infant in Co. Tyrone in November 1925. She pleaded guilty to infanticide. Although R.G. was sentenced to nine months' imprisonment with hard labour she was allowed out 'having first entered into recognizance in open court in the sum of twenty pounds that she will keep the peace and be of good behaviour ... for ... two years and will remain in the Good Shepherd Convent Londonderry for that period (two years)'.[116] In March 1926 the Good Shepherd Convent in Derry agreed to admit R.G. They had been contacted by a Mrs Lavery. The Mother Superior, who had experience of dealing with similar cases in Cork, wrote to Lavery expressing the hope that R.G. 'will get a long term with us, short terms do little good, as you know'.[117] She also noted that while she was in Cork, female offenders in the convent 'were very good'[118] and stated that some 'stayed long after their time was up and may be still there!!'.[119] Finnegan's study of Magdalen asylums run by the Good Shepherd order in Ireland has shown that order encouraged inmates to remain in the institutions for long periods of time.[120] It is apparent from the contents of the Good Shepherd nun's letter in this particular case that she was also keen for the women sent there by the courts to remain after their sentences had expired.

Many women may thus have been illegally detained in convents and held there after their sentences had expired. However, as the records of convents are currently inaccessible, it is impossible to know how long the women who served their sentences in Magdalen asylums actually spent in those institutions, particularly when their release was at the discretion of the nuns who ran the convent laundries. From the available records it would appear that once the state handed over custody of convicted women to the convents it was the religious orders who determined the women's fates, including – crucially – the length they spent in detention. As Luddy has noted 'care must be taken when generalising about how these institutions operated from the 1920s onwards. The general popular understanding is that Magdalen asylums became institutions of confinement; however, until we gain access to the records this is a view that must be treated with caution.'[121] But some women may have been allowed out of the convents before they had served the full term of their sentences. For instance, in June 1942 Máire C. was allowed to return home having served only one year of a three-year sentence in the Henrietta Street Convent. The circumstances under which Máire was released were exceptional, however, as her father was suffering from advanced cancer of the throat and had requested to see his daughter. From the available evidence it is not possible to know how often an early release occurred during the period under review. As McAvoy has noted, while probation officer Elizabeth Carroll is mentioned in the records of several infanticide cases, it is unclear from the files how closely she or other probation officers were involved with women who agreed to obey the rules of a particular convent rather than serve a sentence in prison. In March 1944, 22-year-old Mary G. was granted permission to leave the Henrietta Street Convent in Dublin for a number of days to attend her uncle's funeral in Co. Meath.[122] Mary had been convicted of the manslaughter of her infant daughter and sentenced to spend eighteen months in the convent.

As McAvoy has observed, 'there was no statutory basis for using convents to detain women convicted of criminal offences. A 1942 Department of Justice memo warned that it was a "makeshift practice" and that "there are no positive means of compelling the offender to remain in the convent if at any time she chooses to leave." '[123] However, it would appear that few women detained in these institutions attempted to leave or were aware of the law. Only two women of the seventy-four women detained in convents in the South objected to serving their sentences in religious institutions. This figure may be higher as it is, of course, possible that other women objected to serving their sentences in convents, but that a written record of their protests was never compiled. Nora H., whose case was mentioned in Chapter 3, 'agreed' to serve her two-year sentence in a convent run by the Sisters of Charity in Donnybrook when she was convicted in June 1931. Less than a year later, the Mother Superioress wrote to the registrar at Green Street Court to inform him that Nora H. was extremely troublesome and had to be 'kept apart from the other inmates of the institution'.[124] She had apparently endangered the life of another inmate on more than one occasion. The Mother Superioress requested that she be removed without delay. Nora was later transferred to prison and ordered to serve two years with hard labour. Presumably Nora was ordered to serve two years in prison even though she had already spent almost a year in the Donnybrook convent because she had broken the terms of the agreement. The hard labour may have been added as an additional punishment.

A Co. Dublin cases highlighted the discrepancy in the manner in which prisoners and women detained in convents were treated. In September 1938 Margaret M. was convicted of the manslaughter of her newborn infant; she undertook to spend two years in St Patrick's Refuge in Dun Laoghaire. Margaret's uncle, Laurence B., pleaded guilty to concealment of birth and was sentenced to six months' imprisonment. Laurence petitioned the Minister for Justice from prison and was released, having only served one month of a six-month sentence. Margaret became extremely distressed on learning that her uncle had secured early release from prison while she had to spend two years in a convent. It seems that she became so distressed that she had to be transferred from the convent to Grangegorman Mental Home. Following her uncle's early release from prison, Margaret M. requested that she be allowed to serve her sentence in prison rather than in the convent where she was held following her conviction. As McAvoy has noted, 'this may have arisen from her uncle's advice and from the fact that the prison sentence was one year long, but the term of detention in a convent two years'.[125]

Most unmarried women incarcerated in convents would probably not have been aware that they were deprived of rights which ordinary prisoners enjoyed, such as the right to petition the Minister of Justice for early release. Petitions for a reduction in length of sentence seem to have had a high chance of success. In a 1942 Co. Waterford case, a woman detained in Mountjoy Prison seems to have successfully petitioned the Minister of Justice for early release. Nora M., a married woman, was convicted of the manslaughter of her daughter's illegitimate infant and sentenced to serve nine months in prison in February 1942. However, she was released on 12 February 1942 by order of the Minister for Justice, having only served several weeks of her sentence in Mountjoy Prison. There is nothing else in the judicial file to indicate why she was released, but she would probably have sent a petition to the minister asking to be released.

It was not only Catholic women convicted of the manslaughter of their illegitimate infants who found themselves condemned to spend a number of years in a reformatory institution in post-independence Ireland. Four of the five Protestant women convicted at the Central Criminal Court, Dublin, between 1922 and 1950 served their time in the Bethany Home in Dublin, a home for unmarried Protestant women and their babies. It operated from 1922 to 1972. Although the Bethany Home was primarily for unmarried mothers and their children, women convicted of crimes ranging from petty theft to infanticide were also accepted.[126] According to Meehan, Protestant institutions such as the Bethany Home willingly participated in the 'Irish culture of containment and control of sexuality in which the hidden shame of its "girls" or "inmates" was transformed into sin'.[127]

While not uncommon, the practice of sending women convicted of infanticide or concealment of birth in Northern Ireland between 1920 and 1950 to institutions such as the Salvation Army Home or Good Shepherd convents was not as widespread as it was in the South. Three women in the northern sample served their sentences in the Salvation Army Home. A.M. was convicted of concealment of birth in November 1931. She paid a recognizance and agreed to spend a period of six months in the Salvation Army Home and to be of good behaviour for a period of two years.[128] When she was convicted of infanticide in Belfast in July 1938, M.M. was sentenced to six months' imprisonment but subsequently released on undertaking to spend two years in the

SENTENCING IN INFANTICIDE CASES: NORTHERN IRELAND, 1920–50

Sentence	Percentage
Sentenced to death	4.1
Imprisoned	20.8
Discharged on entering into a recognizance	45.8
Salvation Army Home	12.5
Good Shepherd Convent	4.1
Acquitted and discharged	8.3
Discharged unconditionally under the Probation Offenders Act	4.1

Salvation Army Home.[129] However, she was later ordered to serve out her term of imprisonment because she refused to remain in the Salvation Army Home. She had apparently caused trouble in the home and threatened to commit suicide if forced to remain there. E.S. was convicted of infanticide and released on undertaking to go to the Salvation Army Home for at least six months.[130] Presumably reflecting religious affiliation, one woman was sent to a Catholic convent.

INFANTICIDE CASES AND MARRIAGE

As noted in Chapter 3, in post-independence Ireland some single women avoided serving time in a religious-run institution or in prison by marrying the putative fathers of their infants. If the father of the infant agreed to marry a woman charged with the murder of her infant, she could often avoid serving a prison sentence. Eight women were released from custody in Ireland between 1922 and 1950 following such marriages. Marriage was a condition of the release of two of the eight women and, although it was not listed as a condition of the release of the six other women who married the putative fathers of their infants, the fact that they married soon after being tried at the Central Criminal Court in Dublin is noted in the Trials Record Books. An impending marriage must have influenced sentencing in these cases. Mary H., aged 19, was convicted of concealment of birth at the Central Criminal Court, Dublin, in June 1931. The father of her deceased infant, James M., a labourer nineteen years her senior, attended her trial. Mary was released from custody on entering into a recognizance and agreeing to marry James M. immediately. The couple married over six weeks later on 5 August 1931. In November 1932, Kate

H. was convicted of concealing the birth of her infant son. Kate was discharged without punishment, presumably because she had married the infant's father in Sligo Jail in July 1932, a number of months before her trial at the Central Criminal Court. No woman in the pre-independence or northern samples was released on agreeing to marry the father of her deceased infant. There is no evidence in the judicial records examined to suggest that such leniency was a feature of infanticide trials in Northern Ireland during the same period, or in pre-independence Ireland. It would appear that release upon marriage to the father of the infant with whose death a single woman was charged was a phenomenon peculiar to the South in the post-independence period. The only logic for this practice is that once they had married, women who had been charged with the murder or concealment of their illegitimate infants no longer posed a threat to Catholic morality. Moreover, they were unlikely to reoffend. In the Twenty-Six Counties sample, the first recorded instance of marriage between a woman convicted of the manslaughter or concealment of birth of an illegitimate newborn and the putative father was in 1930. The last recorded instance of this practice in the cohort of cases studied was in 1948.

'RELEASED FROM CUSTODY AND HANDED OVER TO THE CARE OF HER FATHER'

In her study of infanticide in twentieth-century Canada, Kramar has suggested that the fact that single women who worked in domestic or personal service usually lived and worked on their own may have meant that they were at a disadvantage, as they would not have had a male family member to intervene with the authorities on their behalf: 'Without fathers to shield them from prosecution – either by way of securing a perhaps costly defence attorney or by way of diverting the matter entirely from the criminal system – domestic servants were likely to be in a more vulnerable position than other women.'[131] The evidence in a small number of Irish cases suggests that unmarried women may indeed have benefitted from their fathers' attendance in court. A small number of single women were discharged because their fathers guaranteed to ensure that their daughters would be of good behaviour and would return to court to receive judgement if called upon. Although these women were not juveniles, the authorities still seem to have regarded unmarried women as being, in effect, subject to the control of their fathers. Margaret O.'s father attended her trial at the Co. Cork

Summer Assizes in July 1908 and he undertook to take charge of her and to take her home.[132] Minnie M.'s father was present during his daughter's trial at the Munster Winter Assizes in December 1901. He 'acknowledged himself bound in open court in the sum of 10 pounds the condition being he will produce the said Minnie M. to receive judgement when called on by the Crown'.[133] In the Twenty-Six Counties sample, 2.6 per cent of convicted women were handed over to the care of their fathers, brothers or both parents who were in attendance in court. For instance, in a 1927 Co. Leitrim case, Bridget C. was found guilty of concealment of a birth but discharged on her father undertaking to look after her. Margaret D. pleaded guilty to the manslaughter of her female infant at her trial in the Central Criminal Court in March 1935. The plea was accepted. Margaret entered a recognizance of ten pounds and was released from custody and handed over to the care of her father who was in attendance in court. Margaret D. was 22 years old when she was tried. The ages of the other women are not recorded but it is likely that they were also adult women in their early twenties. At Johanna D.'s trial at the Central Criminal Court in October 1926 it was stated that her parents would look after her. Johanna was placed under a rule of bail for two years and discharged. It appears to have been less likely, but not unknown, for a defendant to have been handed over to the care of another woman. One woman was released upon payment of a recognizance and undertaking to return home to her grandmother.[134] Another woman, Mary F., was handed over to the care of a named individual who may not have been a family member. Convicted of the manslaughter of her illegitimate infant in the spring of 1934, she was sentenced to serve twelve months in prison but this was suspended, as Mrs Anne Jane Bailey 'undertook to the court to take care of the accused if she were released and to keep her so long as she remained with her'.[135] It is not clear from the files who Mrs. Bailey was. However, it is possible that she was a relative or a woman who had agreed to employ Mary. There are no obvious differences in infanticide cases where women were handed over to the care of a father or other relative and cases where women were sent to prisons or convents, other than the fact that the woman's father or other relative was present for the trial; presumably such relatives made their willingness to take the defendant back into their care known to the court. The presence of relatives in court did not always lead to the woman's release; there are instances where a woman's mother or father gave evidence in her defence in court but the woman was sent to a convent to serve her sentence.

Edith A.'s father was clearly concerned about his 24-year-old daughter after finding her outdoors on the night of 3 October 1937. Edith had given birth unassisted and had 'done away' with the baby soon after delivery. In his evidence William A. recalled bringing Edith back to the house and putting her to bed. Edith was, he said, 'in an excited state and asked us to let her go away to drown herself'.[136] He had to hold her in her bed to prevent her from leaving the house again. William A. attended his daughter's trial and gave evidence in her defence. He and his wife (Edith's stepmother) were both anxious to have her home again. William A. did not think his daughter was able to take care of herself: 'She never has been normal.'[137] He seems to have gone to considerable lengths to influence the court's treatment of his daughter. Several letters attesting to the family's respectability, including one from a Church of Ireland clergyman are included in Edith's case file. Despite her father's efforts Edith was sentenced to three years in the Bethany Home, Dublin.

While some women may have benefitted from their fathers' attendance in court, others may have received longer or harsher sentences as a result of a father's intervention. In some cases, the parents of single women convicted of the manslaughter or concealment of birth of an illegitimate infant may have requested that their daughters be sent to a convent to serve their sentences. In at least one case, the father of an unmarried woman convicted of infanticide arranged for her to be sent to a Magdalen asylum. Mary Anne M. was convicted of concealment of birth in June 1927. In this case the original sentence handed down by the judge was replaced by an order to have her escorted by members of the police force to the Good Shepherd Convent in New Ross. In a letter to the court the Reverend John O'Connor, New Ross, explained that at the request of Mary Anne's father he had arranged for her to be taken to the convent: 'This note is to show that all arrangements have been made by me and they will take her at any time that she is sent there now.'[138] The entry into the Trials Record Book dated 27 July 1927 noted that Mary Anne M. 'shall not leave the Convent of the Good Shepherd New Ross to which she is now being sent without the express permission of the Reverend Mother of the said convent'.[139] In this case, the father of a woman who had given birth to an illegitimate child and killed it intervened in the judicial process with the help of a priest to ensure that his daughter would not return to the family home for some time, if ever again. The local priest planned and executed an alternative sentence for Mary

Anne M. and the courts consented to this. The actions of Mary Anne's father give some indication of the level of shame experienced by families whose daughters gave birth to illegitimate children and were tried for infanticide. Yet this is only part of the picture. The fathers of a number of defendants were concerned for their daughters' welfare; some were keen to have them home again.

The practice of sending single women convicted of the manslaughter or concealment of birth of their illegitimate infants to religious-run institutions rather than to prison was not limited to Ireland. Kramar's research on infanticide in twentieth-century Canada has shown that single women convicted of the concealment of birth of their infants sometimes served their sentences in reformatories rather than in provincial prisons, which suggests that the Canadian authorities also sought to reform unmarried women who had been sexually active outside marriage.

Little is known of the fate of unmarried women convicted of the murder, manslaughter or concealment of birth when they were discharged from prison or convents. As Andrews noted in relation to infanticide scholarship generally, 'most of the existing literature, however, has confined itself primarily to the initial medico-legal and penal arbitration and disposal of offenders. Seldom have historians considered in much depth the longer-term disposal of infanticides, their evaluation whilst under detention within asylums (or prisons), and their discharge and restoration to families and communities.'[140] The longer-term disposal of infanticides that Andrews referred to is beyond the scope of this study. However, information is available for a small number of women who feature in the Convict Reference Files in the first two decades of the twentieth century. The Discharged Prisoners' Aid Society appears to have assisted several women prior to independence. For instance, Mary B. spent some time in the Good Shepherd Convent in Waterford in 1906 before she got a 'guarded situation', possibly as a domestic servant.[141] The families of some unmarried women were willing to welcome them back to the family fold. Bridget R.,[142] Julia S.[143] and Mary M.[144] may well have returned to their parents' homes on their release from prison. Evidence in both Bridget and Julia's files indicate that their parents were willing to have them back, while Mary M. expressed interest in her petition for early release in returning to her mother's farm to assist her there. Some women were given assistance in finding work. Hannah A. was handed over by a Crown officer to the Roman Catholic Discharged Prisoners' Aid Society when she was released in August 1911. Hannah K. was released to the Home for

Discharged Prisoners when discharged from prison in December 1901.[145] She would probably have spent eighteen months there before being sent to Canada, where she would have been assisted in finding work as a domestic servant. The Prisoners' Aid Society also found a situation for Hannah M. in June 1919.[146] When Alice K. was released from prison in April 1911, she travelled to a boarding house in Bristol to begin working as a housemaid.[147] Less is known about how single women convicted of murder, manslaughter or concealment of birth in Ireland, North and South, between 1922 and 1950 fared following their release from prisons or convents. Some may well have emigrated; others may have re-entered the workforce as domestic servants. In cases where the evidence of a single woman resulted in the conviction of one or more of her relatives for the murder, manslaughter or concealment of birth of her illegitimate infant, it would be interesting to examine whether family life was returned to normal following their trial or discharge from prison, or whether such cases led to the long-term or permanent severance of family ties.

CONCLUSION

There were some clearly discernable shifts and changes in the manner in which sexually active unmarried women convicted of the murder, manslaughter or concealment of birth of their newborn infants were dealt with in Ireland over the course of the fifty-year period examined. While historians who studied infanticide cases in the post-independence period assumed that convents were not used to detain Irish women convicted of the manslaughter or concealment of birth of their infants as often in the decades prior to independence as they were from 1922 onwards, this chapter has demonstrated that this was so, by analysing ninety-five cases from the pre-independence period. From 1922 onwards, there was a tendency to detain women convicted of manslaughter or concealment of birth in convents rather than in prisons. As Luddy has argued, while Magdalen asylums 'might have been places of welfare in the nineteenth century this may not be the cases in the twentieth century'. It would appear that after independence these women 'were held against their will, that they engaged in unpaid labour and lost whatever rights both the law and the Constitution granted to them as Irish citizens'.[148] The period 1922–50 also saw single women convicted of concealment of birth in the Twenty-Six Counties serve longer sentences than women who had been convicted of the same offence in the pre-independence period. Prior to 1922, sentencing patterns for single women convicted of the murder, manslaughter or concealment of birth of their illegitimate infants was very much in line with practices in England and Scotland. After independence, sentencing patterns in the Twenty-Six County state differed from sentencing patterns in Northern Ireland, Scotland and England, where women were generally not sent to religious-run institutions to serve their sentences. The tendency to send single women convicted of the manslaughter or concealment of birth of their illegitimate infants to convents rather than to prison may reflect increased concern about sexual morality in post-independence Ireland and the desire to stamp out sexually transgressive behaviour by dealing more severely with unmarried women convicted of these offences. In some instances the woman's family were keen to have them detained in a religious institution. The religious orders that ran the institutions where these women were sent, in some cases for several years, may have helped to shape this policy. Catholic probation workers who came into regular contact with the religious orders who ran convents with Magdalen laundries may well have made it known to the court that such institutions were willing to admit unmarried women convicted of infanticide in post-independence Ireland. This eventually became the preferred options of judges in the Twenty-Six Counties. The religious orders would have had a vested interest in detaining these women in their institutions, as they provided them with a cheap form of labour. It also provided the state with a less expensive way of detaining female criminals. Governments in post-independent Ireland, a predominately Catholic state with a conservative social outlook, would undoubtedly have been more receptive to the opinions of religious orders than the administration in the pre-independence period.

After 1922 the convent replaced the prison as the main site for the reformation and correction for unmarried sexually active criminal women. There they experienced an erosion of the rights that women had enjoyed in the pre-independence period, such as the right to petition the authorities for a reduction in their sentences. Only the most determined and disruptive women incarcerated in convents between 1922 and 1950 managed to come to the notice of the authorities and requested to be transferred to prison. Most women may not have been aware that if they had been held in prisons they would have been able to petition the Minister for Justice. This was something that at least one man, who was convicted of the concealment of birth of his illegitimate son, took advantage of. Indeed, single women suspected of the murder of their illegitimate infants in post-independence Ireland may not have been aware of their rights during the pre-trial process. Very few would have had legal counsel when they were questioned by the gardaí. Yet while the sentences imposed on single women convicted of the manslaughter or concealment of birth of their illegitimate infants may have been harsher in the Twenty-Six Counties after 1922, there were nonetheless several instances where there was clearly a considerable amount of sympathy for female defendants at official level. The legal system regarded the murder of an infant less seriously than the murder of an adult and, accordingly, women convicted of the concealment of birth or manslaughter of an infant were treated differently from other murderers. In many instances, convents were viewed as a more appropriate place of detention than prisons in post-independence Ireland.

NOTES

1. National Archives of Ireland [hereafter NAI], Central Criminal Court [hereafter CCC], Co. Galway, 1942.
2. Ibid.
3. NAI, CCC, Co. Clare, 1934.
4. *Clare Champion*, 22 December 1934.
5. S. McAvoy (Larmour), 'Aspects of the State and Female Sexuality in the Irish Free State, 1922–1949' (PhD thesis, University College, Cork, 1998), p.292.
6. NAI, Department of the Taoiseach, S7788A.
7. McAvoy (Larmour), 'Aspects of the State', p.310.
8. *Irish Independent*, 14 February 1951.
9. The murder of an infant by its mother was a capital offence until 1922 in Northern Ireland and 1949 in the Twenty-Six County state.
10. The 15 June 1931 edition of the *Irish News* published an article on the trial of a 17-year old girl for the murder of her newborn infant with the heading 'Painful Case at Ballymena'.
11. The 19 July 1938 edition of the *Irish News* carried a report on the trial of 'a young girl' who pleaded guilty to infanticide and quoted her defence counsel, M.J. McSparran, who described the case as 'pitiable'.
12. The 14 August 1930 edition of the *Irish News* reported on the trial of 'a young domestic servant,' who had been charged with child abandonment, under the heading 'Baby Found at Wayside. Poignant Story told in Newry Court'.
13. *Limerick Leader*, 22 September 1926.
14. NAI, CCC, Limerick, 1935.
15. *The People* (Wexford), 27 April 1929.
16. Ibid.
17. Ibid.
18. Ibid.
19. M. Luddy, *Prostitution and Irish Society, 1800–1940* (Cambridge: Cambridge University Press, 2007), p.117.
20. NAI, CCC, Co. Donegal, 1947.
21. *Connacht Tribune*, 19 January 1935.
22. PRONI, BELF/1/1/2/98/6, 1932.
23. PRONI, HA 9/2/4.
24. PRONI, HA 5/569.
25. *Irish News*, 5 January 1932.
26. *Belfast Telegraph*, 29 January 1932.

27. *Irish News*, 5 January 1932.
28. *Belfast Telegraph*, 29 January 1932.
29. *Belfast Telegraph*, 23 May 1931.
30. *Irish News*, 21 July 1928.
31. Ibid.
32. Ibid.
33. Ibid.
34. Ibid.
35. Ibid.
36. Writing about Edith Roberts's trial for the murder of her newborn baby girl at the Leicester Assizes in 1921, Ward noted that 'a less austere judge might have made some attempt to convey the reality that there was no prospect of the death sentence being carried out'. See T. Ward, 'Legislating for Human Nature: Legal Responses to Infanticide, 1860–1938', in M. Jackson (ed.), *Infanticide: Historical Perspectives on Child Murder and Concealment, 1550–2000* (Aldershot: Ashgate, 2002), p.262. The trial judge donned the black cap when he pronounced the death sentence on Roberts. According to Ward, in 1916 the trial judge 'in a similar case in 1916, declined to wear the black cap and told the prisoner: "It would be a hollow pretence for me to suggest in any way that your life will be forfeit." ' (Ibid.) Although Lord Justice Best donned the black cap when he pronounced the death sentence on J.M. in July 1928 he did reassure her that the recommendation to mercy would be forwarded at once.
37. *Irish News*, 21 July 1928.
38. PRONI, HA 5/1449.
39. Ibid.
40. NAI, Convict Reference File [hereafterCRF] M 37/1916.
41. Ibid.
42. M.L. Arnot and C. Usborne, 'Why Gender and Crime? Aspects of an Institutional Debate', in M.L. Arnot and C. Usborne (eds), *Gender and Crime in Modern Europe*, (London: Routledge, 1999), p.7.
43. *Limerick Chronicle*, 7 July 1910.
44. Ibid.
45. NAI, CRF/1911/A 11.
46. NAI, CRF/1906/B 59.
47. NAI, CRF/1911/A 11.
48. Ibid.
49. Ward, 'Legislating for Human Nature', p.256.
50. *Evening Herald*, 17 September 1900.
51. Ibid.
52. *Freeman's Journal*, 5 December 1900.
53. *Cork Examiner*, 29 July 1916.
54. D. Ferriter, *The Transformation of Ireland 1900–2000* (London: Profile, 2005), p.323.
55. J.H. Whyte, *Church and State in Modern Ireland, 1923–1970* (Dublin: Gill & Macmillan, 1971), p.24.
56. *Irish Times*, 3 October 1928.
57. *Irish Times*, 7 December 1927.
58. Ibid.
59. Ibid.
60. Ibid.
61. 'A citizen of Waterford' clearly sympathised with Mary S., who was convicted of the murder of her daughter's illegitimate infant in November 1938. The unnamed citizen wrote to the Taoiseach to protest at the fact that Mary had been sentenced to death, arguing that 'there is something wrong in the law that allows a seducer to get off scot free and a poor demented mother to be hanged'. Many more Irish people may have shared the citizen's sentiments (NAI, Department of the Taoiseach, S11040).
62. NAI, Attorney General's Office, 2000/10/2921, Letter to the Secretary of the Department of Justice from B. Daly, 28 March 1941.
63. *Cork Examiner*, 30 November 1928.
64. Ibid.
65. J.M. Donovan, 'Infanticide and the Juries in France, 1825–1913,' *Journal of Family History*, 16, 2 (1991), p.162.

66. M.J. Maguire, 'The Myth of Catholic Ireland: Unmarried Motherhood, Infanticide and Illegitimacy in the Twentieth Century' (PhD thesis, American University, Washington DC, 2000), p.38.
67. Sentencing information was not sourced for twelve women in the northern sample, 31.5 per cent of the total sample. In some cases this was because there are gaps in the records, while in other cases the relevant files were consulted but the information was not located.
68. *Nolle prosequi* is a Latin legal phrase meaning 'to be willing to pursue'.
69. Arnot and Usborne, 'Why Gender and Crime?', p.7.
70. Ibid.
71. NAI, Court of Criminal Appeal, 36/1938.
72. NAI, Department of the Taoiseach, S5886.
73. NAI, CCC, Co. Kerry, 1929.
74. NAI, Department of the Taoiseach, S5886.
75. NAI, Department of the Taoiseach, S5891.
76. NAI, CCC, Co. Wexford, 1929.
77. The percentages given here are calculated using the number of cases where information on the verdict is available, rather than the sample total.
78. Ward, 'Legislating for Human Nature', p.256.
79. Catherine A. married the father of her infant shortly before she gave birth in March or April 1929. However, as she was unmarried when she became pregnant and as she lived with her parents rather than her husband after her marriage, it was decided to include her in the sample for this chapter.
80. As McAvoy put it, 'it was open to juries in murder cases to bring in a verdict of guilty of manslaughter, a non-capital offence. In doing so a jury accepted that the accused was culpably negligent but that the killing was not deliberate or malicious.' See McAvoy (Larmour), 'Aspects of the State', p.284. She has noted that 'the factor determining whether the verdict would be "guilty of murder" or "guilty of manslaughter" appears to have been the skill of the defence in establishing that, although not insane, at the time of committing the offence the state of mind of the accused was temporarily unbalanced by childbirth to the extent that she was not responsible for her actions' (ibid., p.283).
81. It is not clear from the available records whether Mary C. pleaded guilty to manslaughter or concealment of birth.
82. T. Ward, 'The Sad Subject of Infanticide: Law, Medicine and Child Murder, 1860–1938', *Social and Legal Studies*, 8, 2 (1999), p.166.
83. Kirsten Johnson Kramar, *Unwilling Mothers, Unwanted Babies: Infanticide in Canada* (Vancouver, BC: University of British Columbia Press, 2005), pp.50–1.
84. NAI, CRF/1906/B 59.
85. Ibid.
86. NAI, Trials Record Book, CCC, Change of Venue Cases, November 1927 Sittings – June 1933 Sittings.
87. NAI, CCC, Co. Mayo, 1943.
88. Fifteen women in this sample were sentenced to serve terms of imprisonment. Eleven women received sentences that included hard labour or suitable labour.
89. Twenty-four women (46 per cent of those convicted) in this sample for whom information is available received non-custodial sentences.
90. *Cork Examiner*, 29 July 1916.
91. *Cork Examiner*, 4 December 1915.
92. *Cork Examiner*, 8 December 1914.
93. Ibid.
94. N. Meehan, 'Church and State Bear Responsibility for the Bethany Home,' *History Ireland* (September/October 2010), pp.10–11, at p.10.
95. Luddy, *Prostitution and Irish Society*, p.113.
96. NAI, Crown Files at Assizes, Co. Limerick, 1915.
97. Luddy, *Prostitution and Irish Society*, p.121.
98. NAI, CRF/1906/B 59.
99. This percentage does not include the women who were sentenced to death but whose sentences were reprieved, as they also served several years in prison.
100. McAvoy (Larmour), 'Aspects of the State', p.287.
101. NAI, Trials Record Book, CCC, June 1925 – June 1927.

102. McAvoy (Larmour), 'Aspects of the State', p.289.
103. Ibid.
104. Maguire, 'Myth of Catholic Ireland', p.93.
105. NAI, CCC, Co. Tipperary, 1928.
106. Maguire, 'Myth of Catholic Ireland', p.117.
107. *Nationalist and Munster Times*, 19 July 1928.
108. Ibid.
109. Trials Record Book, CCC, Change of Venue Cases, November 1927 Sittings – June 1933 Sittings.
110. NAI, Trials Record Book, CCC, 4 November 1933 – 22 April 1941, Letter from Sr Frances Eucharia Greer to the County Registrar, dated 9 July 1938.
111. Luddy, *Prostitution and Irish Society*, pp.117–18.
112. *Clare Champion*, 22 December 1934.
113. Notes on A.H. from the records of the Salvation Army Home, Belfast, courtesy of Leanne McCormick, who was granted access to the files during her research for her PhD thesis.
114. NAI, Trials Record Book, CCC, 4 November 1933 – 22 April 1941, Letter from Sr Frances Eucharia Greer to the County Registrar, dated 2nd December 1938.
115. Ibid.
116. PRONI, TYR 1/2A/3 1921–32.
117. PRONI, TYR1/2B/35, 1925.
118. Ibid.
119. Ibid.
120. F. Finnegan, *Do Penance or Perish: A Study of Magdalen Asylums in Ireland* (Piltown: Congrave, 2001), p.40.
121. Luddy, *Prostitution and Irish Society*, pp.76–7.
122. NAI, CCC, Co. Meath, 1943.
123. McAvoy (Larmour), 'Aspects of the State', p.288.
124. Trials Record Book, CCC, Change of Venue Cases, November 1927 Sittings – June 1933 Sittings.
125. McAvoy (Larmour), 'Aspects of the State', p.290.
126. Meehan, 'Church and State Bear Responsibility' p.10.
127. Ibid.
128. PRONI, BELF1/1/1/76, Belfast City Commission Crown Book, 1930.
129. PRONI, BELF1/1/1/78, Belfast City Commission Crown Book, 1937–40.
130. PRONI, BELF1/1/1/56, Belfast City Commission Crown Book, 1925.
131. Kramar, *Unwilling Mothers*, p.43.
132. NAI, Co. Cork Crown Books at Assizes, 1908.
133. NAI, Crown Book, Munster Winter Assizes, Co. Limerick, 1901.
134. NAI, CCC, Co. Cavan, 1924.
135. NAI, Trials Record Book, CCC, 4 November 1933 – 22 April 1941.
136. NAI, CCC, Co. Donegal, 1937.
137. Ibid.
138. NAI, Trial Records Book, CCC, June 1925 – June 1927.
139. Ibid.
140. J. Andrews, 'The Boundaries of Her Majesty's Pleasure: Discharging Child-Murderers from Broadmoor and Perth Criminal Lunatic Department, c.1680–1920', in Jackson (ed.), *Infanticide*, p.217.
141. NAI, CRF/1906/B 59.
142. NAI, CRF R 26/1912. Bridget R. was convicted of concealment of birth and sentenced to twelve calendar months' imprisonment with suitable labour in November 1911.
143. NAI, CRF S 2/1916. Julia S. was convicted of concealment of birth and sentenced to six months' imprisonment with hard labour in December 1915.
144. NAI, CRF M 37/1916. Mary M. was convicted of concealment of birth and sentenced to eight months' imprisonment with hard labour from July 1916.
145. Hannah K.'s file is listed in the National Archives of Ireland as CRF 1901/K55 but her file is not contained in file CRF 1901/K55. It is attached to Hannah A.'s file CRF 1911/A11.
146. NAI, CRF/1910/M52.
147. NAI, CRF/1911/K15.
148. Luddy, *Prostitution and Irish Society*, p.122.

Conclusion

In December 1949, 21-year-old Margaret R. was charged with the murder of her unnamed female infant. She stood trial over two months later at the Central Criminal Court, Dublin in February 1950. Margaret was from Co. Wexford. Since she was 9 years old she had been living with her aunt Bridget who ran a shop in New Ross. This kind of informal 'foster' system, whereby a child was sent to live with a maiden aunt to help her in the running of her business and to keep her company, was not uncommon in Ireland in this period.

In her statement Margaret said that her periods stopped in the third week of March 1949. A doctor confirmed that she was pregnant in June. Apart from seeking medical confirmation of her pregnancy, there is no other information in the case file to suggest that Margaret took any other steps to deal with her unplanned pregnancy. Her response was, in all other respects, very much in keeping with the other case files examined. Margaret concealed her pregnancy from everyone she knew and gave birth unattended in her aunt's home.

When her infant daughter was born in November 1949 Margaret said she picked her up and held her as she had cried twice. Terrified that people in the street below would hear the baby's cries, Margaret 'put [her] hand to its neck and squeezed a little on its neck to stop it crying'. She continued to apply pressure to the infant's neck with her fingers until the cries subsided and 'it got quiet'.[1] She then put the infant's body in a chamber pot. She knew the neonate was dead at that point. Margaret's mother arrived the following day. Margaret told her what had happened and her mother called a doctor to the house.

Although Margaret was tried for the murder of her infant daughter, she pleaded guilty to infanticide and her plea was accepted. She was sentenced on 17 February 1950. Margaret entered into a recognizance of ten pounds and agreed to immediately enter the Good Shepherd Covent in Waterford for a period of twelve months. Margaret was the first woman in the Twenty-Six Counties case files examined to have benefitted from the passing of the Infanticide Act the previous year. However, Margaret's sentence was much the same as those single women convicted of manslaughter or concealment of birth, in that she was sent to a religious institution. The treatment of unmarried women suspected of causing the deaths of their infants seems to have changed little despite the passing of the Infanticide Act.

The experiences of the unmarried mothers who feature in the judicial records of infanticide trials have largely been overlooked by historians. Often misrepresented and subjected to unfair treatment during the course of their own lifetimes, their voices, perspectives and personal experiences need to be reinstated to the history of single motherhood in Ireland. This book has attempted to piece together some of their experiences by providing a detailed analysis of some of the judicial records of infanticide cases tried in Ireland between 1900 and 1950. In so doing, this book has also engaged with the history of the family, the history of medicine and issues relating to social class, patterns of sexual behaviour, policing methods, and other criminal offences such as rape and incest.

The judicial files provide only a partial record of the history of single women and infanticide. The testimonies contained in the trial records are constrained and distorted to varying degrees. Nonetheless, they provide invaluable insights into the lives of unmarried working-class women. They offer 'a slice of history from below'.[2] The records of infanticide trials involving young, unmarried women are a rich source, capable of adding colour and depth to the history of single motherhood in Ireland during the first half of the twentieth century. This case-by-case analysis of the trial records of infanticide cases involving unmarried Irish women, their partners and relatives has resulted in the most comprehensive profile to date of women who committed infanticide in Ireland between 1900 and 1950. While previous studies have thrown some light on infanticidal women in southern Ireland between 1922 and 1950, little was known about unmarried women who committed infanticide prior to 1922, and still less was known about unmarried women from Northern Ireland who were charged with infanticide during the first half of the twentieth century. We now know that the unmarried Irish woman who committed infanticide between 1900 and 1950 was likely to have been in domestic service and in her mid-twenties. As there was a strong Belfast bias in the northern sample, women in the northern sample were more likely to have lived in urban areas. Poverty is evident in many infanticide cases. Most women, North and South, throughout the period, were from poor backgrounds. In the South the fathers of many women in the samples studied were employed as labourers. Some women and their families experienced serious financial hardship. A number of women charged with infanticide came from broken homes. One woman's father was an alcoholic who often turned his wife and children out on the road.

Where possible, the dynamics of relationships between unmarried couples who had to deal with an unplanned pregnancy were discussed. Men have generally been treated as peripheral to the study of single motherhood in Ireland during the first half of the twentieth century. This is largely due to the nature of the sources that most historians of single motherhood have used. However, this study has shown that case studies of infanticide trials can reveal a great deal about the manner in which Irish men responded to unplanned pregnancy during the first half of the twentieth century. The part Irish men played in infanticide cases was more complex than previous studies have suggested. Men responded to unplanned pregnancy in various different ways. Some came forward to marry the female defendants in cases tried between 1900 and 1950, after they had been charged, and, in some instances, after the women had been tried and sentenced. Other men chose to ignore the plight in which their former girlfriends found themselves, while others clearly colluded with the women who feature in these cases.[3] While the male relatives of single pregnant women were less likely to have been involved in infanticide cases than their female relatives, it is clear that the close male relatives of unmarried Irish women in the samples referred to throughout this book also responded to the prospect of the birth of an illegitimate infant in a variety of ways.

The men responsible for the pregnancy of single Irish women charged with infanticide are only referred to in any detail in a relatively small number of cases, and as a result it was not possible to compile a detailed social profile of the typical male partner of the infanticidal woman. However, it is possible to make some observations about the male partners of Irish women who stood trial for infanticide during the period under review. Firstly, the typical male partner of the unmarried infanticidal Irish woman was likely to have been of the same class background as the woman and, secondly, he was likely to have been of a similar age, although there were one or two notable exceptions. It is hoped that as a result of such detailed case-by-case research and analysis, our knowledge of unmarried women who committed infanticide, their relatives and partners, and the contexts in which they committed the crime, is now less impressionistic and more rounded, and perhaps also more nuanced.

This study has drawn attention to the links between suicide and unplanned pregnancy in Ireland between 1900 and 1950. Unplanned pregnancy had profound and, in some instances, tragic effects on the lives of men and women during this period. The case of John P. was high-lighted in the introduction; conflicting interests between his pregnant girlfriend and family seem to have led the 22-year-old to take his own life. The mental strain that concealing a pregnancy and committing infanticide shortly after giving birth unassisted had on the women who feature in the samples studied was all too apparent. A small number of women attempted suicide and others may well have contemplated tak-ing their own lives. The records of inquests may well reveal instances of unmarried pregnant women who took their own lives. Very few Irish women in the cases examined were deemed insane.

This book has contributed to historical understanding of the way in which Irish families responded to unplanned pregnancy and the manner in which they colluded in infanticide cases between 1900 and 1950. Many Irish families reacted angrily to the news that an unmarried female relative was pregnant. Some women were threatened and intimidated by their fathers, but this is only part of the picture. The close readings of a large number of infanticide cases has shown that some Irish families were willing to accept one transgression and that some single women's illegitimate infants were raised in the family home. However, when some of these women found themselves pregnant for a second time they took their infants' lives. There may well have been limits to a family's tolerance of illegitimate births.

One of the most salient features of infanticide cases tried in southern Ireland between 1900 and 1950 was the degree to which the relatives of single women were involved in the death of an illegitimate infant and the disposal of its body. Relatively little was known about family involvement in Irish infanticide cases. This study has shown that many Irish women seem to have come under sustained pressure from their relatives to kill their illegitimate infants and to conceal all evidence of their existence from the wider community. Some women were turned out of the family home, only allowed to return if they came back without the baby. It is possible that the relatives of some women took the decision to kill their infants for them. The birth mothers may have acquiesced in this, relieved perhaps to have been rid of an unwanted burden. In some cases there appears to have been a somewhat curious combination of concern for the birth mother and ruthlessness in killing a newborn infant and disposing of its body. The relatives of single women who gave birth in the family home in southern Ireland both before and after independence colluded in the crime to a degree that was not matched in cases tried in

Northern Ireland during the same period. In the North the female relatives of unmarried pregnant women may well have been more likely to collude in procuring an abortion than in committing infanticide.[4]

This study has also added to historical understanding of the relationship between fathers and daughters. If historians of infanticide in Ireland referred to the father-daughter relationship in their work at all it was generally to emphasise the menacing, intolerant and unsympathetic father. There is no doubt that many fathers of single pregnant women who were later charged with infanticide did threaten them once their suspicions were aroused. Some fathers turned their daughters out of the family home and at least one father saw to it that his daughter was incarcerated in a convent following her conviction. However, it is also clear from the cases studied in this thesis that the fathers of unmarried Irish women charged with infanticide reacted in various different ways. Some men appear to have been kindly, compassionate and forgiving. The fathers of some women gave evidence in court on their behalf. At least one man wrote to the judicial authorities to appeal to the trial judge to treat his daughter leniently. Another woman's father went to considerable lengths to keep his daughter from being detained in an institution. The mothers of infanticidal women were more likely to have colluded with their daughters and a pregnant woman was more likely to confide in her mother than her father. Nonetheless, there were instances where women referred to their fear of their mothers in their statements.

The level of influence senior family members exerted on younger people, both men and women, during the period is evident in the trial records of infanticide cases. Several men in the cases examined came up against parental disapproval in their choice of spouse. Patrick M.'s mother refused to give her consent to her son's marriage to his pregnant girlfriend in the summer of 1945.[5] Edward C. said that his mother objected to his keeping company with Margaret S. He told the gardaí who questioned him that on one occasion his mother told him that 'she didn't wish [him] to be with Peggy S. She gave [him] a lecture then over it'. Although Edward said that he 'kept away then for a while' he later resumed contact with Margaret but refused to marry her when she told him that she was pregnant.[6]

There was a striking degree of continuity in infanticide cases tried in Ireland both before and after independence. The most significant difference that emerged from detailed analysis of individual cases tried both before and after independence was in terms of sentencing patterns. While historians who studied infanticide cases in the post-independence period assumed that convents were not used to detain Irish women convicted of the manslaughter or concealment of birth of their infants as often in the decades prior to independence as they were from 1922 onwards, this study has demonstrated that this was so by analysing a sample of ninety-five cases. From 1922 onwards, there was a tendency to detain women convicted of manslaughter or concealment of birth in convents rather than in prisons. The period from 1922-1950 also saw single women convicted of concealment of birth in the Twenty-Six Counties serve longer sentences than women who had been convicted of the same offence in the pre-independence period. Prior to 1922 sentencing patterns for single women convicted of the murder, manslaughter or concealment of birth of their illegitimate infants was very much in line with practices in England and Scotland. Sentencing patterns in independent Ireland differed from sentencing patterns in Northern Ireland where women were generally not sent to religious-run institutions to serve their sentences. The tendency to send single women convicted of the manslaughter or concealment of birth of their illegitimate infants to convents rather than to prison may reflect increased concern about sexual morality in post-independent Ireland and the desire to stamp out sexually transgressive behaviour by dealing more severely with unmarried women convicted of these offences. In some instances the woman's family were keen to have them detained in a religious institution. The religious orders that ran the institutions where these women were sent, in some cases for several years, may have helped to shape this policy. They would have had a vested interest in detaining these women in their institutions, as they provided them with a cheap form of labour. It also provided the state with a less expensive way of detaining female criminals. Governments in post-independence Ireland would undoubtedly have been more receptive to the opinions of religious orders than the administration in the pre-independence period.

Women held in convents experienced an erosion of the rights that women had enjoyed in the pre-independence period such as the right to petition the authorities for a reduction in their sentences. Only the most determined and disruptive women incarcerated in convents between 1922 and 1950 managed to come to the notice of the authorities and request to be transferred to prison. Most women may not have been aware that if they had been held in prisons they would have been able to petition the Minister for Justice. This was something that at least one man, who was convicted of the concealment of birth of his illegitimate son, took advantage of.[7] Indeed, single women suspected of the murder of their illegitimate infants in Ireland may not have been aware of their rights during the pre-trial process. Very few would have had legal counsel when they were questioned by the gardaí. Yet while the sentences imposed on single women convicted of the manslaughter or concealment of birth of their illegitimate infants may have been harsher in the Twenty-Six Counties after 1922, there were nonetheless several instances where there was clearly a considerable amount of sympathy for female defendants at official level.

This study has also added to historical knowledge on patterns of sexual behaviour among unmarried working-class Irish women during the first half of the twentieth century. While extra-marital sexual relationships were certainly frowned upon in Ireland in this period, official and indeed non-official forms of disapproval certainly did not deter unmarried women from engaging in sexual relationships. In some cases single domestic servants became involved with men that they did not intend to marry. Some women had several sexual partners. A number of women seem to have become pregnant as the result of short-lived casual encounters, while others had been involved with a man of a similar age and from the same class background for a considerable length of time. These women may well have hoped that their partner would assume responsibility for the infant and offer to marry them once they learned that they were pregnant. This was certainly a source of friction between some couples. Some couples who wished to marry came up against parental disapproval while others were unable to secure housing. For the most part however, single women who became pregnant in this period do not seem to have informed the fathers of their unborn infants that they were pregnant. In many cases this was simply not an option because the woman had lost contact with the man before she even realised that she was pregnant. While there were a small number of cases where women said they had become pregnant as the result of rape or incest, and a very small number of women may have been intimidated or forced into having sex with their employers, the overall picture is one of domestic servants in their twenties seeking relationships themselves and consenting to sex either with men they had been seeing for some time, or with men they may have met only once, men whose names they were unsure of, in some instances. A small number of couples married in the later stages of the woman's pregnancy yet they still felt compelled to kill and conceal the infant that was conceived outside wedlock thus hiding all evidence of pre-marital sexual activity.

Such instances indicate the level of disapproval of pre-marital sex in Ireland during the first half of the twentieth century, particularly in tight-knit rural communities.

As noted in previous chapters, many infanticide cases simply never came to light. During the hearing of an infanticide case in 1927 Mr Carrigan, KC, drew attention to the fact that the proportion of infanticide cases that were prosecuted in the Irish Free State may only have constituted a small proportion of the actual number of infanticides committed in post-independent Ireland.

> Without wishing to exaggerate, he thought that it might be said that latterly, unfortunately – judging by the number of cases that came to Court – which could not be expected to bear any proportion to the cases that never reached Court – there was a great wave of infanticide, of the destruction of illegitimate children, in this country. Week after week there were paragraphs in the newspapers giving the results of inquests on infants. Then there were cases in Police Courts and in that Court, where unfortunate girls were charged with the murder of their illegitimate children.[8]

It is only possible to speculate about how many more infanticide cases may have gone undetected and unprosecuted between 1900 and 1950. The groups of cases analysed have been based, for the most part, on the records of the higher courts, the assize courts in the pre-independence period and the records of both the Central Criminal Court and the Court of Criminal Appeal in the post-independence period. Yet, as Ferriter noted, 'many cases were dealt with by the district courts, with the women charged with "concealment of the birth of an infant", rather than in the central criminal courts as capital offences'.[9] A study of the records of the circuit courts would undoubtedly uncover many more concealment of birth cases where the defendants were young unmarried women. Such a study might also shed light on changes and continuities in sentencing patterns in the lower courts before and after independence. A detailed study of the trial records of the lower courts in Ireland between 1900 and 1950 would allow historians to examine the levels of family involvement in concealment of birth cases and to explore the role played by the fathers of illegitimate infants whose deaths were investigated. The records of child abandonment cases have yet to be explored in depth. It is probable that many women charged with child abandonment in Ireland during the first half of the twentieth century were unmarried women. The records of child abandonment would in all likelihood be capable of shedding more light on the history of single motherhood in Ireland.

As the preceding chapters have shown, the judicial records of infanticide cases are capable of shedding light on the history of single expectant women who chose to kill their newborn infants rather than live with the stigma associated with unmarried motherhood. The judicial records also provide insight into various other aspects of the history of the lives of Irish women during the first half of the twentieth century, such as the working conditions of domestic servants, family life and sexual relationships. Hearn's assertion that premarital sexual relations were fairly common among domestic servants in Ireland was borne out by this study. There are many cases in the samples studied that also point to the fact that there was often a gap between Catholic teaching on sexual morality in Ireland and the private lives of unmarried couples.

Little is known about the history of female criminality in Ireland during the first half of the twentieth century. An analysis of the judicial records of all other trials that went before the Assizes and the Central Criminal Court between 1900 and 1950 where the defendants were women would be particularly useful. It would enable historians to assess the proportion of infanticide cases committed by women compared to all other serious crimes perpetrated by women. What motivated Irish women to commit murder? Were they treated differently from men within the criminal justice system?

Eily Q., who was 17 years old, was charged with the murder of her illegitimate daughter at a special court held in a Co. Limerick Garda Station on Christmas Eve 1945. Eily was remanded in custody until 31 December. She would have spent Christmas in a cell. Eily stood trial over a month later at the Central Criminal Court in February 1946. Eily had given birth at the City Home in Limerick in February 1944. She spent some time with her baby in the county home in Newcastlewest, Co. Limerick and afterwards found a woman to look after the infant. Although Eily's father apparently 'knew nothing about the existence of this child', her mother had agreed to pay a woman for the 'support and keep' of Eily's infant.[10] However, for reasons that are unclear, Eily's mother stopped making the necessary payments and the foster mother returned the child to Eily without warning in December 1945. Eily took her daughter, Mary Teresa, to her parents' house but seems to have concealed her existence from them. She kept her daughter in her bedroom at the back of the house for several days while her mother was away, before removing her to the garden shed where she covered her with bags and fed her bread and butter. The child eventually died from starvation and exposure and Eily was convicted of manslaughter at the Central Criminal Court. She was sentenced to serve five years in prison but this was suspended when Eily agreed to spend five years in the Good Shepherd Convent in Limerick instead. This was the longest period of time any woman in the cohort of cases tried at the Central Criminal Court between 1922 and 1950 was recorded as 'agreeing' to spend in a religious institution. Eily Q. was presumably sentenced to serve five years in the convent because her illegitimate daughter was a year and ten months old when she died.[11]

According to probation officer Elizabeth Carroll, 'the Nuns speak very well of Eily Q., stating that she is a very good "child" who has given no trouble whatever since going there'.[12] Eily Q's story, like the stories of many of the unmarried women who feature in this study, ended behind convent walls. Aged only 16 when she became pregnant outside wedlock, and an unemployed and inexperienced 17-year-old when she attempted to deal with lone parenthood in a society that offered very little concrete support to single mothers, Eily would have spent the first five years of her adult life detained in a convent.

On St Patrick's Day in 1936, Judge Hanna spoke at length about crime in the Irish Free State at the annual dinner of the Companions of St Patrick in the Metropole restaurant in Dublin. He reminded his audience that while independent Ireland was 'a star producing its own brightness',[13] the country's 'dark spots were [also] of its own making'.[14] One of the 'dark spots' staining Irish society was the crime of the concealment of the birth of illegitimate children. There had been, as an editorial in the *Irish Times* noted the day after Justice Hanna gave his speech, 'a shocking increase in cases involving infanticide and concealment of birth'.[15]

Judge Hanna's speech 'received considerable notice in the press'.[16] Correspondence between senior civil servants in the Department of Justice and the statistics branch of the Department of Industry and Commerce reveal a deep sense of dissatisfaction with the judge's frank discussion of sexual crime in the Free State. Thomas Coyne, a Department of Justice employee, found it extraordinary that the judge had quoted figures which were inaccurate and implied that he had drawn faulty conclusions from insufficient data. He also suggested that the figures for the years 1932 and 1934 in relation to sexual crime were 'somewhat abnormal'[17] and should have been disregarded. While civil servants in the Department of Industry and Commerce could not prevent Judge Hanna from accessing the statistical abstracts, they did not discuss statistics in relation to sexual crime with him or assist him in his inquiries. Writing to

Thomas Coyne, R.C. Geary of the statistics branch said: 'I need hardly add that no comment was made on the subject by this branch.'[18] Attempts to publicly criticize moral standards and sexual behaviour in the Free State were always discouraged. As McAvoy has argued, the true extent of the problem of sexual crime was hidden from the public eye.[19]

The murder of illegitimate children by their mothers was indeed, as Judge Hanna noted in his speech, one of many 'dark spots' in the history of Ireland during the first half of the twentieth century.[20] Their treatment by the state, the Catholic Church and indeed Irish society in general constituted another 'dark spot' or blind spot in the history of modern Ireland. The history of single motherhood and infanticide in Ireland is in many ways a painful history and a history that raises uncomfortable issues about the nature of Irish society during the first half of the twentieth century. The records of infanticide trials reflect hidden aspects of Irish life; the judicial files allow Irish people, to quote Joyce, to have 'one good look at themselves in [a] nicely-polished looking-glass'.[21]

This book draws to a close in 1950. The Infanticide Act had been passed the previous year. From then on, far fewer single mothers suspected of causing the deaths of their illegitimate infants would be charged with murder. Once the Infanticide Act had been passed, if it could be proven that 'the state of health of the accused mother effectively contributed to the act or omission constituting the offence alleged', then the suspect could be charged with infanticide, which was not a capital offence.[22] There was very little legislation to deal specifically with unmarried mothers in Ireland until the 1960s. Earner-Byrne has argued that 'abortion proved the key' and that it was not until the late 1960s, after abortion had been legalized in Britain, that the Irish government began to reassess the manner in which unmarried mothers and illegitimate children were treated in Ireland: 'Not until official statistics for Irish abortions in Britain filtered back to the Republic was a thorough re-evaluation of the treatment of the unmarried mother in Ireland undertaken.'[23] However, single mothers would have to wait until 1973 before they were entitled to a state allowance, and contraception was not even partially legalized until as late as 1979.

In 1946 those changes were still a long way off for young women like Eily Q. Many more unmarried Irish women were to face trial and imprisonment or institutionalisation for manslaughter or concealment of birth convictions. Before probation officer Elizabeth Carroll signed off her letter to the county registrar at the Green Street courthouse in

October 1946 she mentioned that she expected to travel to Limerick 'with another girl' the following week.[24] She may well have delivered another woman convicted of the manslaughter or concealment of birth of her illegitimate infant to the Good Shepherd Covent there. While a considerable amount of information about the experiences of unmarried mothers who stood trial for the murder or concealment of birth of their illegitimate infants can be recovered from the judicial records, the history of their experiences in detention remains unrecorded.

NOTES

1. National Archives of Ireland [hereafter NAI], Central Criminal Court [hereafter CCC], Co. Wexford, 1950.
2. M.L. Arnot, 'The Murder of Thomas Sandles: Meanings of a Mid-Nineteenth-Century Infanticide', in M. Jackson (ed.), *Infanticide: Historical Perspectives on Child Murder and Concealment, 1550–2000* (Aldershot: Ashgate, 2002), p.149.
3. See C. Rattigan, ' "Crimes of passion of the worst character": Abortion Cases and Gender in Ireland, 1925–50', in M. Gialanella Valiulis (ed.), *Gender and Power in Irish History* (Dublin: Irish Academic Press, 2009), for a discussion of the role men played in abortion cases involving single women in Ireland between 1925 and 1950.
4. C. Rattigan, ' "Dark Spots in Irish society": Unmarried Motherhood, Crime and Prosecution in Ireland, 1900–1950' (PhD thesis, Trinity College Dublin, 2008).
5. NAI, CCC, Co. Cork, 1945.
6. NAI, CCC, Dublin, 1948.
7. NAI, CCC, Co. Dublin, 1938.
8. *Irish Times*, 7 December 1927.
9. D. Ferriter, *The Transformation of Ireland 1900–2000* (London: Profile, 2005), p.423.
10. NAI, CCC, Co. Limerick, 1946.
11. As Eily Q.'s daughter was over a year old, it was a case of child murder rather than infanticide. However, I have discussed it here as Eily was a single mother, one of the youngest single mothers in the cases examined, and her treatment is similar to that of single mothers convicted of the murder of infants under the age of one.
12. NAI, CCC, Co. Limerick, 1946.
13. Ibid.
14. Ibid.
15. Ibid.
16. NAI, Department of Justice 8/451, Memo from Thomas Coyne to R.C. Geary.
17. Ibid.
18. NAI, Department of Justice 8/451, Letter from R.C. Geary to Thomas Coyne, 12 June 1936.
19. S. McAvoy (Larmour), 'Aspects of the State and Female Sexuality in the Irish Free State, 1922–1949' (Ph.D thesis, University College, Cork, 1998), p.331.
20. *Irish Times*, 18 March 1936.
21. T. Brown, 'Introduction', in James Joyce, *Dubliners* (London: Penguin, 1992), p.xv.
22. NAI, Attorney General's Office, 2000/10/2923, Capital Punishment.
23. L. Earner-Byrne, 'Moral Repatriation': The Response to Irish Unmarried Mothers in Britain, 1920s–1960s', in P.J. Duffy (ed.), *To and From Ireland: Planned Migration Schemes c. 1600–2000* (Dublin: Geography Publications, 2004), p.172.
24. NAI, CCC, Co. Limerick, 1946.

Irish Infanticide Cases, 1900–21 (Pre-Independence Sample)

Name	Reference	Year of trial
Hannah K.	NAI, Co. Dublin Crown Book 1894–1900 & CRF/1911/A 11[1]	1900
Kate B.	NAI, Co. Dublin Crown Book 1894–1901 & *Freeman's Journal*[2]	1900
Anne L.	NAI, Dublin, Crown Files at Quarter Sessions, 1900	1900
Mary M.	NAI, Crown Book, Munster Winter Assizes 1900	1900
Margaret S. & Edward S.	NAI, Crown Book, Munster Winter Assizes 1900 *Cork Examiner*	1900
Ellen A. [birth mother] & Mary A.	NAI, Co. Cork Summer Assizes, 1900 & *Cork Examiner*	1900
Kate M.	NAI, Co. Donegal, Crown Book, Summer Assizes 1889–1904 & Co. Donegal Crown Files at Assizes 1900–1902	1900
Bridget M.	NAI, Co. Donegal, Crown Book, Summer Assizes 1889–1904 & Co. Donegal Crown Files at Assizes 1900–1902	1900
Bessie C.	PRONI, BELF/1/1/2/3/5	1900
Sarah S.	NAI, Co. Dublin Commission Crown Book 1894–1901 & *Freeman's Journal*	1901
Bridget N.	NAI, Co. Limerick Crown Files at Assizes, 1901–02 & Crown Book at Munster Winter Assizes, 1901	1901
Minnie M.	NAI, Co. Limerick Crown Files at Assizes, 1901–02 & Crown Book at Munster Winter Assizes, 1901	1901

Name	Reference	Year of trial
Hannah C.	NAI, Co. Cork, Crown Book at Summer Assizes 1901 & *Cork Examiner*	1901
Bridget S. & Dan S.	NAI, Co. Limerick Crown Files at Assizes, 1901–02	1901
Bridget L. [birth mother] & Mary M.	NAI, Co. Donegal Crown Books at Assizes, 1892–1902 & IC 48 36, Co. Donegal Crown Files at Assizes 1900–02	1901
Lizzie W.	NAI, Crown Files at Quarter Sessions, Dublin 1902	1902
Ellen C.	NAI, Co. Limerick Crown Files at Assizes 1902	1902
Mary G. & Robert M.	NAI, Co. Donegal Crown Files at Assizes, 1903–05 & ID 6 9, Co. Donegal Crown Book Summer Assizes 1889–1904	1902
Catherine O.	NAI, Co. Louth Crown Book at Leinster Winter Assizes 1900–05	1902
A.M.	PRONI, BELF1/1/2/9/5	1902
Kate M.	NAI, Crown Book at Munster Winter Assizes, 1903 & ID 39 126, Co. Clare Crown Files at Assizes	1903
Elizabeth W.	NAI, Co. Cork Crown Book at Assizes, 1903 & *Cork Examiner*	1903
Nora C. [birth mother] & Catherine C.	NAI, Co. Clare Crown Files at Assizes, 1903	1903
Hannah A.	NAI, Co. Limerick Crown Files at Assizes, 1903	1903
Margaret O.	NAI, Co. Clare Crown Files at Assizes, 1904	1904
Mary H.	NAI, Co. Limerick Crown Files at Assizes, 1904–05	1904
Isabella K.	NAI, Co. Donegal Crown Files at Assizes, 1903–05 & Co. Donegal Crown Book at Winter Assizes, 1894–1908	1904
E.B.	PRONI, BELF/1/1/2/15/8	1904
Mary B.	NAI, CRF/1906/B 59, (Co. Westmeath)	1905
Margaret M.	NAI, IC 12 57, Co. Carlow Crown Files at Assizes, 1887–1906	1905
Margaret H. [sister of the birth mother]	NAI, Crown Book at Munster Winter Assizes, 1905 & Co. Clare Crown Files at Assizes, 1905	1905
Maria O. & John O.	NAI, Co. Galway Crown Files at Assizes, 1905–06	1905

Name	Reference	Year of trial
Margaret P.	NAI, CRF/1906/P17, (Co. Westmeath)	1906
Mary G.	NAI, Co. Donegal Crown Book at Winter Assizes, 1894–1908 & Co. Donegal Crown Files at Assizes, 1906–08	1907
L.F.	PRONI, DOW1/2B/15/5	1907
C.G.	PRONI, Belf/1/1/2/24/10	1907
M.G.	PRONI, BELF/1/1/2/25/5	1907
Margaret O.	NAI, Co. Cork Crown Book at Assizes 1908 & *Cork Examiner*	1908
Kate H. [birth mother] & Margaret S.	NAI, Co. Limerick Crown Files at Assizes, 1908–10 & Crown Book at Assizes, 1908–10	1908
Bridget O.	NAI, Co. Louth Crown Book at Assizes, 1902–18 & *Dundalk Democrat*	1908
L.M.	PRONI, DOW1/2B/15/5	1908
K.M.	PRONI, ARM1/2D/9/6	1908
Hannah M.	NAI, CRF/1910/M52 & ID 37 205, Co. Cork Crown Book at Muster Winter Assizes 1909	1909
Margaret D.	NAI, Co. Limerick Crown Files at Assizes, 1908–10	1909
Margaret M. Lizzie K.	NAI, Co. Limerick Crown Files at Assizes, 1908–10	1909
	NAI, Co. Limerick Crown Files at Assizes, 1908–10	1909
Mary K. [birth mother] & Cassie K.	NAI, Co. Donegal Crown Book at Assizes, 1909–15 & Co. Donegal Crown Files at Assizes 1909–11	1909
K.M.	PRONI, BELF/1/1/2/29/6	1909
E.H.	PRONI, BELF/1/1/2/33/6	1909
Maria H.	NAI, Co. Dublin Crown Book 1910–17 & Co. Dublin Crown Files at Leinster Winter Assizes, 1910	1910
Hannah A.	NAI, CRF/1911/A 11 & IC 55 78, Co. Limerick Crown Files at Assizes, 1910	1910
Alice K.	NAI, CRF/1911/K15 (Dublin)	1910
Margaret L.	NAI, Co. Dublin Crown Files at Leinster Winter Assizes, 1910	1910
Margaret M.	NAI, Co. Limerick Crown Files at Assizes, 1910 & IC 38 29, Co. Limerick Crown Book at Assizes 1908–1910	1910

Name	Reference	Year of trial
Sarah Jane B.	NAI, Co. Donegal Crown Books at Assizes 1909–15 & IC 48 39, Co. Donegal Crown Files at Assizes, 1909–11	1910
Mary C. [birth mother] & Margaret C.	NAI, Co. Louth Crown Books at Leinster Winter Assizes, 1906–10	1910
E.A.	PRONI, BELF/1/1/2/31/5	1910
Bridget R.	NAI, CRF R 26/1912 (Co. Wicklow)	1911
Winifred B.	NAI, CIF/1911/B 48 (Co. Limerick)	1911
L.B.	PRONI, DOW1/2B/18/7	1911
L.C.	PRONI, BELF/1/1/2/34/7	1911
Agnes M.	NAI, Co. Clare Crown Book at Munster Winter Assizes, 1908 & ID 39 135, Co. Clare Crown Files at Assizes, 1912	1912
Bridget B.	NAI, Co. Limerick Crown Books at Assizes, 1911–12 & IC 55 80, Co. Limerick Crown Files at Assizes, 1912	1912
Hannah O.	NAI, Co. Clare Crown Files at Assizes, 1912	1912
Norah M.	NAI, Co. Clare Crown Files at Assizes, 1912	1912
Bridget P.	NAI, Co. Clare Crown Files at Assizes, 1913	1913
E.C. [mother of birth mother] & G.C. [grandmother of birth mother]	PRONI, BELF1/1/2/42/5	1913
Margaret C.	NAI, Co. Clare Crown Files at Assizes, 1914	1914
Ellen O. [birth mother] & Hannah O.	NAI, Crown Book at Co. Cork Assizes, 1914 & ID 37 210 Crown Book at Munster Winter Assizes 1914 & Cork Examiner	1914
K.F.	PRONI, BELF/1/1/2/45/7	1914
Bridget W.	NAI, Crown Book at Assizes, Co. Galway 1914–15 & Irish Times	1914
Minnie E. [birth mother] & Susan E.	NAI, Co. Carlow Crown Book at Leinster Winter Assizes, 1915 & Nationalist and Leinster Times	1915
Julia S.	N.A.I., CRF S 2/1916, (Co. Kerry)	1915
Bridget M.	NAI, Co. Clare Crown Book at Munster Winter Assizes, 1915 & ID 39 138, Co. Clare Crown Files at Assizes, 1915	1915

Name	Reference	Year of trial
Kate C.	NAI, ID 38 101, Co. Cork Crown Book at Assizes, 1915 & *Cork Examiner*	1915
Susan M.	NAI, IC 55 83, Co. Limerick Crown Files at Assizes, 1915	1915
E.R.	PRONI, DOW1/2B/22/5	1915
S.G.	PRONI, BELF/1/1/2/48/5	1915
N.G.	PRONI, BELF/1/1/2/47/7	1915
Margaret M.	NAI, CRF M 35/1916 (Belfast)	1916
Mary M.	NAI, CRF M 37/1916 (Co. Galway)	1916
Lilian G.	NAI, City of Dublin Commission Crown Book, 1914–17 & IC 70 48, Dublin Crown Files at Commission, Leinster Winter Assizes, 1916	1916
Mary D.	NAI, Co. Cork Crown Books at Assizes, 1916 & *Cork Examiner*	1916
Mary O.	NAI, Co. Clare Crown Files at Assizes, 1916	1916
K.M.	PRONI, DOW/1/2B/23/6	1916
Annie T. [birth mother] & Annie M.	NAI, Co. Dublin Crown Book & IC 70 51, Crown Files at Commission, Leinster Winter Assizes, 1917	1917
M.S.	PRONI, BELF/1/1/2/53/7	1917
Ann H.	NAI, Co. Limerick Crown Files at Assizes, 1918	1918
Mary B.	NAI, Dublin Crown Files at Leinster Winter Assizes, 1919	1919
Eliza M.	NAI, Dublin Crown Files at Leinster Winter Assizes, 1919	1919
Kate F. [birth mother] & Hannah C.	NAI, Co. Cork Crown Books at Assizes, 1919 & *Cork Examiner*	1919
Mary C.	NAI, Co. Donegal Crown Book at Assizes 1919 & ID 6 13, Crown Files at Assizes, 1919–21	1919
Kate N.	NAI, Co. Clare Spring Assizes, 1920	1920
Catherine M.	NAI, Dublin City Commission Crown Book 1918–21 & IC 71 75, Crown Files at Leinster Winter Assizes, 1920	1920
Margaret M.	NAI, Co. Donegal Crown Book at Assizes 1917–21, ID 6 13, ID 6 13, Crown Files at Assizes 1919–21	1920

NOTES

1. Hannah K.'s file is listed in the National Archives of Ireland as CRF 1901/K55, but her file is not contained in file CRF 1901/K55. It is attached to Hannah A.'s file: CRF 1911/A11.
2. Newspaper reports were used as an alternative source of information for cases in this sample where either the sentencing information or the trial records were not available.

Infanticide Cases tried at the Central Criminal Court, 1922–50 (Twenty-Six Counties Sample)

Name	Reference	Year of trial
Mary H.	NAI, CCC, Co. Clare	1923
Anne F.	NAI, CCC, Co. Cork	1923
Maggie R.	NAI, CCC, Co. Kildare	1923
Isabella S.	NAI, CCC, Co. Cavan	1924
Delia L.	NAI, CCC, Co. Galway	1924
Annie M. [birth mother] & Margaret H.	NAI, CCC, Co. Monaghan	1924
Mary Anne T. [birth mother] & Eliza T.	NAI, CCC, Co. Monaghan	1924
Catherine C.	NAI, CCC, Co. Donegal	1924
Mary O.	NAI, CCC, Co. Donegal	1924
Christina M.	NAI, CCC, Co. Dublin	1925
Mary Anne C. & Michael C.	NAI, CCC, Co. Longford	1925
Mary K.	NAI, CCC, Co. Westmeath	1926
Margaret R.	NAI, CCC, Co. Wicklow	1926
Elizabeth D.	NAI, CCC, Co. Wicklow	1926
Hannah K. & Nicholas K.	NAI, CCC, Co. Cork	1926
Bessie D. [sister of the birth mother]	NAI, CCC, Co. Donegal	1926
Mollie H.	NAI, CCC, Co. Dublin	1926
Annie D.	NAI, CCC, Dublin	1926
Nora K.	NAI, CCC, Co. Tipperary	1926

Name	Reference	Year of trial
Bridget M. [birth mother], Mary K. & Peter K.	NAI, CCC, Co. Longford	1926
Josephine R.	NAI, CCC, Co. Westmeath	1926
Maggie L.	NAI, CCC, Co. Meath	1926
Mary T.	NAI, CCC, Co. Leix	1926
Johanna D.	NAI, CCC, Co. Limerick	1926
Mary N.	NAI, CCC, Co. Clare	1927
Rebecca A.	NAI, CCC, Co. Donegal	1927
Mary D.	NAI, CCC, Co. Donegal	1927
Elizabeth H.	NAI, CCC, Co. Westmeath	1927
Sarah G.	NAI, CCC, Dublin	1927
Mary G.	NAI, CCC, Dublin	1927
Bridget C.	NAI, CCC, Co. Leitrim	1927
Mary B.	NAI, CCC, Co. Offaly	1927
Mary M.	NAI, CCC, Co. Kerry	1927
Nora C.	NAI, CCC, Co. Kerry	1927
Bridget U.	NAI, CCC, Co. Kerry	1927
Mary L. [grandmother of the birth mother]	NAI, CCA, 30/1928, Co. Cork	1928
Mary Anne M.	NAI, CCC, Co. Wexford	1928
Essie D.	NAI, CCC, Co. Dublin	1928
Annie H.	NAI, CCC, Co. Sligo	1928
Patrick C. & Myles D.	NAI, CCC, Co. Wexford	1928
Sabina C.	NAI, CCC, Co. Dublin	1928
Margaret S. & John L.	NAI, CCC, Co. Tipperary	1928
Eileen D.	NAI, CCC, Co. Meath	1928
Margaret M. [birth mother] & Mary M.	NAI, CCC, Co. Leix	1928
Mary D.	NAI, CCC, Co. Limerick	1928

Name	Reference	Year of trial
Bridget D. [birth mother], Mary Kate C. & George C.	NAI, CCC, Co. Louth	1928
Margaret H.	NAI, CCC, Co. Kerry	1928
Bridget N.	NAI, CCC, Co. Kerry	1928
Ellen M.	NAI, CCC, Co. Cavan	1929
Christina K. [birth mother] & Ellen K.	NAI, CCC, Co. Galway	1929
Mary Ann S.	NAI, CCC, Dublin	1929
Gladys M.	NAI, CCC, Co. Wicklow	1929
Lucy B.	NAI, CCC, Co. Carlow	1929
Catherine A.	NAI, CCC, Co. Wexford	1929
Bridie F.	NAI, CCC, Co. Tipperary	1929
Esma M.	NAI, CCC, Co. Monaghan	1929
Mary M.	NAI, CCC, Co. Monaghan	1929
Kathleen M.	NAI, CCC, Co. Monaghan	1929
Bridie C.	NAI, CCC, Co. Limerick	1929
Deborah S.	NAI, CCC, Co. Kerry	1929
Nora C.	NAI, CCC, Co. Cork	1929
Margaret B.	NAI, CCC, Co. Dublin	1930
Mary O. [birth mother] & Kate O.	NAI, CCC, Co. Clare	1930
Ethel D.	NAI, CCC, Co. Sligo	1930
Christina R.	NAI, CCA 24/1930, Co. Dublin	1930
Mary S.	NAI, CCC, Co. Tipperary	1930
Annie C.	NAI, CCC, Co. Galway	1930
Margaret F. [birth mother] & Bridget C.	NAI, CCC, Co. Clare	1930
Kate M.	NAI, CCC, Co. Westmeath	1930
Mary T.	NAI, CCC, Co. Leix	1930
Ellen D.	NAI, CCC, Co. Limerick	1930
Mary F.	NAI, CCC, Co. Meath	1931

Name	Reference	Year of trial
Mary F.	NAI, CCC, Co. Meath	1931
Nora H.	NAI, CCC, Co. Waterford	1931
Margaret H.	NAI, CCC, Co. Meath	1931
Hannah B.	NAI, CCC, Cork	1931
Mary H.	NAI, CCC, Co. Leix	1931
Mary K.	NAI, CCC, Co. Limerick	1931
Rose Anne F.	NAI, CCC, Co. Louth	1931
Bridget M.	NAI, CCC, Co. Mayo	1931
Mary K.	NAI, CCC, Co. Kilkenny	1931
Bridget M.	NAI, CCC, Co. Limerick	1932
Kate B.	NAI, CCC, Co. Cork	1932
Ena P.	NAI, CCC, Dublin	1932
Kate H.	NAI, CCC, Co. Mayo	1932
Annie M.	NAI, CCC, Co. Limerick	1932
Bridget C.	NAI, CCC, Co. Galway	1933
Mary R.	NAI, CCC, Dublin	1933
Norah M. Jnr. [birth mother], Norah M. Snr. & Mary M.	NAI, CCC, Co. Clare	1933
Bridget C.	NAI, CCC, Co. Clare	1933
Kathleen M.	NAI, CCC, Co. Louth	1933
Margaret W.	NAI, CCC, Co. Kildare	1933
Mary M.	NAI, CCC, Co. Tipperary	1933
Mary Anne K.	NAI, CCC, Co. Monaghan	1933
Bridget M.	NAI, CCC, Co. Offaly	1933
Teresa M.	NAI, CCC, Co. Offaly	1934
Mary Kate F.	NAI, CCC, Co. Cavan	1934
Teresa C.	NAI, CCC, Co. Clare	1934
Balbina M.	NAI, CCC, Dublin	1934

Name	Reference	Year of trial
Elizabeth C.	NAI, CCC, Co. Westmeath	1934
Elizabeth M.	NAI, CCC, Dublin	1934
Mary F.	NAI, CCC, Co. Louth	1934
Margaret F.	NAI, CCC, Co. Limerick	1934
Elizabeth E. [birth mother] & Rose E.	NAI, CCA, 13/1935 & NAI, CCC, Co. Roscommon	1935
Annie C.	NAI, CCC, Co. Cavan	1935
Mary S. [mother of the birth mother]	NAI, CCC, Co. Meath	1935
Mary T.	NAI, CCC, Co. Waterford	1935
Delia M. & John M.	NAI, CCC, Co. Mayo	1935
Bridie M.	NAI, CCC, Co. Offaly	1935
Susan D.	NAI, CCC, Co. Dublin	1935
Bridget B.	NAI, CCC, Co. Limerick	1935
Kate K.	NAI, CCC, Co. Limerick	1935
Margaret D.	NAI, CCC, Co. Limerick	1935
Kathleen D.	NAI, CCC, Co. Waterford	1936
Kate Anne F.	NAI, CCC, Co. Sligo	1936
Mary Anne D. & Martin D.	NAI, CCC, Co. Mayo	1936
Mary S.	NAI, CCC, Co. Meath	1936
Elizabeth D.	NAI, CCC, Co. Limerick	1936
Margaret S.	NAI, CCC, Co. Tipperary	1937
Kathleen K.	NAI, CCC, Co. Wicklow	1937
Margaret M.	NAI, CCC, Co. Limerick	1937
Catherine M. [birth mother] & Rosanna M.	NAI, CCC, Co. Kilkenny	1937
Edith A.	NAI, CCC, Co. Donegal	1937
Mary M. [birth mother] & Margaret M.	NAI, CCC, Dublin	1938
Bridget D.	NAI, CCC, Co. Cork	1938

Name	Reference	Year of trial
Mary S. [mother of the birth mother]	NAI, CCA, 36/1938, Co. Monaghan	1938
Celia H.	NAI, CCC, Co. Mayo	1938
Bridget K.	NAI, CCC, Co. Monaghan	1938
Margaret M. & Laurence B.	NAI, CCC, Co. Dublin	1938
Mary B.	NAI, CCC, Co. Tipperary	1939
Bridget C.	NAI, CCC, Co. Longford	1939
Mary M.	NAI, CCC, Co. Wicklow	1939
Mary M.	NAI, CCC, Co. Donegal	1940
James B., Jean B. [birth mother] & Annie B.	NAI, CCC, Co. Cavan	1940
Mary R.	NAI, CCC, Co. Cavan	1940
Annie Christina K.	NAI, CCC, Co. Roscommon	1940
Bridget C.	NAI, CCC, Co. Limerick	1940
Bridie B.	NAI, CCC, Dublin	1941
Christina M.	NAI, CCC, Co. Dublin	1941
Bridget C.	NAI, CCC, Co. Galway	1941
Mary L.	NAI, CCC, Co. Dublin	1941
Mary M.	NAI, CCC, Dublin	1941
Máire ní C. [birth mother] & Cáit ní C.	NAI, CCC, Co. Galway	1941
Eithna M.	NAI, CCC, Co. Cork	1941
Nora C.	NAI, CCC, Co. Limerick	1941
Eileen R.	NAI, CCC, Co. Limerick	1941
Mary C.	NAI, CCC, Co. Meath	1941
Annie T.	NAI, CCC, Dublin	1942
Kathleen M.	NAI, CCC, Co. Kildare	1942
Mary Ellen T.	NAI, CCC, Dublin	1942
Nora M. [mother of birth mother]	NAI, CCC, Co. Waterford	1942

Name	Reference	Year of trial
Margaret R.	NAI, CCC, Co Galway	1942
Kathleen L.	NAI, CCC, Co. Limerick	1942
Margaret R.	NAI, CCC, Co. Kilkenny	1942
Mary Kate M. & John M.	NAI, CCC, Co. Galway	1943
Margaret F.	NAI, CCC, Co. Mayo	1943
Mary G.	NAI, CCC, Co. Meath	1943
Eileen Q.	NAI, CCC, Co. Tipperary	1943
Kathleen L.	NAI, CCC, Co. Tipperary	1943
Mary K. [mother of the birth mother]	NAI, CCC, Co. Offaly	1943
Norah C.	NAI, CCC, Co. Roscommon	1943
Sarah M.	NAI, CCC, Co. Limerick	1943
Kate O.	NAI, CCC, Co. Limerick	1943
Mary C.	NAI, CCC, Dublin	1943
Agnes D.	NAI, CCC, Co. Donegal	1943
Margaret H.	NAI, CCC, Co. Cork	1944
Joan C.	NAI, CCC, Co. Kerry	1944
Mary Bridget B.	NAI, CCC, Co. Leitrim	1944
Mary W. [birth mother] & Catherine W.	NAI, CCC, Co. Kilkenny	1944
Bridget D.	NAI, CCC, Co. Kilkenny	1944
John E.	NAI, CCC, Co. Meath	1944
Mary K.	NAI, CCC, Co. Wexford	1945
Jane M.	NAI, CCC, Co. Sligo	1945
Johanna W.	NAI, CCC, Co. Limerick	1945
Annie B.	NAI, CCC, Co. Clare	1945
Nora S.	NAI, CCC, Co. Cork	1945
Patrick M.	NAI, CCC, Co. Cork	1945

Name	Reference	Year of trial
Annie R.	NAI, CCC, Co. Cavan	1946
Elizabeth D.	NAI, CCC, Co. Offaly	1946
Mary Elizabeth F.	NAI, CCC, Co. Sligo	1946
Eily Q.	NAI, CCC, Co. Limerick	1946
Mary C.	NAI, CCC, Co. Donegal	1947
Margaret H.	NAI, CCC, Co. Cork	1947
Kathleen M.	NAI, CCC, Co. Limerick	1947
Edward C.	NAI, CCC, Dublin	1948
Elizabeth M.	NAI, CCC, Co. Limerick	1948
Katherine N.	NAI, CCC, Co. Cork	1948
Mary Kate M. [sister of birth mother]	NAI, CCC, Co. Roscommon	1948
Bridget F.	NAI, CCC, Co. Mayo	1948
Margaret R.	NAI, CCC, Co. Limerick	1948
Mary M.	NAI, CCC, Co. Kilkenny	1948
Mary M. [birth mother] & Nan M.	NAI, CCC, Co. Tipperary	1949
Mary W.	NAI, CCC, ID 29 11, Co. Offaly	1949
Frances B.	NAI, CCC, Co. Sligo	1949
John M.	NAI, CCC, Co. Wexford	1949
Margaret R.	NAI, CCC, Co. Wexford	1950

Infanticide Cases Tried in Northern Ireland, 1921–50 (Northern Sample)

Name	Reference	Year of trial
S.C.	PRONI, BELF/1/1/2/62/5	1920
M.H.	PRONI, ARM1/2D/14/5	1920
K.C.	PRONI, DOW1/2B/31/5	1923
M.B.	PRONI, BELF 1/1/2/73/7	1923
F.C.	PRONI, DOW1/2B/31/8	1924
M.C.	PRONI, BELF1/1/2/74/5	1924
M.K.	PRONI, DOW1/2B/31/7	1924
J.M. [father of infant]	PRONI, TYR1/2B/34	1924
J.B.	PRONI, BELF1/1/2/76/5	1925
E.S.	PRONI, BELF 1/1/2/77/5	1925
R.A.G.	PRONI, TYR1/2B/35	1925
S.G.	PRONI, BELF 1/1/2/79/5	1926
N.R.	PRONI, TYR1/2B/35	1926
A.S.	PRONI, TYR1/2B/35	1926
C.K.	PRONI, TYR1/2B/35	1926
I.L.	PRONI, BELF/1/1/2/80/6	1926
D.G.	PRONI, BELF1/1/2/86/5	1927
S.M.	PRONI, BELF1/1/2/87/7	1928
C .W.	PRONI, TYR1/2B/37	1928
J. M.	PRONI, HA 5/569 (Belfast)	1928
M.M.	PRONI, ARM1/2D/16/6	1928
J.M.	PRONI, BELF/1/1/2/91/6	1929

Name	Reference	Year of trial
L.R.	PRONI, DOW/1/2B/36/6	1929
S.C.	PRONI, DOW/1/2B/36/6	1929
E.H.	PRONI, BELF/1/2/2/40/67	1930
A.M.	PRONI, BELF/1/2/2/40/68	1930
S.W.	PRONI, BELF/1/1/2/94/6	1930
M.B.	PRONI, BELF/1/1/2/95/6	1930
M.W.	PRONI, TYR1/1B/1/39	1930
A.M.	PRONI, BELF/1/1/2/97/5	1931
A.R. [birth mother] & J.R.	PRONI, DOW1/2B/38/7	1931
J.V.	PRONI, TYR1/2B/40	1931
A.H.	PRONI, BELF/1/1/2/98/6	1932
M.M. [father of infant]	PRONI, HA 9/2/4 (Co. Down)	1933
L.M.	PRONI, DOW/2B/44/5	1937
M.M.	PRONI, BELF/1/1/2/117/5	1938
S.M.	PRONI, TYR1/2B/47	1938
K.M.	PRONI, BELF/1/2/2/56/4	1945

Bibliography

MANUSCRIPT SOURCES

Dublin Diocesan Archives
Catholic Enquiry Office (Edinburgh) Correspondence, 1932, Archbishop Byrne Papers, Lay Organisations 2.

Catholic Women's League of Scotland Correspondence, 1929, Archbishop Byrne Papers, Lay Organisations 2.

Legion of Mary Correspondence, 1941–49, Archbishop McQuaid Papers, Lay Organisations.

Liverpool and County Catholic Aid Society Correspondence c. 1930, Archbishop Byrne Papers, Lay Organisations 2.

Rotunda Girls' Aid Society, Appeal and Annual Report, 1930, Archbishop Byrne Papers, Lay Organisations 3.

St Patrick's Guild, Archbishop Byrne Papers, Lay Organisations 2.

National Archives of Ireland, Dublin
Attorney General's Office Files
Attorney General's Office, 2000/10/2923, Capital Punishment.

Attorney General's Office, 2002/16/480, File relating to John Daly who was charged with the murder of Bridget K. through abortion in 1939.

Attorney General's Office, 2000/10/2921, Infanticide Legislation.

Department of Health Files
Department of Health, A116/167, Illegitimate Infants.

Department of Health, M34/58, Reports on the Inspection of Maternity Homes.

Department of Justice Files
Department of Justice, 90/4/1–31, Evidence submitted to the Committee on Criminal Law Amendment Act (Carrigan Committee).

Department of Justice, H 171/39, File relating to the Criminal Law Amendment Act.

Department of Justice, 9/19, File relating to the Illegitimate Children (Affiliation) Orders Bill.

Department of Justice, H266/61, File relating to Infanticide Legislation.
Department of Justice, H247/41D, File relating to Prostitution.
Department of Justice, 72/94A, File relating to Prostitution, 1946–48. Includes evidence submitted to the Committee on the Suppression of Prostitution.
Department of Justice, H266/40, Letter from Committee for the Reform of Laws relating to the Protection of Women and Girls, 15 October 1926.
Department of Justice, 8/451, Sexual Crime and Juvenile Offences. Memo by Intelligence Division in connection with Judge Hanna's speech (1936).

Department of the Taoiseach Files
Department of the Taoiseach, S10815A, Adoption of Children.
Department of the Taoiseach, S14716, Copy of Frank O'Connor's 'Ireland' in *Holiday* (December 1949) and letters of protest.
Department of the Taoiseach, S5891, Death Sentence on Catherine A.
Department of the Taoiseach, S5886, Death Sentence on Deborah S.
Department of the Taoiseach, S5571, Death Sentence on Elizabeth H.
Department of the Taoiseach, S5884, Death Sentence on Mary Anne K.
Department of the Taoiseach, S5195, Death Sentence on Mary K.
Department of the Taoiseach, S6489A, File relating to the Carrigan Committee.
Department of the Taoiseach, S7788A, File relating to Insanity as a Defence to Criminal Charges and Infanticide.
Department of the Taoiseach, S5931, Illegitimate Children (Affiliation Orders) Bill. Department of the Taoiseach, S14493, Infanticide Bill, Memorandum for the Government.
Department of the Taoiseach, S11040, Letter to the Taoiseach from a 'citizen of Waterford' dated 10 December 1938 to protest at the sentence of death passed on Mary S. who was convicted of the murder of her daughter's illegitimate infant. Files also include a report dated 17 November 1938 from the gardaí in Monaghan as to the circumstances of the crime of which Mary S. was convicted.
Department of the Taoiseach, S5998, *Report of the Committee on the Criminal Law Amendment Acts (1880–85) and Juvenile Prostitution* (1931).

Trial Records
Trials Record Book, Central Criminal Court, 13 October 1941 – 1 December 1945.

Trials Record Book, Central Criminal Court, City of Dublin, 7 February 1928 – 15 November 1943.
Trials Record Book, Central Criminal Court, Change of Venue Cases, November 1927 Sittings – June 1933 Sittings.
Trials Record Book, Central Criminal Court, 4 November 1933 – 22 April 1941.
Trials Record Book, Central Criminal Court, Change of Venue Dublin June 1925 – December 1926.
Trials Record Book, Central Criminal Court, V 14 30 21, 1946–52.

Public Record Office of Northern Ireland, Belfast (PRONI), Sentencing Information

BELF1/1/1/1.	BELF1/1/1/64.
BELF1/1/1/2.	BELF1/1/1/66.
BELF1/1/1/14.	BELF1/1/1/68.
BELF1/1/1/17.	BELF1/1/1/60.
BELF1/1/1/18.	BELF1/1/1/73.
BELF1/1/1/20.	BELF1/1/1/74.
BELF1/1/1/29.	BELF1/1/1/75.
BELF1/1/1/33.	BELF1/1/1/76.
BELF1/1/1/36.	BELF1/1/1/77.
BELF1/1/1/40.	BELF1/1/1/78.
BELF1/1/1/43.	BELF1/1/1/79.
BELF1/1/1/50.	BELF1/1/1/80.
BELF1/1/1/52.	BELF1/1/1/90.
BELF1/1/1/55.	TYR1/2A/4.
BELF1/1/1/56.	TYR1/2A/3.
BELF1/1/1/58.	DOW1/2A/4.

Trinity College Dublin
Lyon, Stanley, 'Report on Survey Covering the Employment, Social and Living Conditions of Irish Emigrants (First Generation) in Great Britain' (1948), Marsh papers, MSS 8297, Trinity College Dublin.

CONTEMPORARY PUBLISHED SOURCES

Devane, R.S., 'The Unmarried Mother: Some Legal Aspects of the Problem: I – The Age of Consent', *Irish Ecclesiastical Record* 23 (1924), pp.55–68.
Devane, R.S., 'The Unmarried Mother: Some Legal Aspects of the

Problem: II – The Legal Position of the Unmarried Mother in the Irish Free State', *Irish Ecclesiastical Record*, 23 (1924), pp.172–188.

Devane, R.S., 'The Legal Protection of Girls: I – Age of Consent', *Irish Ecclesiastical Record*, 37 (1931), pp.20–40.

Devane, R.S., 'The Dance-Hall', *Irish Ecclesiastical Record*, 37 (1931), pp.170–194.

General Index to the Bills, Reports and Papers Printed by Order of the House of Commons and to the Reports and Papers Presented by Command 1900 to 1948–49 (London: HMSO, 1960).

Glynn, J., 'The Unmarried Mother', *Irish Ecclesiastical Record*, 18 (1921), pp.461–67.

McInerney, M.H., 'The Souper Problem in Ireland', *Irish Ecclesiastical Record*, 18 (1921), pp.140–156.

M.P.R.H., 'Illegitimate: Being a Discourse on the Problems of Unmarried Mothers and their Offspring', *The Bell*, 2, 3 (1941).

O'Brien, F., 'The Dance Halls' *The Bell* (February 1941)

O'Connor, F., 'Ireland', *Holiday* (December 1949), pp.34–63

Report of the Commission on the Relief of the Sick and Destitute Poor, Including the Insane Poor (Dublin, 1928).

'Sagart', 'How to Deal with the Unmarried Mother', *Irish Ecclesiastical Record*, 20, (1922), pp.145–153.

Toksvig, S., 'Why Girls Leave Ireland', *Survey*, vol.LXII, 9 (August 1929), pp.482–85.

Anglo-Celt
Belfast Telegraph
The Bell
Clare Champion
Connacht Tribune
Cork Examiner
Dundalk Democrat
Freeman's Journal
Irish Ecclesiastical Record
Irish Independent
Irish News
Irish Press

The Irish Reports
Irish Times
Limerick Leader
Longford Leader
Nationalist and Leinster Times
Nationalist and Munster Times
Northern Whig and Belfast Post
People (Wexford)
The Times
Wicklow People

SELECTED BOOKS AND ARTICLES

Andrews, J., 'The Boundaries of Her Majesty's Pleasure: Discharging Child-Murderers from Broadmoor and Perth Criminal Lunatic Department, c.1680–1920', in M. Jackson (ed.), *Infanticide: Historical Perspectives on Child Murder and Concealment, 1550 – 2000* (Aldershot: Ashgate, 2002), pp.216–248.

Arnot, M.L. and Usborne, C., 'Why Gender and Crime? Aspects of an Institutional Debate', in M.L. Arnot and C. Usborne (eds), *Gender and Crime in Modern Europe* (London: Routledge, 1999).

Arnot, M.L., 'The Murder of Thomas Sandles: Meanings of a Mid-Nineteenth-Century Infanticide' in M. Jackson (ed.), *Infanticide: Historical Perspectives on Child Murder and Concealment, 1550–2000* (Aldershot: Ashgate, 2002), pp.149–167.

Bechtold, B.H., and Cooper Graves, D., 'Introduction: Towards an Understanding of the Infanticide Scholarship', in B.H. Bechtold and D. Cooper Graves (eds), *Killing Infants: Studies in the Worldwide Practice of Infanticide* (Lampeter: Edwin Mellen, 2006), pp.1–20.

Blaikie, A., *Illegitimacy, Sex, and Society: Northeast Scotland, 1750–1800* (Oxford: Clarendon, 1993).

Brookes, B., 'Women and Reproduction c. 1860–1919', in J. Lewis (ed.), *Labour and Love: Women's Experience of Home and Family 1850–1940* (Oxford: Wiley Blackwell, 1986), pp.149–71.

Brookes, B., *Abortion in England, 1900 –1967* (London: Routledge, 1988).

Brown, T., 'Introduction'. in James Joyce, *Dubliners* (London: Penguin, 1992).

Clear, C., *Social Change and Everyday Life in Ireland, 1850–1922* (Manchester: Manchester University Press, 2007).

Conrad, K.A., *Locked in the Family Cell: Gender, Sexuality and Political Agency in Irish National Discourse* (Madison, WI: University of Wisconsin Press, 2004).

Cook, H., *The Long Sexual Revolution: English Women, Sex, and Contraception 1800–1975* (Oxford: Oxford University Press, 2004).

Cooper Graves, D., ' "... in a frenzy while raving mad": Physicians and Parliamentarians Define Infanticide in Victorian England', in B.H. Bechtold and D. Cooper Graves (eds), *Killing Infants: Studies in the Worldwide Practice of Infanticide* (Lampeter: Edwin Mellen, 2006), pp.111–135.

Davidoff, L. et al., The Family Story: Blood. Contract and Intimacy, 1830–1960 (Harlow: Longman, 1998).

D'Cruze, S., *Crimes of Outrage: Sex , Violence and Victorian Working Women* (London: University College London Press, 1998).

D'Cruze, S., and Jackson, L. A. *Women , Crime and Justice in England since 1660* (London: Palgrave Macmillan, 2009).

De Blécourt, W., 'Cultures of Abortion in The Hague in the Early Twentieth Century', in F. X. Eder, L. Hall and G. Hekma (eds), *Sexual Cultures in Europe: Themes in Sexuality* (Manchester: Manchester University Press, 1999), pp.195–212.

De Blécourt, W. and Usborne, C., 'Women's Medicine, Women's Culture: Abortion and Fortune-Telling in early Twentieth-Century Germany and the Netherlands', *Medical History*, 43, 3 (1999), pp.376–392.

Dickinson, J.R. and Sharpe, J.A., 'Infanticide in Early Modern England: The Court of Great Sessions at Chester, 1650–1800', in M. Jackson (ed.), *Infanticide: Historical Perspectives on Child Murder and Concealment, 1550–2000* (Aldershot: Ashgate, 2002), pp.35–51.

Donovan, J.M. 'Infanticide and the Juries in France, 1825–1913', *Journal of Family History*, 16, 2 (1991), pp.157–176.

Earner-Byrne, L., 'The Boat to England: An Analysis of the Official Reactions to the Emigration of Single Expectant Irishwomen to Britain, 1922–1972', *Irish Economic and Social History*, 30 (2003), pp.52–71.

Earner-Byrne, L., 'Moral Repatriation': The Response to Irish Unmarried Mothers in Britain, 1920s–1960s', in P.J. Duffy (ed.), *To and From Ireland: Planned Migration Schemes c. 1600–2000* (Dublin: Geography Publications, 2004), pp.155–173.

Earner-Byrne, L. 'Reinforcing the Family: The Role of Gender, Mortality and Sexuality in Irish Welfare Policy, 1922–1944', *History of the Family*, 13, 4 (2008).

Eder, F.X., Hall, L. and Hekma, G. (eds), *Sexual Cultures in Europe: National Histories* (Manchester: Manchester University Press, 1999).

Fanning, R., *Independent Ireland* (Dublin: Educational Company of Ireland,1983).

Ferriter, D., *The Transformation of Ireland 1900–2000* (London: Profile, 2005).

Ferriter, D., *Occasions of Sin: Sex and Society in Modern Ireland* (London: Profile, 2009).

Finnane, M., 'The Carrigan Committee of 1930–31 and the "moral condition of the Saorstat" ', *Irish Historical Studies*, 32, 128 (2001), pp.519–536.

Finnegan, F., *Do Penance or Perish: A Study of Magdalen Asylums in Ireland* (Piltown: Congrave, 2001).

Garrett, P.M., 'The Abnormal Flight: The Migration and Repatriation of Irish Unmarried Mothers', *Social History*, 25, 3 (2000), pp.330–343.

Guilbride, A., 'Infanticide: the Crime of Motherhood', in P. Kennedy (ed.), *Motherhood in Ireland: Creation and Context* (Cork: Mercier, 2004), pp.170–180.

Haste, C., *Rules of Desire: Sex in Britain: World War One to the Present* (London: Chatto & Windus, 1992).

Hearn, M., 'Life for Domestic Servants in Dublin, 1880–1920', in M. Luddy and C. Murphy (eds), *Women Surviving: Studies in Irish Women's History in the 19th and 20th Centuries* (Swords: Little-hampton, 1990), pp.148–179.

Hearn, M., *Below Stairs: Domestic Service Remembered in Dublin and Beyond 1880–1922* (Dublin: Lilliput, 1993).

Heywood, C., 'Innocence and Experience: Sexuality among Young People in Modern France, c. 1750–1950', *French History*, 21, 1 (2007), pp.44–64.

Hill, M., *Women in Ireland: A Century of Change* (Belfast: Blackstaff, 2003).

Howes (ed.), M., 'Public Discourse, Private Reflection, 1916–70', in A. Bourke, S. Kilfeather, M. Luddy, M. MacCurtain, G. Meaney, M. Ní Dhonnchadha, M. O'Dowd, C. Willis (eds), *The Field Day Anthology of Irish Writing: Irish Women's Writing and Traditions*, Vol. 4 (Cork: Cork University Press, 2002), pp.923–930.

Inglis, T., 'Origins and Legacies of Irish Prudery: Sexuality and Social Control in Modern Ireland', *Éire Ireland*, 40, 3 & 4 (2005), pp.9–37.

Jackson, L., 'The Child's Word in Court: Cases of Sexual Abuse in London, 1870–1914', in M.L. Arnot and C. Usborne (eds), *Gender and Crime in Modern Europe* (London: Routledge, 1999, pp.222–237.

Jackson, L A., *Child Sexual Abuse in Victorian England* (London: Routledge, 1999).

Jackson, M., *New-Born Child Murder: Women, Illegitimacy and the Courts in Eighteenth-Century England* (Manchester: Manchester University Press, 1996).

Jackson, M., *The Borderlands of Imbecility: Medicine, Society and the Fabrication of the Feeble Mind in late Victorian and Edwardian England* (Manchester: Manchester University Press, 2000).

Jackson, M., 'The Trial of Harriet Vooght: Continuity and Change in the History of Infanticide', in M. Jackson (ed.), *Infanticide: Historical Perspectives on Child Murder and Concealment, 1550–2000* (Aldershot: Ashgate, 2002), pp.1–17.

Jackson, M., 'Fiction in the Archives? Sources for the Social History of Infanticide', *Archives*, 27, 107 (2002), pp.173–185.

Johnson Kramar, K., *Unwilling Mothers, Unwanted Babies: Infanticide in Canada* (Vancouver, BC: University of British Columbia Press, 2005).

Johnson Kramar, K., 'Unwilling Mothers and Unwanted Babies: Infanticide and Medico-Legal Responsibility in 20th Century Canadian Legal Discourse', in B.H. Bechtold and D. Cooper Graves (eds), *Killing Infants: Studies in the Worldwide Practice of Infanticide* (Lampeter: Edwin Mellen, 2006), pp.137–166.

Kennedy, F., *Cottage to Crèche: Family Change in Ireland* (Dublin: Institute of Public Administration, 2001).

Keogh, D., *The Vatican, the Bishops and Irish Politics 1919–39* (Cambridge: Cambridge University Press, 1986).

Kiernan, K., Land, H. and Lewis, J. (eds), **Lone Motherhood in Twentieth-Century Britain: From Footnote to Front Page** (Oxford: Clarendon, 1998).

Kunzel, R., *Fallen Women, Problem Girls: Unmarried Mothers and the Professionalization of Social Work, 1890–1945* (London: Yale University Press, 1993).

Lambert, S., 'Irish Women's Emigration to England, 1922–60: The Lengthening of Family Ties', in A. Hayes and D. Urquhart (eds), *Irish Women's History* (Dublin: Irish Academic Press, 2004), pp.152–167.

Luddy, M., 'Moral Rescue and Unmarried Mothers in Ireland in the 1920s', *Women's Studies*, 30, 6 (2001), pp.797–817.

Luddy, M., *Prostitution and Irish Society, 1800–1940* (Cambridge: Cambridge University Press, 2007).

Luddy, M. and Murphy, C., ' "Cherhez la Femme": The Elusive Women in Irish History', in M. Luddy and C. Murphy (eds), *Women Surviving: Studies in Irish Women's History in the 19th and 20th Centuries* (Swords: Littlehampton, 1990), pp.1–14.

Lyder, H., ' "Silence and Secrecy": Exploring Female Sexuality during Childhood in 1930s and 1940s Dublin', *Irish Journal of Feminist Studies*, 5, 1 & 2 (2003), pp.77–88.

Maguire, M. J., *Precarious Childhood in Post-Independence Ireland* (Manchester: Manchester University Press, 2009).

Mahood, L., *Policing Gender, Class and Family: Britain, 1850–1940* (London: University College London Press, 1995).

Marks, L., ' "The Luckless Waifs and Strays of Humanity": Irish and Jewish Immigrant Unwed Mothers in London, 1870–1939', *Twentieth Century British History*, 3, 2 (1992), pp.113–137.

Marland, H., 'Getting away with Murder? Puerperal Insanity, Infanticide and the Defence Plea', in M. Jackson (ed.), *Infanticide: Historical Perspectives on Child Murder and Concealment, 1550–2000* (Aldershot: Ashgate, 2002), pp.168–192.

McAvoy, S., 'The Regulation of Sexuality in the Irish Free State, 1929–25', in E. Malcolm and G. Jones (eds), *Medicine, Disease and the State in Ireland, 1650–1940* (Cork: Cork University Press, 1999), pp.253–266.

McAvoy, S., 'Before Cadden: Abortion in Mid-Twentieth Century Ireland', in D. Keogh, F. O'Shea and C. Quinlan (eds), *Ireland in the 1950s: The Lost Decade* (Cork: Mercier Press, 2004), pp.147–163.

McCarthy, Á., 'Hearths, Bodies and Minds: Gender Ideology and Women's Committal to Enniscorthy Lunatic Asylum, 1916–25', in A. Hayes and D. Urquhart (eds), *Irish Women's History* (Dublin: Irish Academic Press, 2004), pp.115–136.

McCormick, L., *Regulating Sexuality: Women in Twentieth-Century Northern Ireland* (Manchester: Manchester University Press, 2011).

McCray Beier, L., 'We Were Green as Grass': Learning about Sex and Reproduction in Three Working-Class Lancashire Communities 1900–1970', *Social History of Medicine*, 16, 3 (2003), pp.461–480.

McKenna, Y., 'Embodied Ideals and Realities: Irish Nuns and Irish Womanhood, 1930s–1960s', *Éire Ireland*, 41, 1 (2006), pp.40–63.

McLoughlin (ed.), D., 'Infanticide in Nineteenth-Century Ireland' in A. Bourke et al. (eds), *The Field Day Anthology of Irish Writing: Irish Women's Writing and Traditions, Vol. IV* (Cork: Cork University Press, 2002), pp.915–919.

Meehan, N., 'Church and State Bear Responsibility for the Bethany Home', *History Ireland* (Sept/Oct 2010), pp.10–11.

Oberman, M., 'Understanding Infanticide in Context: Mothers Who Kill, 1870–1930 and Today', *Journal of Criminal Law and Criminology*, 92, 3 & 4 (2002), pp.707–737.

Odem, M.E., *Delinquent Daughters: Protecting and Policing Adolescent Female Sexuality in the United States, 1885–1920* (Chapel Hill, NC: University of North Carolina Press, 1995).

O'Donnell, I., O'Sullivan, E. and Healy, D. (eds), *Crime and Punishment in Ireland 1922–2003: A Statistical Sourcebook* (Dublin: Institute of Public Administration, 2005).

O'Sullivan, E. and Raftery, M., *Suffer the Little Children: The Inside Story of Ireland's Industrial Schools* (Dublin: New Island, 1999).

O'Sullivan, E., ' "This otherwise delicate subject": Child abuse in Early Twentieth-Century Ireland', in O'Mahony, Paul (ed.), *Criminal Justice in Ireland* (Dublin: Institute of Public Administration, 2002), pp.176–201.

Owens, R. Cullen, *A Social History of Women in Ireland 1870–1970* (Dublin: Gill & Macmillan, 2005).

Pomata, G., 'Unwed Mothers in the Late Nineteenth and Early Twentieth Centuries: Clinical Histories', in E. Muir and G. Ruggiero (eds), *Microhistory and the Lost Peoples of Europe* (Baltimore, MD: Johns Hopkins University Press, 1991), pp.159–204.

Prior, P., 'Mad, Not Bad: Crime, Mental Disorder and Gender in Nineteenth-Century Ireland', in I. O'Donnell and F. McAuley (eds), *Criminal Justice History: Themes and Controversies from Pre-Independence Ireland* (Dublin: Four Courts, 2003), pp.66–82.

Prior, P., 'Roasting a Man Alive: The Case of Mary Rielly, Criminal Lunatic', *Éire Ireland*, 41, 1 & 2 (2006), pp.161–191.

Quinn, C., 'Images and Impulses: Representations of Puerperal Insanity and Infanticide in late Victorian England', in M. Jackson (ed.), *Infanticide: Historical Perspectives on Child Murder and Concealment, 1550–2000* (Aldershot: Ashgate, 2002), pp.193–215.

Rattigan, C., '"Crimes of passion of the worst character": Abortion Cases and Gender in Ireland, 1925–50', in M. gialanella Valiulis (ed.), *Gender and Power in Irish History* (Dublin: Irish Academic Press, 2009).

Richter, J.S., 'Infanticide, Child Abandonment, and Abortion in Imperial Germany', *Journal of Interdisciplinary History*, 28, 4 (1998), pp.511–551.

Rose, L., *The Massacre of the Innocents: Infanticide in Britain 1800–1939* (London: Routledge, 1986).

Rose, R.S., 'Induced Abortion in the Republic of Ireland', *British Journal of Criminology*, 18, 3 (1978), pp.245–254.

Ryan, L., 'Negotiating Modernity and Tradition: Newspaper Debates on the "Modern Girl" in the Irish Free State', *Journal of Gender Studies*, 7, 2 (1998), pp.181–197.

Ryan, L., *Gender, Identity and the Irish Press 1922–1937: Embodying the Nation* (Lampeter: Edwin Mellen, 2002).

Ryan, L., 'Sexualising Emigration: Discourses on Irish Female Migration in the 1930s', *Women's Studies International Forum*, 25, 1 (2002), pp.51–65.

Ryan, L., 'The Press, Police and Prosecution: Perspectives on Infanticide in the 1920s', in A. Hayes and D. Urquhart (eds), *Irish Women's History* (Dublin: Irish Academic Press, 2004), p.137–151.

Schulte, R., *The Village in Court: Arson, Infanticide, and Poaching in the Court Records of Upper Bavaria, 1848–1910* (Cambridge: Cambridge University Press, 1994).

Smith, J., *Ireland's Magdalen Laundries and the Nation's Architecture of Containment* (Manchester: Manchester University Press, 2007).

Smith, J., 'The Politics of Sexual Knowledge: The Origins of Ireland's Containment Culture and "The Carrigan Report" (1931)', *Journal of the History of Sexuality*, 13, 2 (2004), pp.208–233.

Valiulis, M., 'Neither Feminist nor Flapper: the Ecclesiastical Construction of the Ideal Irish Woman', in M. O'Dowd and S. Wichert (eds), *Chattel, Servant or Citizen: Women's Status in Church, State and Society* (Belfast: Institute of Irish Studies, 1995), pp.168–178.

Valiulis, M., 'Virtuous Mothers and Dutiful Wives: The Politics of Sexuality in the Irish Free State', in M.G. Valiulis (ed.), *Gender and Power in Irish History* (Dublin: Irish Academic Press, 2009).

Ward, T., 'The Sad Subject of Infanticide: Law, Medicine and Child Murder, 1860–1938', *Social and Legal Studies*, 8, 2 (1999), pp.163–180.

Ward, T., 'Legislating for Human Nature: Legal Responses to Infanticide, 1860–1938', in M. Jackson (ed.), *Infanticide: Historical Perspectives on Child Murder and Concealment, 1550–2000* (Aldershot: Ashgate, 2002).

Weeks, J., *Sex, Politics and Society: The Regulation of Sexuality Since 1800* (London: Longman, 1989).

Whyte, J.H., *Church and State in Modern Ireland, 1923–1970* (Dublin: Gill & Macmillan, 1971).

Zedner, L., *Women, Crime, and Custody in Victorian England* (Oxford: Clarendon, 1994).

UNPUBLISHED THESES

Earner-Byrne, L., ' "In Respect of Motherhood": Maternity Policy and Provision in Dublin City, 1922–1956' (Ph.D thesis, University College, Dublin, 2001).

Fink, J., 'Condemned or Condoned? Investigating the Problem of Unmarried Motherhood in England, 1945–1960' (Ph.D thesis, University of Essex, 1997).

Guilbride, A., ' "I Went Away in Silence": A Study of Infanticide in Ireland from 1925 to 1957' (Minor MA thesis, University College, Dublin, 1994).

Maguire, M.J., 'The Myth of Catholic Ireland: Unmarried Motherhood, Infanticide and Illegitimacy in the Twentieth Century' (Ph.D thesis, American University, Washington, DC, 2000).

McAvoy (Larmour), S., 'Aspects of the State and Female Sexuality in the Irish Free State, 1922–1949' (Ph.D thesis, University College, Cork, 1998).

Rose, R.S., 'An Outline of Fertility Control, Focusing on the Element of Abortion, in the Republic of Ireland to 1976' (Ph.D thesis, University of Stockholm, 1976).

Index

Gaffney, Sergeant 137
Galway District Court 14
Galway Homes and Home Assistance Committee 143
Garrett, P.M. 10, 17
Geary, R.C. 239
gender ideology 181
gender, and relatives' responses to illegitimacy 76
George J. 142
George P. 27–28
Gibson, Mr Justice 199
Gladys M. 134
Gleeson, District Court Justice Dermot 65
Glynn, Joseph 51
Good Shepherd Convents 51, 114, 210, 214, 215, 217, 221, 222, 229, 238, 240
gossip/rumour and infanticide detection 28, 29, 173–82, 189
Government of Ireland Act (1920) 3
Grangegorman Mental Home 216
Green Street Court 46, 216, 240
Greer, Sister Frances Eucharia 213, 214
Guilbride, A. 99, 102, 106
Guinness, Mrs Noel 51

Hackett, Dr 49
Hackett, Sergeant William 68
Hamilton, District Inspector 44
Hanna, Judge 238, 239
Hanna L. 54
Hannah A. 58, 134, 198, 222
Hannah B. 154
Hannah C. 85–86
Hannah K. 138, 198, 199
Hannah L. 79–80, 82–83
Hannah M. 223
Hannah R. 49
hard labour 216
Harper, Hugh 55
Harriet H. 58–59
Haugh, Mr Justice Kevin 12
Hayden, Garda Michael 106
Hearn, M. 38, 58, 60, 65, 158, 237
Heneghan, Mr 143
Henry, Constable 188
Higgins, Sergeant Peter 43, 185
High Park Convent 36, 211
Hill, M. 81–82, 83
Holles Street Hospital 134, 171
Home for Discharged Prisoners 222
homelessness 61
Hooper, barrister Mr 202
Horgan, Sergeant Cornelius 54
Howe, barrister G.L. 112
Hughes, Sergeant Thomas 171
Hughes, Superintendent John 99

I.C. 39
I.L. 67
Illegitimate Children (Affiliation Orders) Act (1930) 13–14, 54–55

immorality, police attitudes to 130
incest 103–04, 108, 154–57, 162, 235
infant mortality 9
infanticide
  as birth control 70, 136
  figures 5–7, 230
  trials 241–56
  use of term 21
Infanticide Acts 18, 193, 197, 229, 230, 239
Infanticide Bill (1949) 193, 204, 205
informing, by relatives 84–87
Inglis, T. 129
insanity, as verdict 21, 205, 206, 207
insensitivity, among doctors 48–49
institutional provisions, for illegitimate children 136
Intoxicating Liquor Act (1923) 3
Irish Constitution (1937) 4
Irish Women Workers Union 64
Isabella S. 106

Jack W. 144
Jackson, L.A. 24, 58, 60, 76, 83, 131, 145, 159
Jackson, M. 50, 76
Jacob, Edward 198, 206, 210
James B. 98, 118, 151
James H. 138
James L. 13
James M. 150, 218, plate 12, 13
James N. 153, 174
James R. 162–63
Jane M. 134
jazz dancing craze 142
J.B. 90
J.D. 139
J.E. 43, 90
Jean B. 151
Jim M. 153
Jim R. 162–63
J.M. 39, 43–44, 102, 136, 159–60, 163, 196
Joan C. 69
Johanna 194
Johanna D. 114, 220
Johanna M. 92
Johanna W. 56
John C. 154
John D. 142
John E. 46, 108–09, 110, 111
John L. 137, 144, 212
John M. 100, 103–04, 133, 160
John M.G. 46
John O. 43, 176–77
John P. 27–28, 232
John W. 101
Johnston, Mr Justice 49
Josephine B. 80
J.R. 87, 156
Julia S. 47, 50, 52, 82, 108, 116, 222
juries 197, 200
Justice for Magdalenes group 6

Kate Anne F. 154, 182